St.Helens Community Libraries

This book is due for return on or before the last date shown. Fines are charged on overdue books. Renewal may be made by personal application, post or telephone, quoting date, author, title and book number.

11. OCT 02	04. APR 09.	
03. DEC 02	21. FEB 11.	7 - DEC 2018
02. JAN 03	02. AUG 12.	
30. JAN 03		9 - JAN 2019
01. APR 03	02. AUG 12.	
24. APR 03		19 FEB 2019
MAY 03	01. NOV 13.	
31. OCT 03	- 4 APR 2014	15 OCT 2019
02. JAN 04.	- 2 JUN 2014	
18. MAR 04.		- 6 JAN 2020
11. APR 05.	16 MAY 2016	
05. SEP 06.	- 7 JUN 2016	17 SEP 2021
16. NOV 06.	13 MAR 2017	

DUGGAN, Mona   LH. 942.761
ORMSKIRK - The Making of a
        Modern town

D1423140

ORMSKIRK

THE MAKING OF A MODERN TOWN

MONA DUGGAN

SUTTON PUBLISHING
WEST LANCASHIRE DISTRICT COUNCIL
EDGE HILL UNIVERSITY COLLEGE

First published in 1998 by
Sutton Publishing Limited · Phoenix Mill
Thrupp · Stroud · Gloucestershire · GL5 2BU
in association with West Lancashire District Council and Edge Hill University College

British Library Cataloguing in Publication Data
A catalogue record for this book is available from the British Library

ISBN 0 7509 1868 3

Cover picture: Ormskirk in the eighteenth century by M.H. Rawsthorne, 1852.

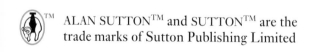 ALAN SUTTON™ and SUTTON™ are the
trade marks of Sutton Publishing Limited

Typeset in 11/12 pt Ehrhardt.
Typesetting and origination by
Sutton Publishing Limited.
Printed in Great Britain by
Redwood Books Limited,
Trowbridge, Wiltshire.

Contents

List of Illustrations

Foreword

Lancashire is a county with a proud past and a challenging future.

Its historical perspective is like a great jigsaw and the full picture cannot be completed without the inclusion of every piece of the puzzle. That is why we, at Edge Hill University College, are pleased to be involved with this contribution to the historical annals of Lancashire.

Since 1933, Edge Hill College – as it was then – has been a fundamental part of the fabric of Ormskirk. From a comparatively modest start in the mid-1930s, Edge Hill University College now employs nearly 1,000 people, caters for more then 10,000 students and contributes around £40 million to the local economy.

Founded in 1885 by a group of Liverpool businessmen who wished to set up a non-denominational teacher training college for women – and based in the Edge Hill area of the city – the University College has since expanded beyond education and now teaches healthcare, humanities, sports science, management and a range of other subject areas at undergraduate, postgraduate and research levels.

As an integral part of the West Lancashire community, Edge Hill University College works in close partnership with major organizations in the area and the student community action organization supports more than 200 voluntary projects each year. A total lifelong learning opportunity is available to the local community alongside the valuable Sporting Edge and the Rose Theatre, to which facilities we warmly welcome members of the public.

We, at Edge Hill University College, look forward to a long and prosperous association with our home town of Ormskirk.

JOHN CATER
Chief Executive

Preface

Since the 1970s, historians have been searching for a model for urban development in Britain in the seventeenth and eighteenth centuries. Despite various theories being advanced, early modern towns defy easy generalisation. Some historians, notably Peter Clark and Paul Slack, have advanced theories of urban crisis and decline during the period covered by this book, while others, such as A.D. Dyer and John Patten, believed that there was overall economic and social progress in towns after 1700. In the 1980s Peter Borsay produced his theory of urban renaissance in many early modern towns, and Angus McInnes favoured the concept of a period of revival throughout the period.[1] Meanwhile, Penelope Corfield has cautioned that it is unwise to generalise about the fate of market towns. She believes that the rationalisation of the market network meant that, while it was true – as reported in the *Essayist* of 1718 – that 'in many of these Places once populous and flourishing, the Fairs and Markets are become strangely thin; and where one can see little besides Toy-shops and Stalls for Baubles and Knicknacks', yet for other, more strategically placed market towns the eighteenth century was a period of consolidation and prosperous expansion.[2]

Evidence in support of these arguments has been provided by the larger market towns, such as Norwich, Exeter, Warwick, Preston, Bath and Shrewsbury. However, a significant gap emerged in the evidence concerning smaller market towns.[3] As J.D. Marshall wrote in his study of the Cumbrian market towns, 'a town has to be substantial and respectably urban-seeming to merit the attention of practitioners; but,' he continued, 'it is difficult to see how any meaningful discussion of urbanism can take place without careful consideration of the embryonic form.' In Ormskirk we have that embryonic form.

Gradually, as I examined most aspects of life in Ormskirk, I witnessed the birth of an early modern urban community. Rural pursuits were abandoned, a new social urban hierarchy was born, new social relationships were established and the town acquired a completely different and characteristically urban economic profile. Some of these adjustments arose from a response to national initiatives – for example, changes such as the provision of a charity school following the Established Church's support for the idea. Others were a reflection of national attitudes – for instance, the growing antipathy in the eighteenth century towards sports involving animal cruelty. In many ways, life in Ormskirk proved to be a microcosm of national life, while in others it retained a character all its own. Many of its distinctive features could be attributed to its location in what was regarded as a remote corner of north-west

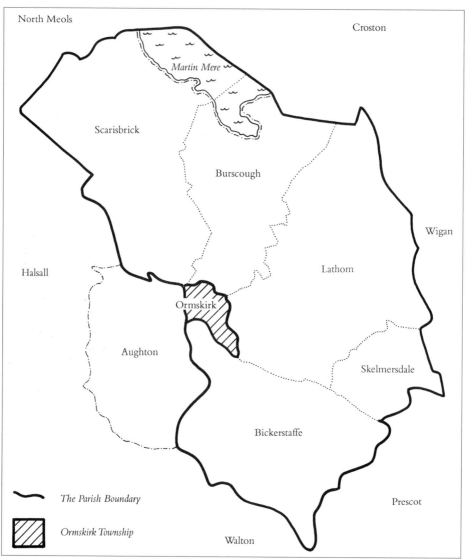

1. The parish of Ormskirk.

England. That location – between the emerging commercial town of Liverpool, the mining and industrial centre of Wigan and the successful provincial centre of Preston – made it a prime candidate for Corfield's process of 'rationalisation'.

This study is based on an array of sources. Whatever gave me a glimpse of life in Ormskirk during my period[4] I have used as evidence of the state of the town. In particular, as William Haller advised, I have tried 'to hear the quiet voices'[5] that tell the story of an archetypal early modern English provincial small market town.

Acknowledgements

Initially I should like to acknowledge my debt to the Open University for awakening my interest in urban history.

Then I should like to record my thanks to all those who have allowed me to use their private collections of records, especially to Lord Derby and to the authorities at Douai Abbey. I am also grateful to the staff of all the many public record offices and libraries I have visited, particularly to the staff of the Lancashire Record Office.

Others to whom I owe special thanks include Dr John Walton who initially had confidence in my abilities and supervised my studies for a short period.

Finally I must thank the two to whom my debt of gratitude can never be repaid: Dr Michael Mullett, my supervisor during my studies at Lancaster University; and Heaton, my husband and constant supporter. Michael has guided, sustained and encouraged me, while, without Heaton's help, patience and confidence in my efforts, this work would never have reached completion. Thank you all.

Abbreviations

PRO	Public Record Office
LRO	Lancashire Record Office
CRO	Cheshire Record Office
QSP	Quarter Sessions Petitions
DDK	Derby Muniments
THSLC	*Transactions of the Historical Society of Lancashire and Cheshire*
TLCAS	*Transactions of the Lancashire and Cheshire Antiquarian Society*
TCWAAS	*Transactions of the Cumberland and Westmorland Antiquarian and Archaeological Society*
CS	Chetham Society
TRHS	*Transactions of the Royal Historical Society*
RSLC	Record Society of Lancashire and Cheshire
HMC	Historical Manuscripts Commission
HMSO	Her Majesty's Stationery Office
LPRS	Lancashire Parish Register Society
DNB	*Dictionary of National Biography*
CSPD	Calendar of State Papers Domestic
VCH	W. Farrer and J. Brownbill, eds, *The Victoria History of the County of Lancaster*, vols 2, 3 (London: University of London, 1907)

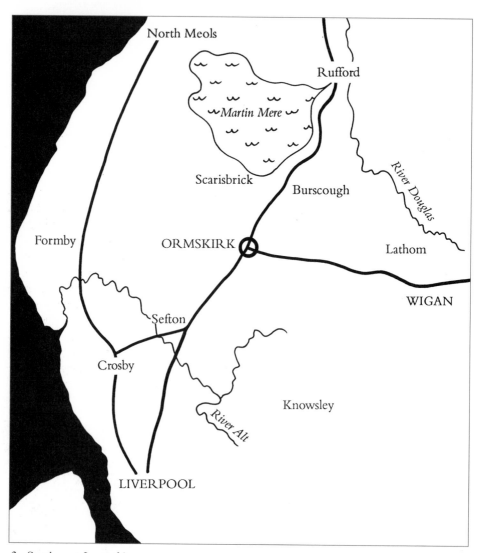

2. *South-west Lancashire.*

Introduction

The origins of the settlement at Ormskirk are obscure. Although there have been finds of small hoards of Roman coins in the vicinity,[1] there is no evidence of a Roman settlement on the site, nor is there any evidence of a powerful overlord founding the town for economic reasons, either in the distant past or in more recent times – as occurred at Whitehaven in the eighteenth century. Instead, the town has evolved from an early settlement built in a dominant position on a sandstone ridge overlooking the south-west Lancashire plain. This ridge marked the western edge of the Skelmersdale plateau – its highest point being 254 feet above sea level – to the west of the south Lancashire coalfield. Until the late eighteenth century, the lands to the west of the ridge were mainly undrained mosslands extending towards the coast and surrounding a large, shallow lake, Martin Mere. To the north of the town, the River Douglas flowed northwards to the Ribble Estuary crossing a floodplain, while to the south the River Alt was surrounded by marshy ground. The plateau provided access to the area from eastern Lancashire and from the main north–south highway, which ran through Wigan.

The place-name of Ormskirk has Scandinavian derivations: kirk is the Scandinavian word for church, and Orm is a personal name.[2] There are various candidates for the identity of Orm, the patron of the early church. Baines[3] credited Orm, the Saxon lord of Halton in Cheshire, ancestor of the Boteler family who held large estates in Lancashire, with the building of the church, but no firm evidence supports this theory. The *Victoria History of the County of Lancaster* (VCH)[4] makes the suggestion that Orm was an early lord of Lathom, and includes the plausible theory of Revd John Sefton that Orm may have been a recluse who built an oratory on the hill. The true identity of Orm is unknown, but the existence of a church on the site was of paramount importance in the evolution of the settlement.

3. Fragment of an ancient cross on the exterior eastern wall of Ormskirk church.

Little remains of the early settlement, but the fragments of a cross dating from the Dark Ages and reused in the construction of the east wall of the church, and the circular shape of the graveyard, indicate an early religious site. An old window – possibly of Norman origin – was discovered within the northern wall of the chancel during the restoration work done during the 1880s. The Domesday survey did not mention the town specifically, but included the area among the lands of Lathum (Lathom). Consequently, we are left to conclude that Ormskirk was an early settlement, probably evolving from a Saxon or Viking village sited above the wetlands, and developing gradually, as the population of the area increased in the thirteenth century, into a market and route centre for the surrounding area. The town's position among the mosslands meant that its market served a large hinterland. In fact, its dominant position in this area remained virtually unchallenged until road improvements were made in the late eighteenth century.

Any detailed account of the medieval period is impossible because of the lack of evidence. However, an overview of the history of the people of Ormskirk since the Norman Conquest reveals that, after long periods of steady development, forces outside their control would suddenly engulf the settlement. On each occasion this caused great changes in the lives of the inhabitants, often overturning the whole political and social structure of the community and leaving the settlement to develop along a completely different course.

The earliest instance of dramatic change occurred when the settlement was granted to nearby Burscough Priory by its lay overlord, Robert son of Henry of Lathom, as an act of religious piety. The foundation charter of the priory, dating from *c.*1189, confirmed the grant of the church of Ormskirk with its appurtenances to the priory.[5] The grant is the first evidence we have to confirm the existence of the settlement, and from it we can infer that, before that date, the settlement's institutional status was that of a rectory manor held by the lords of Lathom. In the cartulary of the priory there is evidence that Ormskirk church was established before Burscough Priory was founded in 1189. Another charter, dated between 1212 and 1232, refers to a grant made by Richard of Scarisbrick's ancestors to the Church of St Mary of Ormskirk. If this grant had been made after the foundation of the priory, it would have been addressed to the priory as holder of the church.[6] Thus, with the foundation of the priory in 1189, the development of the embryonic township suddenly changed direction and it came under the jurisdiction of the prior and canons of Burscough instead of a lay overlord.[7]

The small township then experienced a period of calm progress, increasing in importance during the latter part of the thirteenth century and becoming one of the most valuable assets of the priory. Evidence of the town's success is the fact that, some time between 1260 and 1302, the prior and canons of Burscough conferred on it the status of a free borough, and granted to each burgage (the land held by a burgess) one acre of land for the annual rent of 12*d*.[8] Then another change, coinciding approximately with the enfranchisement of the borough, occurred in 1286, when Edward I granted to the priory the rights of a weekly market in the town and an annual five-day fair, beginning on 28 August.[9] This included the right to stallage paid by those who sold in the market, and tolls paid by those who bought, formerly taken by Edmund, Earl of Lancaster – a fact which attests that the market had been in existence before the date of Edward's grant.

Again the institutional standing of the township was altered, and, as before, these significant changes were followed by a period of calm progress and consolidation.

Trading increased in the fourteenth century, when both a cloth seller and a tailor appear in the records,[10] and in 1461 the right to hold a second annual fair, this time at Whitsuntide, was granted by Edward IV.[11] At some point before the sixteenth century, the borough status of the town lapsed and, as no relevant records remain, we cannot find a reason. The only surviving evidence of the prior and canons' grant of borough status is the long narrow burgage plots which continued to line the principal streets of the town until the twentieth century, and which can still be identified in a few places today.

A third period of sudden change of direction occurred in 1535, when the priory was suppressed and the township became Crown property. The document listing the assets of the priory, gives us some idea of the stage of economic development reached by the town at that date, for the rents of a total of eight shops and ten stallages in the booths were listed, in addition to the profits from the market and the fair.[12] The shops were workshops with retailing facilities, and the booths were a permanent marketing area, probably that listed in a later document as under the stairs of the Town Hall.[13] The court leet records for this period reveal that the activities of traders were strictly controlled to establish the credibility of the market. The traders were frequently presented to the court for such offences as putting grain in pepper, selling bad meat and using incorrect measures.[14] Evidently, the Crown's administration was successful in promoting the town, for in 1598 it was described in the duchy court as a 'great, ancient and very populous town, and the inhabitants are very many, and a great market is kept there weekly besides two fairs every year; and the quarter sessions are held there twice a year, whereunto . . . great multitudes of people continually thither repair'.[15] The town's legal function was increased when Ormskirk was chosen as one of the venues of the quarter sessions in the time of Henry VIII. During the next two centuries, the importance of the town grew both as a centre for the quarter sessions and, in terms of ecclesiastical jurisprudence, as the court for the deanery of Ormskirk.

In 1603, James I granted the township to William Stanley, Sixth Earl of Derby. Subsequently its fortunes were tied to those of his family.[16] When this study begins, Ormskirk had undergone one of the most traumatic periods in its history, as a consequence of the policy of James, Seventh Earl of Derby. During the Civil War the earl supported the King, and his seat, Lathom House, was twice besieged by Parliamentarian troops, finally being taken in December 1645.[17]

During the years 1642–1645, Ormskirk's inhabitants suffered great hardship as the soldiers from each side

4. James, Seventh Earl of Derby, beheaded 1651.

5. An unknown artist's impression of Lathom House before the Civil War.

obtained food and supplies from the town, both legally on credit and illegally by plunder, leaving very little for the townsfolk. The town was the victim of a devastating attack of plague in 1648, actuated by the presence of the military and compounded by the effects of malnutrition. The town and market were closed to avoid the spread of infection, a measure which caused further hardship for the inhabitants. The situation was so critical that the leading townsmen appealed to the quarter sessions for help, claiming that the plague had left 800 people 'not able to subsist without speedy contribution forth of the County'. Using the estimated figure of 950 (see p. p. xvii) for the total population of the town, we can calculate that approximately 84% of its population was suffering extreme poverty, though the numbers may have been exaggerated by the distraught townsmen, anxious to stress their plight.[18] Later petitions prove that the condition lasted for another five years.[19] As a result, Ormskirk joined other Lancashire towns – such as Lancaster, Liverpool, Preston and Wigan – that had suffered from Civil War disruption and its aftermath, in the desperate search for stability that characterised England in the mid-sixteenth century.

It is difficult to estimate the size of the population during the period 1660–1800. As the town served as a centre of trade, law, accommodation, leisure and professional services, people were constantly visiting it. Most of the time the population included many who were not true inhabitants, but it is impossible to ignore these temporary residents and to deal exclusively with genuine townspeople, so the demographic features of this study include many of these outsiders.

The only reliable and, for some years, continuous documentary evidence of the size of the population is the manor court roll, and this has its shortcomings. The papers include the lists made at the view of frankpledge – the medieval enrolment in tithings which had become an annual roll-call of the tenants of the manor. The roll of 1680 recorded 218 'inhabitants' present. If this, the number of heads of households, is multiplied by 4.5, the estimated average size of households,[20] a total of 981 inhabitants is reached. By 1699, some 243 inhabitants were listed, giving an increased population of 1,093. By 1754 the number at the view was 269, giving an estimated total population of 1,210. By 1780 that had risen to 1588.[21]

However, although these listings provide valuable information regarding the increasing population, there is a problem in using them as a basis for the size of the population because subtenants and lodgers are not included. Possibly only a few properties were sublet or subdivided in the seventeenth century. Severe attacks of plague and other economic after-effects of the Civil War had reduced the population. Consequently the estimated size of households (4.5 people) would probably be sufficient to include lodgers and subtenants. However, once the town's economy improved in the early eighteenth century, people moved into the town and there was an increase in subletting and building on land belonging to Derby tenants. There was therefore an increase in subtenants and lodgers. This means that the estimate made from the listing was too low. Indeed, in 1778 the vicar, in reply to the Bishop of Chester's visitation questionnaire quoted a figure of 2,280 for the population of Ormskirk township.[22] This represents an increase of 712 on the 1780 view of frankpledge listing's estimated total of 1588 and includes the subtenants and lodgers.

6. An unknown artist's impression of the town in the eighteenth century.

However, as Prof. Hoskins observed, 'history is not a matter of counting heads',[23] so we must accept a rough estimate of the population as approximately 950 inhabitants in the mid-1600s, increasing to 2,554 by the time of the 1801 census return.[24] This increase provides a remarkable contrast to that of the rapidly expanding northern towns of Liverpool, Wigan and Preston during the same period.[25] These towns were strategically placed to take advantage of the eighteenth-century upsurge in transatlantic trade in the case of Liverpool and Preston, and the increased demand for small ironware – often also associated with the transatlantic trade – in the case of Wigan. However, the statistics for Ormskirk do not describe a town in decline, but rather one making steady progress. As we will see, although the town attempted both to extend its role as a legal centre and to establish new roles either as a spa, or as a racing or leisure town, it was unable to make any permanent change in its established status and remained a successful market town.

CHAPTER I

Economic Change

Most of the phrases used by historians to describe this period (1660–1800) imply general economic change or growth, particularly in the urban setting. 'The commercial revolution', 'the urban renaissance', 'the commercialisation of leisure' and 'the birth of a consumer society' all carry obvious connotations of economic change or progress.[1] Our task is to discover how far this scenario of change affected the lower end of the hierarchy of towns – the small market towns – by examining the progress of Ormskirk. Our first examination will focus on change in marketing, as this was the prime role of these towns. However, before examining that development in Ormskirk, it is essential to consider the state of markets nationwide, in order to set the local market in a wider perspective.

The importance of markets had declined prior to the Civil War, and whereas in Lancashire there had been eighty-five chartered markets and fairs – plus about fifty which were held by custom and had never received charters – by 1640 the number of chartered markets in the county had been reduced to about thirty.[2] The fate of many of the customary markets is unclear. However, between 1650 and 1690, approximately 140 charters were granted and the national total number of markets was increased by 20%.[3] In Lancashire two new market charters were granted: Weeton in 1670 and Martin Mere (Tarleton), also in 1670. Three towns received a confirmation of their grants: Ormskirk in 1670, Garstang in 1679 and Preston in 1685.[4] Although the income from these grants provided a source of much-needed revenue for the Stuart kings, the demand for increased marketing facilities must have existed to provide the initiative and the money for such grants. After 1729, numbers again began gradually to decline, so that by 1792 the number had fallen back to the level of 1673.

This decrease marked a rationalisation of the market network, whereby the larger marketing centres expanded and gradually took over the role of their smaller neighbours. Patten cites the example of Preston, which 'slowly swallowed the trade of the little markets around it, like Kirkham, Chorley and Garstang',[5] but as far as Ormskirk was concerned, 'The Douglas . . . stood in the way of any extension of Preston's commercial links. Though three roads crossed the valley, they were often impassable in winter through flooding, and, beyond the river, Ormskirk was able to dominate the trade of the mosslands'.[6] This rationalisation, which often included an alteration in the role or character of the market, usually occurred when the boundaries of the market catchment area altered as a result of factors such as improved transport facilities, the growth or decay of an important local industry, an alteration in the disposable incomes of the population or even the superior entrepreneurship of a particular town. Although markets usually drew their trade from a 15 mile radius and fairs from a radius of up to 75 miles,[7] their boundaries were inevitably dynamic, being dependent ultimately upon the personal choice of both the buyer and the seller. A market specialising in livestock could draw its stock – which transported itself – from a large area, whereas a corn market's area would of necessity be smaller because of the difficulties involved in transporting grain. Thus a market, like that at Ormskirk, catering for the sale of diverse products would have various catchment areas of differing sizes for its different products. Customers were prepared to travel further to a market supplying unique goods of high value, whereas they were content to attend the nearest market for vegetables and dairy products.

Braudel identified a similar system in France, where he envisaged ever-widening rings of supply areas surrounding the central market. He considered that the central zone was that supplying kitchen garden and dairy produce, then came the cereal zone, the wine-growing zone, the livestock zone, the forest zone and, finally, the zone of long-distance trade.[8] His model differs in detail from the Ormskirk catchment areas, but the concept of progressive zones does apply to the English town. Unfortunately, Braudel's static model does not provide for the dynamic nature of the supply areas and the consequent changing range of products for sale in the market-place.

One instance of a change in catchment areas occurred when transport improved in the eighteenth century. Products could be transported more easily, and therefore could travel to larger, more attractive markets. Also, the fact that customers could travel more easily meant that smaller centres with no outstanding product to offer lost their attraction. Consequently the supply zones and often the complete role of the smaller markets were taken over by their larger neighbours. In 1777, Dr Burn cited a different instance of a change in the supply zones of Kendal market: 'sea-fish caught near Leven Sands were weekly brought to Kendal market. . . . But since the great improvement of the town and port of Lancaster, the market for fish is considerably drawn away'.[9] Although the altering supply zones meant that some markets contracted, others grew. Overall trade in the market-place was not necessarily reduced, but its pattern altered.

Contemporaries were concerned that the practices of forestalling (buying prior to the market), engrossing (buying directly from the producer) and regrating (buying in quantity for resale) were undermining the market's function, and the Tudor acts against these practices were often invoked. In fact, these free-market practices could prove beneficial to the community and indirectly to the market by ensuring a regular flow of commodities not subject to sudden fluctuations in the supply network. As the eighteenth century progressed, the role of these middlemen increased as they supplied large quantities of goods to customers such as the government contractors, who required clothing or food for thousands of soldiers, or the great brewers, who required thousands of bushels of barley. In fact, to quote Porter, 'they were the inevitable off-shoots of concentrated production and the remorseless geographical broadening of the market'.[10] Nevertheless, many consumers from the regulated market-place continued to regard them as profiteers, amassing quantities of goods for resale when there was a shortage or when the price had increased for some other reason.[11]

Sample selling, by which traders met their customers in public meeting places, such as inns, and agreed sales of grain on the basis of a sample – 'parcels of corn in a bag or handkerchief'[12] – also removed the centre of trade from the market-place. M.K. Noble quotes a particularly vivid account of this process in operation at Patrington in the East Riding of Yorkshire: 'the staircase of the inn is all the time a thoroughfare, whereon the farmers continually stump up and down in their heavy boots with a sample bag in one hand and . . . a glass of hot gin in the other'.[13] The main advantages of this method were the avoidance of market tolls by both the buyer and the seller, the reduction of carriage costs and cheapening of the product as a result. The time spent transporting the grain to and from the market was also avoided. These practices became so widespread that in 1733 several boroughs – deprived of their market tolls by sample selling – petitioned the House of Commons against the practice whereby 'millers and mealmen secretly bought great quantities of corn by small sample, refusing to buy such as hath been pitch'd in open market'.[14] Another advantage of selling by sample in regard to corn and grain was evident at Ormskirk in the court leet of 1677 when John Reynold of Altcar was accused of bringing corn to the market 'worse in the bottom of the sack than the top'.[15] Until the corn was taken out of the sack, it was impossible to judge the quality of the whole sackful, but, when a sale by sample was negotiated, the customer received some assurance that the whole load would be of uniform quality, and, if it was not, he had a better chance of redress. One valid complaint was that sample selling prevented poorer people from buying small quantities at competitive prices.

During our period, the development of shops as retail outlets rather than as workshops selling their own products, and their custom of opening daily, also posed a threat to the market. All these factors worried contemporaries, who continued to voice their concern in publications such as the *Gentleman's Magazine* in 1758, which regretted 'the great declension of trade in the market towns'.[16]

Nevertheless, although many ways were found to sidestep market trading, it was not these evasions that were responsible for the closure of markets during the second half of the eighteenth century. In fact, some of these methods were a sign of the extension of trading rather than a cause of its reduction. 'Forestalling', 'engrossing', 'regrating' and all other kinds of wholesale trading actually brought a greater volume of trade into the town. In many towns throughout the eighteenth century there were problems of excess demand, and – for instance in both Lichfield and Walsall – the town authorities responded by maintaining the traditional practice of opening the market at 11.00 a.m. and forbidding outside buyers to buy before 12 noon,[17] thus protecting local consumers from the full weight of market forces. Such close market regulation, dating from Tudor times, lasted well into the era of Adam Smith and 'free trade'. In Preston, as Aikin described in 1795, 'The weekly markets . . . are extremely well regulated to prevent forestalling and regrating. None but the townspeople are permitted to buy during the first hour . . . at nine, others may purchase'[18] These instances are evidence of the persistence of paternalism on the part of the authorities, as they regulated the markets to ensure that both the customer and the trader received their fair share of the benefits. They also reflect the authorities' anxieties about possible food shortages as a result of war. Nevertheless, the dates of this kind of regulation stress the survival of this non-entrepreneurial ethos until the dawn of the nineteenth century. In fact, forestalling remained an offence at common law until 1844.[19]

The fact that so many market-places were enlarged and market halls rebuilt throughout the period 1670–1800 is indicative of a need for larger and better facilities because of the overall increase in trading.[20] By the mid-eighteenth century, commercial considerations were given a high priority in town planning. Reorganised market-places and well-structured trading centres emerged from masses of ramshackle stalls and shambles. The role of both the market and the fair was altering to meet the demand, and it was only the inflexible markets which were failing. *The Liverpool Guide* of 1797 described the two extremes in the one city: 'the fruit and vegetable market, selling oranges and lemons from Spain and Portugal' – the market which had altered its role to supply foreign produce to meet the current demand – and nearby, the old-style shambles where 'the eye should not be turned to either side, as it would be offended at the very indecorous practice of exposing shambles meat in the public street'.[21]

Changes in the volume of trade passing through Ormskirk market are difficult to measure. However, there are facts concerning a definite need for more space and better facilities – indicative of an increase in trade – between the 1740s and 1800. For instance, the market-place was enlarged in 1746 (see p. 55) and the market (or town) hall and shambles was rebuilt in 1779 (see pp. 59–60). Although the need for a larger market-place could be attributed in part to an increase in traffic passing through the town, more traffic meant an inevitable increase in trade in the days before motorised transport.

THE FAIR

Ormskirk Fair was held twice yearly, at Whitsuntide and during the last week of August or the first week in September. According to the *Book of Fairs*, published in 1756,[22] the main purpose of this fair was the sale of horned cattle and horses, and, indeed, there is a record of 'Cavalier' Blundell buying four stirks (heifers of six to twelve months old) and twinters (two-year-olds) at Ormskirk fair in 1664.[23] His grandson, Nicholas, recorded similar transactions at the fair, ranging from 'swopped Bonny Lass for a black mare' (August 1709), to 'bought a Bay Gelding for my Coach' (August 1718). However, his purchases included '83 good sheep for £20' (August 1706) so, evidently the animals sold were not exclusively horned cattle and horses.[24] Indeed, in 1797 a deposition claimed that both sheep and oxen were sold at the fair,[25] and in 1830 another deposition listed the customary tolls charged at the fair: 3*d* for every horse sold, 2*d* for every cow, 1*d* for every pig and 5*d* for every 20 sheep.[26] These tolls were often a cause of conflict, as the court leet book of 1677 attests: in that year, Robert Hitchin was fined 2*s* for 'giving the bailiff undecent language and denying to pay toll for a horse bought in the fair'.[27]

Fairings – traditional souvenirs usually made of pottery – were on sale at Ormskirk Fair, and Nicholas Blundell recorded twice that he bought them for gifts for his nieces and nephews (Butler), who lived in the town.[28] A later deposition confirms that various tradesmen took advantage of the Horse Fair to sell a variety of goods, and stallage was charged on behalf of the Lord of the Manor for these temporary stalls.[29] The accounts of Richard Latham of Scarisbrick record that he spent 5*s* 6*d* on a rug at the fair in 1744, and bought 'ginbread' there for 8*d* in 1741[30] – this item is particularly interesting as it is one of the earliest references to Ormskirk gingerbreads, which became famous in the nineteenth century and are sold in the town today. The sale of a rug at this later date may indicate that the role of the fair had altered slightly, and, certainly, by 1797, clothiers sold their goods (cloth and related goods) at the fair. This was not

7. Selling animals in the market in the early twentieth century.

unusual, for as early as the 1740s, clothiers had grasped the opportunity to sell their wares during the fair in Chester, where they rented shops on Eastgate for the duration of the fair and, as a result, Eastgate was nicknamed 'Manchester Row'.[31] In Ormskirk in 1797, clothiers were charged a toll of 4*d* if they were non-residents, whereas other 'foreign' stallholders were charged only a 1*d* toll. Local inhabitants enjoyed the privilege of being charged only 8*d* annually for the right to have stalls either in the fair or on the market.[32] Evidently, Lord Derby and his advisers wished to protect the local clothiers from competition. Thus the upsurge in the Lancashire cotton and woollen industries during the closing years of the eighteenth century caused change in the traditional Horse Fair, definitely from the late eighteenth century, but possibly, as the sale of a rug in 1744 suggests, from an earlier date. Certainly in the early nineteenth century the annual fair provided an opportunity for the sale of linen in the town (see p. 37).

Several references in Nicholas Blundell's diary attest that in his day the fair was also an occasion for entertainment. He wrote on 30 August 1714, 'it being Ormskirk Fair, I showed my children the strange creatures as were to be seen, I think there was a tiger, a civet cat, &c; I showed the woman dancing with swords and tankards & her husband playing tricks of legerdemain [sleight of hand] to my wife, Mrs Barker and my children.' Then on another visit on 30 August 1715, he 'saw a girl about three years and a quarter old turn round with four swords and put them to her cheeks &c'.[33] These amusements were introduced during the latter part of the seventeenth century after the years of puritanical restrictions, and marked a return to previous customs rather than a completely new development.

A visit to the fair always involved Blundell in socialising with his many friends at one of the Ormskirk inns. He mentioned 'The Lamb' (1706), 'The Golden Lion' (1715) and 'The Talbot' (1725) by name. On one occasion (25 May 1708) the festivities included a dinner, a raffle for a tea table – at 6*d* a ticket – and a supper.[34] Lord Derby's bailiff and steward also went to the fair, as the bailiff recorded in his accounts: 'Spent when I walked the Fair . . . £1 13*s* 2*d*,' – spent, no doubt, again in one of the local hostelries.[35] As the fair was held biannually throughout our period, the inns benefited from this periodic influx of visitors.

THE MARKET

The only existing records which can give us some idea of the character of the market in the period are the court leet records and the town's order book – also compiled by the court leet to regulate the market and to establish a basic respect for public health and safety. As the purpose of these records was to establish order in the town, market users who neither featured in an order nor committed any offence, fail to appear. Consequently the records do not provide a complete picture. Nevertheless, they do offer much worthwhile information. Unfortunately, many of the court leet records have been lost, and those that remain fall into three distinct periods: 1677–1680, 1754–1757 and 1779–1799. These series are used in Table 1, showing a comparison of the products and crafts available in the market during the three periods.

Many instances of change are evident here. One of the most striking is the disappearance of corn and grain from the market-place by the late eighteenth century. Evidently, the practice of selling by sample and the advantages of bulk purchase had reached the north-west and had altered the character of the market.

TABLE 1. Products and craftsmen and the date of their mention in the court leet book[36]

1677–1680	1755–1757	1779–1799
leather (7)	leather (4)	fish (13)
shoes (1)	butter (2)	butter (11)
corn (1)	potatoes (2)	fowls (10)
barley (1)	sheep (1)	meat (3)
beans (1)	corn (1)	peas (1)
hemp seeds (1)	grain (1)	eggs (1)
meat (1)	beans (1)	shoes (1)
Craftsmen	meat (1)	flax (1)
	eggs (1)	soap (1)
locksmith	fowls (1)	
roper	fish (1)	
(see p. 12)		

Numbers in brackets indicate the number of times the product is mentioned. The Order Book[37] supplements the first column by mentioning the following: corn, meat, fowls, fish, fruit, grass, horses, wool, yarn and leather. Potters and 'sivers' (basket makers) are also mentioned.

In 1754, a comment of the traveller Dr Pococke that in Ormskirk 'they subsist chiefly by a great corn market frequented by merchants of Warrington and other parts'[38] suggests that the trade in corn was flourishing. However, an order made by the court leet in 1756,[39] attests that, in Ormskirk, as in the boroughs involved in the 1733 petition, sample selling – though not mentioned as such – was alarming the inhabitants and especially the toll gatherers. The court leet passed an order that 'no inhabitants . . . shall . . . keep in their houses any manner of corn or grain upon any market day after the market bell be rung' for the closure of the market, 'but shall bring or cause the said corn and grain to be brought into the Market (if it is brought into the town to the intent to be sold) upon pain to forfeit for every time so offending to the lord's use 6s 8d.' There were to be no dealings outside the market-place but, if the order was ignored, the fine ensured that the Lord of the Manor would receive more than his toll. The ensuing records are missing, so we have no account of the enforcement of this order, but evidently it did not prevent the sale of grain – other than oatmeal – from moving out of the market. However, depositions made in 1797 attest that some compromise had been made to avoid the loss of tolls from sales of grain made outside the market, but within the town. The toll gatherer explained that, 'such tolls of grain and oatmeal . . . [are] . . . collected whenever such articles are brought into the said town to be sold, as well as on market days'. James Waring confirmed this in his deposition, declaring that there were tolls on 'barley when sent to the maltster in the town . . . [and on] . . . grain sold and sent to the miller in the Manor to be ground.'[40]

From the same depositions the total income from tolls can be used to establish that a considerable amount of grain was sold in the town in 1789. Tolls were paid on approximately 1,020 sacks of barley, 415 of wheat, 238 of oats and 34 of rye.[41] However, nine years later an Ormskirk carpenter, William Maudsley, expressed the opinion that 'of late years very little grain' had been sold in the market, thus providing further evidence that most of it must have bypassed the market. The sale of such a large quantity of barley was the result of the heavy demand made by the brewing industry. In fact, Ormskirk's barley drew customers to the town as early as 1676, for the accounts of Robert Walthew of Preston recorded that he owed money for a load of barley bought in Ormskirk.[42] By the end of the eighteenth century, the trade in grain was so well established in the town that, by the act of 31 Geo III c.30 (an act for regulating the import and export of corn, 1791), Ormskirk was selected to be one of the towns where the price of corn and wheat was to be fixed by an inspector supervised by the Justices of the Peace.

The success of the trade increased Lord Derby's reluctance to forfeit the tolls and led to confrontation. In 1797 the toll gatherer explained that 'The tolls of barley . . . have very much decreased . . . owing to the payment thereof having been resisted . . . such resistance originated chiefly from a dispute having arisen . . . [with] . . . John Chadwick, the occupier of Greepy Mill within the said manor of Ormskirk.' A settlement was reached, but conflict continued and in 1830 counsel's opinion[43] was sought to define explicitly Lord Derby's right to the tolls of the market.

Oatmeal was sold on market days in the mealhouse, a large room on the ground floor of the town hall. Evidently the trade in meal had not slackened towards the end of the century, for in 1779, when it was decided to rebuild the town hall, the mealhouse was an integral part of the plan. It was essential that such a basic food should be available for sale in small quantities to the poorer townsfolk, because oatmeal was the staple food of the poor, as is attested by the menus of various workhouses where a more meagre version of their regular diet was served.[44]

Grass was so important in the early period that an order was made ensuring that those who sold it had a legal right to it. It was 'ordered that those persons which bring any grass to sell at the cross or other place, and have none growing of their own and cannot presently prove who gave it to them . . . to forfeit 4d'.[45] Evidently, there was enough demand for grass to feed the urban horses and cows to make it profitable to gather it illegally from the hedgerows and from the common, where the whole community had grazing rights. Although grass disappeared from the market-place in the eighteenth century, the demand for it cannot have decreased because the amount of horse carriage had increased, wagons and coaches had been improved, and later turnpike trusts and canals had been constructed. Again, its sale must have been negotiated directly with the grower. Although grass seeds were still to be bought in the market in 1830, the grass was not.

Court leet cases involving the sale of peas and beans in the market illustrate the development of the wholesale trade. An early example is implicit in the indictment in 1677 of 'John Linacre serv't to Hugh Rimmer of Alkar for selling beans twice over in the market'.[46] Evidently, Linacre, a budding entrepreneur, had bought beans in quantity and had resold them at a profit, thus, in the opinion of the court, forcing prices to rise and threatening the stability of the market. However, by 1756 such middlemen were accepted, and the complaint against William Lunt, described as a higler or middleman, was not that he resold beans but that he sold them 'a quart short of measure'.[47] Lunt came from Longton, near Preston, so it is likely that he had bought his beans cheaply in the larger market to resell in the smaller. Meanwhile, direct selling continued parallel to these developments, as cottagers brought beans and peas for sale from their gardens and smallholdings. One such cottager was Margaret Lea of Maghull, who was fined 5s in 1791 for 'selling peas short of measure'.[48] In the early days of the Order Book (1617–1721), anyone 'forestalling or regrating any manner of wild fowl' was fined 6s 8d, and evidently similar restrictions applied to the sale of butter and eggs, and their dealers' hours for trading were limited. However, by the 1750s the court began to recognise the importance of the trade in butter, eggs and fowls, and in 1755 it lifted all restrictions on their marketing hours. They were 'free to buy fowls, butter and eggs without regard to any fixed hours' on market days.[49] The freed trade grew as dealers collected the poultry, eggs and butter brought into the market by farmers and cottagers on a Thursday, and resold them in Liverpool the following Saturday.[50] As the population in Liverpool expanded and was increased by more temporary residents awaiting passages abroad, so did the demand for produce,[51] and gradually the inhabitants of Ormskirk found that the competition for the available poultry, eggs and butter was too great. Restrictions on marketing hours were reintroduced,[52] and, in the 1780s and 1790s, several higlers trading in fowls and also some women dealing in butter were charged fines varying between 6s 8d and 13s 6d, for buying 'before the appointed time'.[53]

A similar development of middlemen trading in the market occurred in the fish trade. An early order concerned with the cleanliness of the town decreed that 'no fisher whatsoever shall leave any garbage of fish or other filthy matter within this town or market.'[54] Here, the use of the word 'fisher', implies that the seller of fish was the man who caught it. However, a later order concerned with the freshness of the fish warned that any 'fishmonger' who offered for sale 'any stinking fish' would

8. Woman selling fish from the fish stones in the 1880s.

'forfeit 3*s* 4*d*'.[55] By describing the trader as a fishmonger, the order implied that he was a middleman – someone who bought the fish from the fisherman and resold it. In response to an increase in the numbers of fishmongers, restrictions similar to those in the poultry trade were enforced. The sale of fish in the streets before it was brought to 'the fish boards or to the usual place' was forbidden,[56] and the hours of the fish market were controlled: no person could 'either publicly or privately . . . offer to buy or sell any . . . fish before the lord's bell be rung for the beginning of such fish market'– 7.00 a.m. in the summer months and 8.00 a.m. in the winter.[57] However, the inclusion of the word 'privately' in this last order is a tacit admission that already trading was conducted away from the fish boards.

Nevertheless, in the eighteenth century, fishmongers were penalised for dealing in fish. For example, in 1756, the year after middlemen had been accepted in the poultry, butter and egg trade and had been freed from restrictive trading hours, James Fallows of Ormskirk, an opportunist barber, was fined 3*s* 4*d* for 'buying up fish and selling the same on the same day and in the same market.'[58] Although indictments for dealing in fish gradually stopped, the orders regulating trading hours were strictly enforced until the end of the century. Fishmongers from inland areas were repeatedly fined for buying outside market hours. Evidently, they had confidence that their customers would pay high prices for really fresh fish – and knew that there was no sale for 'stinking' fish – and so decided to risk being fined for trading too early. James Atherton from Pemberton, near Wigan, was indicted three times between 1785 and 1798, while the Thompson family, also of Pemberton, and the Lowe family of Wigan incurred several fines.[59] By selling fish so far inland, these fishmongers faced little possibility of competition from fishermen selling directly to the public, but the distance they had to travel before reselling the fish, and the need to sell it quickly, explain their repeated disregard of the restrictions on the hours of trading.

Freshwater fish presented no problems: they were transported around the markets in tanks from which they were offered for sale, but large seawater fish were difficult to keep in such conditions. A quick sale of sea fish was essential to avoid indictments such as that for 'selling stinking fish' brought by one of the Wigan dealers against Michael Brookfield of North Meols (Southport).[60] Salmon was one of the more popular large fishes sold on Ormskirk market, but eels caught in Martin Mere or in the ditches of the mosslands, along with cockles, mussels and shrimps from the shores of south-west Lancashire, were also available. By the end of the century the trade had increased, and the fishmongers at Ormskirk were dealing in large quantities of fish. For instance, in 1794 John Wright was indicted for buying a cartload of mussels before the bell, and also for stopping and buying three packhorse loads of fish before they reached the market-place.[61]

Wholesalers and middlemen seemed to have had little interest in the fruit trade, even though the quantity that passed through the market was sufficient to warrant charging a toll: '1d to 2d per basket according to size'.[62] Only one order concerned them: that allowing the clerk of the market to alter the position of their stalls to cater for the seasonal nature of their trade. Although they used Ormskirk Market throughout our period, the market authorities never came into conflict with these traders, so few records of them remain.

Potatoes entered the market midway through our period, the result of changes in the area's agriculture. In the seventeenth century, potatoes had been grown in the suitable climate and soil – a sandy loam – of south-west Lancashire, as a novelty crop to add variety to the diet.[63] Elsewhere in England they were rarely cultivated. As the eighteenth century progressed, the wetlands around Martin Mere were reclaimed as a result of the drainage schemes of first Thomas Fleetwood and later Thomas Eccleston.[64] These projects provided the area with acres of very fertile peaty soil, ideal for the growing of potatoes. At the same time the potato increased in popularity,[65] and so by the 1750s the cultivation of potatoes had intensified in the Ormskirk district and they were sold in the market. In 1757, two farmers, Thomas Johnson and Andrew Goore of Aughton, were fined for selling their potatoes in the market 'by half a peck which was short of measure'.[66] Johnson refused to hand over his measure either to the officers or to the magistrates, who consequently fined him £1 1s.

Gradually, potatoes became a very profitable crop. In fact, by 1771, according to Arthur Young, an acre of potatoes was worth £10 and yielded 150 bushels in the Ormskirk area.[67] The sale of potatoes continued to increase and by 1830 market tolls had been levied on them: 2d on each cartload of winter potatoes and 1d on a basket of new ones.[68]

The sale of livestock had expanded from the biannual fair into the market before 1660. However, according to Nicholas Blundell's diary, serious horse dealing was reserved for the fair.[69] Nevertheless, the clerks of the market found the need to allocate specific areas for the sale of horses on market days, and it is significant that these areas were east of the town away from the prevailing west wind. Horses, geldings, mares and colts for sale were restricted to the eastern end of Moor Street, no nearer to the cross than where the pump stood,[70] while the pig market was behind the houses in Moor Street;[71] thus keeping any disturbance and dirt away from the market centre and the larger houses nearby. The market trade in cows and pigs continued until the nineteenth century, and during the 1830 case concerning Derby's rights it was claimed that no tolls were charged for the cows and pigs sold on market days.[72] As there is no mention of tolls on horses, it can be assumed that by then horses were sold only at the fair, a practice which continued until the twentieth century.

Contrary to the trends we examined earlier whereby the sale of products was expanding outside the market, the sale of soap expanded into the market in 1796. The inventory of James Berry (1686) listing over 11 lb of Castile soap (a hard soap containing olive oil) confirms that soap had been sold in local grocers' shops from the 1680s,[73] but it did not appear in the market records until the 1790s. In the early modern economy, market retailing of a product indicated its local (rather than national or even regional) production. Thus the sale of soap in Ormskirk presumes a local manufacture of soap, and indeed soap boilers had been operating in the town and selling from their own workshops, certainly since the early 1700s. The industry had grown up to supply the linen producers and the dyers, both established in Ormskirk from the early seventeenth century – if not before. Soap was produced by boiling potash – burnt vegetable ashes, usually from ferns or bracken – and skimming the alkali lye off the surface of the brew. This was mixed with some form of fat, tallow or oil to produce an early form of soap. Usually the boiling was done in a small building outside the house, and indeed a 'house for boiling soap' is listed at the rear of the house in Church Street belonging to Margaret Moorcroft, the widow of James, the earliest soap boiler in the Ormskirk records, who died in 1709.[74] Although soap boilers continued to operate in Ormskirk,[75] it was not a lucrative trade and one boiler, Silvester Moorcroft, became bankrupt in 1719. However, he was discharged a year later because his debt amounted to less than £50.[76] In the 1770s, the national production of soap climbed steadily in response to increasing demand, partly from the burgeoning textile industry. Then in 1787 the Leblanc process was discovered whereby the strong alkali, caustic soda, could be produced from salt, but it was not until 1823 that an alkali works for the production of this chemical was established in the Mersey basin. Caustic soda then replaced lye, and soap more akin to the modern product was manufactured to meet both the industrial and the domestic demand. As habits of personal cleanliness improved, and fashions dictating pristine white linen filtered down through the middle and lower social classes, they needed soap for laundering their linen, unlike 'a good lady of [Cavalier Blundell's] . . . acquaintance . . . [who] . . . was so curious in her attire as to send out of Lancashire to London her linen to be washed and starched as often as they were fouled; such fine linens, . . . as were used about her neck and shoulders.'[77] In response to this demand, particularly from the domestic customer, George Brewer brought soap to Ormskirk Market in 1796. However, his trading methods were suspect and the clerks of the market indicted him for 'selling soap short in weight and for refusing to part with his light weights when ordered'. The court imposed a very heavy fine upon him, 39s for each offence, thus discouraging practices which would endanger the credibility of Ormskirk Market.[78]

By contrast, various craftsmen, prominent in the market in the seventeenth century, disappeared completely from the records in the eighteenth century.

Among these were the 'potters and sivers' whose trade was sufficiently important to the economy during the period 1613–1721 to be designated to a specific area in Church Street.[79] As the order book described these craftsmen as 'resorting to this Market', they were not inhabitants of the town. Probably the potters came from Rainford, 6 miles south-east of Ormskirk, where archaeological excavations have discovered the remains of a pottery, and where a farm still bears the name of 'Pottery Farm'. An inventory of 1661, listing the goods of an Ormskirk shoemaker, William Livesey, mentions 'Rayneford mugges',[80] which confirms that this pottery was used in Ormskirk homes at that time and possibly was bought from a market stall in Church Street.

The 'sivers' pose some difficulty. 'Sivers' was probably an alternative spelling of sievers – the makers or users of sieves. In the seventeenth century a sieve also meant a large basket containing approximately a bushel, which was often used for carrying potatoes, apples or fish.[81] Presumably, then, a 'siver' was a basketmaker, a conclusion supported by the fact that basketmakers do not appear in these records, and yet basketry was a traditional craft in the area using the abundant willow trees which grew on the mosslands. In fact many of the Ormskirk inventories contain references to sieves and very few mention baskets or wiskets – another local name for a marketing basket. One, that of William Watkinson (1671), combines the two – 'in wiskets and sives 2s'.[82] Thus we can deduce that the sieves in the inventories were often these large baskets. Again, like the potters, the sivers 'resorted to the town', probably from Maudesley or Lydiate, two neighbouring villages which maintained a tradition of basket making until the twentieth century. A possible explanation for the disappearance of these two groups of craftsmen from the market may be that they preferred to supply an established shopkeeper with their products, and thus benefit from daily sales with a slightly lower profit margin, rather than wait for the weekly market.

Certainly other craftsmen followed this course: for instance, the locksmith indicted in 1679 for refusing to pay the market toll.[83] He never appears again in the records and, seemingly, after this encounter with the authorities, he decided to sell his locks through James Berry, the local grocer. Certainly, in 1686, six house locks featured in the grocer's inventory.[84]

A Wigan roper, whose customers would include farmers, millers, wagoners, a range of craftsmen, and the sailors and fishermen of the west Lancashire coast, was also indicted in 1679 for toll avoidance. Although some ropers continued trading in the market, for instance, James Rothwell, who was also fined 6s 8d for not paying his market dues in 1782, by the end of the century the main sources for ropes were the town's many rope walks and workshops where both tolls and stallage could be avoided.[85] Hemp, the raw material for rope, was grown extensively in the district and hempyards appear in the early deeds and surveys of properties on the periphery of the town.[86] The preparation of hemp included 'retting', during which the fibres were soaked for two or three weeks until they decomposed. This process left the water poisonous to animals, and this caused great difficulties for the town authorities. One of their first orders prohibited people from 'retting' hemp in 'any watering pool within this manor'.[87] Hemp, flax and yarn came into the market in such large quantities that the clerks of the market designated a special area for their sale: 'Betwixt the sign of the White Horse and Black Horse in the Church Street'.[88] Ropers and weavers would buy the raw materials for their crafts from these stalls. Hemp seed was also sold in the market and was the subject of a case of toll avoidance in 1677, when Margaret Billinge was fined for 'suffering hemp seed to stay in market times'– keeping back her wares until the market had closed and tolls no longer applied, and possibly selling at a higher price when her competitors had sold out.[89] The sale of hemp, flax and yarn continued in the market throughout our period. In fact, a case in the court leet in 1797 concerned the sale of flax by the same unscrupulous George Brewer who sold soap under weight. This time he was fined for selling flax also 'short in weight'.[90]

The greater part of the cloth and haberdashery trade also moved out of the market, not only to avoid the dues, but also to provide a greater choice for their customers of both goods and shopping hours. Only one inventory remains which can be identified as that of a market trader – that of Ann Weeming, 1681. Among her possessions were her stall and the tilt cloth to protect it from the rain, together valued at 3s, and a pair of little scales valued at 6d. Her wares included linen cloth to the value of £11 2s 5d, woollen cloth (7s), fustian cloth (1s 6d), galloon (braid, 18s) and various kinds of buttons, threads and laces.

Her competitors, also trading in the town, were the chapman, Peter Swift, the grocer, James Berry, and the woollen draper, Henry Tarbuck.[91] Swift supplied haberdashery and silk to both the townsfolk at their doors and the villagers from the surrounding area, all potential customers for the market stall. Many similar items were also sold by James Berry, whose shop was open daily – unlike the market stall. Among his stock were sewing thread, pins, tapes, seven-and-a-half gross of small buttons, four dozen tailors' bones (whalebone) and a small quantity of cloth. Meanwhile, the woollen draper, Henry Tarbuck, supplied an immense selection of cloth and some haberdashery. His inventory was valued at £476 5s 6d and included over 300 lengths of cloth, gold and silver lace, whalebone, plated clasps and buttons. This was the shop which would be patronised by the gentry when they selected material for their clothes. Ann Weeming had little chance of competing for these wealthy customers, but there would be trade for her in smaller items, and from impulse buying by passers-by.

The court leet exerted some control over each of these cloth traders in order to maintain the standards of the trade in the town. An order was made that 'every person . . . selling or buying any cloth in the market or elsewhere within this manor . . . shall use . . . such cloth yard as shall be found and allowed lawful by the clerks of the market.'[92] Similar regulations governed the weights used by other traders.

Customers at the market were also protected against poor quality goods. For instance, in 1677 John Valentine was fined 'for bringing to the market three pair of shoes not marketable and giving the officers undecent words'.[93] The officers often complained about the use of colourful language. Strict quality control continued in the town, even outside the market, and in 1756 Thomas Shorlock of Ormskirk was indicted for 'exposing for sale within this manor, horse leather shoes'. This leather was inferior to leather from cow hide and Shorlock had tried to sell shoes made from horse leather as the better quality product. The searchers and sealers of leather (see p. 14) had reported him and he was fined 5s.[94]

On the other hand, shoemakers themselves were protected against unfair competition by another order regulating the market hours – after 11.00 a.m. in the winter and 10.00 a.m. in the summer – which gave shoemakers from outlying villages time to make the journey to Ormskirk before the market opened.[95] Again, the market trade in shoes, like that in haberdashery, continued parallel to an increasing amount of trade conducted directly from shops. As early as 1689 Richard Morecroft had a shop where seats were provided for his customers,[96] and yet, 100 years later, William Latham, another of the town's many shoemakers, still sold from a market stall and was fined for not paying tolls.[97] There was a great range of wealth among Ormskirk's shoemakers. At one end of the scale were those like William Livesey (1661) and William Watkinson (1671), who had a very comfortable lifestyle judging from their inventories.[98] Although Livesey claimed to be a shoemaker in his will, he also kept two heifers, a calf, a sow and piglets. His house had ten rooms, including the shop. These were furnished with many expensive items, such as carved chairs, 'throne' chairs, feather beds, a looking-glass, a carved tester (canopied) bed, a standing bed (four-poster) covered in gilt leather,[99] linen sheets edged with lace and eight silver spoons. In the shop there were only four pairs of shoes, one pair of boots and one pair of slippers of gilt leather intended as patterns from which people could order their shoes. Surprisingly, he had thirty-four seats in the shop, so perhaps a visit to the shoemakers was a social occasion when the customer's family and friends sat around watching the expert shoemaker at work. However, the fact that a Christopher Livesey applied for an alehouse licence in 1661,[100] suggests that possibly the trades of both father and son blended in the one shop. A clock, another valuable item, stood in the shop – possibly to discourage too much socialising.

William Watkinson, also styled as a 'shoemaker' in his will, kept animals – five kine, two hogs, two mares and a gelding – and had quantities of barley and wheat. Over his brewhouse was a loft, possibly a workroom used by the shoemaker, his apprentices and family, where he kept a spinning wheel, leather and shoemakers' tools. Although it was mentioned in the context of other rooms, the shop did not appear in this inventory. However, William had two sons, one of whom, James, was later listed as a shoemaker,[101] so probably the shop had already passed to the sons before the father died. Watkinson lived in a large house with seven rooms, some of which had window curtains – an expensive luxury in those days. His court cupboard, virginal and books are some indication of his lifestyle. Among the poorer shoemakers was Richard Morecroft, whose total wealth amounted to £8 14s. His sparsely furnished cottage had only four rooms, including the shop, where he displayed eight pairs of little shoes valued at a total of 10s.

In 1705 a petition submitted to the Bench by ten local shoemakers gives an insight into their working practices.[102] Seemingly, Thomas Croxton had been 'pressed for her Majesty's service' and his fellow shoemakers appealed for his release. They explained that, as Croxton was a heel maker who supplied them all, they knew 'not how to carry on trade without' him. Evidently, these shoemakers divided their labour for their mutual advantage, seventy years before Adam Smith promoted a similar system in his *Wealth of Nations*.[103] One of the shoemakers, Richard Withington, claimed that Croxton was his servant, and it is possible that several – if not all – of the ten shoemakers worked for Withington in a large workshop, a forerunner of the nineteenth-century factory. Another possibility is that the ten were outworkers employed by Withington. Certainly, by the eighteenth century, that system had spread to the footwear industry, thereby providing employment for shoemakers who had insufficient capital to set up an independent business.[104] In response to the act of 1604 (Jas.I, c.22), the court leet annually appointed searchers and sealers of leather – usually the most

9. Tanner preparing hides, by Hans Sachs, 1568.

respected leatherworkers – to examine all the leather brought for sale and, if it was up to standard, to guarantee its quality by putting their seal upon it. During the first hundred years of our period, there was a series of indictments at the court leet against various Ormskirk tanners for offering leather insufficiently tanned for sale in the market. In order to cheapen the process, tanners used less oak bark, with the result that the leather was less tanned and therefore heavier. As leather was sold by weight, the tanners benefited on two counts. The London cordwainers' company were concerned about this practice and, during the parliamentary debate on tanning in 1675, one of their arguments was that often, when exporters bought directly from a tannery, the leather had not been submitted to the sealers to be examined, thus encouraging the tanners to produce poor-quality leather.[105]

Oaks could only be barked successfully in the spring. Consequently, tanners were compelled to invest capital in large stocks of bark.[106] For instance, the inventory of Henry Walton (1691) reveals that he had bark worth £35 at his tannery, and £112 worth of leather in various stages of preparation.[107] In 1701, during a court case between Thomas Stanley of Bickerstaffe and his stepfather Charles Davenport,[108] seven Ormskirk tanners claimed to have bought £150 worth of bark between them, again a very large outlay at that time. By contrast, between 1752 and 1788, Thomas Barton and Thomas Brandreth, leading tanners in the town, bought bark from the Derby estate for various amounts ranging from £5 10s to £1 0s 6d.[109] This reduction in the amount of bark purchased suggests that some change in the process had occurred in the interim.[110] Possibly specialisation in the supply of bark or an improvement in the extraction of tannin had been introduced and the tanners no longer needed to hold large stocks of bark.

During the last twenty years of our period, no indictments were made for leather being insufficiently tanned. Possibly this was the result of a more efficient tanning process, but, of course, it may have been that the tanners were selling directly from their yards, thus avoiding the sealers. There was little change in the occupation of the curriers, who bought the leather from the tanners, dressed, finished, graded it and cut it into appropriate quantities to supply the town's various leather workers.

Obviously the leather trade was closely linked to the butchery trade. In fact, by 1675, butchers had caused a surplus of leather countrywide, by slaughtering an increased number of beasts, as a result of the non-observance of fast days.[111] During our period, most of the thriving butchery trade in Ormskirk was centred beneath the Town Hall, where their stalls and slaughterhouses, 'shambles' or 'shops', were situated alongside the mealhouse,[112] but extra stalls were erected in the open street. Meat was sold in the market on Thursdays throughout our period, but by the end of the eighteenth century, a special market for meat was held on Saturdays. Of course, the butchers' shops, which had spread throughout the town by the mid-eighteenth century, were open daily for the sale of meat. All these many facilities for the sale of meat are evidence of the quantity of meat consumed in the district and confirm that meat was a common food in the north of England during the eighteenth century.[113] The butchers were particularly disorderly, especially in the early part of our period. They deceived their customers by 'blowing' or stuffing their meat to make it appear larger, 'so that the same is infectious and not marketable'– a common practice in markets in the seventeenth century.[114] They sold cheap meats in the guise of expensive meat, leading the clerks of the market to order that if a butcher brought mutton or lamb to be sold, he was to 'bring the skins of the said muttons or lambs with them'. They had no respect for their environment. For instance, in 1756 one butcher, Samuel Heys, was fined 3s 4d 'for suffering a cask to stand with blood and other dirt in at the end of butchers' shambles as a common nuisance', and quarrelled amongst themselves until an order was made forbidding them to 'discommend or misreport . . . or call any person from any other man's . . . stall, being bargaining with him for any victuals'. They allowed men's children and servants to 'rifle for flesh,' among the discarded carcases, causing 'great inconvenience and discord' to 'daily arise'. They kept mastiff dogs which attacked cattle. They sold meat 'not good and wholesome to men's bodies'. However, the clerks of the market were especially vigilant in these cases, and frequently presented offenders to the court leet, as for instance in 1754, when John Tatlock was fined for selling 'a slaughtered sheep that was not marketable' to the workhouse in Moor Street. In 1780, when the Town Hall was rebuilt and new shambles were erected on the same site (see pp. 60–1), the butchers refused to co-operate until orders were made compelling them to return to the new buildings. Even in the closing decades of our period, quarrels continued among the disruptive butchers, and in 1787 Valentine Coupland was presented for 'throwing down' the stall of Jonathon Rogers, butcher, and was fined 13s 4d.[115]

Admittedly, the butchers experienced many difficulties in their trade, especially concerning credit. For instance, in 1694, James Heyes, one of a family of butchers who traded under the Town Hall during our period, sold beef and pork on credit to

William Burke, a victualling agent for William III, to feed the militia during a muster at Ormskirk. By 1703 the debt of over £150 had not been paid, and in his letter to Queen Anne, Heyes explained his plight: 'for want of the said money, your petitioner is utterly ruined and undone, all he had being seized and his wife and ten small children living upon the charity of his neighbours; your petitioner himself being forced to abscond.' No result of this petition is recorded, but the Heyes family continued as butchers in the town, so presumably the debt was paid.[116]

Difficulties of a different kind, this time of their own making, were experienced by a group of entrepreneurs who established a sugar-refining operation in the town in 1676, thus participating in one of the rapidly increasing processing trades based on imports entering the western ports of England from the colonies in the New World.[117] Jane Laithwaite,[118] her daughter and son-in-law, Henry Barton, an innkeeper who kept the Eagle and Child in Church Street,[119] realised that there was a potential profit to be made from the sale of refined sugar. They concluded an agreement with John Woosey, a sugar boiler who had experience of refining both in Liverpool and in Chester, whereby they would provide premises for the work in addition to the raw sugar, fuel, moulds and all the other necessary basic materials. They also agreed to provide him with board and lodging for seven years. In return, Woosey would provide the expertise and would hire any assistants he required, at his own expense. At the end of each year of the operation, the profits were to be divided into two equal parts – one for Woosey and the other for the investors.

It was intended that a house at Moor Street End belonging to Ann Laithwaite should be converted into a sugar house. The subtenants, the Whalley family, were evicted, but Ann had difficulties and the house was never converted. Instead, they prevailed upon John Woosey's father, Henry Woosey, to allow John to boil sugar in his kitchen in Bickerstaffe[120] in a 'pan' – probably what we would call a vat – previously used for soap boiling. The operation proved to be very successful, so much so that the Laithwaite–Barton family decided that John Woosey was having 'too great a bargain of them' and insisted that he should also teach Henry Barton how to boil sugar. John Woosey refused to do this, 'having spent a great deal of time and with great charges and labour having attained to the art and skill' when he served his apprenticeship. Finally, the family refused to supply any more materials, secured Woosey's arrest for debt, and the whole operation was abandoned.[121]

Most of the ports on the western seaboard and several of the nearby towns successfully established industries processing imports from the American colonies. The tobacco and sugar processing of Bristol and Liverpool, the furniture manufacture of Lancaster, and the cotton industry of south Lancashire are well documented examples. Ormskirk was situated to take advantage of one aspect of Liverpool's trade, but a scheme which had the potential to form the focus of extensive economic activity foundered and came to naught. It is significant that this scheme was abandoned only two years before the leading lawyers in the town proposed an extension to the courts and to the legal function of the town (see p. 26). Evidently, in the early 1680s, confidence was high in the town. At last the recovery from the effects of the Civil War was complete and the townspeople were ready to explore any economic options open to them. Unfortunately, although sugar was refined successfully and sold in Ormskirk for about three years, its permanent establishment as one of the town's leading products was doomed by the greed of the investors and a clash of personalities.

10. Ormskirk Market at the beginning of the twentieth century.

From our examination of the market in Ormskirk, it can be seen that a rationalisation occurred within the market-place similar to that identified by Corfield as taking place between markets. Bulky products which were difficult to handle in the market-place moved out and were sold by sample. Plentiful products in excess of the demand of local people were bought wholesale and transported to other areas, or acquired by middlemen who stored them until they could make a profit. Craftsmen whose goods were in steady demand opened retail shops, often trading from both market-place and shop, while other manufacturers, such as the soap boilers, grasped the opportunity to dispose of their goods to a new clientele in the market. While all these changes were taking place, a steady trade continued in the market-place, providing the inhabitants and people from the surrounding villages with their needs. Each market day the lanes were thronged with people just as they had been on the day of the great storm of 29 April 1697, when 'they could hardly pass in the lanes for the baskets, panniers, sacks and people which the horses had thrown down in their return from Ormskirk market'.[122]

Similar conditions to those in Ormskirk existed in other successful markets in the north-west. The markets in two Cheshire towns were analysed by Mitchell, and Table 2 gives a comparison between the goods sold in those markets and those available in Ormskirk Market in the eighteenth century.

TABLE 2. A comparison of stalls in the markets in Stockport, Macclesfield and Ormskirk in the eighteenth century[123]

Stockport	Macclesfield	Ormskirk
meat	meat	meat
bread	bread	bread
fruit & vegetables	fruit & vegetables	fruit & vegetables
dairy products	tobacco	dairy products
seeds	salt	hempseed
honey	gingerbread	poultry
lard		fish
bacon		leather
		flax
		soap

The location of the individual towns and their specialisation in locally products explain the differences. For instance, the salt for sale in Macclesfield was a product of the nearby salt mines, while the fish on sale in Ormskirk came from the nearby coast. Ormskirk was a centre for the sale of livestock and of meat, and consequently a centre for the leather industry. Similarly, flax was a local product and soap was produced locally for use in the preparation of cloth for dying. The goods in the Stockport market indicate that pig farming on the lower slopes of the Pennines produced a surplus of bacon and lard for disposal in the market, while honey originated in the heather on the nearby moors. Tobacco in the Macclesfield market defies an easy explanation. Perhaps it was an entrepreneur's answer to local demand.

CHAPTER II

Trades and Occupations

As we have seen, as long as demand remained low and could be met by a weekly market, most trading remained in the market and workshops. However, as a society evolved which felt the need for more goods and could afford them, trading extended into retail shops and the occupational profile of the town altered.[1] The emergence of retail shops came late in the north-west. For instance, in Manchester in 1755 the retailing of milk, butter and coal were described as 'new methods of gaining a livelihood unknown in the Town till very lately'.[2] A change in the demand also caused a change in the products supplied by the producers. In order to chart these changes, I have compiled Table 3, which lists all the occupations followed by Ormskirk people mentioned in any of the documentary evidence I have found.[3]

The range of sources consulted has ensured that the evidence is less biased than if it was drawn from one source, but it is impossible to collect a perfect sample of the occupations of the townspeople without a contemporary document specifically drawn up for that purpose. To enable comparisons to be made, I divided the occupations into ten categories.

agricultural	metal
building	professional
distributive	service
food and drink	textile
leather	others

Table 3. The numbers of workers in each category of occupations

Workers in the food and drink trade		Agricultural workers	
innkeeper	119	yeoman	104
victualler	43	husbandman	43
butcher	40	labourer	29
maltster	35	farmer	18
grocer	28	gardener	5
miller	16	cowman	1
baker	6	swineherd	1
vintner	3	Total	201
fishmonger	2		
confectioner	1	Building and woodworkers	
distiller	1	carpenter	23
Total	294	joiner	16

cooper	15
glazier	14
bricklayer	11
cabinet maker	11
mason	10
plasterer	10
slater	8
plumber & glazier	4
pavier	3
white washer	3
millwright	2
painter	2
sawyer	2
glazier plumber	1
organ builder	1
plumber	1
timber merchant & builder	1
chairmaker	1
ship's carpenter	1
stone carver & builder	1
wheelwright	1
wheelwright & innkeeper	1
Total	144

Professions

schoolteacher	25
attorney	22
surgeon	17
apothecary	15
clerk	15
doctor	10
vicar	7
minister (Presbyterian)	8
priests (Benedictine monks)	3
bailiff	2
curate	2
coroner	1
auctioneer	1
barrister	1
tutor	1
Total	130

Leather trades

shoemaker	64
saddler	16
tanner	15
cordwainer	9
currier	9
glover	8
skinner	4
clogger	2
skinner	
ale house keeper	1
whipmaker	1
Total	129

Textile workers

tailor	30
weaver	24
hatter	12
flax dresser	10
rope maker	8
cotton manufacturer	4
dyer	4
feltmaker	4
mantua maker	3
bodice maker	2
breeches maker	2
cloth worker	2
collar maker	2
milliner	2
periwig maker	2
stay maker	2
dressmaker draper	1
flax merchant	1
checkman (weaver)	1
serge weaver	1
silk weaver	1
woolcomber	1
Total	119

Distributive trades

shopkeeper	19
woollen draper	18
ironmonger	10
linen & woollen draper	10
mercer	8
chapman	6
draper	6
tallow chandler	6
merchant	4
carrier	3
haberdasher	3
higler (middleman)	3

bookseller	2	waiter	1
bookseller & ironmonger	2	workhouse master	1
East India merchant	1	**Total**	**85**
grocer & hosier	1		
grocer & mercer	1	**Miscellaneous workers**	
grocer & nurseryman	1	gent	43
haberdasher hats	1	soldier	11
linen draper		gauger (exciseman)	5
tea dealer	1	captain	4
chandler	1	mariner	3
tallow chandler & soap boiler	1	soap boiler	3
traveller	1	horn comb maker	2
wine & oil seller	1	colonel	1
Total	**110**	sailor	1
		Total	**73**
Service industries			
servant	31	**Metal workers**	
barber	16	blacksmith	30
midwife	7	clock & watch maker	7
housekeeper	5	brazier	6
ostler	4	nailer	6
postmaster	3	watch maker	6
bellman	2	balance maker	3
nurse	2	card maker	3
organist	2	farrier	3
excise officer	1	locksmith	1
perfumer & hairdresser	1	pump maker	1
hairdresser & whipmaker	1	smith	1
officer of Excise	1	toolmaker	1
hairdresser	1	umbrella maker	1
ratcatcher	1	whitesmith	1
chaise driver	1	**Total**	**70**
scrivener	1		
sexton	1	**Grand Total**	**1,362**
stableman	1		
toll gatherer	1		

Many difficulties were encountered in compiling this table, among which was the widespread practice of multiple occupations, particularly before the 1760s. For instance, the inventory of Richard Woods (1667) listed cooper's vessels, currier's working boards and unthreshed corn, indicating that he followed three different occupations. Similarly, William Moorcroft, whose inventory included a shop stocked with pottery, was described as a plasterer in his will (1727), while Thomas Hodson, described as a skinner, left a fully equipped 'drinkhouse' (brewhouse). Others actually claimed two occupations. For instance, in 1750 James Stuart described himself as a bookseller and ironmonger in an advertisement.[4] If one of the occupations seemed to be predominant in other documents, I have included that and discarded those which represented a by-employment. When both occupations have more or less equal coverage, I have included both.

Another problem in charting occupations was that of differentiating between individuals with the same name and occupation. I have opted for a period of thirty years as the average number of years during which a working man would be likely to appear in legal documents. So, if a second individual of the same name and occupation appeared after thirty years, I have included him as a different individual, possibly a son with the same name as his father. Yet another difficulty was the fact that, as the signatories in the parish registers claimed that they lived in Ormskirk, meaning the wider parish, not the township, the registers could not be used.

The description of a man as a 'gentleman' was problematic because the term had so many meanings. It could mean that he belonged to the gentry, it might denote that he had a university degree, it might have been applied to an elderly retired man or it might have been used as a courtesy title. In fact its use was becoming broader and less specific. The term 'yeoman' was also an imprecise description which could denote a farmer, a man who cultivated a smallholding in addition to his usual occupation, or, like 'gentleman', could denote status rather than occupation. Consequently, the numbers in the agricultural category may be inflated by many who had only a slight connection with agriculture or who qualified only on the grounds of status. This category may also include some whose permanent home was outside the township but who came to Ormskirk for seasonal work. That is a danger in any survey of this kind for, as we have seen, the population of a market town is not a static body but is continually expanding and contracting as temporary residents come and go.

11. James Stuart's advertisement, describing himself as bookseller and ironmonger, and selling Jackson's tincture and various pills.

TABLE 4. Summary of Table 3

Occupations	No. in Sample	Percentage
Food and drink trade	294	21.58
Agricultural workers	201	14.76
Builders and woodworkers	144	10.57
Professions	137	10.06
Leather trades	129	9.47
Textile workers	119	8.74
Distributors, shopkeepers and merchants	110	8.08
Service industries	85	6.24
Miscellaneous	73	5.36
Metal workers	70	5.14
Totals	1362	100.0

Table 3 illustrates the immense diversity of occupations in the town. This summary (Table 4) shows that, taking the period as a whole, the leather trade for which Ormskirk had been renowned in Tudor and early Stuart times employed only slightly more people than the textile trade. By far the largest employer was the food and drink trade, with innkeepers and victuallers constituting 54.7% of those employed. Ormskirk's many roles as a market town, a legal centre, a staging post between Liverpool and the North, a centre for horse racing and, for several years, a spa town, explains the need for such a large catering trade. These roles and the dominance of the catering trade in the town may also explain the large number employed in the building and woodworking trades, for many innkeepers, townspeople and visitors to the town updated their inns and homes, or built new ones during this period, in response to the 'urban renaissance' and 'the extraordinary pressures on them to engage in conspicuous consumption merely to maintain, let alone improve, their status'.[5] Although a large number of lawyers could be expected in a town where both the quarter sessions and the deanery court met, the size of the whole professional sector, which also included schoolteachers, apothecaries and doctors, exemplifies the emergence of an important professional class in its own right.[6] The large number of professional people in Table 4 is particularly remarkable, though their numbers fell dramatically in the later years of the eighteenth century (see pp. 25–8).

In tables 5 and 6 the samples are divided into three periods to illustrate the changing occupational profile of the town. Before summarising the results in Table 6, I have listed the more unusual occupations in Table 5. These required a specialised skill, and the fact that the specialists found sufficient need for their skills to provide them with work, pinpoints a change in demand and the emergence of a consumer society. Admittedly, the 1750–1800 sample contains many more examples which, of course, would increase the number of specialist occupations recorded. Nevertheless, their appearance in such large numbers reflects an economic trend towards specialisation.

TABLE 5. Specialist occupations found in Ormskirk

1660–1699	1700–1749	1750–1800	
stone carver	organ builder	cabinetmaker	organist
horn breaker and	haberdasher of	chairmaker	perfumer
combmaker	hats	painter and	ratcatcher
bodice maker	confectioner	gilder	waiter
milliner	whipmaker	stone mason	cotton
	gauger	higler	manufacturer
	clockmaker	tea dealer	mantua maker
	pumpmaker	brandy merchant	breeches maker
	organist	clock maker	stay maker
	scrivener	balance maker	checkman
	collar maker	umbrella maker	milliner
	periwig maker	coroner	chaise driver
	silk weaver	hairdresser	peruke maker

The emergence of such occupations as cabinetmaker, chairmaker, gilder, organist, chaise driver and brandy merchant, and the marked increase in the luxury trades evoke the luxurious style of living characteristic of the affluent in the Georgian era, while the mantua maker, the breeches maker, the stay maker, the periwig maker and perfumer give us a picture of the elaborate costume and vanity of the townsfolk. Certainly, Ormskirk was one of those towns where, as John Trusler observed in 1777, 'the notions of splendour that prevail in the capital are eagerly adopted; the various changes of fashion exactly copied . . . the great degree

TABLE 6. A summary of the changing categories of occupations*

1660–1699	No.	%	1700–1750	No.	%	1751–1800	No.	%
Food	45	22.39	Food	60	19.23	Food	144	25.49
Professions	37	18.41	Professions	52	16.67	Building	75	13.27
Leather	32	15.92	Building	43	13.78	Textiles	67	11.86
Building	24	11.94	Leather	41	13.14	Distributive	64	11.33
Textiles	20	9.95	Textiles	32	10.26	Leather	57	10.09
Distributive	19	9.45	Distributive	28	8.97	Services	56	9.91
Services	11	5.47	Metal	25	8.01	Metal	48	8.5
Others	8	3.98	Services	21	6.73	Professions	48	8.5
Metal	5	2.49	Others	10	3.21	Others	6	1.06
Total sample	201	100		312	100		565	100
gents	10			17			16	
agricultural	34			68			99	
Total	245			397			680	
Total in this dated group of samples			1322					

* I have excluded both gentlemen and yeomen from the percentages because of the uncertainty surrounding their titles. Agricultural workers, too, are excluded because without the addition of the yeomen, their numbers would be distorted. To correct the picture the numbers in these classes are included separately.

of luxury to which this country arrived within a few years [was] . . . astonishing'.[7] Meanwhile, the inclusion of a ratcatcher provides a glimpse of the less salubrious aspects of Georgian life. In fact, 'the multiplication of new specialist trades and the decline of the old-style multiple occupations was one of the more radical and modern aspects of urban development in the late eighteenth century'.[8]

The ability of these specialists to earn a livelihood resulted from a great surge in demand in the late eighteenth century. That demand's growing strength can be monitored in the increasing proportion of unusual occupations, expanding from 1.99% of the total trades in the period 1660–1699, to 3.85% in the period 1700–1749, and to 4.25% in the period 1750–1800. From these figures the consumer-led change in the economic profile of Ormskirk can be dated as occurring from the 1730s.

THE PROFESSIONS

The importance of Table 6 in providing a picture of the varying occupational profile of the town warrants a full examination of each category. First we will consider the category of professional occupations: doctors, apothecaries, teachers and lawyers, whose position among the hierarchy of Ormskirk trades experienced a most remarkable change, caused by the dramatic reduction in numbers during the 1750–1800 period. Their high profile in the early years was characteristic of the position in the majority of eighteenth-century English towns. For instance, in Shrewsbury, McInnes identified a similar rise in the numbers in professional employment in the century 1660–1760.[9] Although the overall number of lawyers in such towns increased, many barristers deserted the smaller towns nationwide in the eighteenth century, as the two functions of the legal profession gradually separated and the manorial courts decayed. The number of barristers fell nationally, and those remaining abandoned day-to-day legal work for work in the central courts.[10] Nevertheless, the sharp reduction in the overall number of professional people in Ormskirk after the middle of the century was unusual among market towns.

As we have seen, Ormskirk had a long tradition as the venue of both the quarter sessions and the deanery court. In 1682 an attempt was made to extend the area covered by the town's quarter sessions court. A local attorney, Thomas Dod, was engaged to approach the clerk of the peace, Roger Kenyon, with the proposition that 'The good town of Ormskirk' wished to make an application to Lord Derby that 'all four sessions' were held in the town instead of alternating between the towns of Wigan and Ormskirk. (By 'four sessions' they meant the two actual sessions and the two adjournment sessions held in the south of the county.) They stressed that there was a 'commotion of affairs' in Wigan, which in their eyes was setting 'up for a principality of itself'.[11] They were referring to the Wigan riots of that year when Kenyon had enforced the penal laws in the borough, sending bailiffs into the town to distrain for recusancy fines. The townspeople attacked the bailiffs and a riot ensued.[12] The leaders of Ormskirk, grasping the opportunity to increase the town's share of legal business, pointed out to Kenyon that Ormskirk 'lies convenient to the country'. After admitting that 'it would conduce to the benefit of the place', they assured Kenyon that Lord Derby was 'much interested' in the town and had 'been pleased to manifest his favours thereunto upon all occasions'. If their enterprise had succeeded, it would have guaranteed an improvement in the whole economy of Ormskirk. As it stands, it provides positive evidence of the entrepreneurial skills of the town's inhabitants, particularly the lawyers, in the 1680s but, unlike the situation in many towns, that initiative did not continue. Nevertheless, in the early years of the 1700s, Ormskirk continued to be a thriving legal centre.[13]

The reason why the pattern of Ormskirk's professional profile differed from that of the majority of other towns can be explained by a close examination of the careers of three members of the professional sector. Firstly, we will consider the Entwistle family of lawyers. John Entwistle lived and worked in Ormskirk, but acted as the recorder of Liverpool until he was eighty-four, in 1709. His son Bertie, brought up in Ormskirk, later moved to Wigan, where he became a member of the common council. In 1697 he was proposed by Lord Macclesfield to oppose Kenyon for the post of recorder of Wigan, but although he did not receive that appointment he was appointed recorder of Liverpool in 1709 in his father's stead. Later he became vice-chancellor of the duchy of Lancaster, an honour which it is doubtful that he would have received had he remained a resident in the small market town.[14]

Secondly, a similar pattern is evident in the career of Joseph Brandreth, born in 1745 in Upholland, and brought up in Ormskirk where the family moved in 1748 and where his father owned a tannery. He studied medicine in Edinburgh (1767–1770) and returned to practise in Ormskirk for six years. Then he moved to Liverpool to become one of the first three physicians on the staff of Liverpool Dispensary. In 1780 he joined the staff of the infirmary and gained a reputation as one of the founders of Liverpool's medical establishments.[15] Both the lawyer and the doctor moved away because there were fewer opportunities for advancement in Ormskirk than in either Wigan or Liverpool.

Similar reasons prompted the move of Thomas Ball, an attorney 'of Ormskirk, later of Liverpool'. He moved to the port again because its expanding population generated work, and also because out-of-town clients found it easier to contact him in Liverpool than in Ormskirk.[16]

Despite the importance of Liverpool, the quarter sessions and the deanery courts continued to meet in Ormskirk until the last quarter of the eighteenth century, when certain sessions of the deanery court moved to Liverpool. Some sessions were held in Liverpool in 1770, and others reverted to Ormskirk in 1790. Later a similar pattern was followed by the quarter sessions.

The departure of members of the professional classes from Ormskirk to the rapidly expanding towns nearby was one of the causes of the tragedy which finally

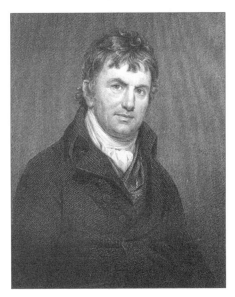

12. Joseph Brandreth MD (1745–1815), by E. Scriven.[17]

13. House of the Brandreth family in Burscough Street. The tanyard and pits were behind it.

overtook the town in the mid-nineteenth century. Without the support and money of these pseudo-gentry, the town lacked initiative, and when it was confronted with a large influx of Irish refugees fleeing from the famine in the 1840s, it became one of the most unhealthy and squalid towns in the country.

THE FOOD AND DRINK TRADE

The immense importance of the food and drink trade to the economy of the town is indicated by the proportion of workers employed in that trade, which never dropped lower than 19.23% and rose to 25.49% towards the end of our period. As mentioned earlier (see p. 24), the town's many functions necessitated a large-scale catering trade, but the numbers of those selling food for home consumption also increased, as Table 7 illustrates.

The marked increase in workers engaged in the preparation and sale of food in the period 1750–1800 was a response to a sudden demand caused by a change in consumer habits rather than by the gradual increase in Ormskirk's population. At that time, many townspeople had a surplus of wealth, the result of the alleviation of several causes of poverty. The plague had been conquered, general health had improved, and towards the end of the eighteenth century, medicine and medical advice were freely available in the Ormskirk dispensary.[18] The long-term effects of civil war had been overcome, and the political climate was more settled. The increasing numbers of foodsellers evident in Table 7 suggest that much of this newly acquired wealth was spent on meat, fish and groceries, thus improving the diet of the townspeople both in the range and quantity of foods consumed.

This was true nationwide. As Barry Coward commented, 'ordinary Englishmen and women began to eat and wear a wider range of commodities than ever before' in the early eighteenth century.[19] As usual the north-west followed

TABLE 7. Food and drink suppliers 1660–1800

Food producers and/or sellers	1660–1699	1700–1749	1750–1800
Butchers	8	9	23
Grocers	5	11	12
Millers	5	3	8
Bakers and confectioners	–	2	5
Fishmongers	–	–	2

London's lead and the widening of the range of consumer goods happened later in this area. The large-scale development of cattle-rearing at that time indicates a rise in meat consumption, while the frequent references to the poorer people insisting on wheaten bread instead of that made from rye or barley, which was considered inferior, provide further evidence of increased affluence. The sale of imported foods, such as tea, coffee, rice and sugar, increased so much that the quantity available for re-export was vastly reduced.[20] Initially sugar was re-exported in large quantities to Europe, but by the 1750s nearly 1 million hundredweight, or 90% of the total imported, was retained for the domestic market.[21] There was also an increased demand for home-grown produce. As Joseph Massie wrote in 1757, 'it is well-known that gardening hath much improved in this kingdom within the fifty years last past, and that vastly greater quantities of roots, fruits, greens, such as Turnips, Potatoes, Cabbages, Colliflowers etc. have been grown of late years.'[22]

The increase in bakers and confectioners in the eighteenth century also proves that the customs of food preparation were changing. Bread and cakes were now bought on a more regular basis from shops which were open daily instead of being baked in the home or bought occasionally from hawkers in the streets. The earliest specialised confectioner recorded in Ormskirk was Robert Moore, who died in 1719.

When all the food and drink makers and suppliers are included among those engaged in the catering trade, the proportion among the whole workforce increases from 10% (1660–1699), to 11.9% (1700–1749) and to 17.1% in the later period (1750–1800). When only innkeepers, alehouse keepers and victuallers are included, the proportion shows similar increases from 8% to 8.2% to 13.2%. This general trend is confirmed by the number of alehouse licences issued during this period. Unfortunately, the licences for the middle period (1700–1749) are missing, but during the period 1662–1699 a yearly average of twenty-three licences were granted, which increased to an average of thirty-five for the period 1750–1800.[23]

The Hearth Tax returns also confirm the expansion of the catering trade during the period 1661 to 1675.[24] Although their dates do not coincide exactly with those of the alehouse licences, the two records are combined in Table 8 to show that over 55% of the Ormskirk inns expanded in size between those dates, 31% remained the same and 14% decreased in size, the least successful inns being divided to provide private accommodation or shops. Three of the five inns which decreased in size conformed to the general pattern of increase in the 1660s but were reduced in size in the 1670s. Of course, some of these reductions may represent tax evasion rather than any real reduction in the size of the inn.

However, evidence remains of one inn which lost its prominent position in Ormskirk between 1680 and 1700.[25] The Eagle and Child on the corner of Aughton Street and Church Street was an 'ancient' house, and its sign, based on a Stanley family legend, visibly illustrated the influence of the earls of Derby in the town. In the 1640s, Hugh Lathom rebuilt part of the inn and made 'a very strong and substantial building of very good timber and other materials . . . very commodious and fit for an inn with necessary and convenient rooms and chambers (the chambers above stairs consisting of a fine dining room with other fair lodging rooms) all being very well boarded and the floors laid with oak.' The inn had sixteen or seventeen beds, and sometimes catered for as many as two

Table 8. Innkeepers and the number of hearths in the inns

		Dates of licences A=1661, B=1662, C=1675	Number of hearths taxed in 1664	1666	1673	Increases etc.		
Ambrose	Daniel	C		3	6	+		
Ball	James	ABC	2	4	2			*
Barton	Henry	ABC		7	9	+		
Barton	John	A	2	2	2		=	
Berry	John	A	2	2	2		=	
Bickerstaffe	Hugh	AB	1	1			=	
Billinge	Richard	A C	1	2	4	+		
Billinge	Thomas	C	1	1	2	+		
Garner	John	ABC	3	4	4	+		
Greenhalgh	Thomas	C	3	4	4	+		
Heyes	John	AB	6	8	8	+		
Heyes	Phillip	A C	4	5	4			*
Jackson	James	A	2	2	3	+		
Johnson	John	B	2	1		−		
Keaquick	Thomas	C	2	3		+		
Livesey	Chris	A C	1	2	3	+		
Morecroft	Margery	A	3	3			=	
Morecroft	Richard	A	1	1	1		=	
Morecroft	Thomas	AB	5	8	8	+		
Morecroft	William	A C	1	2	3	+		
Oliverson	Thomas	A		1	3	+		
Pemberton	John	ABC	2	2	2		=	
Poole	Robert	A	2		4	+		
Scarisbrick	Alex	C	3	5		+		
Seddon	William	C	2	3	2			*
Shaw	John	A	1	1			=	
Sutch	Silvester	C		3	4	+		
Swift	George	AB	1	1			=	
Taylor	John	A	2		3	+		
Walker	Raph	A C	2	3	3	+		
Webster	James		1	1	2	+		
Webster	John	C	1		2	+		
Winstanley	John	A	2	2			=	
Woods	Anne		1	1			=	
Woods	Robert	C	2		1	−		
Worthington	Edward	ABC	3	3	3		=	
			20	2	11	3		

No. of alehousekeepers 36

*	alehouses where hearth numbers increased and then decreased	3
+	alehouses where hearth numbers increased	20
=	alehouses where hearth numbers remained the same	11
−	alehouses where hearth numbers decreased	2

hundred in the dining room. It was 'of good repute and esteem and much resorted to by the gentry and people of quality' – including James, Seventh Earl of Derby (1642–1651), his countess, their retinue and guests – 'being looked upon both for building and recreation as the best inn in the said town of Ormskirk'. However, Hugh died, leaving the inn to his son, Henry, who sold it to an apothecary, John Cooper, who lived in part and converted the rest into two large dwellings and an inn, the Red Lion. The two houses were sold to John Entwistle, barrister, and to Samuel Andrews, an attorney – further evidence of the wealth of the local members of the legal profession at this time. Later, John Entwistle sold his house to Thomas Dod, yet another lawyer. Meanwhile, Margaret Billinge, a widow, kept the Red Lion, and her inventory (1695) shows the great reduction in the innkeeping capacity of that one property during the thirty years since Henry Lathom was innkeeper.[26] Although she had a great variety of mugs, dishes, tankards, possett cups, plates and porringers, only five bedsteads remained to provide overnight accommodation. However, as we have seen, most of the Ormskirk inns increased in size, thus conforming to the trend prevalent in the many English towns as noted by Borsay, 'by the late seventeenth century . . . individual premises now began to benefit from greater investment, with a new emphasis on size, quality and respectability.'[27] Certainly, many Ormskirk inns were of a very high quality. For instance, the inn kept by Gilbert Ambrose, who died in 1692, had eleven rooms, including a gallery and its furnishings, including court cupboards (sideboards often used to display plate), oval tables, carved chairs, mirrors and pictures. In 1690, as we shall see (p. 147), Henry Jones provided viols and 'books of divers sorts' for his guests' enjoyment.[28]

The ever-increasing provision of inns in the late seventeenth century was mainly the result of the expansion of Ormskirk's role as a legal centre. The meeting of the courts created a need for food and accommodation as, for instance, Lord Derby's bailiff recorded in his account for Ormskirk: 1687, 'Spent in ordinaries and extra ordinaries at the court £2 1s 6d', 'at the ending and affearing of the said court 6s 8d.'[29]

He incurred similar expenses in 1689 and the churchwardens also recorded expenses when the ecclesiastical court met in 1666: 'March 6th Spent when we met to attend ye Deanes Court 4s March 6th Spent for a quart of sack given to ye Deane 2s 6d.'[30]

In fact the churchwardens resorted to an inn after the court throughout the eighteenth century. For instance, in 1779 they spent 'at Swan – Court Day 3s 6d'.[31] The inns' private – neutral – meeting rooms were also in demand. For example, the ninth Earl and Countess of Derby used rooms in the Wheatsheaf in 1697, during a family dispute concerning their rights to tithes.[32] Blundell also frequently met his lawyers at inns, as on 18 August 1714, when he 'went . . . to Ormskirk and . . . met Mr Plumb at the Talbot and consulted with him about my going to Lancaster assizes'. Frequently he arranged to meet his doctors at various inns, as, for instance, at the Swan on 3 January 1719 when he 'payed Dr Longworth for physic'.[33]

Traditionally the inn was the venue for celebrations, as when the vicar and the churchwardens met at the Wheatsheaf with the churchwardens of various neighbouring churches after they had taken their oath of office.[34] Blundell often resorted to inns after various social occasions, as he did to the Golden Lion in August 1715 after a visit to Ormskirk Fair.[35]

The turnpiking of the road between Preston and Liverpool in 1771 led to an increase in carriers and coaching, and a parallel increase in the demand for the services of the local inns. For instance, in 1776 the churchwardens paid the innkeeper at the Talbot for his services in receiving goods.[36] Improvements in transport and communications were generally responsible for much of the increase in Ormskirk's catering trade at this time.

Thus Ormskirk expanded its role as a service town, particularly as far as innkeeping was concerned. In Table 9 a comparison of the facilities available in the inns and alehouses in various towns is made from a government survey of 1686. Whenever a muster was called, the large influx of men stretched the amenities of the venue to their limit. Consequently, to avoid any breakdown in the provision of accommodation and stabling in the event of a major military operation, this nationwide survey was commissioned at the time when James II was building up his army, to discover how many beds and stables were available in the inns and alehouses of certain towns to accommodate soldiers.[37] Ormskirk was the traditional venue for musters of the militia. For instance, at the time of the Rye House Plot in April 1683, there was a muster of the Earl of Derby's troop and regiment in the town.[38]

The difference between the facilities in Manchester and Liverpool emphasise the fact that, although Manchester was an established route centre, where stabling was needed, its role as an important industrial town had not yet emerged. By contrast, Liverpool, as a port, already provided ample accommodation for travellers. The same was true of Preston, another port and the principal crossing place of the Ribble. Preston's fast-developing role as an important provincial centre is reflected in the exceptionally high total of both rooms and stabling in the town. Similarly,

TABLE 9. *An abstract of 'A Particular Account of all Inns, Alehouses etc. in England with their Stable Room and Bedding, 1686'*

Towns	Guest beds	Stabling for horses
Ormskirk (A)	67	117
Wigan	33	101
Prescot	43	75
Manchester	128	305
Liverpool	202	333
Preston	217	520
Kendal (B)	279	439
Kirkby-Lonsdale	153	190
Penrith	136	214
Appleby	117	126
Milnthorpe	25	37
Ambleside	18	31
Shap	17	20

Sources:(A). PRO War Office Records, W.O. 30/48.
(B). J.D. Marshall, *Kendal 1661–1801, the Growth of the Modern Town* (Kendal: CWAAS and the Curwen Trust, 1975), p. 7.

Kendal's results reflect both its commanding position and the lack of similar towns on the route north. However, Ormskirk's impressive total of facilities compared with those of Wigan stresses the importance of the town's catering establishments and their part in establishing it as one of the leading market towns in the area.

Between 1700 and 1750 the number of workers in the catering trade remained fairly static, only increasing from 20 to 24 in fifty years. Also, very little construction work for the trade is recorded until 1734, when Thomas Barton, a maltster, erected a new brewhouse. Then in the following year, Thomas Plumbe extended the Queens Head in Burscough Street.[39] As we have seen (p. 26), this was the period when the economy of Ormskirk was changing direction. The spa had decreased in popularity, and the races and cockfights had lost their appeal to the Derbys and their monied set, who moved to more sophisticated venues, leaving Ormskirk to abandon its role as a leisure town.

Ormskirk was not alone in experiencing a slight halt in the expansion of the catering trade at this time. In fact, this static period for the trade has been recognised as a characteristic of the urban scene in the mid-eighteenth century.[40] In the late eighteenth century there was actually a nationwide decline in the provision of inns in consequence of the building of specialised theatres, assembly rooms, estate agents' offices, auction rooms, warehouses and corn exchanges.[41] The construction of canals lessened the wagon traffic through towns which had no canals, but often, as in Ormskirk, this reduction was offset by the increase in carrier and passenger traffic following the turnpiking of major roads. To cope with these changes, many inns were updated and became eating houses or hotels providing accommodation, thus reverting to their earlier, more specialised role.

This happened in Ormskirk, and the need for more staff would explain the rapid increase in the catering trade at the end of the century, for as we have seen (p. 29), the percentage of the workforce rose from 11.9% (35 workers; 1700–1749) to 17.1% (96 workers; 1750–1800). The change in the role of the inn also explains the modest increase in alehouse licences issued. Certainly, one new inn – or hotel – was built in Burscough Street in 1798. This was the new Wheatsheaf,[42] which took the same name as the inn which had been used by the court leet for its adjournments in the mid-1700s.

THE DISTRIBUTIVE TRADES

The size of the distributive trade is distorted in Table 4, because food and drink salesmen have been removed from this category and included elsewhere in order to avoid the difficulty of differentiating between food producers and food distributors. Nevertheless, the sharp increase in the number of shopkeepers is evident in the late eighteenth century, despite the fact that the figures do not include many for whom shopkeeping was a sideline. The documentary evidence resulting from the enforcement of the Shop Tax (1785–1789) provides statistics whereby the number of shops in various towns can be compared. Exemption from the tax was granted to warehouses, to premises selling wholesale, to shops selling only flour, bread, meal or bran, and also to small shopkeepers who paid neither the church nor the poor rate.[43] The returns attest that in Ormskirk 52 shops paid tax, in Lathom 6, in Halsall 1, in Rufford 4, in Everton 1, in Chorley 14 and in North Meols (Southport), Maghull,

Aintree and Burscough no shops at all are recorded as paying tax. Further afield in Kendal, 29 paid tax, in Penrith 15, in Appleby 8 and in Huddersfield 3.[44]

Although three or four chapmen are recorded in Ormskirk during our period, only one, Peter Swift, who died in 1686, left an inventory describing his stock.[45] It included 'gloves, and silk and ribining', but unfortunately the appraisers, tiring of itemising his possessions, concluded with 'other goods he traded in', leaving an imperfect account of his stock. Nevertheless, it appeared to be that of the traditional pedlar. Travelling salesmen caused great anxiety in market towns, because their doorstep selling meant that people would 'have little or no occasion to come to . . . Market Townes for anything' and 'if suffered will in time be the utter ruin of all Cities and Market Towns in England'.[46] This anxiety was further increased by the growing number of Jews who had come to England following Cromwell's reopening of the country to Jewish settlement in the 1650s. The Jews' lack of capital, experience and local connections, and the strict regulations of their religion, forced them to join the ranks of itinerant tradesmen.[47] As a result of this anxiety and to discourage any expansion in the numbers of chapmen, an act was passed in 1696/7 requiring all chapmen to be licensed at £4 per person. Three chapmen were licensed in Ormskirk: John Carmont, Mathew Nicholson and John Gilbertson,[48] but very little is known of them.

Some chapmen were, in fact, yarn badgers (travelling salesmen) who bought spun yarn from the domestic spinner and sold it to the weavers. This trade was often followed by Scotsmen, who travelled on foot.[49] Certainly Scotsmen came to Ormskirk, for in his reply to the Bishop's visitation enquiries in 1778, the vicar of Ormskirk wrote that there were Presbyterian Scottish pedlars in the town 'who after they are quite weary of their packs and burdens choose to settle with us and open peddling shops here, this being the centre of their late customary walks and circulating perambulations'.[50] The register of Aughton Street Presbyterian chapel lists five Scotsmen between 1744 and 1759. One of them, Andrew Carruthers, was a linen draper, while another, Peter Ross, followed the allied trade of tailoring.[51] In other parts of England these Scottish chapmen were remembered by inn signs such as the Scotsman's Pack in Hathersage in Derbyshire. The Scotch Piper in Lydiate near Ormskirk was once known as the Scotsman – probably another reference to the Scottish pedlars.

BUILDERS AND WOODWORKERS

The increase in the percentage of building workers and woodworkers during the early part of the eighteenth century and the slight decline in their numbers in the latter part reflects the same change of direction in the economy of Ormskirk that affected innkeeping. By the 1740s, the development of Ormskirk as a leisure town halted, together with the building boom it helped to fuel. Building continued to be an important industry in the town, but towards the end of the century most of the workers were employed in building small houses in yards behind larger properties, and in dividing larger buildings to cater for the increasing population, rather than in constructing splendid townhouses.

TEXTILE WORKERS

Textile workers, particularly those producing linen, had formed a large proportion of the workforce of Ormskirk since Tudor times, possibly earlier. One early weaver, Robert Mawdesley, paid 20s to join the Liverpool Weavers' Guild in 1591, because Ormskirk had no guild, and he wanted both public recognition of the quality of his work and the privileges conferred by membership of a guild.[52] At that time, linen produced in the Ormskirk area was sold as far away as Coventry, Banbury and Witney, as is attested by the trading connections listed in the will of a 'linen man', William Banester of Croston near Ormskirk, who died in 1595.[53] This shows how important Ormskirk was as a centre of linen production, for, although linen was woven in many parts of the country, and 'perhaps as much as a third of the labouring population might have been involved in the linen industry as a by-employment',[54] that production was usually absorbed by the needs of the workers' families or of the gentry families who owned the estates.[55]

Like the rope industry (see p. 12), the linen industry in Ormskirk was a typical pre-modern industry, governed by its geography – the low-lying mosslands, and climate – mild and damp, and using local organic raw materials. According to James Brome in 1707, 'the county [abounded] with flax to make linen'.[56] Indeed, although most of the flax was grown outside the township, flax dressers, flaxmen, flax women and flax merchants figure as inhabitants of Ormskirk during our period, and an area 'betwixt the sign of the White Horse and the Black Horse in the Church Street' was allocated for the sale of flax on market days.[57] Usually flax was prepared on the farm where it was grown, as Nicholas Blundell and Richard Lathom of Scarisbrick described in their diaries.[58] Then the flax surplus to the family's needs was sold to middlemen who 'put it out' to various workers for spinning and weaving. John Hill of Ormskirk, a 'gentleman' according to his will, was probably engaged in this kind of dealing, for flax worth £29 15s and weights and scales valued at £1 are listed in his inventory, while his total wealth was only £46 19s.[59]

J.D. Marshall found that in the eighteenth century great quantities of linen from West Lancashire were exported through Liverpool,[60] and possibly linen from Ormskirk was in the vanguard of this trade. Indeed in 1666, William Blundell indulged in a financial gamble and bought 3,332 yd of linen for £40 to export to Barbados in the *Antelope* of Liverpool.[61] The deal was successful and he doubled his investment, thus becoming one of the pioneers of the trading connection between the West Indies and Liverpool. Although C. Northcote Parkinson suggested that the cargo had been illicitly collected in Ireland, it seems more likely that William, already under suspicion as a recusant, would export linen made in his own locality so avoiding any unnecessary risks of prosecution for illicit trading in Ireland. Certainly, his grandson, Nicholas Blundell bought sailcloth in Ormskirk from the 'Quaker' – possibly John Crosbie – for renewing the sails of his windmill.[62]

As the shipping industry in Liverpool expanded, so did the demand for sailcloth from Ormskirk. Nevertheless, foreign competitors were producing both sailcloth and fine linens, which undermined the sale of west Lancashire linen. Petitions were sent to Parliament asking for support against foreign competition, and the government, realising the national importance of the linen trade, responded by passing various acts to protect the industry.[63] Duties were imposed on imported linen in 1713, and exported linen was charged no duty at all after 1717. In 1736 an act required foreign cloth to be stamped on landing, and all British vessels to have sails of British sailcloth. In 1742, bounties were granted to those who exported linen.[64] However, there was no great increase in linen production in Ormskirk.

Towards the end of the century, Ormskirk continued to spin linen thread for the sailcloth industry[65] – probably as a by-employment – but the weaving of sailcloth gradually moved away to other centres, such as Warrington, where, at that time, half of the heavy sailcloth used by the Navy was manufactured.[66]

Meanwhile the demand rose for fustian, a finer cloth with a linen warp and a cotton weft, as the introduction of American cotton cheapened the product. Cotton first gained a viable role in the English textile industry in the production of fustian, and, as Sir Charles Wilson observed, 'in Lancashire, cotton manufacture was grafted on to the earlier linen technology'.[67] By the 1770s two weavers specialising in weaving fustian joined Ormskirk's textile workers to supply the increased demand. Possibly these weavers used the cotton which, according to Arthur Young, was spun in the workhouse by the paupers.[68]

In the early eighteenth century, silk production was introduced into Ormskirk from Macclesfield,[69] and in the second decade one Ormskirk weaver, William Hewitt, specialised in weaving silk.[70] Included in his inventory was silk 'in the knot', worth 10s and 'ribband in the looms' (3s), suggesting that his main occupation was weaving ribbon, not cloth. Although silk ribbon was fairly expensive, it was in great demand, and in 1680 Anne Weeming, the market stallholder, carried a stock of ribbon worth £6, approximately 19% of her total outlay on haberdashery.[71] The lifestyle of a successful silk weaver is evoked by the many luxuries listed in Hewitt's inventory, while the virginals, pewter salver, pewter mustard box, the pictures, the carved chairs and the long-case clock also indicate the amount of financial security necessary to follow that trade.[72]

Very few Ormskirk workers were employed in this craft during the early eighteenth century, because of the shortage of raw silk and its cost. The shortage was so severe that waste silk, discarded by the silk-throwsters, was boiled, combed and spun again into second-rate thread. This process was so profitable that, as Arthur Young reported, a waste silk industry was established in Kendal by the London silkmen who found it worthwhile to transport the waste silk from London to be reconditioned in the north-west.[73] Although no similar industry was set up in Ormskirk, the local silk weavers would certainly use cheaper reprocessed silk whenever possible. Competition from continental and eastern silk manufacturers meant that the export market was virtually closed to English silk, and imports of foreign silk reduced the home market.[74] Nevertheless, handloom silk weaving continued in Ormskirk until the end of the nineteenth century,[75] during which time supplies of raw silk had improved. There was a silk factory to the west of Burscough Street in 1825,[76] but that was probably a nineteenth-century development.

The woollen industry had a long history in the town and, during the seventeenth century, at least four feltmakers were at work. The inventory of an Ormskirk woollen weaver, John Prescot (1716), gives us a comprehensive picture of the production of cloth from wool. The weaver had in his workshop 'whole wool' (the raw material), comb wool, short wool, worsted ready spun, woollen yarn, warping bars – on which to wind the warp ready for the loom – one chain of wool ready warped, and 'goods ready woven'. The loom is not mentioned, possibly because it belonged to a 'putter-out', or it may have already passed to another member of the family, but that is unlikely because he still owned the other implements and his only 'reputed' son was a child. The total value of the goods in the inventory was £20 13s 10d, of which the wool, cloth and tools amounted to

£16 8s 4d, approximately 75% of his total wealth. The humble lifestyle portrayed by Prescot's three stools, a table, two cupboards, bed and bedsteads, wooden vessels and two brass kettles is in stark contrast with that of the affluent silk weaver.[77]

Wool was spun as a by-employment by the Ormskirk womenfolk whenever time permitted. The skill of northern spinners was well known, and during our period Norwich weavers sent wool by land carriage to be spun in the northern counties.[78] Thomas Crossley of Bradford gave an interesting account of 'putting out' wool to Ormskirk spinners towards the end of the eighteenth century. The wool was sent in packs of 'tops' (1 lb weight of wool) by the Leeds and Liverpool canal via Skipton. The pack was consigned to a small shopkeeper, who received a halfpenny a pound for putting out, a task he gladly undertook for it brought him customers. Crossley explained that 'much difficulty was experienced with the yarn, we had to sort it and from the same top there would be yarn as thick as sixteens and as small as twenty-fours showing the difference in the spinners'.[79] Certainly this would happen as young children were often given the task. In the 1780s this difficulty was overcome by setting up factories where, in the words of Matthew Boulton, workers could be kept 'under our eyes and immediate management'.[80] When that happened in the woollen towns, the hand spinners of Ormskirk were redundant.

Although factories appeared in Ormskirk at the end of the eighteenth century, it is unclear whether any of them were woollen spinning mills. Factories were mentioned under three different descriptions: in 1787, Plumbe and Woods' cotton manufactory was recorded;[81] during the period 1790–99, Davenport's factory repeatedly appeared in the Derby rental accounts;[82] and in 1792, William Green's factory was mentioned.[83] Whether these describe the same factory at different dates, or whether two or three different factories existed, is uncertain. It is also unclear what kind of process took place within them. William Green was not recorded as a tenant of the Derby estates, but, as Davenport's factory and that of William Green were contemporary, it is possible that Green was Davenport's manager. Certainly cotton was woven at at Green's factory, for in 1793 a pauper apprentice, Thomas Wright of North Meols, was bound to learn cotton weaving there. However, despite the success of the cotton industry elsewhere, the factory in Ormskirk experienced hard times, and during one of these, Wright absconded and returned to his father.[84]

In the early nineteenth century the upper floor of a cotton factory – again to the west of Burscough Street[85] – was converted into a hall for the sale of linen. Thus handloom linen weaving continued alongside the manufacture of cotton. In 1819 the hall was described as 'built for canvas over the cotton manufactory on an extensive scale, which did not answer the purpose of the erection. It is now used as a linen hall and is only open at the annual fairs'. Evidently, the tradition of selling linen at Ormskirk Fair continued until the nineteenth century. The spinning of cotton 'for the Manchester trade' was described as 'the principal manufacture' of the town until the mid-nineteenth century, but cotton weaving seems to have been abandoned earlier.[86]

Despite the introduction of factories to the town, the proportion of those employed in the textile industry during the period 1750–1800 only increased from 10.26% to 11.86%, and much of that increase was accounted for by more specialised finishers: the breeches maker, the mantua maker, the stay maker, the milliner, the tailor and the hatter. Indeed, the town was little affected by the boom in cotton production sweeping the north-west at that time.

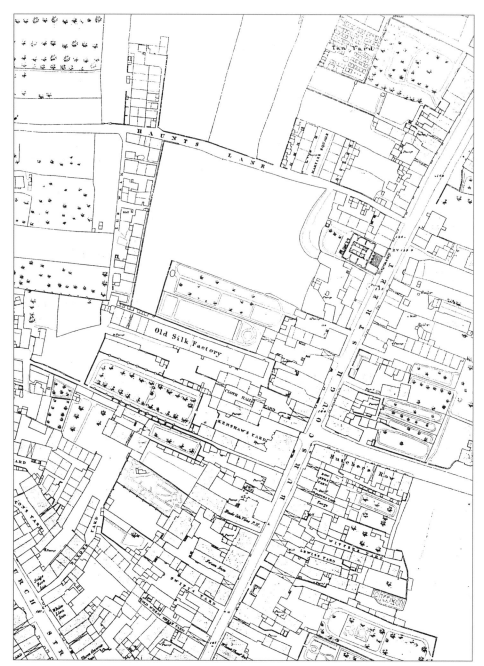

14. Location of the factories and linen hall, 1850s.

THE LEATHER WORKERS

The importance of the leather industry in Ormskirk can be gauged by the fact that whereas in most urban centres it employed about 8% to 10% of the working population, in Ormskirk that proportion ranged from 10.09% to 15.92%. However, late in the eighteenth century there was a relative decline in the English leather industry, a fact observed by Macpherson, writing in 1805. Clarkson noted that in Leicester, Chester and Nottingham, 'as the industrial revolution gained momentum, the leather industry gradually slipped from its leading place in the economy'.[87] In Ormskirk, too, there was a decline in the proportion of leather workers, but here another factor contributed to the decline. Leather processors from Ormskirk gradually withdrew into the rural areas surrounding Liverpool. Some of the names of farms to the south of Ormskirk, such as Tanpit Farm in Downholland, still bear witness to their location.

Indeed, as Table 10 shows, whereas processors – tanners, curriers and skinners – initially made up 34.4% of the leather workforce, that proportion fell first to 27.5% and then to only 13.8%. The majority of Ormskirk's leather workers at the close of the century were shoemakers, saddlers and cordwainers – those who made leather goods.

TABLE 10. The various types of leather trades[88]

Trade	1660–1699		1700–1749		1750–1800	
Occupations using leather						
Shoemakers	15		22		27	
Heelmakers					1	
Cordwainers					8	
Cloggers					1	
Glovers	4		3		1	
Whipmakers			1			
Saddlers	1		3		12	
Total and percentage of leather workforce	20	62.5%	29	72.5%	50	86.2%
Leather processors						
Tanners	9		11		3	
Curriers	2				4	
Skinners					1	
Total and percentage of processors	11	34.4%	11	27.5%	8	13.8%
Total leather workforce	32		40		58	

THE METAL WORKERS

Ormskirk's metal industry also altered during our period, as the workers gained greater skills and adapted to the needs of the new consumer society. In the seventeenth century only four blacksmiths and one nailer worked in the town. By the eighteenth century, specialists such as the pump maker and the three clockmakers appeared. By the close of that century, work demanding greater precision was undertaken by a gold balance maker, three cardmakers for the textile trade and five clock and watchmakers. The excellence of Ormskirk's long-case clocks was acknowledged nationwide and the reputation of the watchmakers of Ormskirk and Prescot was such that their watches were often sold at three guineas apiece – more than three times the price of a London watch.[89]

THE SERVICE INDUSTRIES

The service industries echoed the same trends as the other industries. Again, skilled specialists appeared. For instance, in the early period there were only two barbers in the town, and by the last period there were nine barbers, three hairdressers and a peruke maker. Similarly, in the early period there were two servants, and by the later period that had increased to twenty-one servants, five housekeepers, one waiter, three ostlers and a stableman. New occupations emerged, such as chaise driver and perfumer, while, as we have seen, other specialised occupations, such as organist, sexton and ratcatcher, previously regarded as by-employments, grew in importance. The steady growth of the service industry from 5.47% (1660–1699) to 6.73% (1700–1749) to 9.91% (1750–1800) was very similar to that in other towns. For instance, in Shrewsbury[90] and in Preston there was only one barber recorded on the Guild Rolls of 1702 and by 1742 there were thirty-three.[91]

A COMPARISON WITH THE OCCUPATIONAL PROFILE OF OTHER TOWNS

C.B. Phillips compiled a table of the freemen's occupations in Kendal during the 1690s,[92] which is compared with the early period for Ormskirk in Table 11.

TABLE 11. The occupational profiles of Ormskirk and Kendal

Occupations	Kendal 1690s		Ormskirk 1660–1699	
	No.	%	No.	%
Textiles	170	43.0	20	9.9
Leather	81	20.5	32	15.9
Services	36	9.1	11	5.5
Distributive	33	8.4	19	9.5
Metal	28	7.1	5	2.5
Building	25	6.3	24	11.9
Professions	13	3.3	37	18.4
Food	9	2.3	45	22.4
Others			8	4.0
Totals	395	100	201	100

15. *Examples of long-case clocks made in Ormskirk: by John Wignall, c. 1786; by Thomas Helm, c. 1780; by Thomas Helm, c. 1780; by Jon Taylor, c. 1725. Photographs courtesy of R.W. Baxter of Southport.*

Surprisingly the two market towns did not have similar profiles. Kendal's woollen industry outstripped Ormskirk's linen industry, while the catering industry in Ormskirk employed many more workers than that in Kendal, despite the fact that the War Office documents recorded a far larger provision of inns in Kendal. There was also a larger proportion of professional people in Ormskirk, possibly on account of the spa attracting apothecaries and doctors. However, both towns employed exactly the same proportion of distributive workers.

The comparison shown in Table 12, between Preston and Ormskirk, was compiled using Borsay's findings from the in-burgesses of the period 1702–1742,[93] which I have edited to correspond to the Ormskirk summary table within the same period.

Again, the comparatively large proportion of professionals employed in Ormskirk emerged, while the textile industry in Preston far outstripped that in Ormskirk, even in the early 1700s.

Birmingham's occupations in the 1770s from trade directories[94] provides the comparison in Table 13, but the number of professionals are excluded from the Birmingham sample. In order to compare similar sources, the Ormskirk directory for 1786 is used, but the sample was so small that I have included the general occupational profile of Ormskirk to provide a better comparison.[95]

Birmingham resembled Ormskirk in the high proportion employed in the food and drink trades. Those included among 'other' trades in the Birmingham sample were button makers and toymakers, neither of which featured in Ormskirk. Whereas the metal industry was the major productive trade in Birmingham, textiles held that position in Ormskirk. Table 14 provides comparisons with Manchester and Appleby using data from directories,[96] and with Shrewsbury using the register of freemen admissions.[97]

TABLE 12. *A comparison between the Occupational Profiles of Preston and Ormskirk, 1700–1750*

| Occupations | Preston | | Ormskirk | |
	No.	%	No.	%
Building	95.3	22.1	43	13.8
Textiles	91	21.2	32	10.3
Food	72.3	16.8	60	19.2
Leather	53.6	12.5	41	13.1
Services	36	8.4	21	6.7
Metal	32.3	7.5	25	8.0
Professions	27.3	6.3	52	16.7
Distributive	16.3	3.8	28	9.0
Others	6	1.4	10	3.2
Totals	430.1	100	312	100

TABLE 13. A comparison between the occupational profiles of Birmingham (1770) and Ormskirk 1751–1800

	Birmingham 1770 directories		Ormskirk all sources		Ormskirk 1786 directory	
	No.	%	No.	%	No.	%
Food	387	31.4	144	27.9	10	16.1
Others	224	18.2	6	1.2	1	1.6
Metals	173	14.0	48	9.3	7	11.3
Distributive	137	11.0	64	12.4	10	16.1
Leather	99	8.0	57	11.0	6	9.7
Textiles	98	7.9	67	13.0	17	27.4
Builders	69	5.6	75	14.5	10	16.1
Services	46	3.7	56	10.8	1	1.6
Totals	1,233	99.8	517	100	62	99.8

The profiles of Appleby, Ormskirk and Shrewsbury are similar. The high proportion of professional workers in Appleby reflects its position as a parliamentary constituency and legal centre for Westmorland, and the low proportion in Ormskirk reflects the drift of professional workers into larger towns at this time, as examined earlier (see pp. 26–8). The lower proportion of workers employed in the food and drink trade in Shrewsbury is problematical. Perhaps the through traffic was not so great as that through Appleby and Ormskirk, or perhaps other towns provided accommodation nearby, which reduced the demand. Manchester differs from the other towns in its high proportion of textile workers, indicating its future development. Perhaps the surprisingly low proportion of building workers in Manchester can be explained as a distortion of the evidence resulting from the choice of only one year for the statistics.

Table 15 concerns only shopkeepers, which have been divided into various categories.[98] The figures for York were taken from directories, while those for the Provinces came from the *Gentleman's Magazine*.

TABLE 14. A Comparison of the occupational profile of four northern towns

Occupations:	Manchester 1772		Appleby 1793		Ormskirk 1751–1800		Shrewsbury 1750–75	
	No.	%	No.	%	No.	%	No.	%
Food	181	25.6	14	29.8	144	25.5	60	21.7
Builders	34	4.8	7	14.9	75	13.3	23	8.3
Textiles	254	35.8	6	12.8	67	11.9	38	13.8
Distributive	128	18.1	6	12.8	64	11.3	37	13.4
Leather	27	3.8	4	8.5	57	10.1	34	12.3
Services	26	3.7	–	–	56	9.9	30	10.9
Professions	45	6.4	10	21.3	48	8.5	27	9.8
Metal	–	–	–	–	48	8.5	26	9.4
Others	13	1.8	–	–	6	1.1	1	0.4
Totals	708	100	47	100.1	565	100	276	100

TABLE 15. A comparison between the various types of shopkeepers in York, the provinces in general and Ormskirk

Type of shop	York 1784 %	York 1797 %	Provinces 1748–1770 %	Ormskirk 1750–1799 %
Wearing apparel	37.5	33.6	44.5	35.5
Food	19.2	27.2	20.5	25.9
Drink	4.5	6.3	4.9	1.8
Sundry consumables	14.7	5.7	13.1	16.3
Household durables	2.3	4.6	3.6	6.6
Hardware	9.1	9.1	5.2	5.4
Special services	12.5	13.7	8.1	8.4
	99.8	100.2	99.9	99.9
Numbers in sample	88	176	283	166

The similarity between the pattern of shop types in the provinces and those in Ormskirk is remarkable, and confirms that in this respect the experience of Ormskirk was typical of economic change in a small market town.

Having analysed the reasons for the success – or otherwise – of the different occupational groups in Ormskirk, we will now review the general causes of the town's changing economic situation. Many of these causes affected towns nationwide, while others were purely local or regional. Our whole period was marked by confusion in the English currency caused by two problems: the insufficient issue of money of smaller denominations and the gross undervaluation of the British silver coin, which encouraged counterfeiting and clipping. The shortage of silver coin was exacerbated by the practice of melting down and selling British silver coin in both Europe and the Orient, where the value of silver was much higher. Counterfeiting, clipping and coining were so widespread that shopkeepers had to weigh coins before accepting them, while to replace the scarce coins some of them issued their own coin or tokens and others used small change in foreign currencies. Gradually, various financial reforms were enacted and a more reliable banking system established. However, as late as 1787 a mint enquiry found that 43% of all copper coinage was 'blatantly inferior' and a further 37% was described as 'trash'. One result of these problems was the increasing use of long-term credit for retail sale, an important feature in eighteenth-century trading. Ormskirk traders experienced two particular problems with this shortage of currency in the 1660s and 1670s. Firstly, payment for labour in kind was gradually being replaced by cash payment, which created a great demand for coins of small denominations, and secondly the establishment of retail shops as an extension of market trading also increased the need for coins. The more progressive traders issued tokens for use as change, and as the tokens circulated in the town they were accepted as a form of local currency, with the added bonus for the traders of advertising their businesses. Altogether, eight different tokens are known to have been issued in Ormskirk: by Thomas Crosbie, the Quaker grocer, and Thomas Farrar and Henry Torbock, both drapers, in

16. *Tokens issued by Ormskirk tradesmen. Tokens issued by William Haydock in 1671, with the steeple at the east end of the church; Henry Torbock in 1666; Thomas Farrar in 1666; Ambrose Jackson in 1667; Henry Atherton in 1671; Thomas Crosbie in 1666; Joshua Crosbie in 1668; and John Berry in 1667.*[99]

1666, by John Berry, another grocer, and Ambrose Jackson in 1667, by Joshua Crosbie, another member of the Quaker family of grocers, in 1668, and by William Haydock and Henry Atherton, both in 1671.[100]

Issuing tokens did not solve the local currency problem, because a ring of clippers and coiners was operating in the district in the 1670s and traders were a vulnerable target. In fact, one of these coiners confessed to buying corn at Ormskirk Market, 'where he did put off his counterfeit money'. Clippings were collected from several sources, ranging from Jane Smolt, a poor widow living in Scarisbrick, to William Laithwaite, a rich alderman in Wigan. Also, collection places such as the alehouse of Peter Woosey – close to the Stanley Gate at Bickerstaffe near Ormskirk – were arranged, where the silver was passed to larger dealers. The collectors' usual procedure was to pay for the clippings of silver in clipped money or in a larger amount of counterfeit money, which was then 'passed' in Ormskirk, Wigan or Preston. The actual coining was done mainly at Rawcliffe in the Fylde, where there was 'a very safe roome to coin in'. The ring was broken in 1680, when one of the leaders was caught carrying his apparatus to London, where he intended to set up another operation.[101]

All these difficulties with coinage inhibited trade in Ormskirk until the mid-eighteenth century, but gradually the national improvement in currency affected the town, indirectly causing some of the alterations we have noted in the occupational profile. Nevertheless throughout the whole period credit trading hindered progress and stretched the resources of local traders. Several Ormskirk inventories illustrate the existence of widespread credit dealing. In 1661 the total value of the goods of Thomas Smith, blacksmith, amounted to £49 12s 11d, out of which he owed £24 6s 8d and was owed £13s 14 2d. The 'debts good and bad' of Henry Torbock, woollen draper in 1670, totalled £63 13s 3d, about 13% of his total assets, while the inventory of the humble bricklayer, John Vause (1671), whose total wealth amounted to £36 2s 9d, listed £3s 10d 'owing for work and lent money'. At the other end of the scale was Isaac Woods (1677), the wealthy woollen draper with assets of £596 18s 5d, personal goods worth £25 3s 2d, the stock for his business worth £115 4s 10d and debts 'doubtful and desperate' of £20 11s. In 'specialites and other security', he had £434 19s 4d.[102] In the seventeenth century a substantial cash float was the basis of a trader's credit rating. This guaranteed his credit-worthiness to all with whom he dealt, and without it he could not obtain goods for his trade. As Defoe wrote concerning tradesmen, 'credit is the choicest ware he deals in and he cannot be too chary of it when he has it or buy it too dear when he wants it. . . . Credit is the tradesman's life; it is by this that all his affairs go prosperously and pleasantly.'[103] When that credit was lost, the tradesman could not obtain stock or raw materials and often became bankrupt. Such casualties in Ormskirk included Andrew Wilding, the blacksmith in 1719, Henry Rutter, the wheelwright, and Peter Billinge, the surgeon in 1743, James Prescott, the brazier, and Robert Barton, the maltster in 1769 and Henry Cook, the victualler in 1772.[104] Some of the 'lent money' in the inventories was a form of early banking. John Windle, an Ormskirk maltster in 1673, was owed £62 8s 5d or 62% of his total assets, so he was probably acting as an informal banker, supplying cash and charging interest.[105] As Adam Smith noted, towns were both accumulators and circulators of capital,[106] a 'banking' role common in towns from the seventeenth century. For instance, in 1692 a lady from Preston lent £260 through an Ormskirk attorney – probably Thomas Ball –

who specialised in such transactions, to two Liverpool merchants at 6%.[107] Similarly, Margaret, the wife of Silvester Moorcroft, ironmonger of Ormskirk, explained in her will of 1704 that £33 had been 'delivered to William Hill [a lawyer] to put out at interest for me'.[108] As John Walton noted, 'Lancashire attorneys played a particularly prominent role as loan brokers, finding investment outlets for capital'.[109] Gradually, as the eighteenth century progressed, 'regional webs of credit began to grow',[110] and trade in the north-west began to expand. As this happened in Ormskirk the number of specialist craftsmen and tradesmen increased.

Another precondition for successful commerce in England during our period was adequate transport and communications. Throughout the seventeenth and eighteenth centuries the highways in this area were extremely hazardous. In 1646 the highway between Ormskirk and Liverpool was 'so far worn out that . . . [it] . . . cannot be made passable'.[111] In 1719, during the debate about the Douglas Navigation, it was reported that 'the highways which [were] upon deep clay [were] . . . very much cut up by the land carriage of goods . . . and [were] . . . scarce passable in a wet season'. A pamphleteer replied that 'it [was] the custom of this part of the country to carry most of their goods on horseback, the causeways being generally very well paved'. No doubt that custom arose from necessity.[112] In 1724, Blundell's coach overturned and 'laid fast the road being so deep, so . . . [they] . . . left it and went with [their] horses to Wigan'.[113] A year later Blundell recorded that the roads were so bad that coals had to be carried by packhorse to Crosby.[114] On 27 December 1755 James Stanley sought permission

17. An unknown artist's impression of Church Street in the eighteenth century.

from Lord Derby's chief steward to use the road through Knowsley Park for a return journey to Ormskirk, because 'the roads from hence [Ormskirk] to Warrington are almost impassable, so very bad that the horse and coach were two days in performing so short a part of their journey'.[115] Finally, in 1771, Arthur Young reported seeing ruts measuring 4 ft deep floating with mud near Ormskirk during one wet summer. His remark that 'agriculture, manufactures and commerce must suffer' was perceptive,[116] for poor road communications undoubtedly influenced the town's belated response to the influences of London and to various national economic trends. In fact one of the causes of the spa's failure was the condition of the roads in the area (see pp. 166–7).

Towards the end of the eighteenth century, efforts were made to improve transport. The Liverpool–Ormskirk–Preston turnpike was opened in 1771, and that same year the Leeds to Liverpool canal was begun. The stretch to the Douglas Navigation and so to Wigan was completed by 1774.[117] As the canal carried much of the heavy goods traffic across the Lancashire plain to Liverpool, it relieved congestion in Ormskirk, while the turnpike improved the route through the town. As a result the town's trade altered and expanded.

Unfortunately for Ormskirk, improvements to the roads were Janus-faced. The improved roads also led away from the town, and other sections of the community followed the example of the professional classes and emigrated to Liverpool. Gore reported in 1794 that in Liverpool there were 'numerous erections for most of the manufactures hitherto carried on in the inland towns'.[118] Liverpool's population expanded from 22,000 in 1750 to 78,000 in 1801 as workers flooded into the town.[119] However, this boom lasted only twenty years, then factories moved closer to their raw materials, leaving Liverpool to revert to its former role as a leading seaport. The effects of that temporary boom reverberated in Ormskirk for the first fifty years of the nineteenth century, resulting in severe economic difficulties for the town and appalling conditions for its inhabitants.

CHAPTER III

Development of the Townscape

ROADS AND THEIR UPKEEP

We saw in Chapter II that few improvements had been made to the inter-town highways until the 1770s. Here we will examine the improvements in conditions within the township. As Ormskirk was a manor belonging to the Earl of Derby, any change to the townscape needed his approval. Much of his authority had been delegated to the court leet and its officials. Consequently, the initiative for change often emanated from the townspeople through the court leet, in response to a need they recognised in their economic or social environment. Thus the orders and presentments of the court leet often reveal both cause and effect of many of the town's economic conditions, and also provide evidence of change in the townscape. Roads and amenities in a town were a sensitive barometer of economic conditions. For instance, bad roads discouraged trade and were a sign of apathy among the townspeople, while attractive conditions were evidence of economic success.

There was a two-tier responsibility for the roadways in the town. The justices at quarter sessions had the overall responsibility for the highways between the towns – the King's Highway[1] – while the court leet was responsible for the highway within the township. It was incumbent upon the court leet to maintain those roads in good repair, otherwise the justices could decree that unless repairs were done within a certain time, a large fine would be imposed on the townsfolk. For instance, in July 1675 the inhabitants were indicted at the quarter sessions for not repairing 'the King's highway lying within the said town containing in length 20 roods upwards' [about 110 yd if statute rod or 160 yd if Cheshire rod], 'leading between the market towns of Ormskirk and Prescot'. A fine of £20 was to be levied if the repairs were not done. Consequently, by October the supervisors were able to certify that the road was 'well and sufficiently repaired and amended

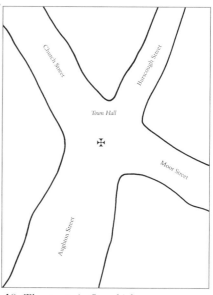

18. The streets in Ormskirk.

and safe for the passage of the King's subjects'.[2] Similarly, in 1745 when Aughton Street again needed repairing, the reluctant inhabitants were threatened with a £100 fine. This brought results and Charles Stanley JP was able to examine the repair and pronounce it 'well and truly repaired'.[3]

Thus, the upkeep of Ormskirk's roads was a major concern of the court leet and as early as the sixteenth century four supervisors of the highway were appointed to inspect the roads, to oversee work on them and to report any who caused the surface to deteriorate.[4] By the Restoration, these officials had been increased to eight: four 'street lookers' and four supervisors of the highway.[5] The court leet's order book, compiled during the period 1617–1721, guided these officials and was continually revised. Nevertheless, the problems of administrating the road repair programme – one of the supervisors' most controversial duties – were immense.

Armed with the order book and the customary rights to call upon townspeople to repair the highway, the supervisors set about their task. A highway rate was levied by the constable to pay for materials, and defaulters were presented to the court leet, as for instance in 1677, when several inhabitants were fined 'for refusing to pay their taxes for the repair of the highways'.[6] The differences in the amount levied on each defaulter suggests that the highway rate in Ormskirk was not a flat rate, as was customary in many parts of the country, but was assessed upon the amount of property held by the payee. A letter from the constable asking the steward to register the defaulters also asks him to add the sums 'charged on them for the use of the highways'.[7] This suggests that a toll system was in operation, but there is no further evidence of such a charge, so it was probably a temporary arrangement never imposed officially. Among the defaulters was the Countess Dowager of Derby, who had been assessed on her mill and kiln for 2s. The defaulters were fined, but the money was not forthcoming from six of them – including the countess. The steward abandoned further action against her and charged the amount to the Derby estate in 1683.[8]

Another difficulty was recruiting labour for each project. From medieval times it was customary for all inhabitants to be bound to provide annually six days' unpaid labour towards repairing the roads. Later, those with a holding of £50 annual value or over were bound to send a cart and two men to work under the direction of the supervisors.[9] However, in seventeenth-century Ormskirk, although the supervisors called upon inhabitants for their customary labour, the evidence suggests the amount of labour demanded of each inhabitant was also assessed according to his land holding. For instance, in 1680 the supervisors indicted fourteen townsmen for refusing to 'come to the repair of the highways'.[10] Their fines ranged from 1s to 6d, the size of the fine presumably depending on the difference in amount of labour they owed. It is significant that already the power of the court was insufficient to secure an immediate response to the supervisor's orders.

Even when they had their money and their labourers, the supervisors still needed road-mending materials. They had an arrangement with the tenant of the local 'delphs' (quarries) to provide stone, but sand was also needed for drainage and to bed down the stones. It was available in some parts of Ormskirk, but often that was not convenient. This was the case when James Hey and Robert(?) Molyneux were appointed supervisors.[11] Immediately across the Ormskirk boundary was Aughton Moss, a good source of sand, so the supervisors instructed their labourers to collect sand from that common. Unfortunately they did not seek the permission of John Plumbe, lord of the manor of Aughton and a prominent lawyer in Liverpool. He served them with a writ out of the King's Bench at Westminster for trespassing and carrying away sand and soil. However, 'the mediation of friends prevailed upon . . . Mr Plumbe to accept a small satisfaction' of 1s and the case was dropped. After that case it seems that the supervisors decided to pay people for ashes and cinders for roadworks and so avoid using sand. However, the authorities refused to reimburse the supervisors if they 'pay anything to any person for his rubbish brought to the highway', so the payment ceased.[12]

A letter from Charles Stanley JP to Lord Derby's chief steward, during the repairing of Aughton Street in 1745, describes some of the difficulties in coordinating the project. He wrote, 'You know Aughton Street is now new paving and all at the expense of the public, except each person's front, which most people have consented to do themselves; you will please let my Lord know it and I daresay he will not be against doing the front belonging to Lord Strange; and as the street has been raised, it will be necessary to raise the cellar floor in proportion to preserve the fall. I should be glad to receive orders about the paving etc. as soon as you can, for fear the pavior should be gone out of town'.[13] Lord Derby, like the manorial lords or corporations in most towns, knew little about such road improvement schemes. The initiative was the responsibility of road users,[14] and its implementation was the concern of the steward.

In most areas, due to the decay in the court leet's power, the responsibility to maintain the highways was transferred to the parish authorities in 1555.[15] However, throughout the seventeenth century Ormskirk court leet still fulfilled its medieval duties of maintaining the roads and appointing supervisors annually, despite finding it increasingly difficult to get the cooperation of the inhabitants. However, in 1691 a permanent Act of Parliament was passed enabling the quarter sessions to levy an occasional highway rate based on the same assessment as the poor rate.[16] This act removed the financial responsibility and, consequently, the repair of the highways from the control of Ormskirk court leet to the quarter sessions. In the next extant court rolls, dating from 1754,[17] the appointment of the supervisor of the highways had been dropped and all that remained was the appointment of street-lookers, whose duties were to report any kind of nuisance in the streets. This changeover of administration occurred in Ormskirk between 1680 and 1754, the period for which the court rolls are missing, so we have a record neither of the change nor of the court leet's reactions. However, one case in 1680 attests that the court leet resisted any erosion of its jurisdiction. The jury presented Thomas Moorcroft for 'bringing a presentment at Wigan Sessions concerning the slutch [mud and vegetable matter] cast out of the watercourse at Aughton Street End out of our Court Leet contrary to our Ancient Orders made in the said court wherefore he is to be amerced'. He was fined 10s – a large fine when compared with the 4s a quarter given in relief to a destitute woman in 1678 by the quarter sessions.[18] Although the court leet's jurisdiction over road repairs was forfeited, it retained its powers controlling obstructions to the roadway and the maintenance of the pavements until the end of our period.

All inhabitants were liable 'to repair and amend their pavements over against their fronts', and if they refused they were charged 6s for every yard of neglected pavement.[19] Although this order was commendable, the result was less than perfect, as a description of English streets written in 1754 attests, 'now one householder minds or paves with small pebbles, another with great, a third with ragstones, a fourth with broken flints, a fifth is poor, a sixth is able but backward and unwilling'.[20] As a contrast we have Dr Pococke's description of Ormskirk being 'exceedingly well paved and . . . neatly kept . . . ',[21] and also the letter to Lord Derby in 1745 concerning the 'new paving' of Aughton Street. However, that letter excepts 'each person's front, which most people have consented to do themselves', so perhaps Pococke was only referring to the actual roadways, and indeed later court leet rolls confirm that both the level of the pavements were uneven and the surface materials were irregular. In 1783 several people were amerced 'for suffering the pavements in the front of their houses to lie so low as to be a nuisance to the road by lodging dirt and other rubbish'.[22]

The boundaries of the roads were defined and preserved by an order of the court leet that the inhabitants should 'well and sufficiently repair, maintain and uphold all their hedgebolts, hedges, ditches and other . . . fences'.[23] This also prevented livestock from straying into the roadway. The most troublesome animals were the pigs, which often escaped and grubbed up the surface of the roadway. Consequently an order was made that all swine were to have rings inserted into their snouts to make grubbing painful, and a penalty of 12d was imposed on the owners of pigs which went 'abroad at large unpeg'd or unrung'. Nevertheless, that did not solve the problem and in 1755 the court employed Henry Moorcroft at a salary of 10s a year to find the owners of straying pigs and amerce them.[24] This had the desired effect and resulted in a greatly increased number of people accused of that offence. By the time of the next extant court rolls (1779–1799), the town had no further trouble from swine – a sign of the gradual urbanisation of the manor.

Running water also destroyed the roads' surface, so it was important that ditches should be cleared. Henry Latham, an innkeeper, was fined 3s 4d by the court leet in 1677 for not cleaning and scouring his ditch.[25] James Stuart cleaned his ditch satisfactorily, but dumped the 'slutch' on Aughton bridge 'to obstruct the same and cause a common nuisance'. He was fined 5s 'for every week the same shall lie there.'[26] The lord of the manor was responsible for keeping water courses crossing the waste or common land, clear of muddy deposits, and his steward paid someone to dispose of this mud. However, in 1745 the steward received an offer for the 'slutch' dredged from the 'bridge hole', and sold it, so that instead of paying 10s for the removal of the mud he received £3 15s.[27] It is significant that the value of the deposits as a fertiliser was realised at this time of widespread agricultural improvements. Later it is possible that another use was found for the mud by Dr Barton, who bought the mud. Did he use it as a treatment? Certainly Ormskirk already had the reputation of being a spa town.[28]

Another tenant whose land abutted the highway flooded a field called Fox Meadow, allowing the water to run on to the roadway and so damaging the road surface. Possibly this tenant was fertilising his fields by flooding them and allowing them to stand waterlogged over the winter – a method popular at this time. To avoid any recurrence of the problem, the jury ordered that anyone flooding that particular field would be fined 20s.[29]

Similar problems occurred within the more 'built-up' area. In 1680, nine men were accused of 'suffering their fronts to be uncleansed'. Each was fined 6d and an order was made that 'each of the inhabitants . . . shall weekly cleanse his respective front from the new pavement to the channel'.[30] The orders give us some idea of the conditions that existed to cause them to be issued. A glimpse of the state of the streets is provided by the order that every Wednesday and Saturday each inhabitant was to 'Scour, Sweep and make Clean all . . . their fronts from the Middle of the Channel . . . that no Dung or Corrupted thing . . . be left unswep'd or remain there or put upon any of his Neighbour's . . . Fronts', or forfeit 12*d*.[31] The high fine of 3*s* 4*d* was imposed on those who laid 'dung, muck or timber in the street to touch or pollute the wall of the churchyard'.[32] Possibly the 'pollution' of the churchyard wall was still regarded by many as sacrilege – as it had been in pre-Reformation times[33] – or possibly, as the churchyard was the focus of many activities, any 'pollution' in that vicinity would offend both townsfolk and visitors.

The justices exerted their authority in 1670 when eight townspeople were indicted at the quarter sessions for making dung hills on the King's highway in Ormskirk. They were given notice to remove them and to level and pave the highway concerned within a fortnight, 'so that the King's liege people [could] pass over', or face a fine of £5.[34]

Dung was a continual problem, aggravated by the twice-weekly market, the pig market and the fair. Consequently the beadle was ordered to 'scour and make clean' the market-place each Wednesday and Saturday and to 'carry away all such dung as shall be gotten'.[35] Horses were brought into the town's inn-yards for stud, and of course animals provided all the transport in the town. Beasts were brought on the hoof to be slaughtered by the butchers in the market-place, and one of the orders gives a vivid picture of the scene: 'Divers Butchers within this Town are Guilty of Emptying Paunches in the Open Street, and Throwing of Tup-horns, Blood and other Dirt to the Annoyance of the Inhabitants'.[36] These actions also polluted the watercourse which ran down the centre of the main streets. As we have seen (p. 8), fishmongers, too, often left 'garbage of fish and other filthy matter' around the fish stones.[37] In desperation the tradesmen were ordered to clean the roadway in front of their shops or around their stalls and were fined 6*s* 8*d* if they neglected that duty.

Eventually a solution was reached which greatly improved conditions. A scavenger was employed to 'go thru' the town

19. *Advertisement for a stud at the George and Dragon, Ormskirk, 1815.*

every Monday 'with a cart (if need be) and take and carry away all small heaps and cobs of dung that he shall find so lying in the streets upon anyone's front whatsoever'.[38] He received 5s a year and the manure for his own use. The earliest scavenger was Henry Haddock, who appeared at the view of frankpledge in 1680,[39] so we can date this improvement to that time.

By appointing its first scavenger, Ormskirk conformed to the general trend among market towns. By the 1700s most towns paid for scavenging and similar activities.[40] Leicester appointed a scavenger in 1686, Hereford in 1694 and Lincoln in 1707.[41] Shrewsbury did not follow suit until 1728, when two were appointed to remove all 'street muck and ashes'.[42] However, market towns were not permitted to levy a local rate for scavenging until 1736, so until then the scavengers' wages were paid from the highway levy.[43] Henry Haddock's duties did not include removing general rubbish, and even in 1755, when William Moorcroft was appointed at an increased salary of 10s, he was only to remove dung.[44]

Another of the supervisors' duties was to prevent any part of the highway being appropriated into neighbouring property. In 1679 they presented William Rostorne for 'carrying away part of the highway into his field', and he was fined 3s 4d. In 1754 John Lyon and Peter Pooley were accused of damaging and not leaving a sufficient foot road. The court increased the fine to 13s 4d to deter others.[45] However, it was not only fields but also buildings that encroached upon the already narrow roadways. In fact a glebe terrier for 1696[46] describes Burscough Street, one of the town's main streets narrowed by several encroachments, as 'a small bridleway'. This was the road carrying all the traffic going north to Preston from Liverpool and the packhorses and carts bringing goods to the market.

In 1771, Arthur Young commented on the state of the road to Wigan from the south, 'The only mending it receives is the tumbling in some loose stones, which serve no other purpose but jolting a carriage in the most intolerable manner . . . I actually passed three carts broken down in these 18 miles of execrable memory.'[47] As Wigan is only about ten miles from Ormskirk, similar conditions would exist on that town's approach roads. The repair of important bridges and inter-town highways was the responsibility of the quarter sessions throughout our period, and they certainly tried to improve their condition. For instance, in 1686 the main road to Preston was repaired and the costs beyond the boundaries of Ormskirk were divided between the townships through which the road passed.[48] The bridge at the southern end of Aughton Street, spanning the boundary between the townships of Aughton and Ormskirk, repeatedly caused trouble. In 1682 it was certified as very ruinous and £90 was needed to rebuild it. The justices, who could raise funds for the repair of bridges in each hundred, levied a rate and the bridge was repaired. It is unclear in this case whether the rate was levied only on the two townships concerned, or on all the neighbouring townships. However, in 1707 more repairs were needed, and an account presented by William Grice, a supervisor, to the justices illustrates one of the hazards of holding public office in early modern England. He complained that, although he had received a payment from the high constable of West Derby Hundred, he was still out of pocket. The justices paid him the 2s he claimed.[49]

However, as the volume of traffic entering Ormskirk increased, the small bridges on the outskirts of the town were inadequate to carry it. As early as 1726, Thomas Stanley JP had certified that Brookhouse Bridge on the road to Halsall was repaired 'as well and sufficiently as . . . can be without enlarging which there is a necessity for'. Later, after the turnpiking of the Liverpool to Preston road through the centre of Ormskirk in 1771, the amount of traffic in the town rose dramatically, and expanded further as more carriers stopped in the town.[50] The narrow bridge at the southern end of Aughton Street constricted all the traffic entering the town, causing the equivalent of today's traffic jams. Finally, in 1785, it was decided to widen the arch by 12 ft. The walls of the bridge were to be of dressed stone from the local 'Grimshaw delph', and 240 yd of paving were used for the approach roads.[51] A substantial bridge was erected and no further repairs were needed in our period.

Since there was nowhere specially cleared for Ormskirk market-place, the intersection of the roads served that purpose, further congesting the highway. Despite the court designating certain areas some distance from the crossroads for the horse market and the yarn market,[52] the problem became critical in 1746. It was decided to acquire land from three tenements to enlarge the highway. Altogether 26.5 perches were taken from Mr Wood's tenement on the corner of Aughton Street and Moor Street. A further 6.5 perches were taken from Mr Entwistle's land on the north-east corner and 8.75 perches from Christopher Aspinall's tenement on the south-west corner.[53] The Town Hall-cum-market hall standing on the north-west corner could not be moved back. Thus, in 1746, Ormskirk joined the many market towns finding their market-places too small for the burgeoning traffic and trade of the mid-eighteenth century. For instance, between 1776 and 1778, property was demolished in Macclesfield to enlarge the market-place. Similarly, after the fire at Blandford Forum in 1731, almshouses, the shambles and the Guildhall were all relocated away from the market-place. In Bath, too, the High Street was enlarged 'to contain all the stalls which on market days encumber the street'.[54] This was the only occasion when the actual plan of the town was altered for, until the 1740s, the roadways could cope with the demands made upon them, a fact which further confirms the extension of trading at that time.

It is significant that there was no initiative to alter the plan of Ormskirk for aesthetic reasons. The attitude was that if the town could cope with the traffic and the market, there was no need to alter it. If not, then the offending part was widened. There was no proposal to move the market to its own site, or to build a market hall to provide cover for all the traders. The butchers did benefit, reluctantly, from the new shambles under the rebuilt Town Hall in 1779, but conditions for the other traders remained virtually the same as they had been for generations.

PUBLIC HEALTH AND AMENITIES

The court ensured that the supervisors and street lookers maintained constant vigilance over the town. In fact, in 1781, when the street lookers failed to persuade the butchers to move 'out of the public streets' into the newly built shambles, the court fined the unpaid officers, William Scarisbrick and Luke Gore, 6s 8d each for neglecting their duties.[55] The preservation of the environment was another of the street lookers' duties, and in 1755 they presented John Clark, the rope maker, for sinking 'a midden stead on the front facing his house in . . . [Aughton] . . . street'. He was ordered to fill up the offending midden immediately and a fine of £1 19s 11d – the highest fine they could levy – was imposed on him if the work was not done promptly.[56] Similarly, Ann Shaw was presented 'for not having a door to screen her necessary [privy] and dunghill from public view, they being a nuisance'. Again, if she delayed, a fine of £1 1s was to be imposed.[57]

The safety of the town's inhabitants was another responsibility of the court leet. In the late 1700s, fines ranging from 6s 8d to 13s 6d were imposed on townspeople who left their cellars uncovered.[58] Similar difficulties were encountered in Ulverston where, at a similar date, the court leet ordered cellars to be covered with strong doors flush with the pavement.[59] Preston had similar problems as early as 1680, but it expanded earlier than Ormskirk or Ulverston.[60]

The inhabitants were also protected by the court from the effects of structural damage. For instance, in 1791, orders were issued to secure flying slates 'for the safety of His Majesty's subjects', and also in 1799, Jane Caunce of Rufford was warned to demolish the unsafe buildings opposite the Wheatsheaf or secure them sufficiently, or she would be fined 13s 4d.[61]

It is questionable whether the court's intention in keeping the property in good repair was to improve living conditions or merely to ensure that the earl's property was well maintained. Whatever the motive, presentments for the neglect of property increased dramatically. In the eighteenth century the three rolls record a total of only six people amerced for 'their housing in decay for want of repair'.[62] By 1755 the presentments increased and became more explicit. That year John Lyon and James Fithian were threatened with a 10s fine if their roofs were not repaired, and, the next year, seven townspeople were presented for 'suffering their houses or outhousing to go out of repair'.[63] The cases escalated, until by the mid-1790s the court's main concerns were property repairs. In 1790 there were fourteen cases and only three other types of case. Whether this was due to a zealous officer, or whether the earl's property was lapsing into acute disrepair, is unclear. However, the trend continued until 1796, when there were only seven marketing offences compared with eighteen presentments for decaying thatch, rotten doors, the lack of repairs to walls and window frames, the lack of pointing, a decaying kitchen roof, a 'necessary' roof in need of repair, broken back walls and the need for new gates and new doors. As the court leet's authority over other matters was eroded, the steward used the court increasingly to enforce the obligations of manorial tenants to keep their holdings in good repair. In fact, the court evolved into an estate manager's court, which dealt with a few market-related offences.[64]

During the latter years of our period, water running off the housetops directly onto the street – and its occupants – was another nuisance common in the town, and offenders were instructed to fix gutters and down-spouts to their roofs.[65] A blocked drain which damaged a neighbour's property was also ordered to be repaired,[66] and, similarly, water flowing off the cornice of one building directly into a neighbour's cellar had to be diverted.[67] James Riddiough, the last offender, was also presented for 'a necessary being a nuisance to James Walmesley's back kitchen by the privy water issuing through the foundations into the said kitchen'.[68] The reason given for this conviction was that it was a nuisance. Nevertheless, there was a new consciousness of dangers to health in the town in the 1790s. A good example locally of a whole new national attitude to hygiene is the presentation of James Ormishar in 1791 'for making a hole and laying dung therein within his premises so near to a public pump from which a drain issues into the well of the same pump to the injury of the water and the neighbours'.[69] The town's realisation of the threat posed by impure water had increased since the late 1600s, when the jurors ordered that 'no inhabitants . . . shall empty any paunch or paunches of any beast, sheep or calf or otherwise to pollute the . . . wells'.[70]

There is no record in our period of culverting the channel down the centre of Moor Street and Aughton Street, which was virtually an open sewer. In fact, in his report to the General Board of Health in 1849, the inspector reported that there was 'no public sewer, except one of about 20 yds which empties itself into the open street under the fish stones in Aughton Street', and commented, 'For want of proper connection, fall and regular flushing, the sewers frequently become the greatest nuisance in the town.'[71] This was half a century later, but even in our period, an open sewer flowing down the centre of Aughton Street would constitute a grave health hazard, especially on market days. Little was done about it until the 1850s, when the Board of Health was forced to intervene.

As there was no piped drinking water, the townsfolk had to rely on wells throughout our period.[72] The original excavation of the town's wells is not recorded, but, according to the order book (1617–1721), wells were already in existence 'erected to and for the use of the inhabitants . . . and chiefly for the good of the poorer sort', presumably by the lord of the manor. Wealthier inhabitants sank their own wells whenever they were needed. Fire was a hazard in the early modern town – a danger acknowledged by the Ormskirk order 'that no Inhabitant of this Town shall fetch or give any fire to any Neighbour, to be carried into the Street uncovered, upon pain, both of the fetcher and giver thereof, to forfeit for every time so doing, each of them [6d].'[73] The Ninth Earl of Derby provided the town with a fire bell in 1684, and in 1876 this was hung in the clock tower built to replace the ancient market cross.[74] After many disastrous fires, especially those in London (1666) and Warwick (1694),[75] Parliament passed several acts to prevent the spread of fire. Initially these applied only to London, but in 1773 they were extended to every parish. Churchwardens were required to maintain one or more manual engines and also ladders to assist escapes.[76] At this time an engine was a tank on wheels with a leather hose and some simple pumping device. The first evidence of the implementation of this act in Ormskirk was in 1787, when four 'engineers', Ormskirk's first firemen, were elected by the court leet.[77] At their instigation, George Hesketh was fined 7s 6d in 1790 for refusing to assist at the fire at Thomas Wood's.[78] Another example of their influence was the order, made in 1791, that whoever set fire to his chimney in the future would be fined £1 11s 6d.[79] Ormskirk's earliest fire station was a small building against the eastern end of the workhouse in Moor Street, where the fire engine was kept in the care of the governor.[80]

A move from individual to communal responsibility can be traced in this account of Ormskirk's roads and amenities. Gradually the community became aware of its collective responsibility to care for its environment, and reaped the benefits accruing from any improvements. At first its concerns were, literally, with what was under its feet – scavenging is a particular instance – and gradually it became conscious of neglected premises and eyesores which offended the public and spoilt the appearance of the town. Finally, invisible dangers to public health, such as polluted water, were acknowledged and attempts were made to eliminate them.

Another discernable trend is the gradual replacement of the rural element by urban concerns. The nuisance caused by wandering swine is replaced in the second half of the eighteenth century by that caused by uncovered cellars. Concern about unscoured ditches is replaced by concern about overflowing gutters. The

20. House of Industry, later the workhouse.

expansion of the town, as both commercial and domestic buildings were erected on 'backsides' and former small holdings, was responsible for this change.

Although a continuous effort was made to maintain the standard of the roads and amenities in Ormskirk throughout our period, the lack of sufficient funds and entrepreneurial ability prevented any significant progress. Most improvements were responses to immediate need rather than investments to promote long-term development. Investment in the future required large cash injections, and the proximity of the expanding towns of Liverpool and Preston meant that there were more exciting and more profitable projects to attract investment by the Derbys, the gentry and the pseudo-gentry of the neighbourhood, than improvements to the amenities of Ormskirk. As we have seen (pp. 27–8),during the eighteenth century this situation was further exacerbated by large numbers of professional townspeople, who could have provided the impetus and funds for improvements, leaving the town.[81]

THE TOWN HALL

The most important – and, arguably, the only real – amenity in Ormskirk, which attracted investment from the Earl of Derby, was the Town Hall, which served as a market hall and court room. The earliest illustration of this building is on a map produced in 1609 as evidence in a case between the earl and some of his tenants concerning encroachments onto the roadway.[82] It was 60 ft long and 20 ft wide, with three large arches on the corner of Church Street and Burscough Street (see p. 62). On the ground floor were seven small shops, occupied mainly by butchers,[83] and a market hall used as a mealhouse. Upstairs were two rooms: an outer chamber where the quarter sessions and the court leet met and an inner chamber which housed the town's chest containing bonds, documents and other articles of value.[84]

Throughout the seventeenth century the earl maintained the old building, re-roofing it in 1683, glazing the windows in 1687 and renewing the ridging stones in 1696.[85] Then on 29 April 1697 a disaster occurred. A severe storm swept the town, doing 'incredible damage, . . . scarce leaving any whole panes in any of the windows where it passed'.[86] Afterwards the bailiff recorded that the Town Hall was 'very much in decay both in walls, glass and roof', and repairs were ordered immediately.[87]

During the early years of the eighteenth century, one of the shops 'under the stairs' of the Town Hall was tenanted by the Crosby family, grocers, who had extended their premises to provide living accommodation. However, in 1753 the roof of the Town Hall, which also covered the Crosby's home, was in a very bad condition and Hugh Crosby sought permission to alter his house, reroof it independently of the Town Hall and extend it into part of the sessions room.[88] As we shall see (p. 64), these plans, coinciding with a building boom in Ormskirk, provide further evidence of the town's increasing prosperity during the mid-eighteenth century.

Lord Derby delayed at least nine years before consenting to extensions into the sessions room, because a company of travelling players had rented that room at various times between 1697 and 1752 for charges varying between £1 10s and 16s.[89] When these payments are added to the butchers' rents, which in 1683 amounted to £10 19s 2d,[90] it is evident that the building was yielding a steady income for Lord Derby.

Then, in 1757, 'the gentlemen of the town' approached him for permission to use the sessions room for assemblies during race week, adding that there was 'no place in town so proper as the town's hall . . . for that purpose'.[91] Here we can trace genuine civic pride and signs of a social 'renaissance' similar to that happening in the spas and many other towns during the mid-1700s. The proposed assemblies would operate in Ormskirk as one of the 'arenas for personal display'– including the church (see pp. 87–93) – where the 'battle' for urban status could be waged among the emerging middle classes.[92] This social renaissance was another indirect result of Ormskirk's economic progress and increasing prosperity at that time.

These two extensions to the use of the Town Hall are also symptomatic of the changing emphasis in the town's economy. Before the 1690s, the Town Hall was the home of the market and the butchers' shops, the quarter sessions and the court leet. After that date, although marketing and legal business remained important features in the local economy, leisure pursuits rose in prominence as the spa and the races increased in popularity, and the Town Hall's function expanded to become a focus for the attendant activities.

By the late 1770s the Town Hall was proving inadequate for all these activities and Lord Derby decided to rebuild it. Although the workmen agreed that the work was to be done 'in a good and workmanlike manner to the best of their art and skill',[93] they were given only three months to complete the rebuilding. In 1780 the Town Hall, the butchers' shambles and the house formerly tenanted by the Crosby family were mostly demolished,[94] leaving portions of old brickwork which the bricklayers agreed to 'dress of'. The new building was to be slightly larger, encroaching over a public passageway alongside the old shambles. When the Crosbys' house was enlarged into the old Town Hall, it had appropriated the corner site between Burscough Street and Church Street, and the earl decided to build a new house in the same position. This resulted in the Town Hall being orientated towards Church Street instead of dominating the whole market-place.

Much of the labour and cartage was provided by the earl's tenants as boons and services owed to him as part of their rents[95] – a very late example of the survival of feudal duties not commuted into money rents – while many of the materials came from the quarries and woodland on the Derby estate. One payment listed among the earl's costs was 12s 6d for ale, a customary boon for the workmen.[96]

The plan resembled the previous hall – a large room for the mealhouse on the ground floor and a sessions house on the first floor – but instead of seven shops, there were only two, later let at 5s and 8s per annum,[97] and to compensate for the lost revenue the new house was built,[98] 'partly on the original Town Hall site and partly on the earl's land'.[99] It is unclear whether 'the earl's land' referred to an encroachment onto Burscough Street, or the passageway already mentioned.

As a final touch of extravagance the earl decided to emblazon his coat of arms on the front of the building on the pediment – a classical feature typical of public architecture at that time. He ordered Benjamin Bromfield, a Liverpool stonemason, to carve it and transport it by canal to Ormskirk. The carriage and the stonework cost £13 18s 6d – almost as much as the cost of the slates to cover the whole building.[100] To crown the building, an octagonal cupola was built to house either the fire bell or the market bell.[101]

The butchers' stalls were moved into the main street while the rebuilding was done. Their rents were cancelled and, instead, they were charged a toll. This caused problems later because, although the earl built new shambles, the butchers refused to leave their temporary stalls, which had proved to be far better trading positions. In fact, the location was so good that four other butchers joined them to take advantage of the situation. Eventually the court leet made an order that 'whereas the Right Honourable the Earl of Derby has at a considerable expense erected and built a shambles in the most commodious part of the town and near its centre (And it is not doubted by this Jury but the same will be let at a fair price) that the present situation of the butchers is a nuisance to the town in general, it is therefore ordered . . . that they [the butchers] do remove their standings or stalls out of the public streets.' A fine of 39s 6d – almost the maximum fine that the court could levy – was to be imposed on any who remained in the market-place. This was no empty threat for the following year eleven butchers were presented for ignoring the order and were fined the 39s 6d.[102] This had the desired effect, and later in the same year several of those recalcitrant butchers paid rents for the new shambles.[103]

These improvements coincided with those taking place 'in many strategically sited inland trading towns . . . [where] . . . the market house and town hall were rebuilt, refronted and refurbished'.[104] Most of these displayed some aspect of classical architecture, like the pediment at Ormskirk. Wigan's hall was built to a similar plan in 1720 to serve as both market and Town Hall with butchers' stalls on the ground floor. Its railed balcony gave the local politicians a platform from which to address the crowds.[105] In Preston, the corporation ordered the Town Hall to be refaced in brick in 1727,[106] and planned to rebuild it in 1761 to make it 'more structurally ornamental'. Eventually the old Town Hall fell down in 1780, and a new one was constructed in 1782.[107] Leeds Town Hall, built in 1710–1711, and Chichester's council house, built in 1731–3, were of a similar plan, with an open arcaded ground floor and a council chamber above. Bath replaced its old Town Hall in 1777 and erected it on a new site in the High Street.[108] Sheffield's market hall was built in 1786, at the cost of £11,000, and the one at Gloucester cost £4,000 in the same year.[109] This building marks a rise in confidence in the respective towns. The council of Preston, a thriving provincial town, felt the need for a larger administrative centre. Gloucester, as the county town, had similar requirements. Sheffield, Leeds and Wigan, emergent industrial towns with ever-increasing populations and booming economies, wanted sufficiently imposing control centres to impress their customers. Even Bath, the leading spa resort in England, required a nerve centre from which to administer the town. Most of these towns had their own speciality,[110] and the new town halls catered for the needs of that speciality.

By contrast, Ormskirk seemed to be a town in search of a speciality. Traditionally it had been the legal centre of south-west Lancashire and the leading market town for the west Lancashire plain, but, as we will see (Chapter VIII), during the period 1670–1750 the town aspired to the roles of a spa town and of a leisure resort, but neither of these initiatives proved successful. In the 1770s even the town's speciality as a legal centre was in danger as the legal fraternity moved into Liverpool, the source of much of its work (see pp. 27–8), and Ormskirk's position as the continuing venue for the quarter sessions in south-west Lancashire was threatened. Possibly the reason why Lord Derby decided to build a new sessions room was to persuade the legal fraternity that his manor of Ormskirk still had much to offer as a legal centre with the attendant social facilities.

In fact the court rolls for 1754 reveal that already the steward, lawyers and jury were finding the local inn far more convenient than the old Town Hall. After meeting in October that year, the court adjourned until December 'to . . . [meet in] . . . the Wheatsheaf.[111] This arrangement for adjournments continued until the rebuilding of the Town Hall in 1780. Then it was significant that, although the court ordered the butchers to return to the newly built shambles, the court did not alter its arrangements in 1781 but adjourned as usual to 'Sam Hamner's',[112] and continued that practice until the close of the century. Possibly Lord Derby was influenced by these arrangements when he incorporated a large house into the new Town Hall. Whether he originally intended to convert the house into an inn when the tenancy terminated is unclear, but that happened in the 1790s and the lawyers gained a new venue for adjournments.[113]

The new position of that inn commanding the market square can be interpreted as making a definite statement about the town's economy. The dominant roles of both the marketing and the legal functions of the town had moved from their central position in the economy and their place had been taken by a variety of service industries and commercial undertakings.

THE DEVELOPMENT OF PROPERTY

While Whitehaven, Bath and Warwick were built or rebuilt according to the classical ideals of the eighteenth century, no attempt was made to create a new townscape for Ormskirk. The earl allowed the wealthier tenants to update their property and to build various small cottages, outhouses and workshops on their holdings but, otherwise, repairs and renovations were ordered only when absolutely necessary, a policy which resulted in many parts of the town decaying into slums by the end of the eighteenth century.

As we saw, vestiges of the town's history as a seigneurial borough can be traced in the few remaining long narrow plots, which constricted the shape of later houses

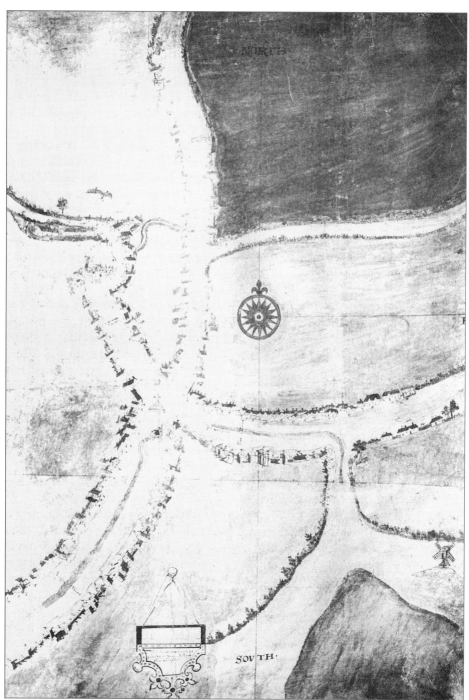

21. Map of Ormskirk, 1609.[114]

and resulted in many being built gable end to the street.[115] Even today, several houses have this form, but there are few visible signs to identify early properties.

The earliest illustration of Ormskirk's townscape is the 1609 map. Despite being dated before our period, it makes a reliable basis for an examination of the town's future development. Although it is impossible to distinguish between houses and other properties on the map, the construction of the buildings can be deduced. Only one house, situated opposite the market cross, has more than two storeys, suggesting that it was built of a superior material. Indeed, on the Derby rental of 1746, that house was described as 'a stone house'.[116] The other properties are of cruck-framed construction, the walls of wattle and daub, and the roofs of thatch or thin stone slabs, described by contemporaries as 'slates'. Some have an upper floor, but usually this is in the roof space, with windows cut into the thatch rather than being a true upper storey. Only one building has vertical banding indicative of box-frame construction. This problematical building was possibly a lock-up, or a mill, built over the stream in the centre of the market-place. No other evidence remains of this building, so it must have been destroyed soon after the map was drawn. A stone chimney and a brick wall are mentioned specifically in the map's documentation, indicating that these building materials were unusual in Ormskirk at that time.

An account of the town's property was compiled for the Hearth Tax in 1664, but, unfortunately, it is unreliable due to the doubtful number of exemptions listed. Certain properties such as those using industrial hearths and houses 'not of greater value than twenty shillings per annum upon full improved rent [and] have not above two chimneys' were exempted from the tax.[117] This caused great dissension nationwide as to what constituted an 'industrial hearth', but eventually it was ruled that smiths' forges, stills and bakers' ovens were not exempted.[118] As Ormskirk had no industries needing hearths other than those, no exemptions could be claimed on that account, but many poor cottagers qualified for exemption. As the unlikely total of only four people 'not chargeable' is listed in 1664, those returns are suspect. The declaration made in 1672 by John Entwistle JP, listing 59 exemptions, is more realistic, and, when those exemptions are added to the 1673 returns charging Hearth Tax on 120 properties, it gives the realistic total of 179 houses in Ormskirk in 1673.[119]

Table 16 has been compiled using the Hearth Tax returns of 1673 and the exemptions allowed in 1672 gives a comparison of the sizes of Ormskirk's houses. Inns, identified from the alehouse licences, were excluded from one column to show a more accurate proportion of large private houses. Nick Alldridge compiled a similar table for Chester including alehouses, and his resulting proportions are included inside brackets. The difference in the results is slight considering the difference in both the size of sample (1648 houses for Chester) and the economic profiles of the two towns. As Alldridge commented, 'this proportional pyramid can be paralleled in many other towns'.[120]

The Derby rentals dating from 1746 listed those paying chief rents, reserved rents and rack rents, and included most of the property in Ormskirk at that date.[121] The earliest rental listed 214 properties,[122] and so, by comparing it with the Hearth Tax returns, we find that, in seventy-three years, approximately thirty-five new properties had been built in Ormskirk. The rental for 1799[123] listed a total of 271 properties – an increase of 57 houses. Thus, whereas the earl's housing stock increased by 19% between 1673 and 1746, in the next fifty years it increased 25% – further evidence of Ormskirk's economic success in the period 1750–1800.

TABLE 16. *The size of the houses in Ormskirk, 1672–1673*

No. of hearths	No. of households including inns	%		No. of households excluding inns	%
1 or 2	130	72.7%	(66.9%)	130	75.6%
3 or 4	31	17.3%	(17.0%)	31	18.0%
5 to 8	16	8.9%	(12.7%)	11	6.4%
Over 8	2	1.1%	(2.2%)	–	–
Total	179	100%	(100%)	172	100%

A great transformation had taken place in the town by 1754, for that year Dr Pococke described Ormskirk as 'a well built town, *mostly of brick*, exceedingly well paved and so neatly kept that it appears more like a Dutch town than any place [he had] seen outside Holland'.[124] Details of this transformation can be traced using the earl's periodic surveys. The earliest one (1702)[125] described in detail the stone house in Aughton Street, tenanted by Samuel Woods, gentleman, with nine under rooms, eleven upper rooms and four garrets, all roofed with slate. It also gave an interesting account of the tenement of James Barton, a clockmaker, at the corner of Aughton Street and Church Street. His traditional wattle and daub cottage consisted of two bays containing three lower rooms, all roofed with thatch, and alongside it was 'another new building consisting of four bays containing six lower rooms, three upper rooms and two garrets'. The number of storeys implied the use of a stronger building material. Indeed, eleven years later the property was listed as 'brick covered in slate'.[126] James Barton had led the way in the transformation of Ormskirk.

In the 1707 survey,[127] several houses were in a transitional state. Bertie Entwistle's house on the corner of Moor Street and Burscough Street was 'part . . . being brick and the other part post and potrill' – the local description of timber framing. Another house at Moor Street End consisted of three bays of brick covered with slate and one bay of daub with thatch. A house on Burscough Street belonging to Ralph Whalley combined stone, brick and 'post and potrill'. A house made completely of brick was a rarity in Ormskirk in 1709, for an indenture[128] used the sole description 'the brick house' to identify a property – possibly Barton's new house. However, by 1715[129] there were eight wholly brick houses, two stone houses, four houses of brick and stone combined and one of brick and daub. All these houses, except the last, were roofed with slate.

The vicarage was one of the last of the larger houses to be converted into brick. In 1778 the vicar, Revd Mr Knowles, wrote to Bishop Porteus, 'I am going to take down a post and potrill wall which was reared 250 years ago and use in its place brick as more durable'.[130] The conversion of the town's buildings into brick continued into the nineteenth century, for in 1819 Roberts[131] described several small cottages of wattle and daub with clay floors and thatched roofs at the north end of Church Street. In Aughton Street, he described some houses as having the 'post and petrel' style with projecting upper stories. Then he commented, 'The repairs they have undergone have been made without any regard to their original

22. Old House, Moor Street.

character which is nearly effaced' – a complaint often repeated today, especially when interior wattle and daub walls are found, as happened during recent renovations in Burscough Street. Robert's comment confirms that most of the early buildings had been refaced in brick by his time – a process that happened during the eighteenth century in many other market towns.[132]

As the town was 'improved', the expectations of the townsfolk also altered and, as early as 1732, Anne Scarisbrick's cottage on the west side of lower Aughton Street was described as having 'very ordinary clay walls and thatched buildings'.[133] This changed attitude was vividly described by Edward Heally, deponent in a case in 1693, when he said, about his employer's property in Church Street, 'the same not being modishly built and the rooms thereof not being so gentle and fashionable as they are now commonly made in fine new houses . . . the said Mr Dodd . . . desired a more pleasant and finer house and . . . gave directions to take down the said old house and make the new structure.' Another deponent declared that Mr Dodd had altered the house 'to make it more pleasant and agreeable to his temper and fancy'.[134] This attitude motivated the nationwide urban renaissance.

As we have seen (pp. 16, 44), when more workers were paid regularly in cash instead of in kind, consumer demand increased, and this fuelled a demand for permanent shops to replace or supplement market stalls. One early Ormskirk entrepreneur who answered this demand was Miles Gerrard. In 1662 he inherited property including an inn, on the corner of Burscough Street and Moor Street facing the market cross, and later, realising its potential as a prime site, converted it into three shops.[135] The new building encroached on the public highway and, in 1677, he

23. Knowles House, built in Burscough Street for Thomas Knowles, Vicar of Ormskirk, 1727–1780, and demolished to make way for the public library.

was presented at the court leet 'for erecting . . . shops near to the market stead further than the ancient buildings'.[136] Similarly, Thomas Crosby, grocer, was presented for an encroachment on Aughton Street made when he extended his shop in 1680.[137]

Domestic buildings were also being extended onto the highway. For instance, in 1677 Robert Heyes was fined the relatively small amount of 3*s* 4*d* by the Court Leet for 'making a cross building into the street something further than the ancient foundation'.[138] As we have seen (p. 51), the justices could impose higher fines to prevent any obstruction of the highway, and encroachments posed a real threat to free passage. One such case was presented in 1699 by John Entwistle against Thomas Houghton, the local cooper,[139] who had built 'a certain edifice with brick and stone'– an interesting mention of the 'new' building materials to stress the intended permanence of the structure. Seemingly, it had encroached 2 yd into Church Street for a distance of 10 yd, and then 'two several pairs of stairs' had been erected still further out into the street, with the result that the townspeople could 'not pass without danger to their lives to the common nuisance of all the King's subjects . . . passing' that way. Houghton was ordered 'to remove and amend the several nuisances and threatened with the particularly high fine of £20 if he defaulted. The 'edifice' is not specifically described, and although Houghton's inventory compiled ten years later[140] mentions the 'new house', the contents – 'broken and sawed timber in the bay at the New House' – suggests a workshop.[141] Nevertheless, this 'edifice' ranks alongside Barton's house as pioneering the use of brick in the town.

It is difficult to identify whether eighteenth-century encroachment rents referred to extensions on existing properties or to completely new buildings. Certainly one concerned a complete cottage, built in 1743 by William Battersby 'by his own expense' on Scarth Hill, where he also enclosed two crofts of 0.25 acres 'out of the waste'.[142] When refacing a structure with brick, some tenants took the opportunity to enlarge their property, while others upgraded the building to Georgian standards by extending the front of the building to the level of a projecting roof or upper storey and so achieving a fashionable facade. On the first encroachment rental in 1734, George Hewitt was charged 2s 4d per annum for an extension in Moor Street, and William Benyon had to pay 6d for a smaller encroachment in Church Street.[143] In 1747, James Clark was charged for a porch in front of his house in Aughton Street.[144] The only extension specifically to a shop was that of Richard Lea – in Moor Street in 1735.[145] Fourteen encroachments are listed between 1734 and 1799, and again their dates – mainly in the 1730s – coincide with the growth of Ormskirk's 'consumer society' and record the increased building activity of that time. Towards the end of the century, encroachment rents were charged for weighing machines belonging to Mr Cooper in 1774, Mr Ashurst in 1786 and Mr Martin in 1789.[146] These also provide indisputable evidence of increased commercial activity during those later years.

The tenants resented paying encroachment rents, for the bailiff's accounts record: '1734 Thomas Carter – never paid, George Hewitt – never paid, 1735 Thomas Plumbe – never paid'. Yet the bailiff continued demanding payment, for instance, from Mr Mollineux, who refused to pay for thirty-three years, and then in 1779 paid only 1s, refusing the extra 6d demanded because he maintained that his property had not extended beyond his boundaries.[147] John Hulme, who extended his house in 1735, paid rent for fifteen years and then refused for eight years. Finally the bailiff recorded, 'this pulled down', which closed the matter.[148] Jacob Stuart took a more aggressive stance in 1780. After extending a building 'further into the street than the site of his old premises' and onto the site of the old pig market north of Moor Street,[149] he claimed it was 'his own absolute right'. Lord Derby consulted his lawyer, who proved that the land was indeed part of the street and that, as Lord Derby was the owner of the soil, he had every right to charge encroachment rents.[150] That silenced the protests, and, although in the 1780s three more encroachments were made – two into Burscough Street by Thomas Helsby and Thomas Brandreth and one into Moor Street by Ralph Kerton – the rents were paid, if slightly in arrears.[151]

The bricks for all this new building were made locally, and a letter to Lord Derby from an Ormskirk builder in 1757 gives an insight into the process.[152] He asked permission to burn a few bricks on Brookfield Green, in neighbouring Aughton, in order to repair an adjoining house. The clay was dug on the common, where it was made into bricks. This was a long-established custom in Ormskirk too, and the Order Book (1613–1721) decrees that 'no person or persons shall make or dig any holes to get clay in any of the waste ground of this manor unless the getter thereof do fill up again every such hole immediately after the getting of such clay'.[153] The trades of brickmaking and bricklaying were combined, and often stocks of bricks were amasssed for later use. For instance, in 1671 the inventory of John Vause, bricklayer, listed bricks valued at £8 and moulding tools worth 4s 6d, while his possessions totalled only £36 2s 9d. Almost a quarter of his capital was invested in bricks.[154] The demand for bricks in Ormskirk became too much to continue to allow the common to be dug for clay, and by 1727 a field had been allotted for that purpose.[155] Possibly it was the same field mentioned in the 1769 rental, recording that 407,603 bricks were made in a certain field.[156] The availablility of cheap coal from the nearby coalfields facilitated the large-scale baking of bricks. Indeed, the production of such a quantity of bricks indicates an emerging brickmaking industry, which, when brickmaking became independent of bricklaying, developed in nearby Burscough and continued until recent times.

Towards the end of the century, the few remaining wattle and daub cottages decayed rapidly. In 1777, Michael Spence's house, outhouses and cottage were listed as 'all in a ruinous condition'.[157] Six years later William Eccleston's holdings were 'going very much out of repair', but stoically he commented that he did not 'mind if they will do during his life'.[158] By contrast, Henry Ashton, Luke Goore and Miss Hesketh refused to pay rent in 1781, claiming that the landlord had neglected their property.[159] In 1794, even the steward acknowledged that, although James Wood had paid no rent, the 'cottage [was] of little or no value'.[160]

Towards the end of the eighteenth century, wealthier tenants, and some of the neighbouring gentry who also held Ormskirk property, invested in new housing in the town. Again this was a nationwide trend, and many great landed fortunes drew income from urban rents and property developments. For instance, Thomas Eccleston of Scarisbrick commissioned the building of six new dwellings on his holding in Church Street, Ormskirk, and in 1789 and 1799 these were sold together with 'several cottages at the back thereof'.[161] Another development in Church Street occurred on the site of the old horse mill and drying kiln belonging to John Irving, a linen draper, who converted the complex into six cottages.[162] A cottage at the rear of his home in Aughton Street was erected by Andrew Rutter for his wife. The astute Rutter, realising that improved property meant increased rents, also sold two old cottages in Croston and invested the resulting £50 in rebuilding two old houses in Ormskirk, sublet to two shoemakers.[163]

Infilling was a common mode of development in eighteenth-century towns, as happened in Leeds, Liverpool, Kendal, Nottingham and Burford. The infilling in Ormskirk, resulting from Lord Derby's reluctance to release land for housing, marked the beginning of courtyard developments, which multiplied in the next century and caused great problems of slum dwelling and overcrowding parallel to those in many other northern towns.[164]

Although the appearance of the town had changed drastically, the actual accommodation within the houses altered very little before the 1730s. Then the proportion of houses with a large number of rooms decreased as bigger houses were divided to accommodate smaller families. Table 17, compiled from inventories, shows the accommodation within houses between 1660 and 1740. The sample for 1720–1740 included four widows all occupying houses with fewer than four rooms, so they were probably larger houses divided. Although the inventories provide somewhat selective evidence, they cover a good cross-section of society.

24. Courtyard developments, Ormskirk, 1850.

25. Ormskirk township from the tithe map of 1845.[165]

So far our examination has been confined to new building and extensions, but old property was divided and altered too. Although this was rarely recorded, the eighty-seven inventories taken between 1660 and 1740 listing rooms, provide evidence of how slowly alteration or extension occurred. In eighty years only four chambers, one parlour and two houses were described as 'new'.[167]

Richard Wood's new house actually meant a new kitchen–cum–living room, for it contained a table and a frame. Similarly, as we saw earlier, Thomas Houghton's new house, containing only timber, was probably a workshop. Very few inventories exist for the later period (1740–1800).

Although Pococke's report described a transformed old town, there had not been the expected increase in new houses nor a parallel increase in accommodation. The only conclusion to be made is that the transformation was a gradual process of renovation and refacing, undertaken as old materials decayed. The fact that new building materials were readily available which needed less attention, were more durable and less inflammable, influenced the townsfolk's choice far more than fashion. Thatch could become infested with pests and was a serious fire hazard, so much so that towards the late eighteenth century, insurance companies discriminated against it in their schedules in favour of slate.[168] Wattle and daub decayed very rapidly if it was not given constant attention, so the emergence of a brick town indicates that the inhabitants had wearied of constantly renovating their homes. They had decided to reface and renovate their property

TABLE 17. House size in Ormskirk 1660–1740[166]

No. of rooms	1660–1680		1680–1700		1700–1720		1720–1740	
	No.	%	No.	%	No.	%	No.	%
1–3	–	–	2	9.1	1	7.2	6	28.6
4–6	7	43.7	11	50	5	35.7	9	42.8
7–9	6	37.5	4	18.2	7	50	4	19
10+	3	18.8	5	22.7	1	7.2	2	9.5
No. in sample	16	100	22	100	14	100	21	99.9

N.B. These figures exclude inns.

with a more durable and less flammable material, which, incidentally, provided the opportunity to indulge in a modest acknowledgement of the latest fashions of symmetry and classical detail.

Ormskirk's slow transformation can be contrasted with that of some of the more successful spa towns such as Bath, Scarborough, Weymouth, Margate and Brighton, which blossomed at this time.[169] Industrial towns such as Wigan and Sheffield were also extending rapidly,[170] and Pococke's comments encouraged us to expect similar developments in Ormskirk, but that was not the case. Nevertheless, this study of the townscape of Ormskirk has demonstrated how far the movement towards an 'urban renaissance' affected the northern market town and provided further evidence of the changing economic pattern in the town during the years 1660–1800.

CHAPTER IV

The Established Church

One aspect of life in early modern Ormskirk not dependent upon the town's economic situation was its religious belief and organisation, both of which responded to a series of different stimuli, often far removed from the area. Although R.C. Richardson's observation that 'Puritanism of the diocese of Chester – like its Catholicism – appears . . . as primarily local in character, local in organisation, local in structure and above all, local in its impact',[1] is true of Ormskirk's religious life throughout our period, outside influences did penetrate the town and introduce changes beyond local control. The Established Church, its local character and the religious orientation of its local leaders responded to changes in religious policy at national level. The local Nonconformists, including the Quakers, were harried – at least until 1689 – as the result of the Clarendon Code and various other Acts of Parliament. The local Catholics came under the influence of the Jesuits and Benedictines in various continental seminaries, who trained Ormskirk boys, and also sent others to minister to the Ormskirk Catholics as they struggled under the threat of strict laws against recusancy.

To gain a balanced picture of the local impact of religious change, we will examine the local response to changing national policies in religion, as well as the uniquely local development of the various congregations. It will emerge how closely the position in Ormskirk mirrors the national situation. In fact, Ormskirk can be seen as a microcosm of national religious development. For instance, we shall see that the affront against traditional Protestantism by the Laudians in the 1630s was reflected locally in the experience of John Broxopp, while the dominance of the Puritans nationally during the middle decades of that century was mirrored by Nathaniel Heywood's dominance in Ormskirk. At the Restoration, the successful national offensive against the power of the Puritans was repeated at local level by the challenge of two pro-Laudians – Dr Richard Sherlock and Peter Stanynought – to the Puritan, Heywood, and his eventual ejection. Then the problems of staffing the Church after the ejections were repeated locally and a neat, eirenic compromise was found. In the mid-1660s, Charles II's misgivings over the first Conventicle Act were mirrored in the local magistrates' unwillingness to enforce it and, later, by outright opposition to it by certain local gentry. In addition, the national enforcement of toleration had local echoes as first Nathaniel Heywood, in 1672, then later other local Dissenters registered their meeting houses. In the national Anglican–Tory revival under Queen Anne, the Sacheverell affair had its local repercussions, while the establishment of Queen Anne's Bounty benefited the local clergy. As at national level, local fear and hatred of 'Popery' resurfaced during the 1745 Jacobite

Rebellion, before toleration was truly accepted in the town. Alongside these microcosms of events surrounding the Established Church, throughout our period, there existed similar local illustrations of national attitudes to both Quakers and Catholics and their religious convictions.

First, to set the scene for developments in the Anglican Church both locally and nationally, we must look back to the third decade of the seventeenth century and Archbishop Laud's attempt to establish a 'new' Anglicanism. Laud abhorred the laxity and disrespect which, he believed, had developed in the Church since the Reformation. Holy Communion was rarely administered and it had become customary to administer baptism in the parents' home. In order to restore dignity and respect to the Church's ceremonies, Laud attempted to restore 'the beauty of holiness'[2] by reinstating visible signs, such as vestments and images. However, Laud's programme, the antithesis of Puritan beliefs, reawoke among the more Protestant element a fear of 'Popery'.

One particular incident in Ormskirk reflects this national issue of 'Laudianism' versus traditional Elizabethan Protestantism. Among the Puritans supported by the Derbys to redress Catholic influence in the area was John Broxopp, who was presented to the living of Ormskirk by Lord Strange in 1628 and appointed to the post of King's Preacher.[3] In 1633, when Archbishop Laud succeeded to the see of Canterbury, Broxopp was indicted at Chester consistory court for not wearing his surplice. In his defence, an excellent example of the Puritans' evasive attitude to vestments, he claimed that he did not wear the surplice because 'sometimes it was at the washing, sometimes at making and sometimes at mending, so as he could not always have the same to put on him'. The same year, Bishop Neile, head of the Northern Province, ordered the communion table to be removed from the centre of the chancel to an 'altarwise' eastern position in Chester Cathedral. This 'Laudian' reform in the cathedral happened the same year as Broxopp's indictment for breaching the 'Laudian' code. Thus, these happenings in Ormskirk mirrored those not only in the diocese but also in the country at large.[4] The Puritan vicar was also indicted in both 1630 and 1637 for holding conventicles in the vicarage – another breach of the Laudian 'code'.[5] When Broxopp died in 1643, he was replaced by John Dunn, 'a painful preaching Minister'[6] with similar beliefs.

This was the Puritan tradition of Ormskirk Church when Nathaniel Heywood was presented in 1656 by Charlotte, Countess of Derby, for the position of vicar. At that time Puritans dominated the Church nationwide, and again Ormskirk reflected the national picture. Four years later, Charles II was restored and religious change followed. Before his return in April 1660, Charles reassured those holding divergent beliefs by issuing his Declaration of Breda, declaring 'a liberty to tender consciences and that no man shall be disquieted or called in question for differences of opinion in matters of religion which do not disturb the peace of the kingdom'.[7] However, when he returned, Charles found himself in an isolated position over toleration, and was unable to challenge the the Cavalier Parliament (elected in 1661) and the predominately Laudian bishops, both of whom wanted to reinstate the Anglican Church to its former position. Finally, after Venner's Fifth Monarchist Rising in 1661 had terrorised London for three days, fear of Presbyterians, Papists and Nonconformists and of a return to civil war spread. Consequently Charles had to agree to the Act of Uniformity (1662), ejecting ministers from their churches if they would not accept the guidelines for the re-establishment of the Anglican Church.

In Ormskirk, these rapid changes in national religious life (1660–1662), and particularly the displacement of the Puritan element in the Church, were clearly marked. Nathaniel Heywood and Dr Richard Sherlock represented the warring elements in the Church nationwide. Nathaniel Heywood[8] welcomed the Declaration of Breda, and with other Puritans signed a petition to the King, pledging his loyalty, and asking him to continue to search for a 'liberty to tender consciences'.[9] Then on 11 May 1660 James Grice, the Ormskirk parish clerk, proclaimed Charles, King of England, 'To the Joy of all Good Christians' – words which stressed the hopes of many townspeople for an establishment of the Breda 'liberty' for all 'tender consciences'.[10]

Meanwhile, the earl and countess decided to join the townspeople in a service at Ormskirk parish church to celebrate the King's return. Dr Richard Sherlock, Lord Derby's chaplain, 'was a Papist in disguise', according to a rumour, 'raised and industriously spread abroad'. When Sherlock served as Vicar of Winwick from 1662 until his death in 1689, the false rumour was scotched. Nevertheless, it reflected some local Protestant opinion of a clergyman who supported the 'Laudian' reforms. When the time for the celebration came, Dr Sherlock, rightly suspecting that the chancel of the parish church 'had been as little regarded as the Lord's Supper, which had not been administered in that church for some years past', went to prepare the church. He was horrified to find that the building 'had been more frequented by dogs and swine than men', and immediately ordered it to be cleaned.[11]

Although no record remains of the event, it is likely that Ormskirk church was originally desecrated by Cromwellian troops during the Civil War.[12] This fact and the Puritans' lack of respect for the church building and its ornaments would account for the disgusting state of Ormskirk church. The cleaning resulted in 'such an insufferable stench' that Dr Sherlock – according to his biographer, defending him against the 'Papist' rumour – 'was obliged to order frankincense to be burned the day before the solemnity, that his congregation might not be discomposed by such an unexpected nuisance'. Whether this burning of frankincense was in truth only to dispel smells, or whether it was a 'High Church' purification rite, is impossible to tell. Nevertheless, the incident vividly illustrates in Ormskirk the collision of the two opposed traditions in the seventeenth-century Church of England, and represents in Sherlock's dominance a microcosm of the 'triumph of the Laudians'.[13]

The Anglican Restoration was further consolidated and ecclesiastical discipline was tightened in Ormskirk indirectly by the Countess of Derby, the church's lay impropriator, when she donated a font to the parish church in 1661. As already mentioned, Puritan parents often preferred to have their children baptised privately at home, and the clergymen acceded to ensure that the child was baptised. The countess's gift of a font to celebrate the King's return can be seen as a way – undoubtedly suggested by the 'Laudian' Dr Sherlock – of encouraging parents to bring their children into church to be baptised – if only to use the new font. Once the habit was re-established, home baptisms could be discontinued, except in cases of dangerous illness. It is significant that, when the prevalence of home baptisms worried the Church authorities, so many new fonts were installed in northern churches. For instance, one at Warton (1661), in Croston (1663), in Great Harwood

26. Font donated by the Countess of Derby in 1661, showing representations of the royal insignia and the Derby coat of arms.

(1663), in Hoole (1663) and in Penwortham (1667).[14] The number of new fonts is also another instance of 'the triumph of [new] Laudianism', for, as Tyacke explained, 'during the Arminian ascendancy [when Laud was Archbishop of Canterbury] altars and fonts came to dominate church interiors, for the two were logically connected, sacramental grace replacing the grace of predestination'.[15] The font's return to prominence, an example of the return to Laudian ideals, illustrates how such changes in national worship were made visible in the local parish church. First nationally then locally, the power of the Presbyterians declined as the Episcopalians' grip on the Established Church tightened.

This nationwide trend is again well illustrated in Ormskirk, where the first sign of declining support for the Presbyterians came in the appointment of a new King's Preacher, a position earning a salary of £50 a year. Sir Henry Ashurst, a Presbyterian sympathiser, described what happened: the position 'had been long fixed upon the Minister of that place'.[16] 'At the return of King Charles II, one, Mr Stanynought, Parson of Aughton, worth £140 a year, rode up to London, and, by the help of friends, surreptitiously obtained this £50 a year to be settled upon himself'. Heywood had fully expected to be appointed, and with nine children to support he needed to augment his meagre salary of £30. Disappointed, he responded by preaching at the celebratory service on an extraordinarily apt text from II Samuel 19, verse 30: 'Yea, let him take all, forasmuch as my Lord, the King is come again in peace unto his own house'. His reaction was 'highly applauded by all especially the gentry'. Nevertheless, those – presumably pro-Laudian – laymen who petitioned Charles to appoint Stanynought had inserted the first wedge to remove Heywood, the Presbyterian, from his position as vicar.[17]

Puritan influences were finally eradicated from the Church of England by the Act of Uniformity in 1662. The clergy were ordered to use the *Book of Common Prayer* and no other form of service, and to declare their 'unfeigned assent and consent to all and everything' within it. They had to be ordained by a bishop, take oaths pledging non-resistance to royal authority, disclaim the Covenant and subscribe to all Thirty-Nine Articles. Those who failed to meet these requirements before the deadline of 24 August (St Bartholomew's Day) were to be ejected from their livings.[18]

Heywood, a graduate of Trinity College Cambridge, studied under Edward Gee, parson of Eccleston, and became minister of Illingworth Chapel, Halifax, during the 1650s. He had received a Presbyterian ordination when four local ministers 'laid hands upon him', but had not been ordained by a bishop.[19] Episcopal ordination was only one of the guidelines of the Act Heywood was unable to meet, so he relinquished his post as Vicar of Ormskirk. Thus he joined 935 other Nonconformists – 39 from Lancashire – who also could not conform, and had therefore left their posts as ministers, curates, lecturers or assistants in 1662.[20] A vignette illustrates the feelings of many of Heywood's former parishioners: 'A poor ignorant man came to him, when he was turned out, saying, "Ah Mr Heywood, we would gladly have you to preach again in the Church." "Yes", said he, "I would gladly preach as you desire it, if I could do it with a safe conscience in conforming." The man replied, "Oh, sir! Many a man now-a-days makes a great gash in his conscience, cannot you make a little nick in yours?".'[21]

According to Robert Bosher, 'the bishops as a whole regarded with honest regret the exodus of so many conscientious and worthy divines',[22] and indeed, the behaviour of the Church authorities towards several ejected ministers in the north-west suggests that they were not harried.[23] Heywood was not so fortunate. He was allowed to continue his duties only until 29 January 1663, when his successor, John Ashworth, master of Merchant Taylors' School, Crosby, was appointed. However, Ashworth did not move into Ormskirk, but rode the eight miles from Crosby on a Saturday, stayed in the vicarage on Saturday and Sunday nights, and rode back to Crosby for school on Monday. Consequently, 'Mr Heywood still seemed to have the sole charge of that Town and Parish, visiting the Sick, instructing them, preaching privately to them as occasion was offered.'[24]

Non-residence and pluralism were great problems for the Church during the late seventeenth and early eighteenth centuries, resulting in many parishioners being deprived of pastoral care. However, as most stipends were low, it was the only way some clergymen could obtain a living wage. Others took teaching posts or other employment to supplement their incomes, and even then their appointments often depended on their influential connections rather than on their aptitude for the posts.[25]

Ashworth's career as vicar illustrates the 'staffing' difficulties of the Anglican Church after the Act of Uniformity had caused so many vacancies. Possibly when the dowager Countess of Derby presented Ashworth for the post at Ormskirk, she hoped that, as Ashworth could only serve the Church at weekends, his appointment would result in Nathaniel Heywood, her protégé, virtually retaining his place as minister. Although Ashworth was not strictly a pluralist, he was the only vicar during our period who did not live permanently in the vicarage. Like many other clerics described as absentees, he lived only a short distance outside his parish boundary, and so would actually be more familiar with the needs of the far-flung members of his congregation than many vicars living in the centre of their parishes. This solution to the problem of Ashworth's semi-absenteeism proved to be a very popular compromise in the town.

Ashworth's hopes of continuing financial improvement from this appointment were blighted four years later when the Fire of London destroyed many of the Merchant Taylors' properties and the company was unable to pay his salary for several years. Fortunately, in 1674, John Stanynought died, and the office of King's Preacher with its £50 per annum salary was returned to him as Vicar of Ormskirk.[26]

After the ejection of Puritan divines, the Anglican Church expressed its reaction to Puritanism and its new-found sense of security by rebuilding and restoring neglected church buildings nationwide. The 'Laudian' insistence upon decency, seemliness and even the holiness of those buildings was restated. As we have seen (p. 53), one Ormskirk court order epitomised this re-awakened respect towards the church's property by decreeing that no inhabitant should pollute the churchyard wall.[27]

In common with most of the authorities in English churches of the 1660s, Ashworth and his churchwardens strove to repair the structure of his neglected church. The earliest churchwardens' accounts (1665) describe their struggle.[28] A month after taking office, May 1665, they 'met several workmen to agree . . . about repair of the lead, clock, bells and other things', and in June the work began. Their main concern was the leaking roof, for the lead had oxidised and cracked and needed replacing. They encountered great difficulty hoisting the lead on to the roof, and helpers had to be enlisted from the watching crowds. For their efforts these locals were paid 1s 6d.

Once the roof was secure and watertight, other repairs were needed. The church walls were mended and the windows were repointed,[29] stonework was installed around the new font and paving stones were laid at the west door. Interestingly, local stone from Scarth Hill Quarry was used by the mason, James Webster, for this work. The church dial – possibly the sundial still to be seen on the southern wall – required attention and the clock cost £1 to repair. The bells were in a very dangerous condition and it took two years to repair them. On one occasion the great bell leaned to the west and 'several persons' had to be paid to raise it.

The references to 'several persons' – always around when help was needed – invite speculation. Were they parishioners, demonstrating concern for their church as part of their pride in the restoration of 'Anglicanism'? Were they townsfolk, showing a new-found consciousness of the need to improve their urban environment?[30] Or were they the ever-present unemployed, always available if there was the chance of earning a pittance? We will never know. Certainly in 1665 the churchwardens, representatives of the parishioners of Ormskirk, had spent £13 14s 3d – about 50% of their total budget of £26 7s 2d – on repairing the church and its fittings, thus providing evidence of this Anglican community's willingness to invest in improvements to its parish church.

In this project, a new communal spirit of co-operation is evident in one section of the community. A need was identified and work was undertaken to achieve the object, rather than waiting passively for the lord of the manor or the bishop to impose change. The change in attitude of the vicar, the churchwardens and the parishioners towards the church premises is also significant. The place formerly allowed to be 'frequented by dogs and swine' was transformed.

Meanwhile, Dissenting clerics nationwide sought new ways of following their vocation outside the Church. Parliament was not satisfied that the Act of Uniformity alone solved the problem caused by what they viewed as the politically dangerous Nonconformists. Consequently, it passed a series of acts, the 'Clarendon Code', to curb still further the Nonconformists' activities. This 'Code', rooted in earlier repressive acts such as the Act against Sectaries (1593),[31] included the Corporation Act (1661), decreeing that all officeholders in boroughs, cities and ports should be practising Anglicans,[32] the Conventicle Act (1664, renewed 1670) forbidding attendance at religious meetings other than those conducted according to the liturgy and practice of the Church of England,[33] and the Five Mile Act (1665), forbidding ejected ministers from preaching within five miles of a corporate borough or places where they had formerly held positions.[34] The Licensing Act (1662) also suppressed Dissenting literature as well as all politically seditious material.[35] One significance of these acts was, as J.P. Kenyon observed, that they 'tacitly accepted the existence of a separate Protestant community',[36] and, according to R.A. Beddard, caused 'a lasting division in society between the privileged conformist and the unprivileged nonconformist'.[37] The enforcement of these acts varied from place to place, reflecting the differing attitudes of county magistrates, and from time to time, depending on the current political climate.

The Corporation Act did not apply to Ormskirk, but the Licensing Act prevented any religious literature from being published in the town until 1679, when Zachary Taylor became vicar. The ejected Heywood ignored the Five Mile Act and the Conventicle Act and, as we have seen (p. 76), he 'still seemed to have the sole charge of the Parish'. He travelled and ministered to 'Wigan, Warrington, Liverpool, Preston, Eccleston and other, more remote places',[38] a circuit similar to that covered by another ejected minister, Henry Newcome.[39] Like most Puritans, Heywood considered preaching extremely important, and usually preached 'twice on the Lord's Day and several times in weekdays'. His lengthy sermons sometimes lasted three or four hours when 'his heart was so fully set upon his Master's work that he forgot his own strength and his hearers' patience'. However, the threat of prosecution was always present, and 'in times of great danger' he 'preached at one house in the beginning of the night and then . . . [went] . . . two miles a foot over mosses and preached toward morning to another company at another house'.[40] Although his activities were known to the authorities, who in 1665 listed him among 'persons fit to be secured' as 'one of the nonconformist, secluded, pretended Ministers and such as frequently hold conventicles, giving the people opportunities of meeting to hatch mischief',[41] he was not apprehended at this time. His brother Oliver wrote on 19 April 1666 that Heywood, 'who hitherto hath been wonderfully hid in his own house, secured from danger, hath larger opportunities for study than ever before'.[42]

Despite rejoicing in 1666 that 1,500 Nonconformists had been presented at Lancaster Assizes, the Bishop of Chester had to admit to Sheldon that conventicles continued to be held by Nonconformists, Papists and Quakers in Ormskirk in 1669.[43] The lack of any prosecutions during 1664–1672 at Ormskirk quarter sessions confirm that local magistrates turned a blind eye to conventicles, thus – perhaps unintentionally – supporting Charles II's tolerant religious policies. Many magistrates nationwide were disinclined to enforce the first Conventicle Act. Consequently, Parliament renewed the Act in 1670, with a new clause imposing fines of £100 on justices who did not act against conventicles, and granting a substantial reward to informers.[44] Two years of keen persecution followed, but the Dissenters experienced some respite in 1672, when the King issued the Declaration of

Indulgence. By this, Charles suspended the penal laws and allowed Nonconformists to meet in places licensed by magistrates. His action was vigorously opposed by the bishops and Parliament, and he was forced to withdraw the Declaration in 1673. Two years passed before the licenses were recalled, but it signalled a much stricter enforcement of the law – helped by informers only too ready to claim a reward. Nevertheless, even when magistrates conscientiously administered the law, their action was often frustrated by public sympathy for those prosecuted.[45]

The struggle between the King and Parliament in alliance with Archbishop Sheldon was re-enacted locally in a confrontation between Lady Stanley of Bickerstaffe – a member of a cadet branch of the Derby family and a supporter of the Parliamentarians during the Civil War – and militia soldiers under a deputy lieutenant acting in response to a directive from John Wilkins, Bishop of Chester. When the declaration was issued, Heywood took out licenses for two meeting places: one at Scarisbrick and another adjoining Lady Stanley's house in Bickerstaffe, both within the 5 mile limit of Ormskirk parish church. A year after the withdrawal of the declaration, April 1674, the harassment of Heywood began. On eighteen consecutive Sundays, the constable of Bickerstaffe and several officers came to arrest him for contravening both the Conventicle and the Five Mile Acts. However, the local officers, sympathetic towards Heywood, refused to use force, as Heywood described in a letter: 'Two warrants (one for £20 and one for £40) have been out against me these seven weeks, but we keep our doors fast barred and the Officers are very civil to us.' In fact, Robert Holland, the constable of Bickerstaffe wrote, 'Let your Master [John Entwistle JP who issued the warrants] do with me what he pleaseth, I am resolved I will never break any door here'.[46]

Then, altering his tactics, the Bishop offered Heywood the living of Aughton if he would conform. However, although the salary tempted Heywood, he refused. The crisis came when soldiers of the militia were sent to take Heywood while he was preaching in the Bickerstaffe chapel. Lady Stanley 'placed herself near the pulpit door, hoping to overawe their Spirits and obstruct their Designs'. When Heywood finished praying, the soldiers rushed forward and 'the Lady would have stopped them, but they pressed forward' and, according to Heywood, he 'was pulled out of the pulpit with a pistol lifted up at . . . [his] . . . head and a God-dam-me in . . . [his] . . . ears'.[47] In January 1674 he was taken before a magistrate, where 'many considerable Gentlemen, and some that were no friends to his Cause, mediated for him'. He was bound over to next quarter sessions, where 'old Lady Stanley and her Husband, Mr Henry Houghton, a Justice of the Peace and several others spoke on his behalf'. The justices, swayed by Heywood's defence and his impressive array of supporters, released him.

Heywood's opponents, including the Anglican magistrate, John Entwistle, next tried to prosecute him under the Five Mile Act, but 'nobody could be brought to swear that he lived in the town'.[48] A warrant was issued to distrain his goods, but the officers said that the doors were shut and that they had no orders to break them. In fact, throughout his troubles, Heywood was supported by most of his fellow townsfolk of whatever creed. As Michael Mullett observed, 'neighbourliness came first, uniting communities in defence of a neighbour . . . when some elementary popular sense of justice was outraged and regardless . . . of that neighbour's religion'.[49] This was as true of the Catholic squire, Nicholas Blundell, and of a Catholic widow at the centre of a religious riot in Wigan in 1681, as it was of the Dissenter, Heywood.[50]

Another confrontation between Conformists and Nonconformists occurred in 1674, again involving Lady Stanley, but this time against the Ormskirk churchwardens. The leaden roof of the Bickerstaffe chapel within the church was leaking badly and, as the Stanleys of Bickerstaffe were responsible for this chapel, Lady Stanley was informed. Although the wardens wanted the lead repaired, she wanted to replace it with slates. Then to harass the Anglican Church authorities, she had the lead stripped off the roof, leaving both the chapel and the church open to the weather for months. The furious churchwardens indicted her at the quarter sessions, and later, when the magistrates refused to help, presented her at the consistory court. The Bishop persuaded her to act, but not as the churchwardens wished. The chapel was reroofed in slate. According to Silvester Moorcroft, 'Dame Elizabeth gave . . . [him] . . . and his fellow churchwardens a great deal of trouble in the matter by causing indictments at the quarter sessions and put them to charge both there and at Chester where they expended £24 or thereabouts.'[51]

Shortly after his trial, Heywood's health failed and he died in December 1677. All the town turned out to watch the funeral procession, each 'in their several capacities doing him honour in their peculiar way'. The coffin was preceded by the town's constable, who carried the staff, and the mourners followed it 'in their due and decent order'. Mr Starkie, a Nonconformist minister, preached the sermon in the parish church, 'no man forbidding him; nay all that were any way concerned, consenting',[52] and Heywood was buried in the chancel in the vault of the Stanleys of Bickerstaffe. Thus in death he was accepted and honoured by the parish church he would never have left, if his Puritan scruples had allowed him to conform to its dictates. The response of the townsfolk to his death again illustrates the sense of community and neighbourliness which prevailed at that time.

Later, in 1685, other local divisions were healed by the marriage of the vicar of Ormskirk (1679–1692), Zachary Taylor (whose father had been chaplain to the Royalist army), to Barbara, the second daughter of Parliamentarian Sir Edward Stanley of Bickerstaffe and the formidable Lady Elizabeth,[53] thus healing the rift between the Ormskirk church authorities and the Stanley family and also uniting Royalist and Parliamentarian families. Zachary Taylor's appointment reflected the earlier dissenting tradition of the Ormskirk vicars. Although Zachary jnr conformed to the Anglican Church,his father had been ejected as assistant to the vicar of Rochdale and later became master of Kirkham Grammar School.[54]

Titus Oates's allegations, the Exclusion Crisis and the Rye House Plot had little impact in Ormskirk. When the accession of William and Mary caused the question of the hereditary divine right of kings to trouble consciences nationwide, Zachary Taylor published a pamphlet *The Vindication of a Late Pamphlet . . .* in 1691.[55] He tackled the problem of the 'non-jurors' who felt unable to swear allegiance to William and Mary while James, to whom they had already sworn allegiance, still had the 'Authoritative Right and Title' to the Crown. Taylor's view was that, although James had the hereditary right to the throne, that authority was conferred by God. If God transferred that authority, the subject should transfer his allegiance. To deny allegiance was to deny obedience to God.

After leaving Ormskirk, Taylor published several pamphlets, including one concerning the Lancashire demonomania.[56] This was addressed in scathing terms to several Dissenting ministers, including Nathaniel Heywood the younger, Oliver Heywood and Richard Frankland (the head of the Dissenting Academy), who claimed to have cured Dugdale, a gardener from Surey near Pendle, who was thought to be possessed by a devil. Taylor accused the Catholics of manipulating Dugdale to appear to be possesssed, and the Dissenters of seeking self-glorification by performing 'miracles'. Possibly Taylor's attack was aimed indirectly at Nathaniel Heywood who, with his father, had challenged the domination of the Church of England in Ormskirk, and rivalled Taylor for many years. Evidently the passing of the Act of Toleration had not restored harmony.

Zachary Taylor's use of the written word extended to inscriptions on the walls of Ormskirk church, which were whitened and inscribed with the Lord's Prayer, the Ten Commandments and verses from the scriptures at the cost of £6 in 1685.[57] The majority of the congregation could read the texts, and for those who could not, the verses were read aloud regularly, a practice in many post-Reformation English parish churches. Taylor agreed with George Swinnock who, in 'The Christian Man's Calling . . . ' (1663), asked, 'How many for the want of reading have lost their precious souls . . . how can they know God's will that cannot read it?'[58]

During the late seventeenth century, the plight of the extremely poorly paid lower clergy caused concern nationwide. Finally, in 1704, Queen Anne founded her 'bounty' to supplement the salaries of the poor clergy out of the proceeds of the Crown's tenths and first fruits. Payment was delayed until 1715, and then only clergymen earning £10 per annum or less benefited. However, in 1707–1708, livings of up to £50 were exempted from payment of both first fruits and tenths, and, in 1715, a scheme was introduced to make payments to livings of between £10 and £35, if an independent benefactor made a donation towards increasing that living. The bounty was paid in sums of £200, to be invested in land approved by the commissioners.[59]

Eventually Ormskirk's vicars benefited from this scheme. The annual stipend of the vicars of the parish covering the townships of Ormskirk, Burscough, Lathom, Scarisbrick, Bickerstaffe and Skelmersdale, was £30.[60] Despite the salary of £50 a year for the office of King's Preacher, most Ormskirk vicars were in straitened circumstances. However, in 1708 they benefited from being exempted from paying tenths. Then in 1719 William Taylor, an Ormskirk gentleman, gave a donation[61] which enabled the vicar, Christopher Gibson (1718-1727), to receive £200 from the bounty for investment.[62] Difficulties arose finding suitable land, and eventually in 1729 a small estate in Lathom was acquired and the vicar benefited by £17 per annum from the investment.

Queen Anne's bounty resulted from a widespread fear that general apathy was endangering the Church. This fear was manipulated by Dr Sacheverell who, despite swearing allegiance to William and Mary, had never abandoned the High Anglican concepts of divinely appointed authority. As Geoffrey Holmes described, Dr Sacheverell's inflammatory sermons and his consequent trial and release on 21 March 1710 resulted in a riot in London, supported by apprentices, white-collar workers and many professional people.[63]

There was a parallel to this affair at Ormskirk quarter sessions in 1711, with the roles being reversed. The high churchmen were the prosecutors and a Presbyterian teacher was indicted. Peter Steynhead of Warrington was accused of publishing scandals against the Queen and the Church of England, and was arrested under the Licensing Act. His book, a fiery expression of Presbyterian beliefs, described the practices of the Church as those of the devil and concluded that 'whosoever vindicated and tolerated the practices of the Church of England, vindicated and tolerated the practices of the devil'. This was interpreted as an attack on the Queen as head of the Church. He was found guilty, fined £20 and sentenced to stand upon the pillory in Ormskirk market-place on market day with an inscription above his head: 'I stand here for libelling the Queen and the Church of England as by the law established.' He had to give security for his good behaviour for seven years, and remain in prison until he had paid his fine – probably a long time, for £20 would be difficult to raise. His heavy punishment reflects the same 'High Church' intolerance as that demonstrated by Dr Sacheverell and his supporters.[64]

The rapid growth of Nonconformity after the Act of Toleration alarmed the bishops, who determined to improve the Church's image and provide adequate accommodation in churches for the increasing population. Inadequate provision for parishioners was not new. Collinson cited many examples from London (1609) and Exeter (1601), while Wrightson quoted an instance in Terling (1630), where one parishioner complained that 'he could not get into the church by reason of the crowd of people'.[65] Increasing population in the early eighteenth century exacerbated the problem and Nonconformists grasped the opportunity to fill the gap. For instance, a petition for Holy Trinity church in Whitehaven in 1715 voiced the fear that 'several others may be induced for want of other accommodation to resort to the places of worship amongst those that dissent from the Church of England'.[66] In 1711 the Fifty New Churches Act provided churches in London, but although the problem was nationwide, only three new churches were built in south-west Lancashire immediately following the Act: at Burtonwood in 1716, at Billinge in 1717 and at Tarleton in 1719. Later, St George's in Liverpool (1726–1734) and St Luke's in Lowton (1732) were built, while the Georgian restoration of an earlier church in North Meols was completed in 1730. The majority of churches in south-west Lancashire responded to the movement by renovating and adding galleries and extensions, rather than by rebuilding.[67] Albers found evidence that in the whole of Lancashire during the period 1689–1800, 67 churches were completely rebuilt, 19 were substantially enlarged and 35 others added galleries.[68] Although the Church could not respond adequately to the demand in new industrial districts, such as Sheffield, Liverpool and Manchester, especially later in our period,[69] the pattern of building and renovation of churches in small and medium-sized towns, where the population increased more gradually, indicates an adequate response to their needs.

Ormskirk church was already too small for the number of parishioners before the Act of Toleration. In 1682, John, Bishop of Chester, had granted a faculty to erect a gallery because 'the parishioners complain that they are incommoded on the Lord's Day for want of seats in their parish church, insomuch that some well-affected persons cannot deport themselves at divine service with that decency which they desire, and others make a pretence of their too frequent absence'. The gallery – 9 yd long and 6 yd wide – was to be erected at the west end of the church.[70]

Then in 1690, a vestry was built on the northern side of the chancel, where there were remains of an ancient chantry chapel dedicated to St Nicholas.[71] Many repairs and improvements were carried out in 1711, including resoldering the lead on the church roof, replacing slates, mending windows, doing pointing, repairing the gates and fitting the great door with bands to strengthen it. Slates were fixed in the belfry 'windows' and the bells' mechanism was renewed. The clock was kept in working order and the walls were whitened.[72] As Norman Sykes observed, whitening 'possessed for that age a symbolic value as typifying the dispersal of mysticism and obscurity by the penetration of the pure light of reason'. This was true in Ormskirk, where lightness, purity and godliness came to be exemplified in the decoration of the church.[73] One major alteration in 1721 was the demolition of a stone wall which separated the Scarisbrick chapel on the south side of the chancel from the main body of the church,[74] again increasing the seating capacity of the church.

Nevertheless, Bishop Gastrell criticised the inadequate capacity of the church during his visitation of Ormskirk in 1722, a criticism paralleling Parliament's concern over the situation in London.[75] The bishop's comment that 'the church being not capable of galleries, will not hold above 600' is confusing, for one gallery had already been built and is included on the churchwardens' annual lists of properties after 1682. Possibly he was referring to side galleries. Certainly his anxiety concerning the shortage of seats was justified. The population of the township of Ormskirk alone was an estimated 981 in 1677, and increased to approximately 1,210 by 1754.[76] Thus, even without an accurate figure for the population of 1722, we can estimate that there were seats in the church for about half the population of Ormskirk township, and none for the other five townships in the parish. Doubtless the local church authorities also feared that this shortage of seats might encourage parishioners to attend the Presbyterian meeting house in Aughton Street, opened in 1695, and the town's other licensed meeting houses.

Finally, in 1724, Christopher Gibson and his parishioners submitted a petition to the Lord Chancellor through the quarter sessions for permission to rebuild the church. They claimed that the timber and beams were rotten, the north pillars were 23 inches out of square and the south pillars 14 inches out. The church was in such a dangerous condition that, during one morning service, a beam had fallen and the congregation had been 'terribly affrighted and were forced to have the same that day propped and leaned on during evening service'. In their additional plea for help, the justices claimed that the inhabitants were very poor and 'must in a short time be destitute of a church'.[77] They succeeded in obtaining a brief (an official authorisation to appeal for donations), and money was collected in churches throughout the land.[78]

It was decided to demolish the nave and the body of the church, leaving intact the main chancel and the three side chapels. These were to be used while the work was in progress. The whole cost was estimated at £1,856 15s,[79] a substantial sum when compared with £180 – the cost of completely rebuilding the Friends Meeting House in Lancaster in 1708.[80] Unfortunately there is no description of the interior of the new building,[81] but an undated engraving of the church shows that the windows on the south wall were large and attractive in a rounded Georgian style with clear glass, and above them a cornice and a parapet with pedestals supporting vases. In the centre of the parapet was a tablet with a vertical sundial.

Inside, along the south side, the gallery advocated by Bishop Gastrell was built, where seating was provided for 'such as stand in need and will purchase the same at reasonable rates proportioned to the extent, situation and goodness of the seats . . . the whole charge to be expended on the building of the gallery'.[82] More seats were also provided on a similar basis on a new western gallery, alongside the organ donated by Jane Brooke in 1729,[83] the crowning glory of this reconstruction.

27. Ormskirk church, 1742.

Here was an excellent example in Ormskirk of the kind of rebuilding cited by Borsay as a sign of the urban renaissance, and occurring during the period of that renaissance.[84] The building evinced that beauty of design inherent in Georgian architecture and typical of the redevelopment in Bath and other towns. However, unlike many of Borsay's examples, it was erected not as a fashionable addition to the townscape financed by the surplus wealth of the inhabitants, but as a response to the parishioners' desperate need. Nevertheless, the extent of the rebuilding, its style and the amount it cost were all more ambitious than was necessary. Behind the planning of such a building were townspeople who were resolved that Ormskirk should have a worthy parish church to serve the religious needs of its parishioners.

During the next two decades (1730–1750), Ormskirk churchwardens concentrated on maintenance, the largest item of which was rebuilding the spire, which, despite the reconstruction of the 1720s, blew down soon afterwards.[85] Townsfolk with no commitment to the parish church objected to paying for these

28. Ormskirk church before the alterations of the 1880s.

repairs, and in 1738 the churchwardens indicted Oliver Holding, a member of the Holding family who attended the Presbyterian chapel in Aughton Street, for refusing his contribution.[86] Then, in 1746, the wardens reported that the north wall of the church was 'ill decayed and not repairable without being taken down and rebuilt . . . being twenty two inches from its perpendicular'. Sometime during the next four years, it was repaired and in 1750 the wardens were finally able to report 'the Church in good repair'.[87]

In the early 1760s, the usual expenditure on maintenance was recorded,[88] but, despite building an extension to the western gallery in 1762, by 1764 there was a need for further expansion. We have seen from the court leet records that the population of the town increased by 61.8% between 1677 and 1780. However, according to R. Lawton, 'there was a considerable acceleration in rates of natural increase . . . between 1750 and 1780'.[89] Ormskirk must have followed that trend. Another factor prompting expansion was the national Evangelical revival led by such figures as William Law (1686–1761). At first this brought many people back into the Church,[90] but later the movement had the opposite effect by encouraging Methodism. The church authorities strove incessantly to increase their accommodation to discourage parishioners from changing their allegiances.

In 1765 an architect, Mr Lightoller – possibly Thomas Lightoller, who planned the new Guildhall and Octagon chapel in Bath during the 1760s – was paid £7 13s 9d for 'his trouble of drawing plans for rebuilding the north side of the

29. The interior of the parish church, showing the Derby coat of arms on the balcony.

church, journeys and expenses' by the Ormskirk churchwardens.[91] At the eastern end of this aisle was the Bickerstaffe chapel, and, as the Stanleys of Bickerstaffe then the Derbys had owned two chapels within the church since 1736, they agreed to incorporate it into the main body of the church and provide more space for the expanding congregation.[92]

The north aisle extension was completed by the addition of yet another gallery connecting to the 'gallery of the Right Honourable the Earl of Derby' on the east of the north aisle, formerly part of the Bickerstaffe chapel.[93] Again, more pews were sold, and the vicar received the rents from nineteen of them on condition that a sermon was preached in the church every Sunday.[94] According to Roberts in 1819,[95] some of the pillars supporting these galleries were octagonal, while others were circular, carved with foliage and painted green with gilded capitals. Finally, the arms of the Earl of Derby were carved and painted on the front of the western gallery. At last, in 1778 the vicar, Mr Knowles, could report to Bishop Porteus, 'the parochial part is in decent repair'. Unfortunately, his satisfaction was short-lived, for in 1784 the top 15 ft of the ill-omened spire blew down and had to be rebuilt at a cost of £34 in 1787.

This record of the continual restoration and extension of Ormskirk parish church confirms the vitality of the local Anglican community, repeated in many small market towns in the region,[96] and attests that 'a body of conscientious and dutiful men [were] trying to do their work according to the standards of the day'.[97]

THE SOCIAL SIGNIFICANCE OF THE ALLOTMENT OF PEWS

The history of the provision of seating in Ormskirk parish church provides a micro-study in the development of the hierarchical structure of English society in the period. For a comprehensive view of the development of these seating arrangements and their links with the town's hierarchy, we need to trace them from the early seventeenth century.

After the relative egalitarianism of the Commonwealth, an era of renewed jostling for position on the social ladder followed, as first the gentry, then the pseudo-gentry, members of the professions, merchants and, finally, successful tradesmen struggled to gain recognition. Economic growth in the late seventeenth century provided surplus income for the townsmen, whose aspirations then imitated those of the national elite. In the early eighteenth century, 'wealth could be freely transferred into status', and the English townscape and, particularly, the parish church provided both the ideal 'armoury and [the] . . . arena' for the pursuit and display of that coveted status.[98] As the nineteenth century approached, the graduated positions of the middling ranks were consolidated behind the ranks of their 'betters'. In fact, the seating plan of many English parish churches, including Ormskirk's, was a dynamic ' map of . . . [town] . . . society'.[99]

Seating in Ormskirk church in the early seventeenth century was haphazard. Some gentry families erected seats above their ancestors' burial places and claimed those places by carving their names on the seats,[100] while others sat on forms provided by the lord of their particular manor. Then in 1634, by order of the bishop, the seating was made uniform at the cost of the parish. This was another response to the Laudian movement, but exactly what 'uniform' meant, is unclear. However, one Laudian reform, mentioned earlier, was the restoration of the communion table to the eastern wall, resulting in a realignment of the seating to face the new position – in a uniform direction.[101] Certainly new seats of a 'uniform' kind were provided at Broxopp's suggestion.

The parishioners found the new seats uncomfortable and so 'some persons (and more persons after finding benefit of it) did, at their own cost, erect and put wainscot under the . . . benches . . . betwixt their benches and the back rail for warm's sake and to keep the wind and cold from their backs and legs', thus making pews as we know them. None of the parishioners 'pretended to have a particular right there more than any other'.[102] The only exceptions were the Earl of Derby and two members of the local gentry: Mr Laithwaite and Mr Hurleston,[103] who kept their right to pews above their family's burial places. This privilege was connected with their freehold of certain properties: the Laithwaite's on the corner of Aughton Street and Moor Street, and 'one of the best and most principal houses in Ormskirk',[104] the Hurleston's being a manor house between Ormskirk and Scarisbrick.

Gradually the parish elite acquired and embellished their seating and created a status display within the heart of the church. The parish clerk had his seat before our period began, and in 1665 'work [was] done about the clerk's seat'.[105] About the same time, the churchwardens appropriated a wainscotted pew and significantly 'raised it about two foot higher for themselves and their successors to sit in', giving themselves an elevated position, symbolic of their rank as leading officers of the church.[106]

30. Dog whipper's pew.

Then it was the turn of the town's officers to be granted prominent places. The constables' seat was installed in 1668, in the centre aisle 'at the proper cost and charge of several inhabitants'.[107] Each constable paid 10*s* for his seat for life, and it was intended to accommodate as many past constables 'as it [would] handsomely and decently hold and contain' – conditions which suggest some unseemly jockeying for position, unless a form of precedence had been agreed. Incidentally, the owner of one of the prized family pews, James Laithwaite, preferred the honour of sitting among the constables.[108]

Later in the seventeenth century, the leading townspeople wanted their exclusive seats, possibly in imitation of the gentry, the Stanleys of Bickerstaffe and the Scarisbricks, who had their private chapels within the church. However, many of their fellow townspeople regarded the privatisation of pews as trespassing on their communal rights, and this local instance of a gradual shift in emphasis from community to individual did not go unchallenged. This shift had many paradoxical aspects. The townspeople took communal action to preserve their former privileges, yet with the weakening of the Derby interest,[109] a new 'town consciousness' emerged. This created a completely new town status system and led to intense competition between individuals for a rung on the status ladder. Thus we see the dichotomy of co-operation and intense competition appearing concurrently within the same community.

Co-operation emerged uppermost in 1672, when forty-five parishioners sent

Bishop Wilkins an objection to John Hurleston's petition for a private pew. Although Hurleston's family traditionally held a pew, he had moved to Pickton in Cheshire, which prejudiced his case.[110] The counter-petition admitted that others had erected seats but had not enclosed them. It was the proposed enclosure, the exclusion of others and consequent elitism that caused dissension. The outcome is not recorded, but the protests did not stop the escalation of status display inside the church, with the enclosed private pew as the ultimate status symbol.

In 1677, competition for this status symbol was behind Jane Laithwaite's defence of her family's right to a particular pew against the challenge of John Entwistle, the lawyer, who having bought the family's house, thereby – in his eyes – had acquired the family's pew. The house, held by freehold tenure, had been in the possession of the Laithwaite family for several generations and Jane, a widow, was head of the current generation. Entwistle's challenge illustrates locally the expanding role and prestige of the professions,[111] while the details of the case demonstrate the amount of antagonism generated by such rivalry.

As was customary, Entwistle instructed his apprentices and servants to sit in 'his' pew, but Jane Laithwaite stormed into the pew and 'did pull and thrust at . . . [one of the apprentices] and would have pushed him out . . . whereby the congregation was disturbed and many people stood up and stared at them and she pulled an instrument or thing out of her pocket like a bodkin and thrust it several times at this deponent'. The following Sunday, in obedience to their master, the two apprentices again took up their positions. Again Jane Laithwaite 'abused' them and added that 'before he should sit there she would have his life and she would bring chamber pots and throw them in this deponent's face, saying that his said master and all his family were outcomers and lousey beggars all of them'.[112]

Here was one of the local pseudo-gentry vigorously defending her hereditary position against the incursion of a socially mobile professional outsider, for, although John Entwistle came from a gentry family from Foxholes, near Rochdale, he did not qualify as Ormskirk gentry and his only claim to status in the town came through his profession. Later he made an incontrovertible statement of his position by deleting the Laithwaite inscription on the gravestone under the pew and carving his own initials upon it. The depth of feeling inherent in the social rivalries of Ormskirk is evident in this case and is typical of that in many eighteenth-century English towns.

Three members of local gentry families – James Holland, Richard Blundell and 'Mr' Sephton – held pews in the 1680s, according to the lists of church property.[113] As no faculties were granted for their pews, these families must have exerted their right to a privilege belonging to them from pre-Commonwealth times, when competition for these status symbols increased. Meanwhile the 'ordinary' people sat 'seldom constantly in one and the same place, if any other one sit in that place before they came, the meaner sort commonly giving place to those of better quality'.[114] Again, a clear consciousness of social ranking is apparent. The bishop encouraged this discrimination by enquiring into an applicant's ranking before granting permission for a private seat. For instance, 'Mr' William Farrington of the gentry family from Worden Hall near Preston, an apothecary and friend of the Countess of Derby, applied for a pew in Ormskirk church in 1692. He was described on the petition as 'very conformable to the Church of England, a constant frequenter of divine service at his parish church, a just payer of his lays towards repairs and provision of necessarys and ornaments for the church [and] . . . owner of a considerable estate and a house in the parish'. Those were the sort of qualifications needed for a seat in the church 'without contradiction from any person whatsoever'.[115]

Mr Hill and Mr Valentine, local gentlemen with those qualifications, acquired family pews between 1695 and 1699,[116] but they were upstaged four years later by Thomas Dod, another local lawyer, who, wanting visible evidence of his very superior position in local society, bought a pew and the floor space under it in the King's Chancel from Charles, Earl of Dunmore.[117]

By purchasing the plot directly from the impropriator, and sidestepping the bishop's court, Dod gained a prestigious position in the King's Chancel where, according to tradition, Henry VII and his entourage had been seated when they visited Lathom House in 1495.[118] The privatisation and enclosure of pews remained a sensitive issue, despite several more private pews having been acquired by wealthy families, who had no claim to gentry status.[119] In 1718 Heyrick Halsall, a gentleman, and Gilbert Taylor and Edward Ashcroft, both husbandmen, applied for permission to erect 'separate seats for their own use alone' over the burial places of their families. The bishop, noting that two of the applicants were lowly husbandmen, instructed the churchwardens to call a parish meeting to discuss the matter with the 'intent to prevent disputes'. Mr Halsall used several inducements – a silver plate and a legacy – to persuade the meeting to agree to his private pew. Finally a compromise was reached. The churchwardens would erect two seats at the parish's charge, one for public use and one for Mr Halsall's private use.[120] The gentleman obtained his seat, while the two husbandmen were to take their turn with the general public.

As we have seen (p. 83), during the building of the new south aisle gallery in 1730, the bishop allowed the churchwardens to exploit this fashion of owning seats to raise money, thus setting a precedent to be followed whenever there was a need for more seating or more money.[121] In fact, in 1762, when another western gallery was proposed, the churchwardens removed one of their seats so that 'a new, handsome and convenient seat' could replace it and be sold to contribute towards the gallery's cost.[122]

When the initiative to sell came from the churchwardens, a slightly different attitude can be detected. The need of the increasing population was recognised, status moved to second place and seats were allotted 'to those in need' of them. Although the seats were upstairs at the back of the church and not in a prominent position, it was intended that the holders should 'bear a rateable and proportional share of the whole expense'.[123] Nevertheless, the seats' location meant that the status of seatholders was no longer paramount,

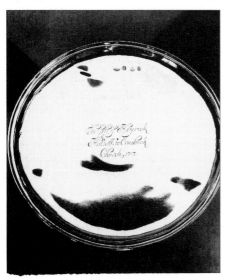

31. Plate donated by Heyrick Halsall.

32. Property in Westhead bought with Heyrick Halsall's legacy.

and only a proportion of the expense was charged to avoid increasing the Church 'ley' (tax).

Similarly no attempt was made to recoup the cost (£4) for 'a new . . . handsome and convenient pew for the use of women to return thanks in after childbearing', again in 1762.[124] The dangers of childbearing at this time led mothers to feel a need to thank God for their safe delivery by observing the rite of churching. The provision of a new pew suggests that more mothers were attending the ceremony in consequence of Ormskirk's rising birth rate, which was also responsible for the recurring demand for more seats in the church. The provision of seating without a demand for complete reimbursement shows a growing concern for the poor, and the increasing ability of the parishioners to meet the cost.

Nevertheless, earlier attitudes to pews as status symbols remained entrenched, especially among the emergent middle class. For example, in 1783 'a new, handsome and convenient seat . . . [together] . . . with the burial place under the same' was granted to 'James Grice [a wealthy cooper] and his family . . . , owners . . . of the said dwelling house . . . [in Church Street] . . . for the use of themselves, families, tenants and servants'.[125] This grant also confirms that status was indirectly attached to properties with rights within the church – and a resultant higher market value. The inclusion of tenants and servants reaffirmed the earlier custom, and provided yet another opportunity to exhibit wealth by displaying their numbers, and thereby the extent of the owner's estate. This grant

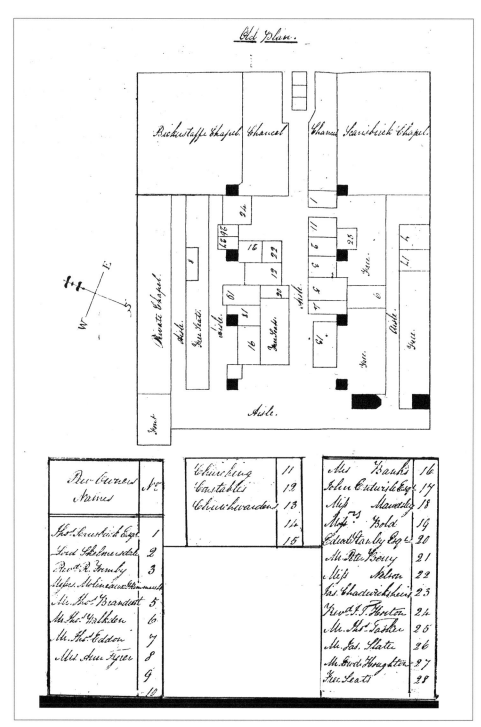

33. Plan of the pews in 1828.[126]

confirms that property and status – lowering as the century progressed – remained the main requirements for acquiring private pews in Ormskirk church, and also that the seating was used to demonstrate – and consolidate – its owner's social position until the end of our period.

Thus we get a dynamic account of the emergence of a hierarchy in the town, and of the success of various groups in establishing in the heart of the church visible evidence of their claim to a position in that hierarchy. This behaviour pattern was not confined to Ormskirk. In fact, throughout the land, 'the physical arrangements at church assemblies and especially the seating were a deliberate demonstration of social difference. Wooden pews and stalls froze the orders of society in a static and visually edifying representation of hierarchy'.[127]

CHAPTER V

The Nonconformists

THE PRESBYTERIANS

The pattern of segregation between the privileged and unprivileged within the parish church was repeated between the privileged Conformists and the unprivileged Nonconformists throughout our period. Although in 1689 the Toleration Act had exempted Protestant Nonconformists from prosecution if their preachers and meeting houses were licensed, the Act of Uniformity (1662), the Corporations Act (1661) and, to a lesser extent, the Test Acts (1673 and 1678) excluded all Nonconformists from educational, civil and political privileges.

After the Act of Toleration, most Dissenters registered their meeting houses, establishing a legal base for their ministry. During the following forty years their numbers increased, and they profited from the Anglican Church's inadequate provision for worship, especially in the northern counties and the emerging industrial centres.[1] Nationally, these were more peaceful years when dissenting sects could minister without fear, consolidate, expand and build new chapels as required.

The Ormskirk Dissenters registered Berry's House as the place of worship 'for . . . a congregation of Protestant Dissenters' in 1689,[2] until their chapel was built in 1693. Then the minister, Nathaniel Heywood jnr, and John Berry registered 'a new building lately erected near the dwelling place of Roger Westhead to be a place for . . . religious worship' for 'their Majesties' Protestant subjects dissenting from the Church of England'.[3] Little is known about this early chapel, which was probably functional rather than ornamental.

Between 1690 and 1695, the Presbyterians and the Independents nationwide explored the possibility of a union. This initiative had two results. The first was the 'Happy Union', an association of ministers – concerned primarily with ordination – known to have been supported by ministers from Lancashire, Devon, Hampshire, Cheshire and the West Riding. The second was the establishment of the Common Fund to provide resources for impoverished congregations and ministers. These attempts at union at the national level were blighted by the two denominations' incompatible approaches to ministry. By 1696, the only remnants were some common funds and a measure of co-operation between neighbouring congregations of the two denominations, especially in the provinces.[4] Provincial Assemblies similar to the Happy Union were set up in various regions during the 1690s and several, including that in Lancashire, survived until the middle of the eighteenth century.[5]

One survey compiled for the Common Fund in the 1690s enumerates the congregations and their ministers and lists ministers' salaries. In Ormskirk, Nathaniel Heywood jnr ministered to a congregation of 250. If the total population of Ormskirk is estimated as 981 (from the court leet returns of 1686), over 25% were Presbyterians in the 1690s. This percentage is extremely high compared with other areas, as seen in Table 18 of the totals and percentages of Dissenters in market towns as compiled by Anne Whiteman using the Compton Census (1676), which did not include the Chester diocese.[6] While the Compton Census included Quakers, the Common Fund enquiry did not. If it had done so, Ormskirk's total would have been still higher.

The Common Fund accounts enable us to compare Ormskirk's 250 'hearers' with Liverpool's 400 'hearers', where two preachers shared an income of £75 per annum, and Rainford's 200 where the preacher received £10 per annum and was considered to 'deserve some encouragement' from the fund.[7] Nathaniel Heywood the younger was paid only £30 per annum – the same salary as his father before his ejection – so he relied on the generosity of his congregation. Bequests, like that of Edward Dicconson in 1717 leaving £5 to the trustees of the chapel, were invested and the interest supplemented the minister's salary. Dicconson also left £6 to be distributed to poor students training for the ministry or to poor ministers of the 'same persuasion'.[8]

Oliver Heywood, brother of Nathaniel, had initiated moves towards Presbyterian–Independent unity in Northowram in 1672, eighteen years before the Happy Union,[9] and in 1681 took part in the ordination of Thomas Jollie, a Presbyterian, as pastor of the Independent chapel at Sheffield.[10] Possibly Nathaniel jnr joined his uncle in 1690 to endorse the short-lived Happy Union. Certainly he was involved in the Lancashire version of the movement in 1694, being present at meetings of the Lancashire United Ministers in Manchester.[11] This Assembly formed in 1691 and was organised in four Divisions: Manchester, Warrington, Bolton and 'the North'. At their biannual meetings the ministers discussed ordination and other relevant matters. Nathaniel Heywood jnr was the delegate for the Manchester meeting in 1695, 1696 and in 1700, and for the Warrington meeting in 1695 and 1697.[12] The available minutes end in 1700, but the Lancashire Provincial Assembly continued and was amalgamated in 1765 with the Cheshire classis, the governing body of elders in that county, to form the Provincial Assembly of Presbyterian and United Ministers and Congregations in Lancashire and Cheshire, a 'union' which existed at least until 1917.[13] Thus the

TABLE 18. The percentages of Dissenters in various towns

Town	Estimated population	Dissenters	%
Stratford on Avon	584	10	1.7
Gisburne	950	21	2.21
Camden	4784	127	2.6
Giggleswick	716	34	4.7
Bakewell	4235	200	4.7
Burton on Trent	1292	65	5
Stow	3856	316	8.2
Bromsgrove	2000	300	15
Ormskirk	981	250	25

Ormskirk Presbyterians through their progressive minister contributed towards the movement for union, long before it came to fruition in the twentieth century.

In Ormskirk the flourishing Presbyterian movement registered two more meeting houses: one in 1697 by Elizabeth Heywood and a second in 1709 by Mary Heywood.[14] Why these houses were needed when a purpose-built chapel was available, and when there was no (recorded) split in the group, is unclear. Perhaps extra accommodation was needed for worship, or for women's or children's meetings. As there was no procedure for cancelling unwanted registrations, all three houses were probably not used at the same time. Perhaps Elizabeth died and the group moved into Mary's house, and the chapel continued to function. Similar expansions were recorded in many areas of South Lancashire, where meeting houses were erected at Tockholes near Blackburn (1710), St Helens (1710) and Chowbent near Leigh (1720),[15] a process repeated in most towns and villages in England.

Nationally the religious scene during the early years of the eighteenth century was dominated by struggles between the Whigs, supporting increased religious freedom, and the Tories, seeking to maintain the privileged position of the Anglican Church. When the Tories were in power, they passed an act preventing Occasional Conformity (1711), excluding Dissenters from public office, and the Schism Act (1714), preventing Dissenters from running schools. As Ormskirk was not a borough, the first statute did not apply, and, although the Schism Act had a devastating effect on Frankland's Academy, where Nathaniel Heywood the younger, Edward Crane (minister in Ormskirk, 1742–1744), John Holland (preacher in Ormskirk, 1744) and several Ormskirk youths, including Ralph Sherdley, Robert Hesketh and Nathaniel Whitfield, were educated,[16] the majority of the Ormskirk Dissenters were not affected by that Act.

The Schism Act alerted the Committee of the Three Denominations, consisting of Presbyterian, Congregational and Baptist ministers, to the Tory threat to the Dissenters. Unlike the Happy Union, this committee was an alliance with no intention of uniting.[17] They commissioned a survey to discover their strength and how many votes they could command in England and Wales. This survey, the 'Evans List', recorded the congregations, their ministers, the number of hearers and the number of votes. The results were collated in 1719, after the act had been repealed. Although its absolute accuracy has been doubted, the list is useful to estimate the current extent of Dissent. Watts calculated from it that 179,350 or 3.3% of the population of England and Wales were Presbyterians, while in Lancashire the figure stood at 16,630 or 8.48% of the population.[18] The proportions in other counties are listed in Table 19, extracted from Watts's table.[19]

TABLE 19. Proportions of Presbyterians in various counties

County	Presbyterians as a percentage of the population
Lancashire	8.5
Cheshire	7.25
Devon	7.2
Kent	2.6
Yorkshire	2
Durham	1.5
Westmorland	1.1

The Ormskirk congregation was listed as containing 286 hearers, which almost agrees with the figure quoted in the visitation report of 1722,[20] listing sixty-six Dissenting families (approximately 297 individuals) and an increase of thirty-six since the Common Fund list of 1692. Using the figure of 1,100 as an estimate of the town's population,[21] and Evans' number of 286 hearers, it can be calculated that the proportion of Presbyterians in the population had risen to 26%. This confirms that the local strength of the movement did not decline before the 1720s. This high proportion could be ascribed to the lack of Independents and Baptists in the town. Certainly the zeal and prominence of the Heywood family in the Presbyterian movement had assured it of support during their lifetimes and the congregation's loyalty after their deaths.

As the eighteenth century progressed, a general malaise spread among Dissenters as many sought 'inspiration from the spirit of reason rather than the Spirit of God'.[22] Individuality of opinion was encouraged in their meetings by an atmosphere of argument quite different from the authoritarianism of the Anglicans and, later, of the Methodists.[23] Meetings of Presbyterian ministers – such as that held in Salters' Hall in 1719 – explored the question of the Trinity, and divisions led to the growth of Unitarianism.[24] Pamphlets appeared, such as those of Strickland Gough enquiring into 'the decay of the Dissenting interest' (1730) and those of Doddridge into 'the means of reviving the Dissenting Interest' (1730). Many vicars reported decaying Dissenting congregations, and between 1714 and 1731 over fifty Dissenting ministers returned to the Established Church. Richey summarises the situation: 'Dissent as a whole was experiencing decline – decline in members, decline in chapels, decline in the percentage of time the Dissenters were willing to devote to religion, decline in morality and most important, decline in financial support'.[25] Presbyterians insisted on highly educated ministers, but adequate salaries were not forthcoming. Although some good-quality candidates came forward, there was a lack of recruits of a high calibre willing to be ordained.

During the mid-eighteenth century, this decline spread throughout the country. Presbyterians increasingly moved away from Independents, the former preaching scholarly expositions of the scriptures and the latter, undergoing a slight revival, concentrating on emotional evangelism and orthodox trinitarianism. This split was slow to reach Lancashire and Cheshire, where the ideals of united Dissent were more persistent. Nevertheless even here, changes were evident as, for instance, in 1750 when Josiah Owen persuaded the Lancashire Provincial Assembly to abandon its usual investigations into the state of congregations, making a break in Presbyterian tradition and supporting Independent Congregational principles.[26]

Although the same decline occurred in Ormskirk, a specific local cause is hard to identify. No local split between Presbyterians and Unitarians is recorded, so seemingly the decline merely conformed to the general pattern. Table 20 charts the decline in Ormskirk using baptismal records in conjunction with the estimated birth rate to calculate the numbers in the congregation. During the period, the average annual birth rate fluctuated between thirty-five and forty per thousand.[27] To set the table in perspective, as we saw, the estimated number of hearers in 1692 was 250 (Gordon's List), while in 1719 it was 286 (Evans' List).

TABLE 20. An estimation of the size of the Presbyterian congregation in Ormskirk, 1743–1783[28]

Years	No. of baptisms	Average per year	Birth rate, per 1,000	Total no. in congregation
1743–1750	49	7	42	166
1751–1760	70	7	36	194
1761–1770	50	5	36	138
1771–1780	38	3.8	38	100
1781–1783	8	2.6	38	68

The low result for the 1743–1750 and 1781-1783 periods may be caused by taking the average of seven years instead of ten. The series could not be continued after 1783 because of haphazard entries in the register.

Using the congregation totals along with the population totals – before 1770 from the court leet records (see p. xvii) and, after 1770, from bishop's visitation returns of 1778 – Table 21 shows the decreasing percentage of Presbyterians in Ormskirk for the period 1743–1783.

Alongside numerical decline, the Presbyterians nationwide underwent social change at this time. Watts commented that social and legal pressure helped to confine Dissenters to the occupations of merchants, tradesmen and self-employed artisans, while the requirements of the Test and Corporation Acts encouraged the aristocracy and gentry to abandon Nonconformity, because it was incompatible with their social and political aspirations.[29] This narrowing social mixture was another case of the decline, for the traditional leaders departed leaving a fiercely independent group, where co-operation was extremely difficult.

Ormskirk Presbyterians' origins among the families of tradesmen and artisans reflected the national position. No gentry or noble families were among their ranks after Lady Elizabeth Stanley's death in the early eighteenth century, and only one member could claim to belong to a profession – Richard Plumbe, the apothecary. The others formed a cross-section of tradespeople, including five

TABLE 21. The percentage of Presbyterians in the population of Ormskirk

Date	No. in congregation	Ormskirk's population*	Percentage of Presbyterians
1743–1750	166	[1041]	15.9
1751–1760	194	1210	16
1761–1770	138	[1379]	10
1771–1780	100	2,280	4.39
1781–1783	68	2,280	2.98

* The population totals in square brackets are approximations based on the known court leet totals.

linen drapers, four innkeepers or victuallers, two butchers, a nailer, a hatter, a tailor, a skinner, a saddler, an ironmonger and a grocer.

During the later eighteenth century, English Presbyterianism, especially in the North and in London, was reinforced by Scots immigration, and, in Ormskirk, several Scotsmen appear on the Presbyterian register at that time. This Scots migration into Ormskirk was important because the congregation received new members. Interestingly, one was listed as a draper, probably one of those travelling salesmen who had settled in the town, mentioned by the vicar in 1778 (see p. 86). As the vicar admitted, the Presbyterians received 'some temporary and occasional additions and increases from Scotch pedlars'. Nevertheless, these were insufficient to halt the decline.

However, during the period 1780–1800, the Presbyterians, nationwide, received increased financial support from families involved in commerce. The denomination acquired an aura of social stability, freedom and progress which attracted young men, ambitious merchants and tradespeople. These newcomers participated in the administration of the chapels, filling leading roles, becoming trustees for chapel property and endowments, improving the chapels' finances and giving a new impetus to the congregations.[30]

Like other Presbyterian groups, the congregation in Ormskirk experienced a short period of expansion. In 1773 they needed a new chapel, and a group of men, not mentioned previously in the Dissenters' records, registered 'an edifice or building in the possession of Edward Pike for public worship'.[31] This was an interim measure. Land was leased on Aughton Street and a minister's house was built with a chapel and yard to the rear.[32] On 26 April 1784, John Irving, a draper whose family had worshipped at the chapel for over forty years, registered 'the newly erected brick buildings situate in Aughton Street . . . for a meeting place for Protestants dissenting from the Church of England'.[33] This was a plain brick building with a paved floor and a pulpit against one wall – probably very similar to the original meeting house and to other meeting houses throughout the land. The architecture was plain and utilitarian with few stylistic details other than a pleasing symmetry. The only visible remains of this development today is the gravestone of the minister, Revd Fogg, and his family.

Despite this initiative to expand, the overall decline in the Ormskirk Presbyterian congregation continued. The register records only thirty-eight baptisms during the period 1771–1780, whereas, during the period 1751–1760, seventy took place. There is a gap in the records between 1783 and 1800, then during the first decade of the 1800s only twenty-two baptisms are recorded, and later Revd Fogg was forced to admit that

34. Gravestone of Revd Fogg and family.

'the congregation is subsisting, but is very small'.[34] The Presbyterian congregation in Ormskirk never regained the prominent position in the town it had held in the days of Nathaniel Heywood.

THE METHODISTS

Dissent was renewed by missionary zeal from an unexpected direction, through a movement within the Anglican community, which the Church rejected. Three ordained preachers of the Established Church – George Whitfield, and the Wesley brothers – led the evangelical revival of the 1730s, which spread to England from the Continent and from the colonies in America.[35]

Wesley regarded the world as his parish and, consequently, during his travels he encroached on the territory of incumbents who often refused to allow him to preach in their churches. Undeterred, he followed Whitfield's example and preached in the open air, attracting many who never went inside a church.[36] He used unconventional venues as preaching houses, such as a malt kiln in Warrington, a cockpit in Denholme in the West Riding and a foundry in London,[37] adapting his services to suit the circumstances. Hymn singing, audible in the open air, was increased and pamphlets were printed for distribution to continue the ministry when the preacher moved on.[38] In the minister's absence, strict organisation was needed to maintain the commitment of each group, so Wesley appointed local preachers who retained their daily occupation, and instituted 'bands' for the more committed members, and 'classes' to which every member belonged.[39] Gradually, as the movement grew, this network of organisations was extended to provide a form of self-help to supplement the periodic visits of the itinerant ministers.

Wesley confined his travels to a triangle between Newcastle, London and Bristol, and rarely ministered outside those bounds. He targeted areas where the orthodox Church of England had made least provision for the parishioners, and large followings were attracted in emergent industrial areas, where many migrants from the countryside lived far from their 'roots'. Wesley found that settled rural communities with a strong presence of a vicar or squire did not respond to his teaching and, as he had encountered violent opposition in several of those areas, he avoided them.[40] Although the Anglican Church distrusted Wesley's itinerant evangelism, he did not wish to sever his allegiance to that Church. However, in the 1780s, after the American War of Independence, he rebelled against the Anglican authorities in America and revised the Prayer Book for that country. He also ordained preachers for American Methodist Churches.[41] Finally, after his death in 1791, the leaders of Methodism broke their connection with the Anglican Church,[42] and Methodists joined the ranks of Dissenters.

During this period of evangelical revival, support for the Established Church in Ormskirk was increasing. In the 1778 episcopal report, the vicar claimed that, despite the late building programme, at least three chapels were needed to provide sufficient accommodation for the parishioners living in the outlying areas.[43] In fact, Ormskirk, with both a keen vicar and an active lord of the manor, was an area which Wesley regarded as unpromising for conversion. It had few emergent industries and so its population, though rising, was not increased by influxes of immigrant workers. Outside the triangle of Wesley's journeyings it remained 'a Methodist wilderness';[44] in fact, in his report (1778) the vicar,

William Knowles (1727–1780), declared that Protestant dissidents other than Dissenters and Quakers would 'not vouchsafe to take any notice or settle amongst us'.[45] Even in 1801 it was claimed that the only Lancashire towns with over 2,000 inhabitants which Methodism had not penetrated were Accrington, Ashton-in-Makerfield, Prescot and Ormskirk.[46]

Actually Methodism had been established in the town by 1792 under the control of the Liverpool Circuit, at the instigation of the superintendent, Revd Thomas Taylor, one of John Wesley's hand-picked preachers. The chapel at Moor Street End was described by Taylor as 'a place to preach in, fitted . . . with a pulpit, benches and a couple of rooms adjoining, one of which we got furnished for the preacher whenever he came'.[47] The location of this chapel suggests that it was the same old 1696 chapel, abandoned by the Presbyterians in 1784 when they built their new chapel in Aughton Street. However, the small congregation had to contend 'with much opposition from mobs and riots'[48] and seemingly the little chapel was wrecked. Certainly, the meeting was indicted in 1795 at the court leet, 'for want of the Methodist Chapel roof being in sufficient repair',[49] and the group were forced to abandon their mission in the town.

Later, when Revd Adam Clarke visited the town in 1801, he preached in true Wesleyan tradition from the fish stones in the market square. By 1804 the Methodists had acquired another centre, described in 1810 in an appeal for a new chapel: ' Our present preaching house is a very uncomfortable place . . . adjoining a public bakehouse and a slaughterhouse . . . underneath is a rag warehouse. The floor is much broken which makes it so cold in winter that many . . . dare not come, and in summer the livestock from beneath are very troublesome – our good women complain of having to undress on their return to "catch and kill".'[50] The discomfort of the Methodist ladies tormented by fleas and lice moved the conference, and the meeting received the help they required to build a new chapel on the northern side of Chapel Lane, probably again on the same old site.

THE QUAKERS

Although changes were occurring in the Anglican Church and among the Presbyterians and Methodists, little changed in the position of those dissidents who completely rejected the teachings of the Anglican Church: the Quakers and the Catholics, outcasts to be castigated and feared for their suspect allegiances. From the earliest days of their movement, Quakers were harried and often imprisoned for their faith, despite the issue of the Instrument of Government in 1653 protecting members of dissenting sects. The Quakers' teaching that 'the Spirit of God is in every man and every man who obeyed this Light could attain perfection' and their rejection of all sacraments and liturgy[51] offended Conformists. Antagonism against them was increased further by their enthusiasm for spreading their message – even within the churches – and by their egalitarianism, which led them to reject several social customs, such as raising their hats to their 'superiors'.[52] Their behaviour appeared to 'challenge the reality of inequality and the existence of hierarchy', the basis of seventeenth-century social life.[53] Quakers were accused of blasphemy because, it was said, they claimed equality with God; of vagabondage, because they travelled around spreading their teachings; rightly, of refusing to pay tithes or their Church 'ley' to a hostile

35. Quaker burial ground, Graveyard Lane.

Church; and of refusing to swear oaths of allegiance. Nevertheless, before 1661 they were usually allowed to meet for worship, and the 1660 Declaration of Breda led them to believe that they would keep that freedom after the Restoration. However, as we have seen, Venner's Insurrection on 6 January 1661 generated widespread suspicion against all Nonconformists, and on 10 January meetings of Quakers, 'Anabaptists' and Fifth Monarchists were forbidden. The establishment's immediate response indicates the extent of this suspicion.[54] As J.R. Jones observed, 'Religious dissent was equated with political faction.'[55]

As in the Established Church, the experience of the Bickerstaffe Quakers demonstrated locally both the national suspicion of their faith and motives, and the nationwide Quakers' response. The Bickerstaffe meeting was founded in 1653 in the parish of Ormskirk outside the boundaries of the township where many of them lived. They refused burial in Ormskirk churchyard and bought land for their own graveyard in 1665.[56] Then, in 1669, the Quaker leader, George Fox, visited the meeting, which thrived for over a century but had to be abandoned in 1786.

The experience of Oliver Atherton, leader of the local Quakers, illustrates how their egalitarianism caused them to break the accepted social code and incur hostility from the gentry. In 1654 he met James Howard, an Ormskirk gentleman, on horseback in Mawdesley, a nearby village. The Quarterly Meeting Sufferings Book[57] describes what happened: 'Oliver passed by and gave him no words [and] the said Howard fell abeating the said Oliver and so continued about a quarter of a mile, often swearing that he could find in his heart to sheath his knife in the said Oliver.' A similar incident occurred in Ormskirk Market when William Langley, an Aughton Quaker, met Richard Germaine, who 'layd hands violently on him and shook him'.

The Quakers' enthusiasm for spreading their faith and challenging the established religion on its own ground also aroused antagonism in Ormskirk.[58] A local example of the kind of invasive behaviour pioneered by Fox in Lancaster in 1652[59] and by other militant Friends, such as Thomas Rudd at Liverpool in 1699,[60] occurred at Ormskirk in 1658, when the same Atherton 'was moved of ye Lord' to go to the parish church and address the people immediately before Heywood came in to take the service. When Heywood entered, the constables jumped up from their pew and escorted Atherton to the Town Hall, where he was imprisoned for the day. Undeterred, he went again to the church in 1660, but this time he waited until Heywood had finished, and then 'in patience and fear of ye Lord' spoke to the people. The congregation was incensed by him preaching an alien doctrine inside their church, and two of them 'pulled him by ye hair of his head and threw him out of the steeple house with much violence'.[61]

Fear and hostility towards the Quakers increased throughout the land in the late 1650s, fanned by anti-Quaker propaganda in pamphlets and sermons. In Cheshire and south Lancashire, this hostility gave rise to an insurrection led by George Booth, ostensibly to prevent danger from the Quakers. The rising in the north-western counties was short-lived, and the nationwide rising, planned in areas as far apart as Derbyshire and Hampshire, never materialised. Gradually, indiscriminate propagandists who labelled the Quakers as 'Papists in disguise' grafted hatred of Quakers on to fear of Popery. As tension mounted, General Monck moved into London to organise a campaign against the Quakers and radicals generally. Indirectly, this same tension led to the restoration of Charles II and his welcome as the saviour of the Protestant religion. This aspect of the Restoration encouraged the authorities to move openly against the Quakers. Meetings were raided in Dorset, Berkshire, Cheshire, Gloucestershire, Merionethshire and Wiltshire, while in Norwich and Cambridge mobs invaded the meetings, breaking up the sparse furniture and causing severe injuries to some members.[62] At Harwich, a Friends' meeting was interrupted and the leaders were sent for trial, accused of inciting a 'mutiny'.[63]

Again Ormskirk was no exception, as attested by a case at Ormskirk quarter sessions in 1660. According to the Quakers' petition,[64] on 18 January, seventeen Quakers were 'not suffered to stay peaceably together' in the house of Peter Leadbetter in Bickerstaffe. A company of soldiers under Captain Houghton by the order of the Earl of Derby[65] took them to Ormskirk, where they were imprisoned, before being taken to the Wigan quarter sessions. There they were tendered the Oath of Allegiance, which they refused to swear 'for conscience sake', and were committed to the sheriff's custody to be sent to Lancaster Gaol. The sheriff hired eight men to escort them during their two-day journey to Lancaster, where they were detained for nine weeks awaiting the Assize. After great hardship to themselves and their families, the judge acquitted them 'no man having anything to lay to . . . [their] . . . charge'. The timing of this acquittal suggests that the judge's verdict was influenced by the Declaration of Breda, made that same year.

Nevertheless, the Quakers' harassment was not over for, although they had paid their expenses while they were in gaol, the sheriff (William Turner of Preston) and the constable (Richard Hawett of Ormskirk) demanded payment for the expenses incurred both during their imprisonment in Ormskirk and on the journey to gaol. The Quakers refused to pay, so they were taken again before the justices, who authorised the constables to seize their goods in lieu of payment.[66] Despite the Quakers' claim that the King had ordered their release without payment being made, the constables seized articles varying from a heifer to a brass pot, which were worth far more than the sum demanded. Similar persecutions were inflicted at Manchester (1661), Aspull (1662), Colne (1662), Yealand (1663), Haslingden (1664) and Bury (1667), according to the Sufferings Book.[67] Nationwide, Quaker Meetings were raided and hundreds were thrown into prison.[68]

Non-payment of tithes also led to the imprisonment of local Quakers. For instance, in 1661 Oliver Atherton was imprisoned in Lancaster Gaol for refusing to pay tithes. He appealed to the Countess of Derby who, as the lay rector and impropriator of the tithes of Ormskirk church, refused to cancel the debt. Atherton kept to his principles and would not pay, and consequently remained in prison, where he died two-and-a-half years later. His fellow Quakers paraded his body around the market towns between Lancaster and Bickerstaffe, including Ormskirk. They put the coffin in the market-places, and on the market crosses they displayed a notice: 'Here lies Oliver Atherton, from the Parish of Ormskirk, who by the Countess of Derby had been persecuted to death for keeping a good conscience towards God and Christ, in not paying tithes to her'[69] – another example of the social militancy of the early Quakers.[70]

The Ormskirk Quakers' refusal to contribute to the Anglican Church resulted in indictments at the consistory court in Chester, where, in 1674, three Quakers were accused of refusing to pay their Church leys towards the repairing of Ormskirk church.[71] The Quakers declared that, 'as to the breaches, ruins and decays of the fabric we are unacquainted, being not concerned to take care thereof'. The court excommunicated the Quakers, barring them from the Anglican sacraments and from burial within the Anglican churchyard, neither of which would trouble them. Nevertheless, the social and economic ostracism and legal penalties following excommunication could be both unnerving and damaging, if the townsfolk chose to apply them. However, these sanctions were imposed irregularly, depending on individuals' attitudes, and in fact the county had developed a tolerant interdenominational culture, which 'preferred tolerance to agreement and had little time for uniformity'.[72] Nevertheless, such toleration could not be guaranteed, for a few years later, in 1679, the chief informer against the Ormskirk Quakers was a Catholic, William Moss.[73]

Following the Second Conventicle Act (1670), the form of harassment inflicted on the Quakers changed and they no longer suffered physical punishment, possibly because they had become more introspective and had abandoned the belligerent evangelism of the 1650s. During the early 1660s many of the enthusiastic itinerant leaders died, and their fervent evangelism was moderated. George Fox was left with a large unwieldy movement, and so he developed more organisation, elaborating the monthly, womens' and quarterly meetings. This unintentionally stimulated conservatism among Quakers,[74] and in response to this moderation, the authorities changed their tactics and attempted to ruin the

Friends financially.[75] Sir Daniel Fleming, a leading instigator of anti-Quaker prosecutions in Lancashire and Westmorland, wrote, 'It is as clear as day that nothing will convince them of their errors as soon as the drawing of money from them; for a great part of their religion – notwithstanding their great zeal and fair pretences – is tyed to their purse strings'.[76] Nevertheless, the Quakers did not alter their ways and continued to be indicted, principally for not paying tithes, but also for holding conventicles, absence from church services, and refusing to pay fines. Consequently, the bailiffs increasingly distrained their goods. The informer's reward of one-third of the distrained goods led to increased prosecutions and much bitterness between neighbours and even within families. One such instance occurred in Ormskirk, as a note in the Sufferings Book describes: 'Peter Andrews, son of Sam Andrews . . . informed, the said Peter being, as he said, spat on by his father who was not a Quaker'. Sam, an attorney, despised his son for informing about a Quaker conventicle. It is significant that, for Sam, loyalty to his neighbours took precedence over strict obedience to the law, especially a law he regarded as unjust. In Sam's eyes his son was a traitor to his neighbours and was contemptible.

The lists of goods distrained in these cases give ample evidence that Ormskirk was part of a national pattern to cause the maximum distress to the Quakers. Tradesmen in Ormskirk, as elsewhere, faced ruin as their essential tools were taken in lieu of tithes and fines. For instance, in 1675 Henry Ashton, a distiller, had his still plus a bucket and chain – very likely from his well – taken, while Joseph Coppock, a grocer, was deprived of his scales and weights. Other tradesmen lost quantities of their stock. John Johnson lost almost 7 yd of coloured fustian, Richard Johnson had 20 lb of bacon taken from his shop and Henry Foster, a weaver, 'had his linen cloth distrained in ye market'. In 1677, Thomas Crosbie lost four pairs of men's worsted stockings priced 4s a pair, while Joseph Coppock had 3½ yd of silk costing 16s a pound taken. No mercy was shown, even to widows like Mary Sutton, who was fined 5s for attending a conventicle at which she was not present. She refused to pay, so her brass, pewter and flax, valued at over 6s, were confiscated. As Alan Anderson observed, 'the local magistrates . . . used every means at their disposal, including the very suspect information of some of the informers to ensure that the Quakers . . . should suffer for their opinions'.[77]

Nevertheless, neighbourliness often triumphed over authority, as a quarter sessions petition in 1676 illustrates. A quantity of distrained goods were in the hands of the constables who had 'many times offered the goods on sale, but none will buy them'.[78] The constables begged the magistrates to order the goods to be restored to their owners because the goods were 'rotting and spoiling'. After this, the constables did not trouble the Ormskirk Quakers, and, in the late seventeenth century, only the tithe farmers continued to distrain goods, ranging from 4 lb of pack thread to cheese, from oats to new 'breeks'.

Despite these regular attacks on their livelihoods, the Ormskirk Quakers continued trading. As they were all either tradesmen (grocers, a tailor and a woollen draper) or craftsmen (a weaver, a flaxwoman, a cooper and a tanner), there were no wealthy members to assist them. However, a mutual help network existed among the sect and it may have operated here.[79] Certainly Joshua Crosby, the grocer, had family connections in Lancaster, for in 1684 he had married Margaret Middleton, who brought him food while he was imprisoned in the castle.[80] Her father, Christopher, made William Stout, the Lancaster grocer, his trustee, so there was contact between the two families. Characteristically, Stout had a poor opinion of Crosby's business acumen, and in 1690 he described him as 'a grocer and an honest man, but not very capable to manage his trade to much advantage'.[81] Doubtless Stout assisted him, for the Crosbys were still trading over fifty years later, when the persecutions had long abated.[82]

After the Act of Toleration, the Quakers registered the house of Godfrey Atherton in Bickerstaffe as a place for public worship and also registered their graveyard.[83] The hatred felt towards them remained in some quarters, and derogatory expressions were often used to describe them. For instance, an Ormskirk farmer wrote to the steward concerning a lease 'you will have some Artfull Quaker to treat for the present year's profit'.[84] Their stereotype had altered from the militant fanatic to the astute trader. Nevertheless, toleration brought apathy, and the sect declined, until in 1778 Bishop Porteus could describe the Quakers as 'a weak and struggling party . . . [the meeting house] . . . is but little frequented and is almost become obsolete'.[85]

THE CATHOLICS

The Catholics, more than most Dissenters, anticipated the Restoration of Charles II with the hope that toleration would be established. The Declaration of Breda encouraged them, and in 1661 some Catholics even took the opportunity to petition the King to repeal the penal laws.[86] Undoubtedly the King and many of his supporters sympathised with the Catholics, but Anglicans dominated Parliament after 1661, and for them the toleration of Catholicism was anathema. They saw it as a threat not only to the Established Church, but also to the sovereignty of the land, for, in their opinion, Catholics owed allegiance to an alien foreign power – the Pope – who had never relinquished his right to depose monarchs and who, they thought, would impose absolute monarchy on any country under Catholic rule. When Charles married the Catholic Portuguese princess, Catherine, in 1662, suspicions grew that foreign Catholic powers were manipulating Charles and were trying to establish a foothold in the land. These suspicions of Catholic plots smouldered among the Protestants, even though many, like Pepys, accepted Catholics among their friends,[87] and tried to reduce the effects of the harsh penal laws on them despite their fears. As Miller observed, 'they distinguished between Popery as a malign political force and Papists as people'.[88] Thus, during this period, Catholics were able to practise their faith as long as they kept a low profile. Then, in 1672, embers of distrust were fanned by Charles' grant of the Declaration of Indulgence, giving Catholics limited freedom of worship. However, as we saw, Charles had to withdraw it almost immediately. The following year, Parliament reciprocated by passing the Test Act to prevent both Catholics and Dissenters from holding public office.

Charles' alliance with Louis XIV and his declaration of war in 1672 on Holland, a Protestant trading rival of England, also aroused suspicion. Finally when James, Duke of York, married Mary of Modena, an Italian Catholic princess in 1673, the flames of anti-Popery were ignited. Processions were organised, effigies of the Pope were burnt, pamphlets were distributed and finally Titus Oates produced allegations of a popish plot to remove Charles II and establish Catholicism in the land. As a result, between 1679 and 1681, many Catholics were imprisoned, sixteen priests and five laymen were executed, and the administration of the penal code was tightened nationwide.[89] During the same period, abortive attempts were made in Parliament to exclude James from the succession. Gradually though, fears of another civil war exceeded the fear of Catholicism and the crisis burnt out. In 1685, when Charles II died, the Catholic James II was accepted as King, despite a revolt in 1685 led by the Duke of Monmouth in favour of his claim to the throne as the Protestant – though illegitimate – son of Charles II.

Again, the national situation was mirrored in Ormskirk. In the 1660s the magistrates ignored the activities of priests as they ministered to their fellow Catholics.[90] An overt rivalry existed between the Anglican vicar and the Catholic priest for the souls of the townsfolk, and when Heywood visited the sick, 'Popish friends would often procure some Popish priest or one of their religion to come also to them, and if they had the least pretence to give it out that the Party had died in their faith, they would wonderfully exult over the Protestants'.[91] This almost friendly rivalry resulted on one occasion in the priest producing a set of questions for Heywood, 'a notable Champion against Papists'. In fact, during the 1660s the penal laws were ignored in Ormskirk by common consent.

Nevertheless, Heywood viewed the challenge of Catholicism so seriously that, after the Declaration of Indulgence in 1672, having being ejected in 1662, he sited one of the two chapels he licensed close to Scarisbrick Hall, where a clandestine Catholic school had been established by the Jesuits, who lodged with the family. Here Heywood exercised his short-lived freedom to campaign against what he saw as the escalating threat of Catholicism. As the licenses allowed by the Declaration were not recalled immediately, Heywood continued preaching 'against the Popish Party at Scarisbrick on November 5th 1673', among other dates.[92]

The experiences of 'Cavalier' Blundell of Little Crosby illustrate the strength of anti-Catholic feeling aroused in the Ormskirk area by the allegations of Titus Oates.[93] As the administration of the penal laws tightened, Blundell wrote to a friend, a bookseller in Dublin, in 1679, 'I was troubled . . . to see my trusty old sword taken from me (which had been my companion when I lost my limb, my lands, my liberty for acting against the rebels in the King's behalf) by an officer . . . who in that former old time had been a captain against the King.' Then, in the same year, to prevent the magistrates from confiscating much of his property, Blundell made an arrangement with the Protestant John Chorley, Mayor of Liverpool (1678–9), whereby some of his land was mortgaged and the interest paid to Chorley. Thus that amount of his property was concealed in order to diminish the two-thirds which were likely to be seized. Nevertheless, Blundell decided not to join the Catholic gentry fleeing to the Continent in the winter of 1678.

The Catholics' plight in Ormskirk resulting from this stricter interpretation of the penal laws prompted the constables, overseers of the poor, and even the churchwardens of the parish church – not completely altruistically – to appeal to the justices in 1679 to release the Catholics from paying their recognisances. Seemingly certain Catholics were 'very poor and indigent and some of them [had] . . . relief out of the parish and the rest by reason of their being continued bound for recusancy from session to session . . . [were] . . . reduced to such a low and mean condition that in a very short time they must of necessity be chargeable and burdensome upon the inhabitants of the parish'.[94] The town authorities' well-founded anxiety prompted John Entwistle JP to add his own request that the justices should act. Although this petition can be interpreted as demonstrating the authorities' self-interest in trying to prevent the escalation of the poor rate, it can also be seen as the result of interdenominational sympathy or the first glimpse of a plural religious culture in Ormskirk.

During his reign the Catholic King, James II, together with both the Catholics and the Protestant Dissenters, hoped that toleration could be granted in a constitutional way. During the latter years of Charles II, some of the Catholic gentry of Lancashire had indulged in toasting James and even left bequests to him such as that of Richard Walmesley of Dunkenhalgh, 'to his Royal Highness, the Duke of York, one black horse'.[95] However, fear and suspicion of dissidents remained nationwide, and James faced great opposition to his plans. Nevertheless, he continued his programme of relief for both Catholics and Protestant Dissenters, issuing his Declaration of Indulgence in 1687, reissuing it in 1688 and removing staunch Anglicans from various positions of authority. Those replaced locally included John Entwistle JP, who served on the Bench at Ormskirk and was 'disgraced' in 1685. By 1688, between twenty-five and thirty Catholics had been appointed to the Commission of the Peace in Lancashire,[96] and between June 1687 and September 1688 the Commission was mainly Catholic.[97] Even the Protestant William Stanley, Ninth Earl of Derby, was removed from his position as Lord Lieutenant of the County in 1687, and the Catholic Caryl Molyneux, Third Viscount Maryborough, was appointed in his stead.[98]

This promotion of Catholics increased the Protestants' deep-seated distrust of James II and of all 'Papists'. Finally, in June 1688, the birth of a prince, a Catholic heir to the throne, exacerbated the crisis and caused the 'Glorious Revolution'. Even before the coming of William III, Catholics were removed from their new positions, and after 1689 the penal laws were vigorously enforced. Cavalier Blundell was again the victim of this hardening attitude when his house was searched by three 'insolent' musketeers. His servant was beaten on the roadway and robbed of 57s, and yet another servant returning from market – very likely from Ormskirk – 'was assailed upon the road with pistol and bayonet (whereby some blood was drawn), because he would not yield his horse to an officer of our County's militia, who refused to shew him an order for seizing the same'.[99] The Lancashire plot of 1692–4 implicated members of the Catholic gentry living in the Ormskirk district: the Blundells, Gerrards, Standishes and Dicconsons. Although they were found not guilty, distrust remained, not only in Lancashire but among Protestants nationally. Double land tax was imposed on the Catholics in 1692, and in 1695 the Disabling Act prevented Catholics from taking any part in public life.

The Catholics' hopes for increased religious freedom were dashed, and they continued worshipping secretly in private houses, where the householders risked imprisonment for harbouring priests. Those who refused to attend Protestant services – the recusants – were liable to fines of £260 per annum, or could choose the long-term alternative of forfeiting two-thirds of their estates to the Crown. It was a criminal offence to give a Catholic education or to make any donation towards 'superstitious uses' – the work of the Catholic Church – and yet Catholicism continued to survive, mainly due to the work of Jesuits, Benedictine missionary monks and other priests trained abroad.[100] These priests lived with Catholic gentry, who provided their board. In return, Mass was said regularly inside the house for the neighbouring Catholics, and afterwards breakfast was usually provided for the congregation. Outsiders had to wait for an invitation to attend – a necessary precaution against informers. These arrangements meant that the Catholic gentry, already leaders of their own communities, had their power increased by their patronal control over the priests, until they virtually dominated the Catholic Church in England.[101] Locally, William and, later, Nicholas Blundell displayed a benevolent despotism towards their – exclusively Catholic – tenantry, and dominated their priests. An instance of the gentry's power is contained in Blundell's letter to the Provincial of the Society of Jesus, asking for another priest to replace Father Poyntz, who did not suit him, and listing the qualities he expected in the new priest.[102]

The secrecy involved makes it difficult to identify which priests served Ormskirk before the 1720s, but one candidate is Richard Mossock, cousin of Sir Edward Moore of Bank Hall, Liverpool, and a landowner from Mossock Hall in Bickerstaffe. Mossock was ordained abroad, returned home and acted as Archdeacon of Lancashire, responsible for the county's Mass centres until his death in 1699. Certainly Mossock Hall was the base for Father Anselm Walmesley, who served the town in the 1720s.[103] Nicholas Blundell mentions many Catholic priests working in the Ormskirk area in the early eighteenth century, particularly those acting as chaplains to the following halls: Lydiate, Crank, Moor Hall (Aughton), Formby, Mossock Hall (Aughton), Scarisbrick, Ince Blundell, Croxteth, Aigburth, Sefton and Fazakerley.[104]

Although the Catholic gentry had provided for their clergy from the 1630s, by the 1720s the rising middle class were taking over their responsibilities. Of course, many of these middle class benefactors had gentry origins and had been forced by the severity of the penal laws to earn their living in the professions or in trade. This new, mainly urban, Catholic middle class contributed much to the survival of Catholicism, and in the early eighteenth century facilitated the decline of 'country-house' Catholicism. As John Barrow, a priest at Claughton, wrote, 'Merchants, manufacturers, tradesmen, etc., are the persons to whom we must, in these days of Dissipation, look up to for our chief support. These can afford to contribute largely, and will not fail to do so.'[105]

Many missionary priests resented their patron's interference, and, when funds allowed – often due to the generosity of 'middle class' Catholics – they left the gentry's homes and moved into towns, where the need for their services was increasing. Often they converted the top floors of their homes into chapels and sacristies.[106] For instance, Father William Gillibrand SJ, who lived in Crosby Hall from 1701, said Mass regularly in Liverpool, but in 1707 he moved into the town and became its first resident priest since the Reformation. He lodged with John Lancaster, a grocer and brother of Dr William Lancaster of Ormskirk, who often attended Nicholas Blundell. The Lancaster family home had been Rainhill Hall, but by the 1700s this Catholic gentry family, like many others, had been impoverished by recusancy fines.[107] By 1736 the congregation in Liverpool was established and St Mary's was built. Similarly, by 1740 a chapel was built in Wigan.[108]

In Ormskirk too, the country house arrangements proved unsatisfactory for an urban ministry. As the religious climate had changed sufficiently to make it unnecessary for Catholicism to remain an underground movement – provided that it maintained a discreet profile – a Benedictine mission was established within the town. In 1732 Dom Maurice Bulmer, the priest at Croxteth Hall, was appointed

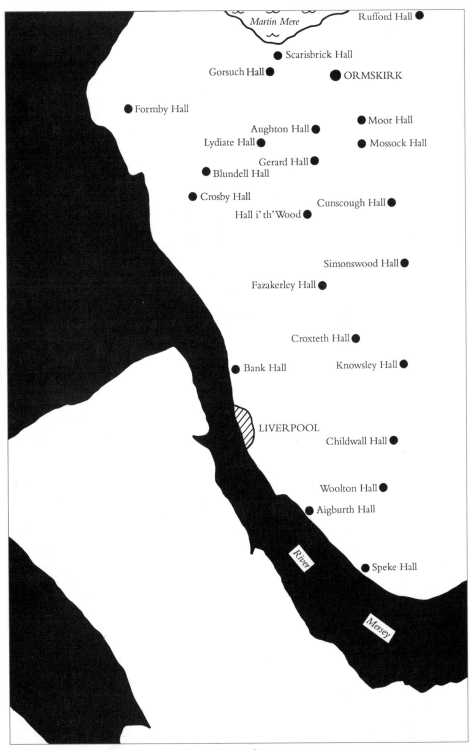

36. Location of secret chapels in south-west Lancashire.

37. *Mossock Hall, long since demolished.*

and he converted John Entwistle's house in Aughton Street[109] – possibly the former home of the Laithwaite family[110] – into the Mass House. There he ministered to the Catholics in relative freedom and taught their children in secret.

Although arranging financial support for Catholic missions in England was difficult due to the prohibitions on donating money for 'superstitious uses', ways were found to evade the law. In the 1720s a donation was made to the Catholic cause by the Ormskirk doctor, William Lancaster – listed as a non-juror in 1715 – giving £100 to the Benedictine Provincial of the North Province responsible for the mission in the north of England. This money was to be put out at interest, and, in return, twenty Masses were to be said every three months and on the anniversary dates of his wife and himself.[111] Lancaster's will – worded to confuse the Anglican probate authorities – had the instruction that his wife should 'covenant to leave the same to such persons as I have hereby given the same, at her death'.[112] In his wife's official will, nothing suggests that money was left to the Church,[113] but, as Bishop Foley explained, Catholics 'disguised their intentions by leaving everything to some trustworthy person (sometimes a non-Catholic) to whom at the same time they consigned a "spiritual will". This . . . showed their real intentions'.[114] Indeed, among the Ormskirk records at Douai Abbey is a secret codicil signed by Elizabeth Lancaster, directing that the £100 'now in Mr Walmesley's hands' should continue for the use of the priest officiating at Ormskirk. Bequests like these gave the clergy independence, and the date of the Lancaster bequests suggest that the £100 enabled the priest to acquire Entwistle's house as a base for his mission. Mrs Lancaster also left £10 to the nuns 'where Mrs Mary Gillibrand lives', £10 'to the cloister nuns

38. House in Aughton Street, reputed to have been the Mass House.

where Mr Scarisbrick's children are' and £20 to be divided between forty priests –
possibly those at Douai – for five Masses. These bequests confirm that financial
support for the Ormskirk mission moved from the landed gentry to the urban
professional middle class. Later, in 1741, Ann Harrison donated another £100,[115]
and during the seventy years 1730–1800, a total of £1,740 was donated as Mass
offerings to Ormskirk Catholic Church, several granted by secret codicils not
submitted to the probate authorities with the will.[116]

The Jacobite Rebellion (1745) shattered the security of the Mass House.
Secrecy veiled the Jacobites' activities, but among them were Catholics from
south-west Lancashire. The Lancashire plot of 1692–1694 involved many local
Catholic gentry, and members of several neighbouring gentry families fought at the
battle of Preston in 1715. Nicholas Blundell was suspected of being a Jacobite, and
on 19 March 1708 his property was searched for horses in response to the law
forbidding recusants to own horses worth more than £5. His two coach horses
were seized, while his other valuable horses were concealed by neighbours.[117]
Although he had family connections through his wife with Lord Widdrington, one
of the Jacobite leaders, his diaries suggest that he was not an active Jacobite.
Nevertheless, as a Catholic he longed for the resumption of the religious toleration

of James II. In 1715 he felt sufficiently threatened to take refuge in a hiding place within the hall, before departing hurriedly to London and thence to Flanders, where he spent eighteen months in exile with other members of the Lancashire Catholic gentry.[118]

Evidently, in 1715, anti-Jacobite feeling was not strong enough to cause trouble among the people of Ormskirk. In fact, on 22 August, two months before the Battle of Preston during the period when houses were being searched for suspects, Ormskirk quarter sessions granted eighteen 'Crown's prisoners' 'the liberty to work and beg in [the] town'.[119] The authorities considered that their presence would not disturb the town, and yet the townsfolk would be sufficiently sympathetic to contribute towards their keep. Certainly some townsfolk had a great interest in the Jacobite movement. For instance, in 1725 William Grice, the local bookseller, owned the *Eikon Basilike*, a book setting out Charles I's vision of kingship – essential reading for Jacobites.[120]

During the 1720s and 1730s, anti-Papism declined both nationally and locally, but the security of the Catholics was breached when England went to war with France in 1743, giving Charles Edward, grandson of James II, an opportunity to invade Britain, thus reawakening both religious and political antagonism nationwide. The prevalence of Catholics in south-west Lancashire made it a suspect area, and even Lord Derby fled to London, commenting in a letter to the Duke of Rutland, 'I think I am at liberty to save myself from the hands of those whose religion, of course, makes them enemies to the constitution under which they live, with which sort of persons this county does too much abound'.[121] Local officials again searched Catholic homes for arms and horses, which they confiscated,[122] and one Jacobite was tied to the 'Rogues Post' in Ormskirk 'stript naked from the middle upwards and severely whipt' for drinking to the health of Prince Charles.[123] In Liverpool there was a clash between the army and the Jacobites who were routed. The mob then turned on the Catholics and destroyed their chapel. Shortly afterwards, a Protestant mob attacked the Mass House in Aughton Street, Ormskirk. They burnt Father Bulmer's library, desecrated his chapel and collected other things belonging to him and set them on fire. It is unclear whether this attack was a continuation of the Liverpool skirmish, carried out as the Highlanders were pursued northwards, or whether it was a spontaneous uprising in Ormskirk, but it was sufficiently serious to be described in the State Papers as 'the insurrection in Ormskirk'.[124] Similar attacks were made on Catholic chapels in other parts of Lancashire, and the homes of some Catholic squires were burnt.[125]

Shortly after this alarming experience Father Bulmer moved into Aughton, a quieter and less dangerous location, and built a presbytery, where the upstairs room was a chapel. Catholics continued to be viewed with distrust, which often influenced their employment opportunities. For instance, in a letter in 1761, the local Catholic smith, Thomas Harsnepp, reminded Lord Derby's steward of his promise to offer him work and complained that William Scarisbrick had declared that he would never employ any Papists.[126]

However, gradually fear and suspicion subsided nationally and, after the passing of the Catholic Relief Act in 1778,[127] the celebration of Mass was no longer illegal. The Gordon riots marked a last stand against religious toleration, but this time anti-Catholic hostility did not spread to Ormskirk. Finally, in 1791, the Catholics gained the right to build their own licensed chapels.[128] Father Bulmer's successor,

39. St Oswald's church in the early twentieth century. The presbytery built following the 1745 'insurrection' is at the back and the church stands in front of it.

Father Crook (1788–1800), immediately drew up plans for a church next to the presbytery in Aughton. This was completed in 1795 and was dedicated to St Oswald,[129] and the old chapel in Bulmer's house was converted into a school.

It is a problem to assess the numbers of Catholics in Ormskirk during our period, because the early episcopal visitation returns list only the parish totals. For the 1722 visitation, the vicar reported a total of 124 Papist families or approximately 558 Papists in the parish, not the township.[130] As the numbers for Dissenters can be proved to be approximately correct, we can assume that, despite their essential secrecy, the number of Catholics is correct. When the 800 Anglican families or 3,600 individuals are added to the Dissenters and Papists, we get a total of 4,455 individuals in the parish. Thus 15.5% of the population of the parish were Catholic and 8.25% were Dissenters.

The earliest reliable nationwide count of Catholics was made in 1767, when 265 Catholic were recorded in Ormskirk township.[131] This compared with 1,743 in Liverpool, 1,194 in Wigan, 1,043 in Preston, 650 in Lancaster, 200 in Blackburn and 351 in Manchester.[132] In the visitation report of 1778, the vicar – admittedly a biased witness – reported that out of a population of 2,280 in Ormskirk township only 188 were Papists.[133] Using the vicar's figures for the town's population and the count of Catholics in 1767, we find that 11.6% of the population were Catholics, assuming that the population had remained static during those eleven years.

This 11.6% can be compared with Kenyon's estimate from the 1676 Compton census, that Catholic laymen made up 4.7% of the national population of five million.[134] Undoubtedly, this 11.6% was a very high proportion for a mid-eighteenth century market town. According to Aveling, until the 1780s 'a great many provincial market towns and some industrial ones (for instance Halifax, Huddersfield and Hull) had practically no Catholic inhabitants' and 'few had sizeable numbers'.[135] In 1767, Bath had a population of 9,000, of which only 200 were Catholic, a proportion of only about 2%.[136] Catholicism was strong in Lancashire and Cheshire, especially in the West Derby Hundred.[137] In fact, the Vicars Apostolic returns of 1773 recorded a total of 14,000 Catholics in Lancashire, while in Yorkshire there were only 1,500 and in Northumberland 1,800.[138] If we use the vicar's figures for 1778, we can calculate that a percentage of 8.2% of Ormskirk townsfolk were Catholic, while in the whole parish, out of a population of 5,700, the number of Catholics was 755 and the percentage was 13.2% – slightly lower than the 15.5% calculated from the 1722 visitation returns.

A much larger total for the township was quoted when the Catholic Bishop Gibson visited Ormskirk in 1784. Reportedly he confirmed 94 people and 260 communicants attended St Oswald's Church.[139] Using the vicar's 1778 estimate of the town's population and these 1784 figures, we find that 11.4% of the townspeople were Catholic, a very similar percentage to that from the 1767 totals. Allowing for the boundary problems, it is valid to claim that approximately 11% of the population of Ormskirk were Catholic during the mid-eighteenth century. Kenyon claims that the anti-Catholic acts and the growth of scepticism and free-thinking had reduced the national Catholic community to 'an attenuated remnant' in the eighteenth century.[140] This was certainly not true of Ormskirk.

The 1767 returns list the occupations of the Catholics. The largest group, 39%, were craftsmen ranging from watchmakers to bricksetters, and from cabinetmakers to shoemakers. A further 13% were journeymen or apprentices learning crafts. Others who were not self-employed included 11 labourers (17%) and 6 maidservants (9%). Farming, including 4 yeomen and 3 husbandmen, employed 11%, while tradesmen – innkeepers, maltsters, grocers and shopkeepers – made up 9%. There were no representatives of the gentry or the professions, and few craftsmen practised the higher skilled crafts, such as watchmaking and cabinetmaking. Many more were the less skilled shoemakers or weavers. By contrast, the majority (55%) of the Dissenters were tradesmen, and only 39% were craftsmen, whereas most (52%) of the Catholics were craftsmen and 9% tradesmen. This was the result of the strict recusancy laws which indirectly created doubts about the Catholics' credit-worthiness, making it

TABLE 22. *The percentage of Catholics in the population of the parish and the township of Ormskirk**

| Dates | Parish | | Township | |
	Totals	Percentage	Totals	Percentage
1767	1086	19	265	11.6
1778	755	13.2	188	12.2
1784	–	–	260	16.2

* The 1778 visitation totals are used for the township's population in 1778 and 1784. The great difference in the number of Catholics between 1767 and 1778 is due to their sources. The vicar's figure (possibly biased) was 1778 and 1767 was the official count of Papists.

TABLE 23. Occupations of Ormskirk Catholics in 1767 and Dissenters 1743-72

	Catholics	%		Dissenters	%
25	Craftsmen	39	10	Tradesmen	55
11	Labourers	17	7	Craftsmen	39
9	Apprentices	14	1	Apothecary	5
7	Farmers	11			
6	Maidservants	9			
6	Tradesmen	9			
64		99	18		99

difficult for them to operate as merchants or tradesmen. It was far easier to sell their skills in such circumstances.

These figures were compiled from the 1767 returns of the Catholics and from the register of Aughton Street Presbyterian Chapel.[141]

A comparison of the Catholics' occupations in various towns is made in Table 24. In many cases that number was too small to warrant inclusion. The percentages of the totals on the bottom line confirm that the largest single group in 1767 were the craftsmen.

A letter from Bishop Beilby Porteus, to the clergy in his diocese of Chester in 1781, is typical of the change in attitude towards the Catholics by the late eighteenth century. He declared that the danger from Papists was not as great as had been feared, and was convinced of the cruelty of suppressing all Catholic schools.[142] At last, suspicion and fear of Papists had waned and Catholics were to be allowed freedoms they had craved for almost 250 years. Although religious freedom had been granted to both Catholic and Protestant Dissenters, full political freedom

TABLE 24. The employment of Catholics in 1767

Towns	Professionals	Craftsmen	Tradesmen	Farmers	Servants	Labourers	Total
Ormskirk		34	11	7	6	11	69
Wigan	9	170	19	20	9	3	230
Preston	2	158	25	41	2		228
Kirkham	1	14	3	2	1		21
Poulton		11	4	8	7	7	37
Garstang		14	2			2	18
Blackburn		10	1	4	2		17
Baldestone		18	1	4	2		25
Bromsgrove		15	9	8			32
Ilkley	1	13		14		7	35
Ulverston		2				2	4
Gisburn			1	2			3
Stratford		1	2				3
Camden		2	1				3
Total	13	462	79	110	29	32	725
Percentage	2	64	11	15	4	4	100

was not to be attained until the next century,[143] but as far as most of the inhabitants of Ormskirk were concerned, secrecy and suspicion had finally disappeared from the religious scene. As John Bossy remarked, 'nothing succeeded like failure . . . the downfall of James II and the Jacobite cause'.[144] These two events revealed how weak the support among Catholics was for any attempt to overturn the status quo, and that revelation quelled the fear and suspicion of most anti–Papists.[145]

Although the eighteenth century has been traditionally described as a period of inactivity and indifference in the religious history of England,[146] our study of Ormskirk reveals a scenario full of change. The Established Church followed a continual programme of repairing, renovating and rebuilding, and the continual expansion of its capacity indicates a real attempt to provide sufficient seating for an increasing congregation. Neither could the Catholics be accused of apathy and inactivity when, despite national opposition, they maintained a constant number in their congregation and were ready in 1791 to build St Oswald's chapel. Only the Quakers and the Presbyterians shared in the national numerical decline of their particular denominations during the latter years of the century.

CHAPTER VI

Education

The provision of education in Ormskirk was dependent on the state of the economy and the strength of religious commitment among its leaders. When the economy boomed, increased funds were available to pay teachers and to found a charity school, but when it slumped the teaching staff were cut and education suffered. Similarly, when the Anglican Church was strong, it extended its influence over the grammar school and initiated the founding of both the charity school and the Sunday school, but when it was involved in crises, such as that caused by the Act of Uniformity, education suffered. The provision of Catholic education is harder to analyse, because it was an undercover operation, but certainly, as soon as Parliament permitted, Catholic education was provided in Ormskirk. In this chapter we will trace the progress of education in the town under the influence of these factors and a parallel theme will be the emergence of a teaching profession with reference to the grammar school. The inhabitants' changing attitudes towards basic education will be analysed as they progressed from regarding it as an essential aid to reading the Bible, to the conviction that education provided a livelihood. These attitudes led to the growth of philanthropy in the town.

Although education was provided in the township for both the townspeople and those from farther afield, the local schools offered few places to pupils until the foundation of the Sunday School in the late eighteenth century. However, judging by the high standard of literacy – to be analysed in a later section – there were either several forgotten petty schools teaching in the town, or else informal teaching was done in the home or workshop. Neither of these possibilities is documented, so we can only base our enquiry on reports from the recorded schools which provided basic education for substantially fewer pupils than those who obtained their literacy skills from their parents or masters.

THE GRAMMAR SCHOOL

The foundation of the grammar school resulted from a bequest by Henry Ashcroft, who died on 7 January 1601. He lived in Preston, but had been born in Ormskirk where he continued to hold land and property. In the foundation decree of 1612,[1] although the King's preacher and the vicar were to be governors, the clergy were to be outnumbered on the board by eighteen members of the gentry, representing each township in the parish. Of course, the bishop had ultimate control through his power to grant or withold the essential licence to teach, but the high proportion of non-clerics among the governors guaranteed a large measure of secular control over the administration. The secular nature of this foundation illustrates the change in the responsibility for the endowment of grammar schools after the Reformation. The commercial elite and the gentry shouldered the task of providing grammar school education and 'took elaborate pains to vest their incorporations in lay hands'.[2] Their concern was 'stimulated by the demand for lay administrators and professional men' after 'the overthrow of the ancient clerical monopoly of culture'.[3]

The school was built in 1618 on the north-eastern side of the church and, although we have no description of the building, the accounts suggest that it was a timber-framed construction with a stone roof. The account does include 'the leading of bricks' at a cost of 2s, and a later 'a cundeth of brick', but the quantities suggest that they were not a major component in the building.[4]

By the early 1660s the town's economy was suffering from the aftermath of the Civil War and the school fell into disrepair. Despite collecting subscriptions from several townspeople, the governors were unable to collect sufficient to restore the building. They appealed for help from the justices, who imposed an assessment on the whole parish.[5] The township of Ormskirk was to supply £13 6s 8d and the only other assessment known was £3 6s 8d for Scarisbrick, so the total amount cannot be calculated.[6] The justices' assessment of the whole parish confirms the extent of the grammar school's catchment area. It was a small school, catering for fewer than forty pupils, but it was adequate to meet the local demand for a classical education.

This financial crisis had serious repercussions. The salaries of the schoolmasters were reduced, causing a drop in the educational standard of the teachers applying for appointment and also a reduction in their tenure at the school. In the foundation decree, the governors were given the opportunity to vary the master's wages by a clause stating that, 'as the profits belonging to the said school will extend and afford . . . they shall conclude and agree with such master and usher for such wage, from time to time, as they in their discretion shall think fit and reasonable'.[7] These fluctuations in teachers' salaries, which were quite normal at this time,[8] meant that the master's salary varied from £12 per annum in 1623, to £15 0s 9d per annum awarded to John Chorley in 1661, to £6 13s 4d per annum given to Thomas Bell (Ball) who, not surprisingly, stayed less than a year in 1664.[9]

Headmasters' salaries nationwide varied enormously, as the fifty replies received by Christopher Wase for his survey of English grammar schools between 1673 and 1675 illustrate. For instance, the master at Nuneaton grammar school received £80 per annum, at St Albans the salary was £50 per annum and at Blackburn Grammar School the master received £25 per annum.[10] By contrast, only three grammar schools offered less than was given to Thomas Bell in Ormskirk; Kinnersley in Herefordshire (£6 2s 0d per annum), Bungay in Suffolk (£5 per annum) and Bitterly in Shropshire, where the master received no stipend at all, possibly because, as the clergyman, he was expected to teach in the local school. As Wase wrote in 1678, 'the maintenance of very few [masters was] . . . such as may vindicate masters from being necessitous and contemptible; of the rest, scarce what may invite the able and give them freedom to be diligent'.[11] Thus in this period teaching became for many 'the sanctuary of . . . idle, insufficient persons, who have no hopes elsewhere, or . . . [those using it as] . . . a step to some church preferment'.[12]

Other financial difficulties affected John Chorley, master from 1654 until 1663. Although he received one of the highest salaries, it was paid seven years in arrears. The minute book records in 1661, 'John Chorley, schoolmaster and present incumbent shall receive £15 0s 9d per annum due to him for seven years already past before any others receive payments',[13] but gives no explanation. According to Ellis Rycroft's reply to Wase in November 1673, the school was 'endowed very poorly, viz £12 per annum; some augmentations have been left by other persons, but I fear they are left very desperate'.[14] The governors had invested some endowments in property, and the rents were intended to finance the schoolmaster's salary. Sometimes such a delay in payment could be ascribed to the rent collectors' negligence or the tenants' reluctance to pay their rents during times of economic hardship.[15] Certainly the governors did lose £100, a legacy from John Fletcher, invested in 1658 in property, which they thought belonged to Ann Holland, but to which she had no legal title.[16] This loss was a disaster for the school, and probably accounted for the arrears in John Chorley's salary.[17] Such a delay was contrary to the original agreement of 1612, which stated specifically that the stipend was to be paid half-yearly,[18] but this was not the only time the governors did not obey those instructions. The will of Richard Birchall (1646–1649) stated, 'there is a debt of the sum of £23 8s due to me from the feoffees of the free school in Ormskirk . . . for my wages for teaching the scholars at the said free school'. Those wages were two years' in arrears.[19] The governors' casual attitude towards teachers' salaries failed to encourage loyalty, dedication or the growth of professionalism among teachers.

However, the arrears in his salary did not greatly affect John Chorley, a Cambridge graduate,[20] for he had other income. Before the Civil War, schoolteachers often came from wealthy families,[21] and John Chorley was a 'cozen' of Thomas Gerard, a wealthy local yeoman.[22] When Gerard died in 1662, John Chorley received an annuity of £3, and this legacy may have been one of the reasons why he withdrew from teaching in 1662. In the Hearth Tax returns of 1673,[23] he was assessed for six hearths, a similar number to the local doctor, Daniel Ambrose, the local barrister, John Entwistle, and the neighbouring squire of Aughton, Thomas Hesketh, for his townhouse. Any local house assessed for more than six hearths proved to be an inn, so, as one of the largest private houses in the town, this ex-schoolmaster's house must have been very imposing. His family's social position was equally elevated. His daughter, Clarissa, married Bertie (or Bertin) Entwistle, son of John, recorder of Liverpool.[24] Bertie later became vice-chancellor of the Duchy of Lancaster – a very eminent son-in-law for the local schoolmaster.

John Chorley's departure from the school in 1662–3 may also have been connected with the ejection of schoolmasters after the Act of Uniformity.[25] This act (1662), an attempt to establish the Anglican church's control over education, decreed that all teachers must be licensed by the bishop and must 'conform to the liturgy of the Church of England as it [was then] by law established'. Although John Chorley does not appear among the thirty-nine schoolmasters listed as being ejected countrywide, Calamy did confess 'that there were many others, who are not now to be recovered'.[26]

Although it is uncertain whether Chorley was a Dissenter, certainly one of his pupils was, as Oliver Heywood's diary related.[27] John Crompton, a nephew of Nathaniel Heywood, was sent from his home at Breightmet to study under Mr Chorley. As Heywood's diary recorded, 'They sent him to school . . . at Ormskirk with Mr Chorley, he profited exceedingly, was sent to Cambridge [and] was admitted to Christ's College.' Thus he became one of the three scholars from Ormskirk Grammar School known to have entered a university in the seventeenth century.[28] After 1653 little is known of Chorley except as an occasional valuer of inventories or witness to wills, until 1674 when he was appointed governor of the grammar school with the Catholic Edward Stanley of Moor Hall, Aughton.[29] This appointment shows how highly he was regarded by his fellow townspeople, and demonstrates his own long-standing commitment to the grammar school.[30]

Chorley's departure came at a critical time for the school. Finances were at a low level and the ejection of the vicar, Heywood, and his replacement by Ashworth, master of Merchant Taylors' School, meant that the new vicar had no time to promote any improvements. The governors decided to reduce the master's salary and, consequently, three masters who made little impact on the school followed in quick succession. Thomas Bell was appointed in 1663 at the salary of £6 13s 4d per annum, very little more than the £6 which had been paid to Roger Cliffe, an usher under John Chorley. Bell had no intention of staying in Ormskirk for, at his appointment, he negotiated terms allowing him to give the governors only one month's notice before leaving, while they agreed to give him three month's notice before replacing him.[31] He left within the year and was characteristic of many early seventeenth-century teachers described by Geoffrey Holmes as 'birds of passage',[32] who regarded teaching not as a profession but as an interim way of earning a living until they obtained a permanent position in the church or elsewhere.

It was rare at this time for teachers to follow a family tradition of teaching,[33] for the conditions and the salaries discouraged it. However, George Birchall (1664), one of the three masters appointed following Chorley's departure, possibly did have family connections with a previous master, Richard Birchall (1646–1650).[34] After the governors' experience of Thomas Bell's short tenure, they increased the salary they offered Birchall to £10 per annum if he would serve as both master and usher. The minute book described Birchall as a 'gentleman', a title rarely used to describe a master. Possibly he, like Chorley, came from a gentry family, but a George Berchall, or Bircher, of Lancashire was admitted to Trinity College, Cambridge, in 1655. Little is known about him and he may have become the master at Ormskirk. If so, the title 'gentleman' was an acknowledgement of his degree rather than an indication of his social rank. However, he made little impression for when Rycroft (master from 1671?–1675) answered Wase's questionnaire, he completely ignored both him and Bell in his list of previous headmasters. Thomas Stamp, who filled the post in the intervening years, is mentioned, but nothing more is known of him.[35]

Rycroft, like Chorley, held a Cambridge degree, but the similarity between the two masters ended there.[36] Rycroft's house featured neither among those assessed for the Hearth Tax nor among those excused payment through poverty. As his inventory lists 'some old lumber above in the school', it is very likely that he occupied rooms within the school, which would not be taxable. The inventory valued all his possessions at £9 4s 4d, of which his books – valued by John Chorley – were worth £3 0s 2d, his bed and bedding approximately £3 2s 0d and his clothes £1 13s 4d. This left his tools, a saddle and other incidentals, including 'a throne chair, a cushion and a seeled [carved] stool in the school' to amount to only £1 8s 10d. He had provided his own chair out of his meagre salary, which may still have been the same as the £10 awarded to George Birchall. The only luxury he possessed was a silver spoon valued at 2s 6d. Rycroft's inventory can be compared with those of the local bricklayer, John Vause, whose possessions amounted to £36 2s 9d in 1671, with a weaver, Henry Swift (1679) whose possessions totalled £34 9s 8d, a shoemaker,

Richard Erby (1674) £28 4s 2d and finally with a tailor whose total possessions amounted to only £3 14s 0d.[37] Nevertheless, his contemporaries would not have regarded him as having a similar social status to these humble craftsmen. His learning earned him respect, but little financial reward. According to Gregory King in 1688, a schoolmaster with a basic salary of £10 had a lower livelihood than most shopkeepers, artisans, tradesmen and lower-paid clergy, who averaged about £40 per annum, common seamen £20 per annum, labourers £15 per annum and common soldiers £14 per annum. The only group having a lower livelihood than the Ormskirk masters of the late seventeenth century were the cottagers and paupers, at £6 10s 0d per annum.[38]

Governors of grammar schools nationwide found it increasingly difficult to find suitable candidates to fill vacancies. As Vincent explained, 'Local schools which were poorly endowed and which continued scrupulously to observe their founder's regulations prohibiting . . . fees, found it increasingly difficult to attract masters of university standing.'[39] Some solved the problem by allowing their masters to accept other positions, as, for instance, the master of Merchant Taylors' school accepted the appointment as Vicar of Ormskirk and held both positions until 1677. It is significant that while John Ashworth was a governor in his capacity as vicar, there was a complete lack of accounts in the minute book, and, possibly, a complete lack of governors' meetings.

During the mid-1670s a pressure group was formed among the governors to improve the schoolmaster's wages, possibly at the suggestion of John Chorley, who was appointed a governor in 1674. The matter came to a head after Rycroft's death in 1675, when the governors wanted to appoint Peter Hindley and he insisted on a higher salary. Eventually a solution was found without relying on the fluctuating profits from investments. It was decided that 'Whereas the stipend is not now sufficient maintenance for the schoolmaster therefore . . . Mr Hindley may also take for every English scholar 16d, for every Latin scholar 2s and for every Greek scholar 3s, quarterly for the present year'.[40] As no other subject is mentioned, Ormskirk school was still a grammar school in the strictest sense. The Ormskirk governors were extremely conservative in stipulating that only the grammars should be taught, for by this time most school governors had accepted that the preparation of boys for university was not their prime function and had introduced new subjects into their curricula. For instance, in the early eighteenth century, Manchester grammar school offered scientific subjects, Hull taught history, geography and divinity, and Birmingham included mathematics in its curriculum. Most of the new grammar schools established between 1665 and 1735 provided lessons in writing and mathematics.[41] The arrangement for charging fees at Ormskirk continued through 1678 and 1679, but at the end of 1680 the vicar, Zachary Taylor, entered a strange declaration in the minute book implying that the charge for teaching had been withdrawn against his wishes. He declared that, 'Not disputing their power and authority at first to order it – yet being ordered, do protest that ye removal or non-continuance of it is against my mind. And do declare that it doth tend to the utter ruin of the school, the decay of religion for want of such catechising as an ingenuous schoolmaster would exercise them in.'[42] Evidently, the vicar failed to influence his fellow governors.

The vicar's declaration was followed by a statement by Silvester Sutch, a governor who opposed the vicar. He maintained that, 'the Feoffees [governors] had no power to make the order . . . that it would tend to the destruction of the freedom of the school, contrary to the intent of the founder and to the damage of the inhabitants of the parish'. Some townspeople tried to solve the problem by bequeathing legacies to supplement the schoolmaster's salary, but these – for example the £3 left by the grocer James Berry in 1686[43] – were so small that they had little impact. The whole incident illustrates the dilemma of the 'free' grammar school governors as to whether to prohibit fees and offer free education to children of all classes, or to charge fees and be able to offer a superior education under a well qualified teacher to those who could afford to pay.[44] As a result of this decision to discontinue the charges, Peter Hindley resigned. The governors appointed Henry Atherton, an elderly man, at the basic salary. Atherton was a graduate; nevertheless he, like Rycroft the Cambridge graduate, died in poverty.[45] Not surprisingly, the percentage of schoolmasters who held degrees decreased nationwide during the seventeenth century.[46]

Atherton served the school from 1681 until his death in 1685. He, like Rycroft, did not feature in the Hearth Tax returns and so probably lived in the school building. His inventory totalled £9 15s 7d – little more than Rycroft's. His books were valued at £2 10s 0d, his bed, its hangings and the bedding were worth £3 9s 0d and his clothes were valued at £2. Again, his other possessions were extremely meagre.[47] Neither of these inventories mention cooking utensils, so the masters probably used the school stove and and its range of irons and pots.

Despite their low salaries, nothing in the inventories suggests that either schoolmaster followed a secondary occupation. Admittedly Rycroft did serve also as curate of Ormskirk parish church, but if he received any stipend at all, it would have been very small. Otherwise, no master had a second occupation until 1744, when the governors gave the tenancy of various closes, at a yearly rent of £8, to the master, Revd Thomas Ellison (1736–1745), on condition that he would 'hedge, ditch, fence, scour and gutter the premises and provide all gates and stiles . . . at his own expense'.[48] Evidently the master intended to farm the land, but he died a year later and so reaped no profit. Later, two other masters served as curates: Revd John Norcross (1754–1756) at Ormskirk and Revd William Naylor (1756–1812) at Altcar. However, as they were both clergymen, these appointments were probably accepted to maintain a chance of promotion in the Church rather than as a lucrative second occupation.

During the late 1690s, the boys subjected the headmaster, Thomas Lawson (1691–1722), to several 'barring-outs'. This was a tradition whereby the boys forcibly prevented the master from entering the school by barring the doors and windows with forms and whatever was at hand. Even by 1818, according to Nicholas Carlisle, this 'innocent and harmless custom was not [then] altogether relinquished in the North of England'.[49] It usually took place immediately before the Christmas holidays and gave the boys an opportunity to vent any wrath they may have been harbouring against their master. This ritual, a release of tension, was recognised in the statutes of some grammar schools which actually encouraged its practice. In 1660 Charles Hoole, an early educational theorist, made rules for the conduct of the 'ceremony', including one specifying that 'the master [should] know of it beforehand, that all things may be ordered handsomely to the credit of the school' and 'that the scholars behave themselves merrily . . . without making use of any weapons whereby to endanger themselves or do harm to anything in the school'.[50] Certainly limits were necessary, for in 1671 a master at Shrewsbury was wounded, and in the 1690s the townspeople provided the pupils of Manchester Grammar School with firearms and food to enable them to continue the ritual – or riot – for fourteen days.[51] The involvement of parents and adults was not unusual, as Nicholas Blundell recorded on 19 December 1704, 'dined at Dungenhall [Dunkenhalgh]. I helped bar out the children's master, Mr Norcross'.[52] Similarly Revd Peter Walkden, Presbyterian minister of Chipping, recorded in his diary on 6 December 1729, 'at Henry's school, the children had barr'd out Mr Nabb. I gave him twopence to spend with the master and fellow scholars'.[53] This typical 'barring-out' illustrates the feeling of goodwill which often accompanied the proceedings. Usually the 'barring-out' constituted a demand for longer holidays, as in the Ormskirk case or, less frequently, it stemmed from excessive beatings.[54]

This ritual, with its element of role inversion, was the remnant of an earlier popular culture. Its occurrence in December associates it with Saturnalian festivals of inversion and misrule, including the ritual of the 'boy bishop', banned in 1541 after the Reformation. Such festivals provided safety valves for protests against authority and also re-established the validity of that authority by farcically inverting it. Thus we get a paradoxical element in the ritual in that, by expressing protest against some section of the social order, it reaffirms that same section in control.[55]

Even so, the ritual could easily become a riot, as happened in Ormskirk in 1699, when things got out of control and windows were broken. The governors acted and decreed that the boys would break up 'an exact fortnight before Christmas and not before', and if any further disturbances occurred the offending boys would be expelled. No further trouble was recorded in the minute book during our period. However, the *Gentleman's Magazine* recorded another undated occasion at Ormskirk, when the boys arrived very early to organise a 'barring-out' and 'found the master at his desk two hours before his usual time and had the mortification of being congratulated on their early arrival with an order to be there every morning at the same hour'. Later, a 'barring-out' was held at end of the eighteenth century, protesting against harsh treatment by Revd William Naylor, 'the flogging parson'. The master brought the constable to deal with the scholars, many of whom fled, never to return to school.[56]

In 1718 the bishop granted a faculty to allow a schoolmaster's house to be built against the eastern end of the school. Lord Derby gave permission for the house to extend into Church Fields Lane, and a house 10 yd by 6 yd was built. Little is known about this building except that there was no internal access between the house and the school.[57] Thomas Lawson, then master, did not occupy the house and it was let to William Greaves. However, in 1724 the master, John Fletcher, took possession of the schoolhouse and afterwards its tenure was included as part of the master's salary. Mr Lawson, who retired in 1721, received a £20 'golden handshake' 'in consideration of his resigning the school' which he had served for thirty years. By this time the salary had risen to £14 15s 4d, almost as much as John Chorley had received sixty years earlier.[58]

Lawson's long tenure suggests that he was one of the earliest Ormskirk schoolmasters for whom teaching was a vocation. Before settling in Ormskirk he had taught for seven years in Preston. His predecessor, James Liptrott, was also committed to teaching and left Ormskirk to become master of Wigan Free Grammar School. These two mark the beginning of an era when Ormskirk

Grammar School was served by masters who regarded themselves as professionals and were no longer 'birds of passage'. If they moved, it was usually to another teaching post. For instance, although John Parke stayed only one year, he moved to Clitheroe Grammar School. The next three masters remained at the school until their deaths. Samuel Robinson moved to Wigan Grammar School in 1722 and John Norcross followed his father to become head at Rivington. William Naylor held the Ormskirk post until 1821 – a remarkable sixty-five years – after which he was granted a pension of £25 per annum.[59] The careers of these masters support Geoffrey Holmes' opinion that, by 1730, the improved level of salaries and the extended length of tenure led to schoolteaching generally being regarded as a vocation for life.[60] Actually, Ormskirk's experience was that here, professional schoolmasters appeared some fifty years earlier.

Table 25 shows that more than 50% of Ormskirk teachers in the seventeenth century held degrees – a higher proportion than in the eighteenth century and a higher proportion than usual countrywide.[61] However, it is doubtful whether the possession of a degree necessarily made teachers more professional. A long, informal apprenticeship under a competent teacher probably trained them more successfully than a university education. A more reliable indication of a teaching

TABLE 25. *Ormskirk schoolmasters, 1654–1821*

Name	Dates	Reason for leaving	Years of service	Degree	Sources
John Chorley	1654–1663	ejected?	9	Cambridge	Wase, Minutes
Thos. Bell	1663–1664		1	Cambridge? Oxford?	Minutes
Geo. Birchall	1664–			Cambridge?	Wase, Minutes
Thos. Stamp					Wase
Ellis Rycroft	1673?–1675	died		Cambridge	Wase, Minutes
Peter Hindley	1676–1681	resigned	5		Minutes
Henry Atherton	1681–1684	died	3	Cambridge?	Minutes
James Liptrot (moved to Wigan G.S.)	1684–1691	'voluntary removal'	7		Call, Minutes
Thos. Lawson (moved from Preston G.S.)	1691–1721	resigned	30	Cambridge?	Call, Minutes
John Parke (moved to Clitheroe G.S.)	1721–1722	'voluntary removal'	1		Minutes
John Fletcher	1722–1736	died	14	Oxford?	Call, Minutes
Thos. Ellison	1736–1745	died	9	Cambridge	Minutes
Thos. Stockley	1745–1748	died	3		Minutes
Abrah. Ascroft	1748–1749	resigned	1		Minutes
Sam. Robinson (moved to Wigan G.S.?)	1749–1754	resigned	5	Oxford?	Minutes
John Norcross (later at Rivington G.S.)	1754–1756	resigned	2	Cambridge	Call, Minutes
Will. Naylor	1756–1821	pensioned	65		Call, Minutes

The Oxford and Cambridge degrees are marked '?' when there is any doubt whether the master was the same person as the graduate listed in Venn, *Alumni Cantabriegiensis*, or in Joseph Foster, ed., *Alumni Oxonienses* (1891, reprinted Neneln, Leichtenstein: Kraus reprint 1968).

vocation is loyalty to the profession and commitment to their work. By these standards the masters at Ormskirk were professionals from the 1680s.

The appointment of ushers to the school was a haphazard affair, depending both on the number of pupils and on the current state of the finances. As we have seen, Chorley had an usher, Roger Cliffe, who was paid £6 per annum. In 1664 George Birchall agreed to combine the two posts for a salary of £10. No separate usher was appointed then until 1686, when William Grice, the local bookseller and parish clerk, was appointed. The post was part-time and Grice taught whenever his other commitments allowed. No salary was quoted until 1723, when the economy of Ormskirk was improving. Then it was £2 10s per annum, confirming that the post was still only part-time. Between 1736 and 1744 the usher received £8 per annum, and then the posts were combined again. In 1749, in line with the improvement in the local economy, the governors increased the headmaster's salary to £25 per annum, but, in the agreement appointing Revd John Norcross in 1754, they inserted a clause that, 'if the trustees find it necessary that an assistant be required, Mr Norcross shall provide one at his own expense'. Needless to say, none was appointed, and that situation continued until the turn of the century.[62]

The influence of the Chorley family over the school continued indirectly throughout the century, for Bertie Entwistle was appointed one of the governors in 1694 and was followed by his son, Alexander, in 1719.[63] This tradition was true of several local families, including the Stanleys of Moor Hall, the Hollands of Latham, the Hills of Burscough and Latham, and the Fazakerleys and Berrys of Ormskirk. These were not exclusively gentry families but, like the governors appointed in 1612, they were a cross-section of the wealthiest families in the neighbourhood and included lawyers, grocers and apothecaries. All the earls of Derby were nominally governors, but only Charles, the Eighth Earl, attended meetings regularly in the mid-seventeenth century.[64]

Wealth and a charitable disposition towards the school were the major qualifications for election to the board in the eighteenth century, as a resolution made in 1720 attests: 'no person is to be admitted feoffee or governor of the school unless he will pay down two guineas at least, one guinea in hand and another at his death . . . with what more he pleases as God Almighty hath endowed and blessed him with worldly riches and charitable heart'.[65] Two years later, a framed list of subscriptions was hung in the school to exert pressure on the governors.[66] This moral intimidation and a lack of real interest in the school gradually eroded the board, and few attended the infrequent meetings. The vicar, the Revd Knowles, was extremely concerned at the standard of education and the school's declining influence in the town, and wanted well educated clerical governors to support his efforts to improve it. In 1798, at his instigation, the constitution of board was changed, altering the original deed stating that only two clergymen were to serve, and six were elected.[67]

Thus, thanks to the apathy of the lay governors, the Anglican clergy finally wrested most of the control of Ormskirk School out of secular hands. Throughout our period the Church authorities nationwide had worked towards the Anglicanisation of education, for they recognised that schoolmasters influenced the formation of opinion and thereby the spread of the Anglican faith. At first through collaboration with the Cavalier Parliament, they secured the Act of Uniformity (1662), ejecting Nonconformists from parish livings and ensuring that all teachers were practising Anglicans. Later, through their bishops, they controlled the teachers' licences, and at the local level influenced the school through the continual presence of the vicar.

Most of the Ormskirk teachers obeyed the provisions of the Act of Uniformity. Certainly the curate Rycroft conformed, and the grants of licences to Atherton, Liptrot and Lawson in the bishop's call books[68] record that they were practising Anglicans. Seemingly, Ormskirk was unusual in conforming so closely, for the Church's right to control education was challenged throughout the seventeenth century. According to Marchamount Nedham in 1663,[69] the Act of Uniformity was 'either so imperfectly worded as to afford an easy evasion or so poorly put in execution through negligence or corruption of officers, that the law had as good never been made'. Gradually, increasing numbers of schoolmasters countrywide did not apply for the bishop's licence to teach, but the proportion of masters holding holy orders increased, and in those cases there was no need to prove allegiance to the Anglican Church.

Table 26 illustrates the rising proportion of clergymen in teaching nationwide, and, despite the much smaller sample distorting the percentages for the town, Ormskirk's teachers conformed to a similar pattern.

The board elected in 1798 became closely involved in the work of the school instead of the previous governors' narrow duties of appointing masters and overseeing the funds. Resolutions were passed, including one prohibiting the admission of any child under the age of seven or before he could read. Examinations were to be held twice a year by the governors and the master's salary was to 'be regulated according to the state of the school' – dependent on the results of the examinations. The following year, after an overall improvement had been recorded by the four clergymen conducting the examinations, the master received an increase in salary of £5 per annum.[71]

These examinations, based on Latin texts and general Latin and English grammar, were graded according to the pupil's standard. The school continued to offer a very limited curriculum, including only the grammars, when commerce and industry were demanding a competent knowledge of accounting and a more general education. Philosophers and educationalists were also demanding a broader syllabus in the grammar schools. French, Dutch and Spanish languages were suggested by Thomas Hobbes and John Evelyn, while John Locke proposed that the curriculum should include law, geometry, arithmetic and French.[72] In

TABLE 26. The percentage of teachers in holy orders[70]

Sample	Dates	No. of masters	No. in orders	Percentage in orders
A	1660–1714	315 (9)	232 (1)	74% (11%)
C	1714–1770	313 (9)	267 (4)	85% (44%)
E*	1660–1770	559 (18)	449 (5)	80% (28%)

*This is another different sample, not the total from the preceding samples. Ormskirk figures are in brackets. I have included Rycroft, a curate, Ascroft (whom David Orritt suggested may have become curate in Prescot) and Naylor (who is entitled 'Reverend' in a contemporary will) among those in holy orders in Ormskirk.

40. Grammar school, rebuilt in 1850 in Ruff Lane and subsequently extended. The earliest building is on the left.

1818 Nicholas Carlisle described the success of this movement in north-western grammar schools: Middleton grammar school 'taught classics only. But for many years past, a commercial education has been preferred and consequently more attended to, for which 6*s* quarterage is paid'; Chorley Grammar School could 'with propriety be styled a "commercial school", the classics being seldom introduced'; Cartmel Grammar School was 'now more a school for trade and commerce than for classical learning'; while Bolton Grammar School could claim the most extensive syllabus, including geography and navigation among the other subjects on offer. Other grammar schools, including Clitheroe, dragged their feet and, like Ormskirk, remained 'exclusively classical'.[73]

The inadequate curriculum in Ormskirk may explain why only twelve boys were listed in the examination results for 1798. Apparently the same texts had been used throughout the school's existence, for alongside their results were the books they had studied, and the same titles appeared among the stock of the local chapman in 1612,[74] the year of the foundation of the school. Despite making great efforts to improve the educational standards of the school, the governors neglected its buildings. In the charity commissioners' report of 1828 they are described as being 'ill adapted for the purposes of a school, as well from the state of the buildings which are very old, as from the badness of the situation'.[75]

Certainly the restricted curriculum, a shortage of adequate funding and a lack of real interest among the governors confirm that Ormskirk Grammar School shared in the 'prolonged educational depression' identified by Laurence Stone as beginning in the second half of the seventeenth century and lasting over a hundred years.[76]

THE CHARITY SCHOOL, THE SUNDAY SCHOOL

AND OTHER SCHOOLS

Nevertheless, throughout that period, some Ormskirk people were conscious of the need for education and of its financial demands. Many testators made provision for the education of their sons, but few considered the cultural needs of the poor. Whenever they were included in wills, it was to provide them with bread or other necessities, but the possibility of a basic education was rarely considered before the 1720s, when this pattern began to change. Local philanthropy followed the national trend, as Charles Wilson observed: 'There was a change in benefactions from passive doles of bread . . . to the active constructive gifts of apprenticeships and training schools.'[77] There was one local exception in 1690, when Henry Jones, an Ormskirk innkeeper, provided a limited means of education for the poor by leaving money 'for buying books to remain for public use in the parish church of Ormskirk'.[78] Although this presupposes a literate public, it showed concern for the poor who could read books but could not afford to buy them.

Very few of the poor could read in 1700. David Cressy estimated that at that date, out of the whole population, over 60% of the men and over 70% of the women were illiterate.[79] As these percentages included the gentry, merchants, clerics and apothecaries, all of whom Cressy counted as 100% literate, the true extent of illiteracy is evident. The fact that a great many were unable to read the Bible and thus were denied one essential means of salvation prompted several early evangelicals to form the Society for the Promotion of Christian Knowledge (SPCK) in 1698, and to open charity schools. Here the poor were given an elementary education in reading, writing, arithmetic and handicrafts, and so, their supporters believed, were given a means of avoiding abject poverty, a grounding in religious knowledge and a means to salvation. These schools were not founded to provide the children with a means to improve their station in life, but as one account written in 1708 declared, that 'from such timely discipline, the public may expect honest and industrious servants'.[80] Nevertheless, opposition was voiced in several publications, including 'The Essay on Charity and Charity Schools' (1723), where Mandeville expressed fears that an educated poor would become dissatisfied with servile work and demand higher wages. He also declared that no nation could become great without vast numbers of people to do the drudgery.[81] Fortunately, his arguments did not deter the philanthropists.

In Ormskirk, by the second decade of the eighteenth century, various testators left money specifically to provide a basic education for the poor. Mary Winstanley left £10 in 1719 for teaching the poor children of the town to read, and in the same year Archippus Kippax, the late vicar, left money for 'Mary School Dame to keep the . . . school afoot as long as it [the legacy] will reach after'.[82] Though this particular school is never mentioned again, it marked the stirring of the charity school movement, and five years later the charity school in Church Street was launched by the Tenth Earl of Derby, who gave a donation of £200 towards it.[83] The earl's lead was followed by a subscription of £4 4s from the Hesketh family of nearby Rufford Hall,[84] and by bequests from townspeople, including William Grice, the bookseller and parish clerk who left £1 1s in 1725, Asa Latham, gentleman, who left the income from various tenancies in 1726 and William Unsworth, barber, who left £10 in 1734.[85] Thus, at that time of economic improvement, we find surplus wealth being channelled into the provision of education.

The court leet also ensured a regular income for the charity school by the order that the constable should give the trustees the money he received from wool weighing. This was collected after a previous order had declared that anyone who sold wool in Ormskirk was to bring the wool to be weighed in the 'usual place where the constable's weights are kept, that the Lord may have his toll and the constable his dues for weighing'.[86] This meant that the burden of supporting the charity school fell directly on the wool traders and, indirectly, on the inhabitants, who had to pay a higher constable's ley [tax] because the wool-weighing toll, which made a large contribution to the constable's expenses, had been given to the school. The administrative skill of the court leet in extracting this income for the school is noteworthy.

The success of the school could be attributed to the vicar, Revd William Knowles, who proudly claimed to be a member of the SPCK in his report to Bishop Porteus in 1778. However, by that time the society had relinquished its involvement in charity schools. In the same report the vicar described the school as 'a small charity school consisting of twenty boys and girls, who are uniformly dressed and taught to read the English tongue. This is the only provision made for them by the public. In all other respects they are committed to the care of the families they belong to, all other parts of their . . . tuition being left to their economy'.[87] This is the first reference to education for girls in Ormskirk, but whether it had been true since the founding of the school is unclear. Certainly girls often received some education in charity schools, for in 1706 a supporter of the SPCK wrote 'the girls learn to read etc. and generally to knit their stockings and gloves, to mark, sew, and mend their clothes, several learn to write and some to spin their clothes'.[88] Seemingly from the vicar's report, the education provided at Ormskirk was much narrower.

Gradually the small size and the resultant limited impact of the charity schools discouraged their financial supporters. Another problem arose towards the end of the century, when children were employed on a more regular basis due to industrialisation and thus were unable to attend school on weekdays. The complete lack of education available for these working children prompted laymen from both the middle and the lower classes to begin the Sunday School movement. At first the Sunday Schools' ties with the Church were tenuous, but later the establishment of the schools in the diocese of Chester was advocated by Bishop Porteus. He waited a year or two for the new schools to prove themselves, then preached a sermon supporting them and sent a letter recommending their establishment to his clergy in 1785.[89] No doubt he also saw an opportunity to extend the Church's influence through these schools.

Porteus's appeal brought results in Ormskirk, and in 1785 Ormskirk's Sunday School was founded to provide a basic education in reading, particularly of the Bible, and later some writing and arithmetic for the poor children of the town. Bequests, subscriptions and yearly contributions poured in and the authorities were able to buy £600 worth of stock, which yielded £18 per annum. By 1795, eighty-two boys and sixty-nine girls attended the school which, by this time, had a revenue of between £50 and £60 from investments and collections.[90] Another of the school's regular sources of income was an annual sermon and collection in the church – the origin of the Sunday School Anniversary. When the vicar replied to the bishop's questionnaire in 1804, he was able to report that the numbers had increased to 200.[91]

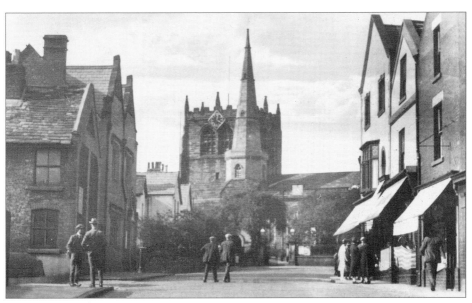

41. Charity school in the early twentieth century. The school is on the extreme left.

The Sunday School movement had many critics. Some even attacked it for profaning the sabbath day by teaching writing and arithmetic. Similar criticism was voiced in Ormskirk, where one of the earliest books printed in the town was *The abuses and advantages of Sunday Schools*, written by Grant Johnson and published in 1800.[92] To counter this criticism, many schools moved their secular classes to evenings during the week and later altered them to daytime classes, thus putting them in direct competition with the charity schools. Whether this happened in Ormskirk we do not know, but gradually the success of the new school overshadowed the old charity school. Finally, in 1819, the two schools were combined to form the united charity school in the 'ancient' school buildings of the 1724 school.[93] In this way, funds were made available to improve and restore the old building in Church Street, which later became the national school, and continued as the centre of elementary education in Ormskirk until the new school in Derby Street – now Stokers Furnishers – was built.

Throughout our period, Catholic children were educated secretly in various private houses in Ormskirk. The Jesuits set up a mission in the area in the 1620s and a school was founded in Scarisbrick Hall.[94] In 1754 an academy for fifty to sixty older boys was set up in Ince Blundell, in the hall of the Catholic Blundell family. This establishment was 'managed' by a secular priest, Father Boardley, from Moor Hall in Aughton, near Ormskirk, and catered for boys countrywide. Those who could not travel daily to the school boarded in houses in the village. There were two masters: John Robinson, a Catholic, and John Berry, reputed to be a Protestant, but who rarely attended church. The local Anglican clergy reported the existence of this academy to the bishop,[95] but he made no attempt to close the school. Older Catholic boys from Ormskirk would be educated at this school during the second half of the eighteenth century. Finally, in the 1790s, the

42. National School, Derby Street.

Catholics were able legally to open a school in their old chapel in Aughton[96] and educate their children in their own faith without duress.

There is no evidence of a Presbyterian school in Ormskirk, but possibly one was attached to the chapel in Aughton Street. Dames' schools in the town also provided education for those who could pay the modest fees, but the existence of these schools is very poorly documented. Certainly in the late seventeenth century the bishop licensed a few Ormskirk teachers who did not teach in the grammar school so, possibly, they taught in small independent schools. However, in the eighteenth century such teachers did not need to obtain licenses, so that evidence disappears.[97]

Despite the patchy nature of the evidence regarding some of these schools, it does provide proof of the concern of the townspeople to cater for the educational needs of Ormskirk and its hinterland. Their success in providing higher education or in persuading townspeople to continue their studies in a university, the Inns of Court or a Dissenting Academy was limited. Only three boys are known to have entered Oxford or Cambridge in the seventeenth century: R. Hill (1638), T. Ashurst (1691) and J. Crompton (n.d.). No figures are available for the eighteenth century.[98] A few may have moved to Edinburgh or to a foreign university to complete their studies, but advanced education was open to very few at this time. Nevertheless, Ormskirk was successful in the field of elementary education. The grammar school, the charity school, the Sunday School, the clandestine Catholic schools, the undocumented petty schools, and the many patient parents and masters who assumed the role of teachers were successful in producing a large body of literate townspeople. The size and composition of that body will be examined in the next section.

The Extent of Literacy in Ormskirk, 1660–1800

Any account of the extent of literacy in Ormskirk during the period cannot be more than an estimate, and it must be stressed that the figures that follow give the most accurate picture possible, but cannot claim to be precise, because of the limitations of the sources. The parish registers, the obvious source of samples of literacy, are no help, because the parish covers six townships including Ormskirk, and only the signer's parish is specified, not the township. Nevertheless, I did collect samples covering twenty years for a comparison with the township samples, and to discover the effect of the inclusion of surrounding rural communities on the results. The omission of the townships meant that the statistical methods of assessing literacy used by David Cressy, Michael Sanderson and Thomas Laqueur, among others, could not be used for Ormskirk. The Hearth Tax Returns – used by R.T. Vann – were not signed for the town, and the Protestation Returns of 1641 were made too early to be applicable to our period.[99]

However, encouraged by David Cressy's statement that signatures on marriage licenses, wills and depositions give a consistent pattern, and following the example of Keith Wrightson and David Levine in their study of Terling, I have adopted a 'magpie' approach, collecting signatures from all the available documents.[100] Probate records were my chief supplier, but deeds, quarter session records – including alehouse licences and bankruptcy papers – estate papers, the records of the consistory court, the assize court and the court leet, and the Association Oath of 1696 have all yielded several examples. This spread of sources avoids some of the difficulties which arise in surveying a single source. For instance, as R.A. Houston acknowledges, surveys made using only the evidence from depositions showed 'a preference for those of maturer years, respectable, socially and economically independent persons whose social credit was high and who were therefore not representative of society as a whole'.[101] A similar criticism could be levelled at the exclusive use of probate records. Although they include some examples from among the poorer classes, they do not include any from paupers. Wills as a single source present another problem in that a literate man might use a mark because of his weakness at the time of signing. Nevertheless, I hope that most of the pitfalls described here will be avoided by the breadth of my research sources.

Once I had amassed the samples, certain signatures began to appear regularly – often on different classes of documents – and had to be jettisoned for statistical purposes. Then the problem arose of two people bearing the same name. In these cases, I tried to identify the occupation of the signer and, if the person of the same name had a different occupation, the name was allowed to stand, but, again from days of dual occupations, a certain amount of error was inevitable. Usually the problem of identity involved father and son, so I retained only one signature for thirty years and then included the next as being of the next generation. I decided again that thirty years would cover the period when most people would be of an age to sign legal documents at that time. Of course, this occurred very occasionally, because very few fathers had sons of the same name among the sample. Some signers had been literate for many years before signing, while others learnt to sign late in life, but this did not affect the results. To all these difficulties must be added the oft-repeated one that a signature is not a proof of literacy. That may be true, but as reading was taught before writing during this period, it can be assumed that most signers were literate. As Cressy declared, signatures, being 'universal, standard and direct', are the best evidence of literate skills and, being 'remarkably sensitive to change in literacy', they are the most reliable guide to literacy available.[102] Their availability is most important. Reliable evidence of literacy covering large sections of the community is extremely hard to find.

Despite all these difficulties, a very clear picture of the state of literacy in Ormskirk 1660–1800 emerged. When all the doubtful signings had been eliminated, a total of 1,433 signings and markings were analysed. Of these, 1,144 were signatures and 285 were marks, which gave a percentage of 20% illiteracy over the whole period. Male illiteracy, calculated from a sample of 1,116, stood at 15% and female illiteracy, from a sample of 317, stood at 37%. These figures denote a very high degree of literacy in the town. As the period covers 140 years, the results have been divided into ten-year periods in Table 27 to facilitate comparisons with other localities.

The pattern of overall increase in literacy was predictable, given the situation nationwide, and the short-term fluctuations must be attributed chiefly to the limitations of the sources. However, the sharp reduction in illiteracy among females after 1690 is remarkable. It is possible that schooling for girls had been introduced into an undocumented petty school during the latter years of the seventeenth century, or perhaps the easing of censorship and licensing laws and the consequent increase in the number of books available motivated females to learn to read and practise their literacy skills. Another possible explanation may be that the economy of the town had altered, demanding literate skills from its female inhabitants, or at least allowing literate mothers the time and leisure to teach their daughters literacy skills in the home.[103] However, from our evidence no real economic improvement occurred until the 1720s, although the townsfolk's

TABLE 27. *Illiteracy in Ormskirk, 1660–1799*

Date	Sample	Total illiteracy (%)	Male sample	Male illiteracy (%)	Female sample	Female illiteracy (%)
1661–1669	68	44	61	39	7	86
1670–1679	90	17	87	15	3	67
1680–1689	56	30	48	21	8	88
1690–1699	141	28	118	27	23	30
1700–1709	106	20	83	16	23	35
1710–1719	83	24	65	22	18	33
1720–1729	141	21	104	13	37	41
1730–1739	116	22	76	17	40	30
1740–1749	130	14	93	6	37	32
1750–1759	86	22	63	17	23	35
1760–1769	101	12	70	4	31	29
1770–1779	113	15	89	4	24	54
1780–1789	90	14	73	10	17	35
1790–1799	112	13	86	9	26	23[104]

confidence was building up during the 1680s as they challenged Wigan as the venue of the quarter sessions (see p. 26) and introduced sugar boiling to the town (see p. 17). Any alteration in the demand for skills would be hard to identify.

A quick comparison with other estimates supports the fact that Ormskirk, indeed, had a unusually low level of illiteracy. Cressy estimated that, at the accession of George I (1714), English men were 55% illiterate and English women 75%.[105] These figures compare with Ormskirk's 22% for men and 33% for women. R.A. Houston estimated that 39% of the population in Norfolk and Suffolk in the 1680s and 34% in the 1720s were illiterate, which can be compared with Ormskirk's total of 30% in the 1680s and 21% in the 1720s.[106] Cressy also estimated that 44% of the females in London in 1720 were illiterate and that later in the century, in 1750, 64% of all brides nationwide could not sign. These percentages can be compared with Ormskirk's 41% in the 1720s and – remembering a difference in the sources – 35% in the 1750s.[107] However, even when the same source is used – the Association Rolls of 1696 – albeit producing a much smaller sample, Ormskirk's illiteracy at 32% was still much lower than the percentage for the whole of Lancashire, which stood at 57%.[108]

The signatures on the Oath of Association (1696) provided an opportunity to grade the signatures according to their fluency without the danger of classing a dying man as illiterate because of his feebleness. These signatures were made by adult males who held some responsible position, to affirm their loyalty to William and Mary. Of the 142 males, 46 put their mark on the document, thereby recording 32% illiteracy among the group – a slightly higher percentage than the 27% in our table compiled from a variety of different sources. When the 96 signatures were graded, 39 or 27% of the whole group were very fluent. Some even indulged in ornamental flourishes. Of the rest, 35% signed their names with less confidence and 23% found the task extremely difficult – judging by the awkwardness of some of the disjointed capitals which often composed the names. The results are summarised in Table 28.

All the preceding comparisons are marred by the fact that they do not show any pattern of progression towards literacy. Fortunately, a few statistical studies are available which make a meaningful comparison between the developing state of literacy in Ormskirk and that in other locations. These include R.A. Houston's study of literacy from depositions made in the Northern Circuit; Robert Unwin's examination of literacy in the Vale of York; Keith Wrightson and David Levine's study of literacy in Terling; R.G. Dottie's study of Childwall, Lancashire; and Michael Sanderson's study of nearby Kirkham and Preston.[109] Thus we have comparisons with the wider area of the north of England, with a northern rural community, with two villages (one in the south-east and one in the north-west) and finally with two towns in the north-west with similar economic profiles to that of Ormskirk.

TABLE 28. Literacy graded from the Ormskirk Oaths of Association, 1696

Grade 1 (fluent)	Grade 2	Grade 3	Marked (illiterate)
39	34	23	46
27%	23%	16%	32%

TABLE 29. *Comparison with deponents from the Northern Circuit Assize, 1661–1749*

	For Northern Circuit				For Ormskirk			
Date	Male sample	Male %	Female sample	Female %	Male sample	Male %	Female sample	Female %
1661–1669	482	54	154	91	61	39	7	86
1670–1679	429	51	143	91	87	15	3	67
1680–1689	416	45	98	87	48	21	8	88
1690–1699	338	41	102	86	118	27	23	30
1700–1709					83	16	23	35
1710–1719					65	22	18	33
1720–1729	178	42	61	74	104	13	37	41
1730–1739	314	27	111	74	76	17	40	30
1740–1749	229	30	78	68	93	6	7	32

The first comparison (Table 29) makes no distinction between urban and rural signers, but gives an overall picture of the north of England. R.A. Houston used only signatures on depositions from the Northern Circuit Assize in his comparison, whereas depositions supplied few of the Ormskirk samples. Yet, although the sources differ greatly, they draw on similar sections of society. The mixture of urban and rural signers may account for the different level in the findings. Nevertheless, a similar pattern to that of the other examples emerged.[110]

Similarly, Robert Unwin made a study of literacy in the Vale of York (1660–1688) using only probate records.[111] Again the samples came from the north of England, but, unlike the Northern Circuit sample and the Ormskirk sample, they came from specifically rural communities. His conclusions are compared with those from Ormskirk in Table 30.

Female illiteracy for Ormskirk was high at the date of the sample in Table 30 and resembled the level in the Vale of York, but during the next decade it dropped sharply, and then would show a similar discrepancy to that shown by the male samples in this table. The difference between literacy levels in a town and those in a rural community in a similar locality provides evidence for a distinctive urban culture. Whereas the culture of rural communities remained predominantly visual

TABLE 30. *Comparison of literacy levels in Ormskirk and the Vale of York, 1660–1688*

Place	Sample	Total illiteracy (%)	Male sample	Male illiteracy (%)	Female sample	Female illiteracy (%)
Vale of York	156	67	139	64	17	88
Ormskirk	214	29	196	24	18	83

TABLE 31. Comparison between Terling and Ormskirk, 1670–1699

Place	Sample	Total illiteracy (%)	Male sample	Male illiteracy (%)	Female sample	Female illiteracy (%)
Terling	83	32	76	29	7	71
Ormskirk	287	25	253	22	34	47

and oral until the late eighteenth century and sometimes into the nineteenth century, literacy levels for the larger urban communities reveal that urban culture in the late seventeenth century became highly literate.

Keith Wrightson and David Levine investigated literacy in the village of Terling for the period 1670–1699 using sources similar to those for Ormskirk. A comparison with their findings[112] is made in Table 31. The size of the village influenced its results, for literacy was more difficult to acquire in Terling than in Ormskirk. The village had no schoolmaster during these particular years, although schooling was available in nearby townships. Literacy levels were also influenced by the differing economies of the two towns: Terling's based on agriculture and Ormskirk's on marketing and the servicing trades, which demanded more literacy from the workers. Prosperity and the availability of leisure time also had an effect on the acquisition of the skill. Surprisingly, Ormskirk in the remote north-west had a much higher literacy rate than Terling in the south-east, where the influence of London had spread to the area, bringing prosperity to those who supplied agricultural products to the city. Admittedly, London would also attract able and educated people away from the village to seek employment in the metropolis, so reducing the number of literate villagers in Terling.[113]

Childwall, a small, north-western township, now absorbed into Liverpool, was studied by R.G. Dottie for the period 1660–1701. He drew some comparisons with the village of Myddle.[114] Although Childwall was much smaller than Ormskirk and did not have the role of market town, its location was very similar. In Table 32, Dottie's findings on literacy, taken from sources similar to those used for the Ormskirk sample, are compared with the figures for Ormskirk.

Again the higher level of achievement of the townpeople of Ormskirk is noticeable, even when compared with a smaller township in a similar location.

TABLE 32. Comparison between the literacy levels in Childwall, Myddle and Ormskirk, 1660–1701

Place	Sample	Total illiteracy (%)	Male sample	Male illiteracy (%)	Female sample	Female illiteracy (%)
Childwall	51	57		55		67
Myddle	41	37				
Ormskirk	355	28	314	25	41	54

TABLE 33. *Comparison of illiteracy levels between Ormskirk, Kirkham and Preston, 1750–1799*

Date	Sample	Total illiteracy (%) Ormskirk	Sample Kirkham	Total illiteracy (%) Kirkham	Sample Preston	Total illiteracy (%) Preston
1750–1759	86	22	350	47	506	44
1760–1769	101	12	420	48	326	41
1770–1779	113	15	426	66	394	49
1780–1789	90	14	430	63	550	66
1790–1799	112	13	460	60	516	53

Comparison can also be made with another larger north-western town, Wigan, where a resolution was made by the parishioners regarding the installation of an organ in the church gallery in 1712.[115] This resolution was made by 338 parishioners, of whom 122 made marks, revealing that 36% of these parishioners were illiterate at that date. Again Ormskirk's illiteracy was much lower, standing at 24% at the same time.

Our last comparison (Table 33) is with the findings of Michael Sanderson, who studied illiteracy in Kirkham and Preston from the marriage signings recorded in 1750–1790.[116]

The difference in the origin of the signings creates difficulties, but does not mar the comparison's usefulness. The samples from Kirkham and Preston taken from parish registers contained many signings from people of a lower social status than the Ormskirk samples. The continuous reduction in illiteracy in Ormskirk contrasts significantly with the continuous increase in the other two towns. Again, the explanation lies in their differing economies. Ormskirk never became an industrial town, despite an attempt to set up a factory during the late eighteenth century. The other two were mill towns and, consequently, child labour was employed and the opportunity for education was lacking. The timing of the increase in illiteracy in Kirkham and Preston – towards the end of the eighteenth century, when an increasing number of cotton factories were being established – lends support to this explanation. John Walton found that literacy levels in many Lancashire towns declined in the late eighteenth century, and he attributed this to economic change coupled with rising population.[117] Although the population was rising in Ormskirk, that did not cause severe problems until the nineteenth century, unlike the situation in Preston and many of its neighbours, which supports John Walton's findings.

The exceptionally low level of male illiteracy in Ormskirk shown in Table 34 could be attributed to the demand for clerical skills made by the majority of employers in the town. The higher level in Table 35 for the parish, including the rural areas, confirms this conclusion. Admittedly, Preston and Kirkham had many workers similarly employed to those in Ormskirk town, but the pressure of population and the presence of industry in those towns had altered the demand for literacy and had left workers with no leisure time to acquire the skills – even if they earned sufficient money to pay for schooling.

TABLE 34. A comparison of male and female illiteracy in Ormskirk, Kirkham and Preston, 1750–1800

Date	Male illiteracy (%)			Female illiteracy (%)		
	Ormskirk	Kirkham	Preston	Ormskirk	Kirkham	Preston
1750–1759	17	23	27	35	70	60
1760–1769	4	30	32	29	66	66
1770–1779	4	38	32	54	73	68
1780–1789	10	46	44	35	79	73
1790–1799	9	44	36	23	75	69

It may be appropriate here to include my analysis (Table 36) of the marriage signings for the parish of Ormskirk, which encompassed five other townships in addition to Ormskirk town. The inclusion of rural communities and the difference in the sources has increased the illiteracy rates, but the rates are still low for such a wide area and follow the same pattern of continuous reduction as those for the township of Ormskirk.

The higher level of illiteracy among females than among males in both Ormskirk town and parish indicate a difference in the expectations of the sexes. In certain sections of the community, literacy was considered unnecessary for females. Nevertheless, the higher level of literacy reached by females in the parish suggest that, in a rural community, seasonal work allowed females an opportunity to acquire these skills. These factors support Jacqueline Grayson's view that 'the relationship between occupation and literacy is more complex than a straightforward "demand-pull" from occupation to literacy'.[118]

Lorna Weatherill suggested that the high level of literacy in north-western towns could be attributed to the influence of religious Dissent.[119] Indeed, extracts from the grammar school records proved that the local Anglicans hoped that literacy would counteract the Catholic threat to their faith. Ormskirk certainly was very active in all religious spheres, and the influence of religion on the literacy of the town cannot be ignored. However, these three north-western townships had similar patterns of religious allegiance, and yet their literacy levels differed. Nevertheless, in most of the foregoing examples, the influence of religion coupled with the difference in both their economic structures and the pressure of their population do provide a satisfactory explanation for their differing literacy levels.

While Keith Wrightson believes that the 'hierarchy of literacy faithfully mirrored the hierarchy of status and wealth', David Cressy doubts whether there

TABLE 35. Comparison of illiteracy: Ormskirk – town and parish

Date	Sample from town	Total illiteracy (%) town	Sample from parish	Total illiteracy (%) parish
1760–1769	101	12	1706	45
1770–1779	113	15	1752	41

TABLE 36. A comparison of male and female illiteracy: Ormskirk, town and parish, 1760–1779

Date	Male illiteracy (%)		Female illiteracy (%)	
	town	parish	town	parish
1760–1769	4	18.9	29	26.2
1770–1779	4	15.1	54	25.6

was any such straightforward correlation between the two.[120] A comparison between the literacy of the males in the Ormskirk sample and their personal wealth as indicated by the Hearth Tax returns (Table 37) seems to favour Keith Wrightson's theory for the period 1660–1680. In Ormskirk a definite association between personal wealth and literacy emerges. However, there is a slight divergence among those assessed for only one hearth, and where many of the signings were made by people whose occupation is not recorded. One explanation for this high proportion of signings among an ostensibly poor group could be the presence in this group of several literate, but elderly, people who had means, but were too old to follow their occupation, and so lived in small houses sufficient for their needs. Thus, although they were assessed among the poorer inhabitants, they did not belong with that group. If this is the explanation, Wrightson's 'mirror' relationship between literacy and wealth is reflected accurately in Ormskirk.

W.B. Stephens has added yet another control to the acquisition of literacy. He suggests that, although it was closely related to prosperity, the requirements of certain occupations also exerted their influence.[121] While it is impossible to determine whether certain occupations attracted the literate members of society or whether they were motivated to acquire literacy in order to follow their chosen occupation, in Ormskirk some occupations were certainly more literate than others. Although over half the previous samples had no indication of the signer's occupation, it was possible to analyse a smaller sample in conjunction with their occupations.

Among those described as 'gentlemen'– a term far from synonymous with 'gentry' at this time – five illiterates were recorded out of twelve signings prior to 1720. As three were on wills, the apparent lack of literacy could be attributed to feebleness. After that date, as most researchers have found, those listed as gentlemen were completely literate, and status, wealth and literacy coincided.[122]

TABLE 37. A comparison between literacy and wealth in Ormskirk, 1660–1680

Number of hearths	Marked	% marked	Signed	% signed
excused payment	2	66	1	33
1	4	20	16	80
2	7	35	13	65
3	4	36	7	64
4	1	17	5	83
5–8			10	100

TABLE 38. *The percentage of illiterate craftsmen, 1660–1800*

Occupation	Sample	No. marked	% marked
Precision workers	5	0	0
Barbers	4	0	0
Woodworkers	24	2	8
Leatherworkers	34	4	11
Bakers	5	1	20
Textile workers	27	6	22
Metalworkers	17	4	23
Innkeepers and alehouse keepers	98	24	24
Builders and decorators	20	8	40
Total	241	49	20

From as early as 1660, the pseudo-gentry of the town – those employed in the emerging professions: the apothecaries, surgeons, doctors, lawyers, clerics and teachers – were 100% literate, as was usual.[123] In these cases, wealth certainly mirrored literacy, for without wealth, few people could train for the professions.

As far as craftsmen and tradesmen were concerned, literacy increased their chances of success, although, as J.A. Sharpe observed, 'illiteracy was not, even in 1760, a bar to economic advancement'.[124] Nevertheless, as tables 38 and 39 show, the more literate tradesmen and craftsmen were, generally, in the more lucrative occupations.

The precision workers were employed in the clockmaking trade and were too highly specialised to include among the metal workers, who ranged from blacksmiths to pewterers, from farriers to cutlers. Similarly, woodworkers included craftsmen such as cabinetmakers, joiners, coopers and wheelwrights. Barbers included periwig makers, who could demand high fees for elaborate hairstyles and wigs, and so were often wealthy, whereas the inclusion of several poor alehouse keepers lowered the rating of the innkeepers.

TABLE 39. *The percentage of illiterate tradesmen, 1660–1800*

Occupation	Sample	No. marked	% marked
Booksellers	4	0	0
Drapers	17	0	0
Grocers	12	0	0
Haberdashers	4	0	0
Merchants	3	0	0
Ironmongers	5	1	20
Chapmen and Badgers	5	1	20
Butchers	8	2	25
Mercers	6	2	33
Shopkeepers (unspecified)	6	3	50
Total	62	9	15

This pattern was predictable, except for the mercers' low position, which cannot be explained either as a 'deathbed' marking, as these particular markings were made by mercers witnessing wills, or as being from the early, less literate years. A possible explanation is that, in Lancashire by this time, the term 'mercer' meant a salesman of mixed wares rather than its original meaning – a seller of fine cloth – a role assumed by the wealthy drapers. These unspecified shopkeepers included those in small general shops where illiteracy was less of a handicap than in the more specialised trades. The tradesmen's lower level of illiteracy than the craftsmen's supports the theory that literacy increased according to the demands of occupations. Tradesmen's employment involved a great deal of accounting in those days of widespread credit, so needed greater literacy than the craftsmen's skill, which could often be practised without recourse to literacy. Admittedly, the craftsman required numeracy to fix his prices and sell his goods, but the evidence confirms that literacy was not as essential for him as for the tradesman. The humbler craftsman could not spare time – or money – to acquire it. It is significant that the balance between craftsmen and tradesmen within a town could affect its overall literacy pattern and, in turn, influence the position of the town in the urban literacy hierarchy.

Jacqueline Grayson observed that, in the predominantly oral culture of the eighteenth century, the lack of the formal ability to read and write held no stigma.[125] However, as Charles Leslie, founder of the Tory newspaper the *Rehearsal*, commented in 1704, 'the greatest part of the people . . . cannot read at all' yet 'they will gather about one that can read and listen to an Observer or Review'.[126] It may be that illiteracy held no stigma among the lower strata of society, but Charles Leslie's comments convey the admiration of that class of people for their literate fellow townsmen, who thereby acquired status. Inevitably, those with means to do so strove to acquire that status and, as Houston suggests, 'the rapid integration of the middle levels of society into a predominantly literate milieu may have hastened their sense of dissociation from the lower social orders'.[127]

Other divisions occurred in society where households were split and illiterate women were unable to share the literate pursuits of their menfolk, and illiterate servants were deprived of the benefits enjoyed by their 'betters'.[128] The illiterate were left clinging to the traditional oral culture and adding their eighteenth-century variations to it. They perpetuated the art of storytelling and kept alive traditional folksongs, until eventually they themselves became literate and many of these arts were lost. Thus, literacy polarised society, isolating the illiterate at the bottom of the social scale and deprived them of an important means of improving their lot.

Although the figures for Ormskirk suggest that the townsfolk were more literate than most of their contemporaries, it must be remembered that the samples from Ormskirk came from documents excluding parish registers, and consequently the lower strata of society who had no occasion to sign the documents, were not included. Those unrepresented people would suffer most from the isolation and deprivation caused by illiteracy. However, among those who were represented in this study, there was a high level of literacy and a steady increase throughout the eighteenth century, associated with a similar improvement in the town's economy after the first two decades. Perhaps this increase in literacy and prosperity was paralleled by an increase in book ownership among the townsfolk. That will be examined in our next inquiry.

CHAPTER VII

Cultural Life

BOOK OWNERSHIP

Although novels, magazines and newspapers were not readily available until the second half of the eighteenth century, reading was a popular pastime in our period. Until 1695, censorship was enforced by the Licensing Act of 1662. All books had to be entered at Stationers' Hall to be licensed according to their subject. Publishers, too had to obtain licenses, and very few were granted outside London. These regulations and the cost of complying with them constricted the publishing trade and limited the range of books produced.[1] For instance, in 1612 the stock of the Ormskirk chapman, Rauffe Burnestone, consisted of primers, psalters, testaments, epistles, devotional books, editions of the classics and herbals.[2] Similarly, Robert Sankey, a mercer in the town who died in 1613, also stocked primers and Greek grammars, among other books.[3] Much of this stock was held for grammar school pupils, but the reading public also enjoyed the classics and devotional literature. Booksellers' stocks altered little during the next fifty years, and the 1,200 books stocked by a Warrington bookseller in 1648 came from a similar range.[4] Unfortunately, no specialist bookseller's inventory remains for Ormskirk from the later seventeenth century, but Ambrose Jackson, grocer, had 'bound books' among the varied stock in his shop in 1683. They were valued at £2 19s.[5] Bound books were expensive, but unbound books were available and could be bound to match previous acquisitions, as Pepys recorded: 'calling for my five books of Variorum print bound according to my common binding'.[6]

Among the stock of Margaret Clarkson, an Ormskirk hardware dealer in 1693, were six broadsheets or chapbooks described as 'rimes called Half a Time', valued at 2s.[7] These were either early examples of light literature reaching the town after the gradual relaxation of the tight controls on publishing, or some small publications which escaped the censors' notice. At 4d each, these 'rimes' were more substantial than the usual broadsheet sold by chapmen in markets and fairs for 1d each.[8]

These two Ormskirk examples were typical of seventeenth-century shops, where books were sold among a variety of other wares. Gradually, as we have seen (p. 25), specialist shops emerged. Cautiously, Ormskirk tradesmen took a half-way position, claiming specifically to be booksellers, yet following another trade as a standby. The Grices, booksellers from the 1720s, were also alehouse keepers, while the Stuarts, booksellers in the 1750s, were also ironmongers.[9] Unfortunately, neither left an inventory, so we have no record of their stocks or of the impact made locally by the arrival of lighter literature by Defoe, and later by Henry Fielding and Samuel Richardson.

Few local inventories mentioned specific books, except the Bible, which featured in thirteen of the fifty-one references to books. In eight cases, the Bible was the only book owned by the deceased, showing how important scriptural reading and the ownership of a Bible was to devout families at this time. Several of the Bibles were large ones, where family events were recorded, and were therefore heirlooms to be bequeathed to specific relations. For instance, both Thomas Pemberton in 1783 and Mary Prescott in 1788 left their Bibles to their nephews as their heirs. This custom may explain why three out of the eight Bible owners – Robert Oakes, yeoman, in 1674, Thomas Keaquicke, alehouse keeper, in 1680, and Mary Prescott, widow, in 1788 – used marks rather than signed their wills.[10] Of course, these three markings may have resulted from infirmity rather than illiteracy, or perhaps a Bible was a desirable possession – a status symbol – even if the owner could not read it. However, two of the Bible owners who marked were alive when reading was taught before writing, so they may have learnt to read the familiar text but not to sign their names.

Bibles are mentioned specifically in 11% of the Ormskirk inventories, a much higher proportion than that in Lorna Weatherill's national survey, where she found Bibles in only 5% of the inventories. Again, this can be attributed to the strength of religious fervour in the district.[11] Table 40 illustrates the incidence of Bibles and the occupations of their owners in wills.

The table charts an incorrect reduction in the number of Bible owners, resulting from appraisers combining articles rather than listing them separately as they had done earlier. However, the fact that later appraisers regarded the Bible as merely another book indicates a change in attitude towards it, and provides unwitting testimony to an alteration in the townsfolk's attitude towards religion.

Several books with biblical themes appear in the inventories, including an *Exposition of Matthew* belonging to Henry Lathom, innkeeper, in 1667, *The Parable of the Prodigal Son*, owned by Thomas Pemberton, yeoman, in 1783, and two *Histories of the Holy Bible*, belonging to John Glover, yeoman, in 1791.[12] Books of sermons were also popular and a book of homilies was listed among the church's property in 1684.[13] Nathaniel Heywood wrote a long homily entitled *Christ Displayed as the Choicest Gift and Best Master* and his brother, Oliver, published it after Nathaniel's death.[14] On one occasion in 1693, John Starkey, the

TABLE 40. *The occupations of owners of Bibles, 1660–1750*

1660–1680	1681–1700	1701–1720	1721–1740	1741–
shoemaker	weaver-husbandman	husbandman	bookseller	widow
felt-maker			glazier	yeoman
widow				
yeoman				
innkeeper				
gent				
yeoman				
alehouse				
keeper				

Nonconformist minister of Ormskirk, used this interest in sermons and recommended his congregation to read Henry Newcome's book *The Plain Discourse about Rash and Sinful Anger*.[15] Probably collections of sermons were among the books of divinity belonging to Richard Sutch, gentleman, who died in 1691, or among the books of devotion left by Elizabeth Wilson in 1735.[16] Sermons were still popular at the beginning of the nineteenth century and were published in Ormskirk by R. Cocker of Church Street and by Fowler of Moor Street.

Accounts of religious controversy were used for reference, and among the books included in the church's property in 1679 was the *Book of Jewell and Hardman*. This concerned the Romish controversy (1565–1568) between the protestant Bishop Jewel of Salisbury and Thomas Harding, who refused to take the oath of supremacy.[17] As we saw (p. 80), the vicar, Zachary Taylor (1679–1692), published several controversial religious works, but the first book printed in Ormskirk was Grant Johnson's *The Abuses and Advantages of Sunday Schools*, published in 1800 (see p. 131),[18] Another book with a religious theme was Henry Lathom's hymn book (1667), which will be discussed later (see p. 159).

The books bequeathed in 1690 by Henry Jones 'for public use in the Parish Church' provide evidence both of the kind of books the public read, and of the religious bias of Ormskirk's Anglican parishioners. Predictably all the books were about religion, but significantly two of their authors were ministers ejected at the same time as Nathaniel Heywood. One was Matthew Poole (1624–1679), a friend of Henry Ashurst, Heywood's biographer, whose series of English annotations for the Bible, completed after his death by other scholars and published in 1683–1685,[19] was among the bequeathed books. The second ejected presbyterian author was Samuel Clarke (1599–1683), vicar of Shotwick near Chester in the 1620s, who wrote *The Marrow of Ecclesiastical History* (1648), an account of the lives of 148 'fathers, schoolmen and modern divines'.[20] A similar account among the collection was John Foxe's *Book of Martyrs* (1563) about the persecution of reformers in Europe from the days of Wycliffe.[21] Another book bequeathed by Jones was a collection of Christian discourses, by the author of *The Whole Duty of Man*, thought to have been Richard Allestree (1619–1681), a royalist divine, later provost of Eton.[22] The final book in the collection was *Discourses on the Whole Common Prayer* by Thomas Comber (1645–1699), Dean of Durham, published in 1684, and was intended to reconcile Protestant dissenters to the Anglican Church.[23] The 1703 list of church property records that the books were given by William Grice, the bookseller, parish clerk and school usher 'pursuant to the will of Henry Jones'.[24]

Another work mentioned specifically in a will was Gerrard's *Herbal* or *The Herball or General Historie of Plantes*, published by the surgeon John Gerrard in London in 1597,[25] bequeathed by the apothecary, William Farrington, in 1693. When he willed his 'books of what kind so ever' to his son, Farrington excluded his Gerrard's *Herbal* and left that to his apprentice, William Barton – along with his case of instruments.[26]

Several legal books were mentioned but, surprisingly, not among the possessions of lawyers. They usually owned too many books to be itemised. For instance, John Entwistle of the Middle Temple and Ormskirk used the collective term 'my study of books' in his will in 1710. Law books featured in the inventories of several innkeepers, including Henry Lathom, who owned *The Statutes at Law* in 1667, and Richard Sutch, who, although described as a gentleman at his death in 1691, held an alehouse licence in the 1660s.[27] Innkeepers certainly needed their law books, for efficient innkeeping necessitated an intimate knowledge of both excise and general law in the late seventeenth century. The role of inns was expanding to include acting both as a centre for the transaction of retail and wholesale trade and as a bank for carriers, drovers and others passing regularly through the town.[28] They were also the venue for various social, political and administrative purposes, such as the adjourned sitting of the court leet at the Wheatsheaf. Meanwhile the innkeeper was expected to keep a watchful eye on visitors in case they contravened the law. Evidently, Thomas Knowles, the parish clerk, found his copy of the twelfth edition of Richard Burn's *'The Justice of the Peace and Parish Officer'*[29] extremely useful, for in 1777 he bequeathed it to William Hill esquire, a local magistrate.

One book of special interest in the will of William Grice in 1725 (as we saw, p. 113)[30] was a copy of *Eikon Basilike*, or *The Protraicture of His Sacred Maiestie in His Solitudes and Sufferings*, which was first published in 1648. As a 'doubtful and suppositious' work, its author was anonymous, but it was attributed to John Gauden, Bishop of Exeter and later Bishop of Worcester. Many editions were published, including extracts commissioned in 1683 for Richard Sherlock, Bishop of Sodor and Man and chaplain to Lord Derby (see p. 74). It was still generating considerable interest in 1691, when a further vindication of it was published.[31] As one of William Grice's prized possessions, this book was bequeathed specifically to his son, Thomas. Whether the family were active Jacobites cannot be proved, but certainly, in 1660, William's father – and namesake – enthusiastically proclaimed the restoration of Charles II at Ormskirk market cross using the meaningful words, 'To the Joy of All Good Christians', and as parish clerk wrote his speech in the parish register as a declaration for posterity.

Lorna Weatherill, in her study of inventories, found that book ownership was high in the north-west. As Table 41 shows, she located books in only 19.33% of inventories nationwide[32], while in Ormskirk I found that a much smaller sample yielded an average of 33.43%. She ascribed her north-western results to higher literacy resulting from the influence of religious dissent (see p. 139).

TABLE 41. Frequency of books in inventories in decades, 1661–1730

Dates	L.W.'s nos. in sample nationwide*	% with books	No. of Orms. inventories	% with books
1661–1670	–	–	22	36
1671–1680	520	18	12	50
1681–1690	520	18	27	41
1691–1700	497	18	17	29
1701–1710	520	19	17	24
1711–1720	455	21	10	30
1721–1730	390	22	17	24
Average		19.33		33.43

* Lorna Weatherill's sample was taken from one year (i.e. 1675) whereas the Ormskirk sample covers ten years (i.e. 1661–1670 inclusive)

TABLE 42. Owners of books listed by their occupations, 1660–1740

1660–1680	1680–1700	1700–1720	1720–1740
gentleman	gentleman	gentleman	vicar
gentleman	gentleman	gentleman	yeoman
captain	steward	gentleman	yeoman
schoolmaster	attorney	vicar	bookseller
yeoman	apothecary	clerk	glazier
yeoman-shopkeeper	schoolmaster	milliner	spinster
yeoman-innkeeper	innkeeper	husbandman	barber
alehouse keeper	grocer		
tallow chandler	grocer		
feltmaker	haberdasher		
shoemaker	saddler		
shoemaker	husbandman-weaver		
shoemaker			
widow			

Predictably, book ownership in Ormskirk was confined mainly to those in the higher status groups: the gentry and those in the emerging professions. These included nine gentlemen, four clergymen, two schoolmasters, an attorney, a steward, an apothecary, a captain and a parish clerk. Yeomen were well represented, with six owning books. However, in other documents, two of these yeomen claimed different occupations, one as an innkeeper and another as a shopkeeper, which would place them among the tradespeople. A barber, a milliner, two grocers, two innkeepers and a tallow chandler represented the book-owning tradespeople, while three shoemakers, a saddler and a glazier represented the craftsmen who owned books. As can be seen from Table 42, no real progressive pattern emerges.

Some of the books, including the hymn book and some of the law books among the innkeepers' possessions, may have been provided for their customers. In fact, the inventory of Henry Jones (1690) lists books in a closet alongside viol cases and the viols, which were used to entertain the patrons of his inn (see p. 158).[33] This provision was not unusual: as Peter Borsay explained, some of the most important 'entrepreneurs of leisure' were the urban innkeepers, whose inns housed theatres, music and even book clubs.[34] I have found no reference to an early book club in Ormskirk, but, as we have seen (p. 129), the same Henry Jones bequeathed books for the public's use. His readers would not be listed among the book owners of the town, but some idea of their numbers has emerged in our study of literacy, which also provides a picture of the cultural interests of Ormskirk's townsfolk in the seventeenth and eighteenth centuries.

THE ROLE OF PICTURES IN THE LIFE OF THE TOWN

Lorna Weatherill also surveyed the incidence of pictures and prints, and found they were fairly widespread (Table 44). This was certainly true of Ormskirk, where out of a total of 110 inventories, 33 (30%) mentioned pictures, but few specified the exact category: print

TABLE 43. *The incidence of picture-owning in Ormskirk, 1675–1745*

	1675–85	1685–95	1695–05	1705–15	1715–25	1725–35	1735–45
No. in sample	15	22	22	9	17	16	6
No. of owners	3	5	5	2	10	9	5
Percentage of sample	20	22	22	22	58	56	83

or painting. Lorna Weatherill found that only 13% of her sample mentioned pictures, but that included many rural inventories where they seldom appeared.[34]

Paradoxically the lower number of inventories in the later samples was caused by an increasing ownership of goods from the late seventeenth century onwards: the appraiser's task became too time-consuming, articles were grouped together, individual items such as pictures were not recorded and inventories were abandoned as a general rule. Consequently, similar surveys are impossible after the late 1740s.

A comparison of the two tables shows a similar rate of change, except that the sudden increase in the 1705–1715 period was delayed in Ormskirk until the next ten-year period, again the time of the town's economic improvement. This delay may also have arisen from Ormskirk's location in the remote north-west, where the influences of London fashion took longer to penetrate.

This is disappointing, because the 1730s marked the 'take-off' in the print industry, when Hogarth's *Harlot's Progress* was so successful that it reached 1200 subscribers, and was pirated in eight different versions. As a result, Hogarth promoted the Copyright Act, passed in 1735, making the production of prints very profitable, especially if the artist, like Hogarth, could engrave his own. Despite the resultant increased cost, prints retained their popularity throughout the social spectrum. For instance, Sir Robert Walpole collected over 300 prints, which eventually were sold to Catherine the Great and are now in the Hermitage Collection in Leningrad.[35] However, many prints were inexpensive, and print shops blossomed in the late eighteenth century. Although no shops sold prints exclusively in Ormskirk, Jacob Stewart (Stuart), the local bookseller, was an agent for printers and supplied the ever-increasing local demand responding to London fashions.[36]

Five categories of engravings were available between 1660 and 1730. The most expensive in limited editions were copies of paintings by great artists, and were bought by collectors.[37] Next were prints from portraits of royalty or other notable people. A few allegorical engravings and some political satires were printed before those of Hogarth, but the only cheap 'pictures' available were woodcuts.

Ormskirk inventories and wills make few specific mentions of prints, portraits

TABLE 44. *Lorna Weatherill's findings based on samples from eight areas of England*[34]

	1675–1685	1685–1695	1695–1705	1705–1715	1715–1725	1725–1735
No. in sample	520	520	497	520	455	390
Percentage owning pictures	7	8	9	14	24	21

or other art forms. Only one gentleman, Henry Tyrer in 1738, and two widows, Anne Bold in 1705 and Ellen Rogers in 1733, mentioned family portraits in their wills, and these are the only paintings which can definitely be identified. Jane Walsh, another wealthy widow proud of her ancestry, left a coat of arms, a most unusual art form.[38]

To be Publish'd by Subscription.

A Just View of the Procession, of all the Companies with their respective banners; the Corporation in their proper Habits: Also the Gentlemen, Ladies, &c. at the GUILD in Preston, 1742. Drawn on the Spot by Mr. WORSEDALE, Painter from LONDON.

To be finely engrav'd with all Expedition; and printed on a Sheet of Super Royal Paper, for J. Hopkins, Bookseller in Preston.

One Shilling to be paid at Subscribing, and another on Delivery of the Print; which will be advanc'd to 2 s. 6 d. after it is publish'd: The Plate will be enter'd according to Act of Parliament, so that it cannot be copied. At the Bottom will be added a Description of the Town, Procession, &c. Also an exact Account of all the Mayors, Stewards, Clerks, &c. of all the Guilds since the first institution

Subscriptions are also taken in by the following Booksellers: Mrs. Hopkins in Lancaster; Mr. Ansdell in Liverpool; Mr. Stewart in Ormskirk; Mr. Laland __an; Mr. Byres in Warrington; and Mr. New

43. Advertisement for prints of Preston Guild procession, 1742.

Some pictures with unusual frames caught the appraisers' attention and were mentioned specifically. Nevertheless, Thomas Tatlock's seven pictures with gilded frames were only valued at 7d.[39] Another unusual artefact was the 'large looking glass and the six small glass pictures fixed around it', bequeathed by Hannah Taylor in 1789. This makes us aware of how far the aspirations of the townsfolk had moved from their sparsely furnished homes of the mid-1600s – before the town's economic improvement – to their highly ornamented rooms of the late eighteenth century.[40]

The appraisers listed some interesting prints in the inventory of Thomas Bradshaw, a maltster (1717) of Church Street.[41] They found 'gild' pictures in the room at the stairhead of his inn. Most likely these were prints of the Preston Guild procession similar to those advertised by Mr Stewart of Ormskirk over twenty years later in the *Preston Journal* of 24 September 1742: 'A Just View of the Procession of all the Companies with their respective banners; the Corporation in their proper Habits: also the Gentlemen, Ladies, & etc. at the Guild in Preston 1742. Drawn on the Spot by Mr Worsedale, Painter from London'. These prints were sold at 'one shilling to be paid at subscribing' (a preprinting deposit) 'and another on Delivery of the Print; which will be advanc'd to 2s 6d after it is publish'd'. The publisher offered a discount of 6d if payment was made before publication, a method of subscribing typical of eighteenth-century publishing. The recommendation of the artist as being 'from London' is similar to that on the Ormskirk playbill, as we shall see (p. 155). A London artist or actor was thought to be superior to a talented local townsman and also to be aware of the latest trends. Mr Stewart realised when he advertised in the Preston newspaper – Ormskirk had no newspaper – that a potential demand for prints existed in the town, especially when various friends could be identified among the crowd at the Guild, in an age before photography.[42] As the Guild is held only once every twenty years, the prints listed in 1717 would portray the 1702 procession. Among those listed as out-burgesses at that Guild were Nicholas Blundell of Crosby and his two brothers, Thomas Clifton of Lytham, William Dicconson of Wrightington, John Entwistle of Ormskirk, his son and four grandsons, Bertie Entwistle of Wigan, his three sons, Robert Scarisbrick of Scarisbrick, Sir William Molyneux of Croxteth, Thomas Hesketh of Rufford and William Farrington of Worden – all of whom were regular visitors to Ormskirk and potential customers at Thomas Bradshaw's inn. Possibly Thomas Bradshaw displayed his print to attract customers, or perhaps he too was among the crowd.[43]

Certainly pictures were displayed in many local hostelries. Possibly some were intended to introduce an element of culture, as Alan Everitt noted, informal exhibitions of pictures were one aspect of the cultural role of some inns.[44] Whether the innkeepers consciously modelled their rooms on those of the gentry to encourage gentry patronage is debatable, but the timing of the arrival of pictures in the inns suggests that possibility. Prior to 1680, no pictures appeared in the innkeepers' inventories, but they featured among the possessions of three local gentlemen and of two wealthy widows. During the next twenty years, pictures appeared among the possessions of no fewer than five innkeepers.[45] At first they were hung in the public places, the parlour or the dining room, where they could be admired and discussed by the customers. Gradually they proliferated, until by 1743 one innkeeper, Mary Stanley, had pictures in most of her entertaining rooms, in several of the bedrooms, and along the staircase and passage was an excessive total of 'eight dozen and eight'(104).[46] At that date, these may have included a series of Hogarth's prints which, according to Sir John Plumb, became 'the favourite decoration of middle-class staircases and dining rooms'.[47] Maps were also displayed in the parlours of inns, for instance in the inventories of both William Bryan in 1727 and James Crane in 1737.[48] Bryan even provided a map in the best bedroom for his guests, most of whom would be passing through the town. These maps would give the visitor some idea of his location and of Ormskirk's relationship to the rest of the county. They would be based on the survey done by Saxton in 1577 and presented in various ways by Speed (1610) or Morden (1695), among others. Few, if any, roads appeared on these early maps. Ogilby was the first cartographer to produce road maps, in 1675. These maps could be bought as single sheets, and were produced on plates 17.5 inches by 13.5 inches, consisting of strips 2.5 inches wide, which charted the roads between various towns and showed the landmarks along the way.[49] These may have been the maps in the inns, or those among the stock of the grocers, Thomas Crosby (1690) and John Crosby (1703), or the bookseller, William Grice (1725), all of whom would cater for visitors to the town.[50]

Once innkeepers began to display pictures on their walls, it was not long before the townsfolk who had cash to spare followed suit. Table 45 charts the spread of picture ownership to representatives of most better-paid occupations in Ormskirk. The barber appears early with the innkeepers because he too was trying to make his premises attractive for his monied customers.[51] The pattern of ownership is predictable, with the wealthy tradesmen owning pictures earlier than the building craftsmen. However, the appearance of John Cuquitt, the husbandman, in 1704 is surprising. His entire possessions were valued at £1 19s 2d, but he had three pictures worth 4d each – treasured possessions indeed.[52]

The few maps and globes appearing in the inventories produced a similar pattern of ownership. As we saw, they featured at first among the grocer's stocks and in the inns. Then by 1727 a framed map was displayed in the 'house' (or living room) of the vicarage. Later, a globe appeared belonging to William Fryer, the plasterer, who also owned many pictures in 1734.[53] Whether this was a globe of the world is not specified, but in this period of 'The Enlightenment', when enquiring minds were probing into science and expeditions were dispatched around the world, it is possible that by the 1730s even humble craftsmen in Ormskirk were interested in using globes to increase their knowledge of the world.

TABLE 45. The occupations of picture owners at twenty year intervals

1661–1680	1681–1700	1701–1720	1721–1740
gentleman	gentleman	widow	gentleman
gentleman	gentleman	innkeeper	gentleman
gentleman	widow	innkeeper	widow
widow	innkeeper	maltster	widow
widow	innkeeper	alehouse keeper	widow
blacksmith	innkeeper	clockmaker	innkeeper
woollen draper	innkeeper	grocer	maltster
yeoman	innkeeper	husbandman	silk weaver
	grocer		bookseller
	barber		vicar
			yeoman
			yeoman
			barber
			bricklayer
			plasterer
			plasterer
			glazier
			glazier

The appearance of tradesmen and craftsmen among the owners of pictures suggests that art was available to most people in the eighteenth century, but two distinct parts existed in the print market: one catering for the wealthy connoisseurs and one for the man in the street. The polarisation of society permeated the art world as much as it did the world of music (as we will see, pp. 160–1). The rich could buy collectable prints and sit for their portraits by Gainsborough or Reynolds, while the less wealthy bought mass-produced copies of inferior works and hoped to see themselves portrayed among the crowd in a Preston Guild procession print. Nevertheless, Samuel Richardson, author of *Pamela* among other early novels, was correct when he labelled the mid-eighteenth century 'this picture-loving age',[54] when both rich and poor ornamented their homes with pictures.

DRAMA AND THEATRE

Another visual aspect of culture in Ormskirk was street theatre, which had been performed in the town since medieval times at the fair or market, or to celebrate some saint day of the pre-Reformation calendar. Remnants of this early dramatic culture remained until the nineteenth century. Each Good Friday, groups of morris dancers toured the district, performing the story of George and the dragon, followed by an 'antic' dance. As a reward they were given 'paste' eggs.[55] It is significant that in Ormskirk this medieval custom, a version of the mummers' play, survived the Reformation unscathed. In other places, Protestants objected to the hint of popery and similar customs were modified to eliminate the saint. For instance in Norwich, the medieval play featuring St George, St Margaret and the dragon was modified in

1552. The revised play, sporting only the dragon, known affectionately as 'Old Snap', survived until 1835.[56] Evidently, in Ormskirk the Catholic influence was strong enough to prevent the removal of St George from the traditional play until the twentieth century. Then all that remained was 'Toss Pot', an amalgamation of St George and the Dragon, but now even that custom has disappeared from the district.

Strolling players had also toured the countryside since medieval times, presenting their shows whenever or wherever they could find an audience. As Sybil Rosenfeld explains, in the seventeenth century, most touring players ' had to make do with barns, stables and haylofts'.[57] Certainly in 1632 several players were indicted at Ormskirk quarter sessions[58] for performing 'a play called Henry VIII' in an alehouse loft during the time of Sunday divine service. The alehouse keeper, 'not thinking that they would have stayed any longer than for the drinking of a can or two of ale suffered them to' use his loft, but confessed that 'they were there for an hour or two'. As the indictment makes no mention of an audience and only nine men were accused, it would be a rehearsal for the play, possibly by Shakespeare.[59] However, it was the timing of the performance, not the fact that players were acting, that offended the authorities.

Gradually, widespread suspicion and hostility grew towards the players, regarded by many as vagrants. In fact, a statute of 1572 included among vagabonds, 'common players in interludes and minstrels' who were not patronised by the Queen or the peerage. The Vagrancy Act of 1597 reiterated these provisions and put players at risk for the next 200 years.[60] The Puritans condemned them as sinners, closed the theatres, and allowed only the clowns, jugglers and puppet showmen to continue entertaining the public with their varied skills. On his return, Charles II restored the theatre, and travelling players were free to tour the country, presenting plays wherever they could command an audience. Nevertheless, this freedom could be lost if their presence was viewed locally as a threat to public order, or their poverty as a threat of an increased poor rate. In these cases, the local justice or the overseer of the poor could have the players whipped and ejected from the town.

Despite Charles II's encouragement of drama, actors and dramatists lost favour during the 1730s because some reckless London players staged burlesques and satires by John Gay and Henry Fielding, such as *The Beggar's Opera*, *The Historical Register for 1736* and *Pasquin*, which gave offence in royal circles. This culminated in the passing of the Licensing Act in 1737,[61] whereby all players, their plays and their playhouses had be licensed by the lord chamberlain. If they performed without a license, players were to be fined, imprisoned or whipped as vagrants. When they were caught, half the fine was given to the informer, while the other half was donated to the local poor, thus encouraging the public to report recalcitrant players. However, most people sympathised with the players and enjoyed their performances, so in practice the justices imposed fines only if there were complaints or disturbances.[62]

During the debate in 1734 on the Playhouse Bill which preceded the Licensing Act, one player-manager, Bill Aston, successfully petitioned against it. He warned that there would be an outcry from 'the frequenters of marts, fairs, horse races and cock matches, who would be robbed of their customary dramatic diversions',[63] because the cost of licenses would prevent the poorer players from performing. Here we have the unrecorded locations of early theatre in Ormskirk. Dramatic performances were additional attractions to commercial and recreational activities, such as fairs, markets and horse races. Roger Lowe described in his diary for

24 August 1666 that 'we went to Chorley, it was the fair . . . we went to see a show concerning the lives of man from his infancy to old age'.[64] Nicholas Blundell's children and the maids also watched a play on 18 April 1715 at Formby Fair, while one of the highlights of his visit to Bartholomew Fair in London in 1717 was watching a farce called *Argulus and Parthenia*. Unfortunately, he never mentioned seeing a play at Ormskirk Fair.[65] Nevertheless, if this happened in nearby Chorley, it can be assumed that Ormskirk townsfolk watched plays at similar events. Plays would be performed either on carts – as the miracle plays had been presented in medieval times – or in booths sheltering the players from the weather and providing a makeshift stage for shows. In 1813, John Brand confirmed that the main attraction at a fair was still the theatrical show, often presented in a booth.[66] Significantly, the rehearsal in the alehouse loft in 1632 took place on 6 May, a few days before Whitsuntide, the time of one of Ormskirk's biannual fairs.

Similarly, the fact that several booths were erected at Ormskirk Races,[67] invites speculation that plays were staged in one of them, as they were at York Races late in the eighteenth century.[68] Traditionally, race week was the time chosen for theatrical performances, because visiting racegoers increased the potential audience. In 1732, players visited Kendal during race week, but by then Kendal had a theatre to accommodate them.[69]

As the eighteenth century progressed, dramatic productions became more sophisticated and audiences demanded more comfort, so better venues were sought by travelling showmen. The upper room in Ormskirk Town Hall was chosen by one group of players. It was also used for many gatherings, including theatrical performances, balls, assemblies and lectures,[70] so the town did not need a purpose-built assembly room or theatre, until the demand outgrew its facilities. As Chalklin observed,[71] the large room over town market halls was usually sufficient to meet the demand for leisure entertainment in the average market town. Specifically, Adrienne Rosen found a similar arrangement in Winchester until 1785; and Angus McInnes noted the same was true of Shrewsbury before 1763.[72] The only details recorded about this use of Ormskirk Town Hall are that, in 1747 and 1748, the 'comedians' hired the room and that, in 1752, the 'show people' paid 16s rent. It seems more likely that, rather than being comedians in the modern sense, the travelling players presented comedies among other plays. Certainly 'comedians' toured the countryside and their performances are recorded at Norwich between 1731 and 1757, at Kendal in 1732 and at Liverpool in 1756, where a traveller reported that the town had 'a neat theatre that maintains a set of comedians for four months in the year very well'.[73] For ten years – from 1747 to 1756 – rents were paid for Ormskirk Town Hall, ranging from £1 10s in the early years to 5s in 1756.[74] As these payments form a continuous sequence, it is likely that all the rents were paid by the same group of players who visited the town regularly. The payments end suddenly without any explanation, but further evidence suggests that one of the local innkeepers offered a cheaper, larger, or more convenient room to the players.

In the early eighteenth century, the travelling players did not only perform in superior venues. Between times, they reverted to their earlier custom of presenting plays in any available barn. Nicholas Blundell mentioned six different occasions when he watched plays at his neighbours' homes – presumably in their barns. In 1708 he mentioned specifically a performance 'in Richard Harrison's barn'.

In 1722 he visited an inn in Preston and 'saw a Droll acted' with conjuring tricks and sword dancing.[75] This is interesting, because of parallels with Ormskirk. An oral tradition declares that a large room behind the 'Buck i'th'Vine'– earlier known as the 'Roebuck'– in Burscough Street was once a theatre, but no documentary evidence remains. Certainly Ormskirk's earliest theatre was built behind the old Ship Inn on Moor Street. Seemingly there was a custom in Ormskirk, as in other towns, that players performed in the inn yards, and later in large rooms attached to inns, where travellers would swell the audience. The more successful players, who could pay higher rents for these venues, organised circuits around inns and later theatres, leaving the barns and less inviting locations for the poorer troupes. Meanwhile, innkeepers sponsored players to attract custom to their inns. In the case of the Ship Theatre in Ormskirk, the landlord erected the building and the players furnished it. One perceptive landlord in Uttoxeter, in 1772, exchanged an outmoded attraction for an up-to-date one when he erected 'a new and commodious theatre in the cockpit at the sign of the Black Swan'.[76] A similar development was the theatre in Moore Street, Liverpool, originally a barn adjoining the cockpit in the early eighteenth century.[77] The cockpit was abandoned and the theatre flourished.

The early theatre in Ormskirk occupied the upper floor of a large, plain brick building behind the Ship Inn.[78] Access was by a narrow wooden staircase from the yard. Many theatres were sited similarly in upper rooms of buildings adjoining inns, such as that in Kendal adjoining the old Foot Ball Inn, which was converted from a weigh-loft over two shops. It was approached by a flight of external stone steps.[79] We have no date for the building of Ormskirk Theatre, but photographs taken in 1926 – long after it had ceased to be a theatre – show an unpretentious building.[80]

Most theatres built at this time were not ornamented externally. For instance, in 1775, when Manchester obtained a license to erect a theatre, it was described as 'a plain brick building'.[81] Perhaps this plainness was intended to contrast with internal spectacular settings, such as the transparent cave of Merlin and the burning lake staged at Manchester in 1777.

Certainly, the actors were proud of the interior of Ormskirk Theatre, as a playbill for 1788 announced: 'Messrs Entwistle and Clarke present their respectful compliments to the Ladies and Gentlemen of Ormskirk, and Neighbourhood, assure them they have spared neither Trouble nor Expence in fitting up the Theatre in a neat and commodious Manner.' The theatre was quite small, 87 ft long and only 23 ft wide, a similar size to Kendal's second theatre, built c. 1778 in the Woolpack Yard, which was approximately 77 ft by 35 ft, and to that built in 1788 in Richmond, Yorkshire, which was slightly smaller at about 60 ft long and 28 ft wide. Evidently, the proportions of provincial theatres were based on London models, for the Kendal theatre was commended as being 'on the plan of the metropolitan theatres'. In the Ormskirk theatre there was a gallery and a refreshment buffet, provided by the innkeeper for his own profit. The ceiling had three domes in it, and from the centre of each was suspended a circular wooden frame holding tallow candles. At the beginning of the performance and at the end of each interval, these were snuffed by a man who was given the nickname of 'Tallow Jack' by the local wags in the gallery. Some other lighting was provided by oil lamps.[82]

Thomas Entwistle, originally from Wigan, and formerly a member of a group of strolling players directed by Thomas Bibby, fitted out the theatre's interior. He accumulated capital, or possibly was a member of a wealthy family[84] – and then started his own troupe in partnership with a fellow actor called Clarke.[85] The 1788 presentation in Ormskirk was one of their first productions, but the fact that the farce was 'as performed at the Theatres Royal [the prestigious theatres privileged to hold an official licence] London, Dublin, Edinburgh etc., etc.' suggests that the company had played a winter season in London before taking to the road, when the London theatres closed for their summer break.[86] The influence of London fashion and opinion was so pervasive at this time that players, like Entwisle and Clarke, used their success in London theatres – where it had been performed 'upwards of a hundred nights with uncommon applause' – to recommend their talents to their prospective audiences.

As was usual in unlicensed theatres, tickets were sold at inns and at hairdresser's, enabling the promoters to avoid taking money at the door. This was one way of sidestepping the requirements of the Licensing Act. Other companies advertised their performances as musical evenings – not affected by that law – to be followed by a rehearsal for a play, included for no extra payment.[87] Other troupes placated local magistrates by donating their takings from one performance to local charities, or by supplying local needs, such as by painting inn signs, giving music lessons or even, in one case, pulling out teeth. Sarah Siddons' company used the same method as the Ormskirk company and advertised, 'There will be no Gold taken at the Door'.[88] Despite all these ruses, playing in the provinces without a licence continued to be illegal until the nineteenth century, and provincial players risked prosecution as vagrants. There was some relaxation in 1788, when Parliament passed an act giving JPs the power to license theatrical productions of certain plays in the provinces for a maximum of sixty days, provided that the players had given three weeks' notice to 'the chief civil officer' before applying for a licence.[89] That meant finding justices favourable to productions, wasting time going ahead to apply for the necessary licence, and spending money the companies could ill afford. Significantly, the much-publicised production at Ormskirk was staged the year when the act was passed. The players were taking advantage of the new climate of toleration.

Considering that tickets were sold beforehand, the doors opened very early – 5.30 p.m. for the 7.00 p.m. show. The timing was similar in London, where doors opened at 4.00 p.m. for performances beginning at 6.00 p.m., and the audience arrived very early to claim the best of the unnumbered seats. For instance, for the first performance of *The Discovery*, Boswell and two of his friends went to the theatre promptly at 4.00 p.m. After claiming their seats, the two friends put their

44. Ormskirk playbill, 1788.[83]

hats on them and went for dinner, leaving Boswell to keep their seats.[90] Presumably, this happened in Ormskirk and the landlord profited from members of the audience having a drink or a meal at the buffet before the show. Actually, theatrical performances in Ormskirk may have been as popular as London productions, because of their comparative rarity, and also because of the large rural area served by the town. It is surprising that no performances were held on Thursdays and Saturdays, the two market days, when a large audience could have been expected. Perhaps the town became too boisterous on those days, or perhaps the innkeeper refused his permission, for he was too busy with regular market customers to cater for his theatre-going patrons.

The Entwistle–Clarke production combined a Shakespearean play with a farce, in what seems to us an over-long and ill-assorted entertainment. However, this agreed with the tradition that some humorous entertainment or frolic followed a more serious play. For instance, when Nicholas Blundell saw *The Soldier's Fortune* at 'Mrs Ann Rothwell's', he 'was present all the time excepting a very few minutes and heard all the Gigg', and on another occasion, after a performance of *The Recruiting Officer* at Great Crosby, he went to watch part of the 'gigg'.[91] By the time of the Ormskirk Theatre, this tradition had been modified by replacing the 'gigg' with a London farce. Compared with a performance advertised in the *Manchester Mercury* (8 January 1771), this was a meagre programme. In Manchester the tragedy was followed by a musical interlude called *Linco's travels*, after which a wooden shoe dance was performed, and that was followed by a comic opera called *The Padlock*. As R.M. Wiles remarked, 'theatre-goers in that "age of exuberance" . . . had come to expect a much longer evening's amusement'.[92]

The division of the audience into those paying 2s to sit in the pit, and the less affluent up in the gallery, visually illustrates the polarisation of society in the late eighteenth century. The grandstand at the racecourse (see p. 173), the pit at the theatre and the private pew were the domain of the elite. Gone were the days when everyone – squire and tenant – crushed into a barn to watch a performance and put whatever they wished into the hat when it was passed round. Urbanisation with its segregating effects had arrived in Ormskirk.

THE ROLE OF MUSIC

Traditionally, musical entertainment took place in the home, particularly among the nobility and gentry. John King, a trumpeter who served the Derby family at Lathom Hall until 1591, had one of the earliest burials recorded in Ormskirk church.[92]

Pepys often recorded domestic musical entertainments, and in 1666, at the height of the Great Fire, he saw the 'river full of lighters and boats taking in goods . . . and . . . observed that hardly one lighter or boat in three that had the goods of a house in, but there was a pair of virginals in it'.[93] This confirms that, in London at least, many people owned musical instruments, especially the relatively inexpensive virginals, and made music in each other's homes. Their music books were supplied by publishers, such as Playford, who sold manuals and songbooks in his London bookshop, opened in 1651.[94]

Probate evidence suggests that this cultural lifestyle was unusual in Ormskirk. Out of the inventories of forty-nine private householders from the period 1660–1690,[95] only three (6%) included pairs of virginals and no other instrument was mentioned. Two belonged to wealthy widows: Jane Tipping and Hannah

TABLE 46. Private individuals who owned musical instruments, 1660–1740

Date	Owner	Status	Housed in	Valued at
1667	Jane Tipping	widow	parlour	£1 10s
1676	Hannah Thompson	widow	(no rooms mentioned)	£2 10s
1689	Samuel Andrews	attorney	parlour	£1
1723	William Hewitt	silk weaver	upstairs	10s

Thompson. The third belonged to the attorney Samuel Andrews.[96] The virginals in Jane Tipping's parlour were listed first, showing both their prominence in her life and also the impression they made on the appraisers. Similarly, Hannah Thompson's virginals were one of five items listed individually. The relatively high value of these instruments – £1 5s for Jane Tipping's and £2 10s for Hannah Thompson's – accounts for their rarity. Even in the home of the lawyer, whose possessions were valued at over £102, the virginals, valued at £1, were prized possessions housed not in a side chamber but in the parlour, ready for entertaining guests or the assembled family, as well as for private enjoyment.

During the rest of our period, only one other pair of virginals was recorded among 110 householders' inventories. These were among the possessions, valued at almost £45, of William Hewitt, a silk weaver in 1723.[97] By this time the virginals – worth only 10s – were housed upstairs in the small cottage, containing only a kitchen and 'house' downstairs and one room upstairs. The position of the virginals among the bedsteads suggests that a change had taken place and that the virginals were purely for private enjoyment.

Table 46 is an excellent example of society's gradual retreat from communal participation in leisure activities – albeit in the home – to a 'privatisation' or individualisation of leisure. The days of uninhibited music-making taking place extemporarily in the heart of the family home had passed. Amateur musicians retreated to their rooms to enjoy making music in private. It was only a small step to dependence on professional performers to provide entertainment outside the home and to what Sir John Plumb called 'the commercialisation of leisure'. Later, music returned to the upper-class Victorian home, where carefully rehearsed programmes were played by talented members of the family in the drawing room, while professional concerts were given on a commercial basis. Meanwhile, among the lower classes where instruments, professional training and entertainment were too expensive, traditional music-making persisted. Folksongs were sung and simple makeshift instruments were played in the cottages, and the gulf between popular and elite culture widened.

Nevertheless, the absence of any kind of flute, drum, viol or other instrument in those inventories was surprising. Of course, music was available outside the home, provided by itinerant musicians or by those too poor to leave inventories. According to the *Gloucester Journal* of 1756, musicians entertained the crowd between fights at the cockpit,[98] while barber-surgeons' shops offered music to their customers.[99] Often music was among the attractions of the strolling players, but there is no specific record of music on any of these occasions in Ormskirk. Even the Town Hall seems not to have been used for musical concerts, although music would form an important part of the balls, assemblies and theatrical performances which took place there.[100] No musical society was recorded in the town during the period (1660–1800) but, doubtless, enthusiastic musicians would join the societies in Preston or Liverpool towards the end of our period.

One place where music was provided during the early eighteenth century was Lathom Spa, where Nicholas Blundell danced with other gentry families in August 1703.[101] The later spas provided music either for dancing or for a pleasant background to other activities, regarded as part of the cure. One of the earliest spas to do so was Islington Spa, in the 1690s,[102] so Lathom Spa in Ormskirk was a leader in providing musical entertainment for visitors in 1703.

The biannual fair and the weekly market in Ormskirk would resound with music as musicians entertained the crowds in return for a few coins dropped into their hats. Borsay noted that race meetings also provided a feast of music, theatre and assemblies,[103] but, although the steward's letters confirm that assemblies were held in Ormskirk Town Hall during Race Week in 1757,[104] neither theatrical nor musical entertainment was mentioned.

Six out of the ten inventories recording musical instruments between 1660 and 1740 belonged to innkeepers, maltsters or brewers. According to Sir John Plumb, many inns, particularly in London, reserved rooms for musical concerts,[105] but again there is no record of such an arrangement in Ormskirk. Nevertheless, from the late seventeenth century, virginals, 'viols and viol cases'[106] appeared in the parlours or dining rooms of several inns, but, as in private homes, innkeepers' musical instruments were mentioned less frequently in the inventories of the early eighteenth century and, finally, were relegated to 'the room over the cellar'.[107] Henry Jones was one innkeeper for whom Ambrose Jackson, the Ormskirk grocer, stocked viol strings – valued at 5s 3d – in 1683. Their inclusion and value suggest that the grocer catered for other musicians from a much wider area who came into the town to make music.

From these facts we can assume that, during the seventeenth century, the townsfolk and visitors to Ormskirk enjoyed impromptu concerts by talented amateurs – often using the innkeeper's instruments – at the various inns. Pepys confirms that this practice was usual in London, where on one occasion, at the Green Dragon on Lambeth Hill, he 'sang of all sorts of things and ventured . . . upon things at first sight and . . . played on my flageolet' (a small flute).[108] However, in the early eighteenth century, the cultural expectations of many changed, and they became critical of such amateur performances. Consequently, to avoid disagreement between customers whose experience – and appreciation – of music differed, innkeepers no longer provided instruments. Their customers had to rely on professional musicians playing at pre-arranged concerts for their musical entertainment, or to be content to join in the less ambitious, and often bawdy, sing-song around the bar.[109]

The void left by the disappearance of amateur concerts from the inns was filled by other leisure activities, which rapidly increased in popularity. As Peter Clark explained, indoor games such as dice, backgammon, shove-halfpenny, card games and a great variety of other games flourished in the alehouses and inns.[110] In Ormskirk in 1700, a shovel board stood in a chamber in Hugh Standish's inn and the inventory taken in 1734 on the death of Mary Stanley, innkeeper, recorded two old backgammon tables in the hall parlour.[111] The appraiser noted 'the men not complete', which could mean that the craze for backgammon in that particular inn had passed but, nevertheless, games of various kinds have continued to have their place – alongside community singing – in hostelries until today.

TABLE 47. Ormskirk alehouse keepers, innkeepers and brewers who owned instruments, 1662–1734

Date	Owner	Occupation	Kept in	No. of virginals	Value
1662	Thomas Gerard	yeoman*	parlour	2	£9
1671	William Watkinson	shoemaker*	parlour	1	£4
1682	Christopher Livesey	innkeeper	parlour	1	£3
1690	Henry Jones	innkeeper	(viols etc. in closet)		£1
1717	Thomas Bradshaw	maltster street	parlour	1	10s
1734	Thomas Barton	maltster	room over cellar	1	5s*

*Although these two men claimed these occupations in their wills, Thomas Gerard held an alehouse licence in 1661 and William Watkinson had a brewhouse attached to his house, so they have been included among the alehouse keepers.

In 1667 the inventory of an Ormskirk innkeeper, Henry Lathom, listed a book of hymns. It is very possible that this was the one published in 1623 by a Puritan poet, George Wither, who had obtained a patent ordering it to be bound with the psalms of Sternhold and Hopkins. This *Hymns and Songs of the Church*, pre-dating the writings of Isaac Watts, John Newton and Charles Wesley, and even those hymns published by Playford, was written when it was more usual to sing metrical versions of the psalms than hymns.[112] As Lathom's denomination is unknown, we cannot be sure whether the hymns were to be sung in church or at a conventicle or, maybe they too were sung in the inn.

The only other places where music could be heard were in the parish churches where organs were being restored after their demolition during the Commonwealth. Their destruction resulted from the ordinance of 9 May 1644, when organs were denounced as 'superstitious monuments' and 'offences and things illegal in the worship of God'.[113] Consequently, in the 1660s, organ music was a novelty to young people such as Roger Lowe, the Nonconformist shopkeeper from Ashton-in-Makerfield, who wrote, 'When I came to Winwick, I went . . . to hear organes. I never heard any before' (17 May 1662–3). Later, he listened to organ music in Manchester (22 December 1665) and Chester (28 June 1666), even though the music formed part of the Anglican services he despised.[114] Pepys, too, mentioned that 4 November 1660 was 'the first time that ever I heard organs in a cathedral'.[115]

In Ormskirk, too, church organs were destroyed. An indenture of the property of the church, made in 1552, mentions 'a paire of organes boght of the Kyng'.[116] These were not mentioned again until 1679, when the churchwardens, listing the church property before transferring it to the newly elected officers, included 'one old organ case with some old organ pipes' in the 'Bell house'.[117] These would be the remains of the 1552 organ, dismantled and relegated to the tower during the Commonwealth. Certainly, Ormskirk church had no functional organ until the third decade of the eighteenth century, leaving the congregation to sing their psalms and hymns accompanied by a viol or flute.

Then, in 1729, Jane Brooke paid £119 12s 4d[118] for a new organ to be installed in

45. *Organ donated by Jane Brooke in 1729.*[122]

46. *Reconstructed organ of 1758, with the Derby arms at the top of the central pillar.*[125]

the church,[119] but, as more money was needed to pay a professional organist, a vestry meeting decided that 'a competent yearly salary shall be allowed for a sufficient organist not exceeding £25 per annum'.[120] The money was to come from an annual levy on all who paid the poor rate, and those who paid the tax could choose the organist. According to Jane Brooke's will of 1742,[121] 'several difficulties . . . [had] . . . arisen concerning the providing of a sufficient . . . salary for an organist . . . and if none should happen to be settled' during her lifetime, she left £300 to the Earl of Derby to invest for the organist's salary. She stipulated that the earl should choose the organist and suggested that the descendents of the first organist, James Parrin, might be suitable.

The parishioners appreciated the organ music so much that in 1758, when Jane Brooke's organ needed attention, a grand new organ was built by Richard Parker of Manchester – another sign of Ormskirk's economic recovery. The first performance on it was given by Richard Bury, the organist of St Anne's church, Manchester, and was reported in the *Liverpool Chronicle* of 23 August 1758.[123]

Thus, although few local households possessed musical instruments in our period – and Owen Ashmore found them uncommon even among the gentry in Lancashire[124] – the townsfolk's need for music was satisfied by music in the church, in the local inns and alehouses, and in the market-place. Those who could afford it shared in an alteration in attitudes to music resulting from professionalisation and commercialisation. Professionals, such as the organist, were paid to make music; amateurs no longer satisfied their audiences and participation waned. Music lovers who had money to spare paid to attend concerts in Preston or Liverpool.

47. Organ on the gallery in the nineteenth century.

Admittedly, the poor, never having experienced classical music, might not have appreciated concerts. Nevertheless, their lack of opportunity led again to a cultural divide, and the polarisation of society spread into the musical aspect of eighteenth-century urban culture. As Peter Burke observes, 'in most parts of Europe, the clergy, the nobility, the merchants, the professional men and their wives had abandoned popular culture to the lower classes from whom they were now separated, as never before, by profound differences in world view'.[126]

CHAPTER VIII

The Spa and the Leisure Scene

Another barometer to measure the changing development of Ormskirk is provided by the town's leisure activities, ranging from the spa in the early years to the races, which continued into the nineteenth century. When the town prospered and the inhabitants had surplus wealth and leisure time, it could be expected that sports such as cockfighting, racing and bull-baiting would flourish. However, such a simple model is inadequate to explain the success or otherwise of the town's leisure pursuits. Other forces counteracted the influence of surplus wealth, and projects which seemed destined for success failed miserably, while others survived, albeit catering for a different clientele than was originally intended. In order to identify these influences, both national and local, and to explain their effect on the leisure situation in Ormskirk, it will be necessary to examine each leisure activity in detail.

The most promising project in the seventeenth century was the spa at Lathom, which relied on Ormskirk to provide accommodation and various services for its visitors.[1] In the early days, Ormskirk seemed destined to become the prototype of a spa town, a forerunner to Bath or Harrogate. However, although Edmund Borlase hoped in dedicating his book *Lathom Spaw in Lancashire* to Lord Derby, in 1670, that 'Time, the Mother of Experience will commend it to Posterity',[2] seventy years later, Thomas Short noted that the spa had fallen into disuse.[3] Both doctors praised the waters for their healing properties, claiming that cures, little short of miracles, had been wrought by their use. Another recommendation came from William Blundell, the 'Cavalier', who, in 1672, declared: 'To these waters next unto God, I do certainly owe my life. Tis now above four or five weeks since I gave them another visit by reason of our old acquaintance. I was pretty well when I went; I drank them eleven or twelve days and returned perfectly well home'. He addens rather ruefully: 'Yet I find them rather costly for my stomach is so good that I eat all before me'.[4] Later, after Dr Short had described the well as derelict, Dr Pococke commended the spring's properties.[5]

The well was popular with the 'common people', who also appreciated its medicinal properties and were allowed free access to it at 'seasonable hours',[6] to use the water for drinking and brewing. Certainly the spring water improved their health, for Borlase declared that they were healthier than most country people, and he used this as further evidence of the water's powers. The quality of the district's spring water contributed to Ormskirk's successful brewing industry, which, as we have seen (pp. 29–33), was an important item in the town's economy.

The well was known in pre-Reformation times as 'Maudlin Well', a holy well dedicated to St Mary Magdalene, but in the years following the Reformation it was abandoned because of its connections with popery. Then, in the period 1651–1672, its 'proprietor', Charles, Eighth Earl of Derby – or rather his tenant, Thomas Hulme of Slade (now Westhead) – restored it. According to Thomas Short, 'a miln stone was laid in the bottom of it, at about a fathom depth, through whose hole in the middle the water constantly boiling up and rising with some force and rapidity, brought up with it plenty of sand and great quantities of cockle and periwinkle shells, which made it very troublesome to the Drinkers, till the proprietor took up that stone and put down others with smaller holes which put a stop to the rising of those unwelcome mixtures'.[7] That was unsuccessful, and in 1670 the problem was solved by collecting the water in a large cistern and then allowing it to pour out through a hole high at the side, leaving the shells to settle.[8] Later, a fixed basin was made below the spout, and by 1740 a deposit of mineral salts had covered it with a yellow rusty deposit. The spring was continually 'brisk boiling up and affording plenty of water',[9] which recommended it to eighteenth-century medical authorities, who considered that spring water which emerged from the ground with some force had additional elements, and was more beneficial than water which oozed from the rocks.

The well was walled with good freestone and, as Borlase described it, 'defended from the violence of weather with a well ordered and decent covering' of wood.[10] According to Short, this shelter also protected drinkers from the weather, so it was probably quite a substantial stone structure with a wooden roof. The ground surrounding the well was paved and a stone gutter was laid to carry the excess water to the highway. This well was maintained much better than most contemporary French wells which, although they were often only a muddy hole in the ground with no paving, attracted a great following among both English and French nobility.[11]

In addition to these improvements, the surrounding area was also upgraded by the 'proprietor'. Seats were provided near the well 'for the ease of weak and weary drinkers'[12] – important considerations, for the spa's clients were usually ill, convalescent or perhaps merely hypochrondriacal. Although these seats were in the open, that was no problem, because the well was closed during the cold weather. Winter closure of spas was quite normal – even when Bath was at the height of its popularity, the season lasted only nine months[13] – and did not detract from their popularity.

In Lathom in the late 1660s, the current passion for parades and promenades was catered for by fine walks 'for both sexes' planted 'thick on all sides with trees which yield a most amiable and reviving shade'.[14] A feature rarely mentioned is best described in the words of Borlase: the field was 'by nature cast into such order as men and women may have a full conveniency for their walks and evacuations without trespassing on either's modesty'.[15] Ormskirk was a leading spa in the development of parades, for the walks dated from the late 1660s. The very earliest in England were in Tunbridge Wells, which were laid out in 1638, paved in 1698, and later became the Pantiles with the addition of colonnaded shops. One of the earliest in Bath was the Kings Mead in 1687, while in Preston, Avenham Walk was gravelled in 1690.[16]

According to Borlase, there was 'a diversity of entertainment', probably itinerant musicians or other entertainers, at the spa. Nicholas Blundell enjoyed these amusements, for on 5 August 1703 he recorded: 'I went with my wife to meet Cozen Scarisbrick, Mrs Hesketh of Rufford etc. at Lathom Spa, we danced with young Mr Hesketh of Aughton, Mrs Entwistle, Mrs Ann Bold etc.'[17] Thus, at that time, the spa was attracting gentry from about 10 miles radius by offering additional leisure facilities and extending its basic therapeutic function. The town on which it depended for

48. Countess of Derby, Charlotte de la Tremouille.

services also profited indirectly from these increased facilities. Unfortunately, the spa and Ormskirk's dependent economic success were shortlived.

The spa did not lack patronage. Borlase lists many who benefitted from the waters. These included the Countess of Derby[18] (who declared it was more efficacious than the German spas she had visited); Major Henry Nowell, deputy governor of the Isle of Man; Lord Strange's nurse; the housekeeper's wife at Cross Hall, seat of another branch of the Stanley family, and her children; Alex Parr – Lord Derby's gamekeeper – and his wife; Richard Dinton, Lord Derby's coachman; and Monsieur Pelate, the countess's gentleman of the horse, who had tried the waters of Bourbon. Borlase was anxious to trace the connections of these socially varied visitors with the Derby family, to convince his readers that the spa was patronised by the north-west's leading noble family and its associates. Lord Derby provided much of the evidence concerning patrons of the spa, as Borlase wrote in his dedication to Lord Derby: 'what I have collected . . . hath been much out of your own observations'.[19] Although Lathom Spa had its noble patrons, it was never patronised by royalty, which would have guaranteed its success.[20]

Borlase was the kind of publicity agent and 'medical economist' who was indispensable in the competitive market for spa resorts. Smollet, recording this need for publicity, had Matthew Bramble say: 'there are fifty spas in England as efficacious and salutory as that of Scarborough, though they have not yet risen to fame, and perhaps never will, unless some *medical economist* should find an interest in displaying their virtues to public view'.[21] However, Borlase's relationship with Derby is puzzling. Whether he promoted the spa purely because he appreciated its benefits, or whether he was commissioned by the earl to write the book, or whether it was written in gratitude for past favours, is unclear. Certainly he 'enjoyed the patronage of Charles Earl of Derby',[22] who gave him free access to the facilities at Knowsley Hall for analysing the water.

As well as commending the spa for its popularity among the fashionable and the associates of the Stanleys, Borlase listed the distinguished physicians, who had recommended the waters. These recommendations were indispensable to the success and reputation of an eighteenth-century spa. His list included Dr Sprattling, Dr Pope (one of the Council of the Royal Society) and Dr Howarth of Manchester. Although Dr Short declared that the waters had 'done many surprising cures and had extraordinary success in the treatment of various ailments',[23] he was mainly concerned with the spring's scientific aspect. In his books he compared the properties of the different waters, the rocks through which they flowed, as well as the various cures attributed to them.

Several of the doctors analysed the water to support their recommendations, for, as Dr N.G. Coley explained: 'It was recognised that the curative properties of mineral water depended not only upon the nature of the substances it contained, but on their proportions in the water and efforts were made to estimate these, so as to compare the potency of one water with another'.[24] Borlase and the earl's personal apothecary conducted several experiments at Knowsley Hall to establish the potency of Lathom water.[25] He used gall – a growth on oak bark caused by parasitic insects – to test the strength of iron in the water, and, as it contained a higher proportion than other springs, he was able to recommend it as more beneficial.

At that time it was believed that spring waters absorbed from the earth a spirit which was responsible for the cures.[26] Although the idea of an aquatic earth spirit seems reminiscent of magic, in the eighteenth century, when knowledge of gases or their properties was in its infancy, this spirit was a valid explanation to contemporary scientists of the chemical changes due to oxidisation which they had observed. The spirit was believed to be volatile and often escaped when spring waters were exposed to the air. Consequently, Borlase performed other experiments to enable him to reassure his readers that, even if Lathom water stood in a bottle for seven weeks, it retained its medicinal properties. Thus Borlase persuaded his readers that Lathom waters were therapeutically superior to others. Possibly he also hoped to create a demand for the waters to be bottled and sold to provide more income for the earl. Borlase made plebeian culture – in this case the traditional belief in the healing properties of water from a holy well – acceptable to the elite by cloaking it in formulas and analyses and giving it the intellectual content required by society during the Enlightenment.

After other tests, Borlase found the water was 'impregnate with vitriol' and some alum.[27] Dr Howarth of Manchester extended Borlase's results, declaring that the waters were 'as deeply impregnated with the tincture of the iron and vitriol minerals as any waters in Lancashire or Yorkshire'.[28] As E.S. Turner said, 'the doctors who pamphleteered on behalf of the spas . . . cloaked their ignorance of physics in rich polysyllables . . . but how the chemical components acted on the body was a matter for the freest speculation'.[29] The doctors of that day had such a limited knowledge of physiology and pharmacology that they could only list the mineral salts as they understood them, and describe how they affected their patients. Thus, Borlase listed the curative agents of the spa water – iron, alum, vitriol and the spirits of the water – but did not specify their effects. Similarly, patients did not expect a detailed diagnosis nor any explanation of the proposed cure. Consequently, Borlase's impressive list of ailments cured, ranging from stones in the kidney, coughs, palsy, scrofula, tumours and strained backs to consumption and dysentry, was quite sufficient to convince prospective clients of the wide-ranging therapeutic benefits of Lathom water.

One of Lathom Spa's most influential promoters was Dr Leigh,[30] a leading analytical chemist, who conducted a campaign in print in 1700 to establish the recognition of Lathom waters' unique properties. Leigh described the waters as being 'one of the best sorts of Vitriolic Chalybeats', and challenged Dr Lister who had declared that 'Vitriol is not to be found in any waters in England, but that all waters of a vitriolic taste are only impregnated with pyrites germinating in the waters'.[31]

Dr Leigh also discovered that Lathom water's strength was 'much the same in winter as summer, which is a conveniency very few in England besides them have'. This was extremely important for any future development of the spa, as the season with all its economic benefits could be extended. Dr Leigh also considered Lathom water unique for other scientific reasons. Amateur scientists were striving to find the origins of natural phenomena, and Dr Leigh's interest was the origin of spring water. In common with most of the eighteenth-century intelligentsia, he consulted classical authorities for a solution. Aristotle claimed that all springs originated in the sea and lost their saltness by passing through rocks. Caesar confirmed this theory, to his satisfaction, by digging on the seashore and finding fresh water, which he supposed had lost its saltness by passing through the sand – the salt particles adhering to the sand.[32] However, Dr Woodward, an eighteenth-century geologist and physician,[33] disagreed with these classical scholars and suggested a subterranean abyss as the source of all spring water. Dr Leigh countered this theory by quoting Lathom Spa water to resolve the argument. Unless spring waters originated in the ocean, they could not bring up marine shells as Lathom Spa water did, so the ancient classical scholars were proved correct. This theory caused considerable interest among amateur scientists, especially among those studying classical scientific theory, and probably brought visitors to Lathom to see the phenomenon for themselves. Indeed, references to the waters by independent agents increased after the publication of Leigh's work.

Leigh's theory was also important because it emphasized the purity of Lathom water. The water's proximity to its source, proved by the presence of shells, guaranteed that the water had less chance of pollution than that of other wells further from their source – an important consideration when the pollution of wells was being recognised increasingly as a danger to health. When Dr Short examined the bedrock through which the Lathom water flowed in 1740, he found that it included white sand, a popular filter at that time. The fact that the water flowed naturally through it stressed again the purity of the water, and was a great recommendation to the more fastidious drinkers. Dr Short also noted 'near it is coal', which contributed to the ultimate disappearance of the well.[34]

Thus, both the 'medical economists' and those interested in hydro-analysis, which had spread from London and the Royal Society, promised a rich future for the well appointed spa, with its associated service town. However, despite all their efforts, they failed to secure Lathom's recognition as a primary spa and could not prevent its eventual extinction. While promoting the spa, Edmund Borlase had expressed the hope that 'a greater Concourse to it may . . . set a larger seal on its power and energy'.[35] That 'Concourse' never materialised. A successful resort needed accessibility, and possibly Ormskirk's rather remote location deterred visitors. Indeed, Borlase acknowledged this drawback in the second edition of *Lathom Spaw* in 1672, when he added a caution that, 'it being remote from the Business of the Nation, the Access to it may not be so universal as is observed in other places'.

Nevertheless, although the Ormskirk area is remote from London, so too are Scarborough, Harrogate and Buxton, and they succeeded as resorts. Of course, they had the advantage of a central or north-eastern position, while Ormskirk was situated on the traditionally remote west Lancashire plain. Even that intrepid traveller, Celia Fiennes, avoided the town in 1698, blaming the dangers in crossing the nearby mosses. She wrote, 'not going through Ormskirk, I avoided . . . Martin Mere . . . it being evening and not getting a Guide, I was a little afraid to go that way, it being very hazardous for strangers to pass by it'.[36] The road from the north was often flooded as it skirted the marshes around Martin Mere, and the bridges over the River Douglas and its tributaries were often in need of repair.[37] Similarly, from the south, the road had to cross the marshes surrounding the River Alt, and improvements were not made to the Preston to Liverpool road until the turnpiking in 1771. Thus the Crosby–Ormskirk–Wigan and the Warrington–Prescot–Ormskirk routes would be the only reliable roads for visitors. These difficulties were not completely detrimental to the spa, for some contemporary doctors regarded the experience of travelling under difficult conditions an essential part of the cure for particular ailments, especially nervous disorders caused by the isolation endured by many seventeenth-century gentlefolk in their country houses. Immediate access was not too difficult, because the spa was fairly close to the Wigan road and to Lathom Hall, which, as the seat of the Derbys, had been the centre of a road network before its destruction in the Civil War. However, the gradual improvement of transport facilities throughout the eighteenth century may have contributed to the spa's failure. Better coaches and the turnpiking of many major roads enabled wealthy northern families, the principal clients of the northern spas, to travel more easily to the fashionable southern resorts.

Despite these difficulties, Charles Stanley, brother of James the Tenth Earl of Derby, was optimistic about the future of spas and decided to invest in cold bathing, another aspect of spa treatment. Towards the end of the seventeenth century he constructed a cold water plunge bath – 'a very compleat Bath with all

49. Bath Lodge.

the usual Conveniences'– in Grippy Wood (now Greetby Hill) in Ormskirk. Cold bathing was publicised by Sir John Floyer (1649–1734), who stressed the Greek and Roman habits of taking cold baths, an argument which appealed to eighteenth-century intelligentsia. Very little is known about this bath, and the only cure recorded for it is that of Thomas Beck, a local 'labouring man', who had suffered from 'aches and wandering pains' and was cured after 'very few Immersions'. However, Henry Prescott, deputy registrar of the Chester diocese, appreciated the bath, for he wrote in his diary on 17 July 1711, 'I rise early, the day very hott, about 7 I go into the cold bath at Grippy, stat in it about 5 minutes and am refresht'.[38]

Lathom Spa had the advantage of being able to use the supporting services of an existing town, a factor which historians have acknowledged to be indispensable to the growth of spa towns.[39] In fact, Fiennes criticised the very inferior accommodation offered by several spas, including Buxton, where visitors often had to sleep three in a bed.[40] When Henrietta Maria visited Tunbridge Wells in 1629, she had to live in a tent, and these primitive conditions were not improved until c. 1680.[41] Borlase drew attention to Ormskirk's superior accommodation. 'Not far from the Spaw,' he wrote,'there are many able tenants sufficient to receive the best Persons with all accommodation and respective conveniences',[42] a fact confirmed by the military survey of 1686 (see p. 32). In 1672, William Blundell, almost certainly, stayed in one of the inns for eleven or twelve days.[43] Admittedly, Blundell did mention a lack of hotels near Lathom Spa – 'the want of convenient lodging makes it less frequented' – but Blundell had been lamed in the Civil War and found walking extremely difficult.[44] However, although the town of Ormskirk was over 1½ miles away from the spa, this was not an unusual distance for a servicing town. Tunbridge Wells in its early days was serviced by Southborough, a hamlet 2½ miles away. In fact, exercise was often recommended as part of the treatment, as Borlase prescribed: 'Let the Patient drink the Water early, on an empty stomach, and walk, jump, ride, swing the Arms, shoot at Butts or exercise gently after'.[45] Therefore, the accommodation for visitors to Lathom Spa cannot have been a great problem, nor can it be blamed for the resort's demise.

Why then did Lathom Spa, which had most of the necessary qualities – a well appointed and medically approved spring, walks, entertainment, reasonable immediate access and plenty of accommodation – never develop and launch Ormskirk as a spa town? The short answer is that Lathom never became fashionable, and in these matters nothing succeeds like success. Another reason provided by Dr Short was that 'later discoveries of several others of the same sort have brought it into disuse'.[46] Specifically, Short recorded the discovery of a spa in 1727 in Knowsley Park, the home of the Earl of Derby. After his father's death, the Ninth Earl of Derby abandoned the rebuilding of the traditional family home at Lathom and decided to build a new wing at Knowsley, which was completed in 1732. His interest in Lathom and its amenities waned, the spa was no longer publicised and its facilities were not updated. As Derby patronage was indispensable to Lathom Spa as a proprietary resort (unlike Bath, which never rested on the patronage of one family), when that patronage was withdrawn the collapse of Ormskirk's promising aspirations to become a spa town was inevitable.

Another, more general, reason for the spa's demise was the prolific growth in the number of spas at that time, when, as William Blundell observed, 'Mineral waters or spaws are abounding everywhere in the kingdom'.[47] The demand was

50. Lathom House in the nineteenth century.

for a few, high-quality, fashionable centres, and, without the earl's support, Lathom Spa was unable to establish a place in that section of the leisure market.

OTHER ASPECTS OF THE LEISURE SCENE: THE RACES

Parallel to the development of Lathom Spa, other leisure facilities, such as race meetings, cockfights, bear-baits and bowling, were developed to draw visitors to Ormskirk in the seventeenth century. Although the lack of consecutive documentary evidence makes it difficult to reconstruct the sporting scene, a problem similar to that of Lathom Spa emerges. The races attracted an enthusiastic following in the late seventeenth century, but by the late eighteenth that had gone, again the consequence of the withdrawal of Derby interest. Another reason was the shadow of religious and political sectarianism that had fallen over the events as they were associated with a regional Catholic and Jacobite circle. Also, national developments in racing were paralleled by changes in the sport at the local level, and those changes did not cater for the type of racegoers at Ormskirk Races. The town's brief spell as a racing centre was doomed, and after a short revival in the early nineteenth century the racecourse became the subject of an Enclosure Award and racing moved elsewhere.

The records of races prior to 1685 are lost, but that year the following advertisement in the *London Gazette* implied an established sporting venue. 'To all gentlemen, that the Ormskirk Plate in Lancashire, which heretofore hath been run for upon the second Tuesday in May is now put off to the first Tuesday in August next'.[48] As the earl was lord of the manor of Ormskirk, he must have been actively involved in establishing the Ormskirk Plate, and the race's success would have relied on his continuing patronage. Certainly, in 1685, the Ninth Earl of Derby negotiated an agreement between various noblemen and gentry from the north-west to provide money to buy two plates for the winners of the races.[49] Lord Derby promised £10, the largest contribution, and received guarantees from the 'founders' to provide plates 'yearly and every year for ever hereafter'. This financial backing by thirty-nine neighbouring nobles and gentry and, through them, by their heirs, assured the races of support and economic success. Derby patronage continued and, in October 1695, the earl initiated a second meeting in the autumn, in addition to the 'founders' event in the summer. A race announcement that 'the winning horse (was) to be sold for £15 at the choice of the Earl of Derby who gives the Plate'[50] confirms the earl's continuing financial support. One of the conditions in the race agreement of 1685 for the entry of a horse whose owner was not a founder was that the horse had been kept in Ormskirk for three weeks before the race. Seemingly, Lord Derby had provided high-quality stabling either at the racecourse or at a nearby livery stable, to cater for the improved standards of bloodstock which were appearing, and also to attract entrants from further afield. Place-names still in use attest that grandstands were constructed,[51] which, with the stabling, would provide revenue for Lord Derby.[52] Thus, as well as supporting the races and subscribing towards the plate, the Stanleys invested capital in the course to improve its facilities, and generally kept it in line with current developments at other racecourses. For instance, among the rules formulated by William Blundell and others for Crosby races was a similar clause requiring entrant horses to be brought to the ground ten days before the race, and to be stabled and fed within 1½ miles of the course. Again, this presupposes the provision of stabling of a sufficient quality to cater for horses bred especially for racing.[53]

The earl's support continued into the eighteenth century, as Nicholas Blundell recorded after the race on 16 June 1724, 'a Gray Hors of my Lord Darby's wann', and on 25 August 1725 'Lord Molyneux' Roan Hors beat Lord Derby's gray Mare'.[54] This Lord Derby was James, the Tenth Earl, who succeeded in 1702, and who lost interest in Lathom Spa. In his weather journal for August 1728, he mentioned a visit to Ormskirk Races,[55] and, two years later, recorded winning the Plate, but added, 'lost it by Rogery at Preston'– by what roguery we may never know. Later, in 1752 Lord Strange, son of the eleventh earl, wrote a letter commiserating with his friend, William Horton of Chadderton, because an attack of gout had prevented him from attending Ormskirk Races.[56] Then, in 1764, Derby subscribed £5 5s towards another annual plate to be run at Ormskirk.[57] Thus, enthusiastic and highly valuable Derby patronage can be traced until the mid-1760s.

An unnamed traveller in 1766 observed that, 'Here [at Knowsley, the tenth earl] . . . used to encourage the people to bring their horses in summer for small plates.'[58] This very significant remark referred to the Knowsley–Prescot races, also recorded by the earl on 12 August 1730: 'Prescot Race in my Park'.[59] Again, the focus of Stanley interest and patronage was moving away from Ormskirk to Knowsley, thirty years later than the spa's experience. Finally, when the twelfth earl inherited the title, he concentrated his racegoing at Newmarket, the favourite racecourse of royalty. There he had a house and stables, and he was understandably reluctant to transport his valuable bloodstock to the North. Thus, Ormskirk Races were abandoned by the family that had been responsible for their foundation.[60]

It is arguable that, though the spa depended almost exclusively on Derby patronage, the races did not, for the early advertisements in the national press – such as that of 1685, which addressed itself to all gentlemen[61] – confirm that Ormskirk's summer meetings were known in the capital and were expected to attract gentry entrants nationwide. These gentry had enough wealth and status to give the races sufficient support, apart from Derby patronage, to have enabled them to continue. The founders' agreement of 1685 included representatives of such leading families as the Brandons (of Gawthorpe near Macclesfield), the Gerards (of Bryn), the Prestons (of Holker), the Standishes (of Standish near Wigan), the Norrises (of Speke), the Banks (of Winstanley also near Wigan), the Bradshaighs (of Haigh near Wigan), the Walmsleys (of Dunkenhalgh) and the Heskeths (of Rufford), who were all supporting the races at this time. They were also involved in the organisation, drawing up rules concerning the entrants, the judging and the general conduct of the race. Disputes were to be settled at their general meetings, and the yearly purchase of the plates by the constable of Ormskirk was arranged.

At the same time the races showed an increasing trend towards gentility, corresponding to the gradual changes in eighteenth-century taste, towards 'refinement'. In fact, Blundell often described taking his wife, her friends and older female relations in their coach to the races at Ormskirk, and his daughters also accompanied him on three occasions. Evidently, he regarded it as a very respectable and genteel occasion.[62] As this change occurred, regional gentry crowded to Ormskirk Races. For instance, Thomas Tyldesley of Myerscough in the Fylde recorded in 1712 that he 'went over Ribble to Ormskirk, where was a great company of ye best in the county'.[63] On the same occasion, Nicholas Blundell recorded meeting 'Lord Peters' and his lady, 'Lawyer Starkey' and 'Parson Letus' (Revd William Latus).[64] Several other lawyers and members of the professional classes also attended the races, and even the nobility were represented, for Blundell recorded that Lord Cholmondley's horse won in 1710, while Lord Molyneux's was successful in 1712.[65] Thus the northern gentry and nobility, in addition to the Stanleys, supported and actively participated in the races.

The aura of gentility was such in 1725 that Nicholas Blundell considered that the racecourse was an appropriate place to arrange a meeting with a view to marriage between his daughter, Mally, and the wealthy – and Catholic – Mr Strickland of Sizergh.[66] Mr Strickland demanded a dowry of £2,000 and Blundell could offer only £1,000, so under the pretext that Mally was not impressed by the gentleman the proposal for the alliance was withdrawn.[67] Thus Ormskirk Races assumed a function similar to that ascribed to York by the Duchess of Marlborough in 1732, where 'all the young women lay out more than they can spare to get good husbands'.[68] Ormskirk Races had become a society venue which the gentry used for a variety of purposes, as we shall see later.

The gentry continued to sponsor the meetings. For instance, in 1696 when the meeting was held, on this occasion, north of the town at Martin Mere, it was sponsored by Thomas Fleetwood of Banks near Bretherton.[69] A subscription list survives for 1764 and includes the names of another generation of well known northern gentry families with notable additions, such as de Trafford (of Croston near Chorley), Blundell, Mordaunt (of Halsall), Patten (of Preston), Clifton (of Lytham), Townley (of Burnley) and Horton (of Chadderton).[70] Sponsorship of the races by major regional gentry and nobility, other than the Derby family, is documented for eighty years and probably started earlier. With such support, the races should have been able to survive without Derby patronage, yet after 1770 their popularity faded and they were not even mentioned in the handbook of the racing fraternity, *The Racing Calendar*. They had ceased to exist as far as the gentry were concerned. Possibly the religious, and even the political, colouring of some of the gentry who supported the races, made the venue at least unfashionable, at worst suspect.

Meanwhile, as we consider the changing support given to a provincial racecourse, we must remember the key changes within the sport of racing nationally, and the changing attitudes towards it. The success or failure of a particular racecourse could be influenced decisively by long-range shifts in attitudes to sport and recreation, and by the progressively widening gap between the leisure culture of the elite and that of the rest of the populace.

This applies particularly to Ormskirk, for in the early years the race meetings were occasions for great jollification to be enjoyed by everyone, and what E.P. Thompson says certainly applied: 'The race meetings of the rich became the poor's popular holidays'.[71] For instance, at the Martin Mere meeting in 1696,[72] footmen were offered a £5 tumbler if they won a race around the same course as the horses. The footmen were expected both to enjoy the experience and to benefit from winning. Indeed a competitive spirit existed between the various gentry households, adding interest for both their guests and their tenants, and ensuring overall success for the event.

Women, too, were invited to run for a smock and a golden guinea – valuable prizes to encourage women (not ladies) to enter the race. The venue for the women's race was advertised by hanging the prize – the smock – on the top of a high pole. Races for women, who were often lightly clad, attracted much attention. As later cartoons confirm, the clear voyeuristic features of the smock race lent another dimension to the race meeting. However, despite these slightly bawdy accompaniments, ladies such as those from the Blundell family did not shun the Ormskirk Races.

The gentry also rode in the races in the early days. The clause in the 1685 advertisement declaring that 'none but gentlemen to ride' was to assure gentleman-owners that the Ormskirk Races were still organised on the traditional principle that horses were ridden by their owners. This was necessary because, following a precedent set by James II allowing professional jockeys to ride at Newmarket, gentry-owners had begun to delegate the riding to stableboys or, later, to trainers. They were usually far more skilled in riding than the owners and so had a better chance of winning the race and the prize money. However, at Ormskirk in 1685 the gentry would not be competing against highly trained professionals, so they could enjoy a participant role in the races. This sports day involved all classes and both sexes, a quality which undoubtedly contributed to its success in the early days.

All this activity drew spectators from every walk of life, including the less desirable 'hangers-on'. William Blundell vividly described a scene which encapsulates the way the early races functioned as a socially heterogeneous festival involving considerable familiarity between classes: 'The same old beggar used to beg in a rhetorical bold way at the races on Crosby marsh and he would flatter the noble gentlemen and tell aloud what gallant houses they kept. I did there once see a gentleman cast a shilling unto him, saying, "a pox o' God take thee!".'[73] The whole occasion vibrated with local life and activity, and necessarily involved the townspeople in catering for the crowd. Two race meetings a year, of several days duration, boosted Ormskirk's economy, adding an economic dimension to the social success that crowned the early races.

Initially, Ormskirk Races enjoyed success largely because in south-west Lancashire an earlier inclusive form of popular culture still lingered long after it had disappeared elsewhere. Deference, albeit informal as in the Blundell vignette, was the key, along with a loyalty to households, to social superiors and to the noble and gentry families. This respect is revealed by some of the wills. For instance, in 1704, Mary Smith chose her 'kind and loving Master' Thomas Stanley to be her executor, while Richard Johnson's will in 1716 illustrates this loyalty to the whole household, irrespective of their social status. He bequeathed 'a pair of gloves to Mr Brooks and my mistress and to every one of their servants likewise a pair of gloves'.[74] Many bequests were made by employers rewarding faithful service, and Blundell's diary contains many examples of his concern for his tenants. This highly traditional social structure was bonded in bucolic play, and the vertical structure of local society was publicly reaffirmed at Ormskirk race meetings.

Although Ormskirk and its hinterland were slow to accept the gradual segregation and stratification in society between the seventeenth and the nineteenth centuries, the area eventually adopted the emergent social structure. The classes were more compartmentalised, especially in cultural and recreational matters. Changes took place in Ormskirk Races reflecting developments in the sport at large, which in turn mirrored shifts in national socio-cultural life. The English monarchy's traditional involvement in horse racing was a major factor, ensuring that the sport would be highly responsive to social trends. Once professional jockeys were allowed to ride at Newmarket, races for gentlemen amateurs were doomed. The role of the gentry now became that of spectators, owners and backers employing professional jockeys, and racing developed into a commercial venture financed by the leisured classes.

Then, in 1740, an act 'to restrain and prevent the excessive increase of horse races' was passed, decreeing that all prizes were to be worth £50 or more, except when they were the annual income from an established benefaction. Borsay suggested that the war against Spain was the reason for this legislation.[75] The government thought that racing obstructed the supply of horses to the battlefield and employed capital needed for the war effort, and so decided to discourage it. Great difficulties were experienced in finding donors to give prizes of £50 in value during the following five years. Consequently, owners concentrated their racing at large racecourses, such as York and Newmarket, where they were sure of competition for several prizes, and the smaller races were deserted. Once the gentry's commitment to the local races was broken, they did not return.

Thus racing at Ormskirk lost the financial support essential for its success. Even after 1745, when racing for lower stakes was possible, it suffered a lack of resources as gentry support moved away. Also, the introduction of professional jockeys effectively separated the pleasures of the lower orders from those of the gentry. As Fielding observed, 'In diversion as in many other particulars the upper part of life is distinguished from the lower'.[76] Splendid new grandstands erected at many racecourses during the 1750s to cater for the monied patrons were a visible expression of this trend and an effective method of segregation. Although the legislation of 1739–1745 effectively reduced the opportunities for amusement for the less wealthy, as Malcolmson observed, 'few were so indelicate as to storm the citadels of genteel pleasure'.[77] This gradual, but unmistakable, recreational polarisation of the classes had far-reaching effects, especially on sports venues like Ormskirk. Once the pleasures of the poor had been separated from those of the rich and the horizontal stratification of society had infiltrated into recreation, the possibility of the whole spectrum of society enjoying a sporting festival together – the kind that Ormskirk had offered – disappeared.

How did Ormskirk adjust to these changing attitudes? Some of the gentry, still loyal to the earlier culture, tried to preserve the meeting, while also supporting other meetings, where their horses could win larger prizes and they could gamble for higher stakes. Despite their efforts, Ormskirk Races suffered financially. For instance, the subscription list for 1764,[78] containing the names of thirty sponsors, is headed by the optimistic announcement that the money is 'towards raising three annual plates or purses of fifty pounds for the term of one year', but, in fact, subscriptions totalled only £35 19s. The Stanleys supported the races regularly until 1730, but eventually they withdrew their support. Although in 1752 Lord Strange was involved in fixing the date of Ormskirk Races and planned to meet his friends there, his real interest was in Newmarket Races, where he planned to enter his colt.[79]

The races continued, but they gradually became occasions for the lower orders alone. In 1782 and 1799, expenses were incurred by Aughton constables after men died at the races.[80] No further details were given, but evidently the men had no money, for the parish was charged. Another glimpse of the scene is provided by the constables' accounts for 1794: 'cash received at the races from those who sold all liquors'. This was not a new departure, for Nicholas Blundell recorded that he 'drank in Rigby's Booth with Mr Heskeine' in June 1726. Nevertheless, the fact that reports of death and drinking are the only ones to survive shows that the character of the races had changed. Ormskirk Races had developed into an *al fresco* plebeian festival with drinking – and deaths – as part of the scene. The compartmentalisation of leisure had reached the conservative north-west.

Certainly the chief explanations for the extinction of Ormskirk Races lie in changes in the gentry's attitude to racing, in increased gambling by all racegoers, in the breeding of superior stock and in the demand for better facilities for both horses and spectators, all of which meant that racing had to be concentrated in a few prosperous centres – preferably those patronised by royalty – and there were only very few of that calibre. Racing in Ormskirk – like the spa – was the victim of the eighteenth-century trend to centralise high-quality leisure facilities, and its demise was accelerated by the resultant fall-off in gentry support.

Two further possible explanations for the gentry's absence at Ormskirk Races during the late eighteenth century are worth exploring. During its early years, Ormskirk Races served as a meeting place for the Catholic gentry, who held considerable estates in south-west Lancashire, despite the punitive economic measures taken against them. They gathered at the races, where they could meet without incurring suspicion. The Scarisbricks, the Cliftons, the Stanleys, the Stricklands, the Molyneux family and Lord Mountgarret all appeared in Blundell's Diurnal as part of a Catholic social network which met at the races, a reflection of the leisure culture of a recusant squirarchy denied the opportunities to take part in political and administrative activities.[81] However, as the century progressed, tension eased and restrictions on their movements were removed. They no longer needed to meet at an 'acceptable' social gathering, so their attendance at the races waned.

The other explanation is rather speculative. Possibly Ormskirk Races were used as a cover for Jacobite gatherings linked to the race meeting's Catholic network. Horse races, involving large gatherings for ostensibly innocuous purposes, made ideal meeting places for political subversion. For example, during Monmouth's quasi-royal progress through the north-west in September 1682, he used Wallasey Races to test and drum up support in strongly Presbyterian and Whig-inclined Cheshire.[82] Later in the Hanoverian period, politics of an entirely different character – those of Stuart legitimism – may have found a convenient and covert home at Ormskirk Races. Among those who attended were Lord Molyneux and Sir Thomas Clifton, both of whom were among the eight accused of taking part in the Lancashire Plot of 1694. Others implicated at that trial included members of the Standish, Dicconson, Tyldesley and Blundell families – all regular attenders at Ormskirk Races.[83] It is true that the accused were found not guilty, but later evidence casts doubt on that verdict. Several documents were found at Standish Hall in 1757 when a wall was demolished, including coded messages and a declaration of loyalty made by many of those implicated in the trial, which was regarded as unsatisfactory at the time.[84] Members of four of the racegoing families – the Butlers, Cottons, Tyldesleys and Standishes – were taken prisoner at the battle of Preston in 1715,[85] while, even after the 1745 uprising, the Standish family still supported the Stuart cause.[86]

Nicholas Blundell cannot be described as an active Jacobite from the existing evidence. Nevertheless, in November 1715, after his house had been searched, he made a furtive journey to London, where he remained until, after several unsuccessful attempts, he obtained a pass to visit Flanders. There he stayed and associated with many of the Jacobite refugees until his return in August 1717. Of course, the whole network would be extremely covert, so written evidence is very difficult to find. Without documentary proof that Ormskirk racecourse was a venue for Jacobite meetings, it would be unwise to presume that the northern gentry attending the races had ulterior motives. Nevertheless, a very real possibility does exist, and it could be argued that, once the Jacobite cause faded, one of the functions of Ormskirk Races had gone, and many of its supporters with Jacobite sympathies deserted it. It follows that if the races had acquired a reputation as a Jacobite meeting place, that would discourage others, not committed to that cause, from attending.

For a whole variety of reasons, Ormskirk Races gradually decreased in popularity in the second half of the eighteenth century, despite the improving economy of the township. After a brief revival lasting only nine years in the nineteenth century, the races ceased to exist, and their contribution to both the economy and the social scene of Ormskirk was lost.

COCKFIGHTING

Other sporting events at Ormskirk followed the same pattern as the races, attracting crowds in the seventeenth century and then losing their popularity and moving away. One of the reasons was that many of them had an aura of bucolic cruelty which was increasingly unacceptable to refined Georgian tastes.

Cockfighting drew crowds to Ormskirk in the seventeenth century. It was well established by 1621, when a lease included 'one cockpit thereunto belonging with all the new building as well . . . standing over the same cockpit'.[87] Originally cockfights took place in an open pit surrounded by spectators. Gradually, tiered

51. Cockpit, formerly in the yard of the Hawk and Buckle at Denbigh, now in the Welsh Folk Museum near Cardiff.

platforms and seats were added to improve the spectators' view. When the fights became more popular, enterprising cockpit owners erected canopies over their pits to protect them from the rain. Later, those shelters were converted into buildings, which could be lit by candles or lanterns, and fighting could continue after dark. The sport had become so popular in Ormskirk by 1621 that Thomas Hesketh of Rufford allowed his tenant to erect one of these more permanent structures over the cockpit. It was situated at Moor Street End beside the house, later called Cockpit House in the Derby surveys between 1727 and 1776.[88] To be mentioned in a lease, it must have been a substantial building – unusual in the provinces. Most seventeenth-century cockpits were improvised or crudely constructed, and indoor pits were usually housed in sheds.

Often cockfighting was associated with horse racing as an alternative amusement during wet weather or after dark, but this was not so in Ormskirk. No documentary evidence from our period mentions 'cocking' at Ormskirk taking place in conjunction with horse racing. Nicholas Blundell visited two cockfights in Ormskirk in February and June 1704, neither coinciding with the races.[89] Similarly, in June 1752 Lord Strange wrote to William Horton of Chadderton, planning a cockfight and, later, two fights in May and June of the following year, all in Ormskirk,[90] again with none coinciding with the horse race. Cockpit Lane, alongside the old cockpit, was near the centre of the town, while the racecourse was on the outskirts, another fact which suggests that cockfighting operated independently. Nor is there any evidence that the cockfights coincided with the biannual fair, held at Whitsuntide and during the last week in August, yet a cockfight was one of the usual attractions of a fair. Cockfighting in Ormskirk seems to have been an ongoing, informal attraction, not tied to any major event but organised on a regular basis, rather like football matches are today, with highlights, such as tournaments, arranged by Lord Strange.

From the meagre documentary records, a pattern of patronage similar to that of the races emerges. The local gentry supported the Ormskirk cockfights during the early eighteenth century, but then gradually abandoned them. In 1704 Nicholas Blundell went to a two-day event where Mr Henry Blundell of Ince won the plate. The provision of a plate suggests that the nobility or the monied gentry were involved. Certainly they patronised the event in the 1750s, when Lord Strange planned the date for the subscription match.[91] Probably these subscribers were similar representatives of the north-west's leading families to those supporting the races in 1764.[92] Certainly, Lord Strange and his close friend, William Horton, were involved in the contest and planned to attend the next fight.

Paradoxically, the Stanleys' enthusiasm for the sport helped to destroy it in Ormskirk. Since the days of the sixth earl, who died in 1642, they had perfected their own breed of black-breasted reds, known as Knowsleys, often rearing as many as 3,000 birds a year. The local lesser gentry could neither finance breeding on such a scale nor meet the challenge posed by such cocks. Nicholas Blundell was typical of most when he enthusiastically attended the cockfights in 1704 and 1705 and noted: 'lost and spent at Ormskirk cocking 8s'.[93] He continued taking an active interest in the sport and built his own cockpit ten years later, where the cocks he bred challenged his neighbour's, but never again did he go cocking in Ormskirk. Lord Strange's letter concerning a 'main', probably in Preston, recorded the consequences of the Derby challenge. He wrote: 'We have beat Mr Morley in the Main by six battles and in the Byes by five and he is satisfied at last that it is not advisable to have anything more to do with us'.[94] After 1770 the *Racing Calendars* recorded that the earl of Derby won most of the cockfights in the north-west, but none was fought in Ormskirk.

The Derbys had so much confidence in their cocks that they bet heavily on them. In the late eighteenth century, the twelfth earl used to wager 5,000 guineas on a main or even on one battle at Newmarket.[95] Gambling was so intense at that time that estates changed owners as the result of one fight. When people could not pay their gambling debts, regulations in Heber's edition of *The Racing Kalendar* (1751) decreed: 'If any man lay more money than he hath to pay or cannot satisfy the party with whom he hath laid . . . then he is to be put into a basket to be provided for that purpose and to be hanged up in that basket in some convenient place in the cockpit . . . and also . . . never be permitted to come into the pit until he hath made satisfaction'. Such ridicule must have been very effective, for this regulation appeared annually until the 1790s. There is no record of the use of the basket in Ormskirk, but a print by Hogarth shows the threat it posed. In 1794, in Preston, the earl challenged John Clifton to a cockfight, where the stakes were 10 guineas for the battle and 200 guineas for the main, the earl's normal level of gambling. In Ormskirk most people were unable – or unwilling – to wager at that level, so the Derby interest moved away and concentrated in Preston, where the Derbys had built a new cockpit off Stoneygate in 1790,[96] Chester, where they had yet another cockpit, and Newmarket, where really high stakes could be won.

Throughout our period this gambling fever, focused on cockfighting, affected all classes, as Pepys wrote: 'it is strange to see how people of this poor rank, that look as if they had not bread to put in their mouths, shall bet £3 or £4 at one bet and lose it and yet bet as much the next battle . . . so that one of them will lose £10 or £12 at a meeting' (21 December 1663).[97] Crowds like these continued to attend the Ormskirk cockfights during the late eighteenth century, but, as the gentry no longer attended, these gatherings are unrecorded.

Inevitably, cockfighting had no future among the leisure activities of an increasingly genteel and refined society. Initially in post-Restoration England, nostalgia for a pre-Puritan 'Merry England' encouraged a revival of animal-torturing pastimes. Indeed, the sport became crueller as 'refinements' were introduced: spurs were attached to the claws to make the injuries more lethal and, later, silver spurs were introduced for battles worth over £5, because they were less deadly and so

52. The Cockpit, by William Hogarth. The shadow shows the debtor in the basket proffering his watch in lieu of payment.[98]

prolonged both the fight and the cocks' suffering. The Earl of Derby used silver spurs, and today one pair of those lethal Derby spurs with the leather guard on which the feeder's name is written – probably used at Ormskirk cockfights – is kept at Knowsley Hall. An example of the carnage involved in the sport is that, during one week in the 1780s in Newcastle on Tyne, over one thousand cocks were slain.[99]

However, men's attitudes to the natural world altered during the early eighteenth century. As Keith Thomas wrote, 'The relationship of man to other species was redefined and his right to exploit those other species for his own advantage was sharply challenged'.[100] This redefinition began among philosophers and poets who re-examined Aristotle's 'ladder of nature' and restated the concept as the 'Chain of Being', in which man's place was below the angels and immediately above the animals. Man's close proximity to the animals made his cruelty to them abhorrent. These arguments convinced the London intelligentsia and – like London's fashions – were quickly accepted throughout the provinces.

The moralists added their opposition by teaching that cruelty to animals had a brutalising effect on the human character.[101] These attitudes spread until people were no longer insensitive to the cruelty and were ashamed of such displays. This revulsion spread in the late seventeenth century, especially among Dissenters. Oliver Heywood made a typical comment at a cockfight in Halifax, when he exclaimed,

'Help Lord! What wickedness committed!'.[102] Roger Lowe, the diarist from Ashton in Makerfield, another Dissenter, wrote, 'I went to see a cockfight. I was ill troubled in my mind that I went'.[103] Defoe also, with his roots in Dissenter thought, was troubled both by the gambling and by the brutalising effect on spectators, and deprecated 'the continual noise among the spectators in laying wagers upon every blow each cock gives'.[104] The spread of these attitudes was encouraged by local newspapers, such as the *Gloucester Journal*, which published an advertisement in 1756 ridiculing this behaviour, declaring that 'music, oaths and curses will not fail to resound round the pit'.[105] Later the Methodists added their disapproval. Eventually the cockpit crowd consisted mainly of the rougher element, and many who did attend took 'greater pains for the concealment of their identity'.[106] Consequently, few records of the personnel involved now survive. Thus another sport which attracted crowds to Ormskirk and also benefited the town economically in the early eighteenth century, lost the gentry's support, became morally repugnant, unfashionable and plebeian, until it was finally abolished by law in 1835.

OTHER SPORTS

Other barbaric sports, such as bear and bull baiting, took place in the district, but again little evidence remains of them. In the early seventeenth century, Ormskirk was renowned for the bear, 'Chester', whose owner had invested heavily in the animal, hoping for large profits. It was valued in an inventory at £12, when two mares and a colt together were valued at only £4.[107] In 1637, Chester wounded his keeper, who appealed to the justices for relief claiming that he was unable to earn a living.[108] Possibly 'Chester' was shot afterwards, for he disappears from the records. Later, someone in the Ormskirk district also invested in a bear, and in 1680 it was baited at Melling near Ormskirk, where two spectators were involved in a fight, received serious injuries and were eventually tried for affray in the assize court.[109] After that the Ormskirk records are silent on bear baiting, which seems to have ceased in the district. Nevertheless, bears continued to feature in the leisure activities of the area. For instance, at Farnworth, at the start of Wakes Week, the mock corporation welcomed the bear with great ceremony as he entered the town. Bears, being so expensive, were usually taken around the district, so the Ormskirk bear may well have been involved in this custom.[110]

Although bear baiting ceased in Ormskirk much earlier than cockfighting, its disappearance can be attributed to the same change in attitude towards cruelty to animals. At the beginning of the period, the activities of 'Chester' were enjoyed by the townspeople, but by the end the sport had retreated to a remote location to avoid the attention of the increasing 'Puritan' element with strong feelings against such savagery. The town's magistrates dealt harshly with the offenders, possibly with the express intention of discouraging the cruel sport.

Keith Thomas suggested another reason for its decline: a 'desire to discipline the new working class into higher standards of public order and more industrious habits'.[111] This concern, evident in the Melling case, could account for the abrupt end of bear baiting in Ormskirk. The men involved had been drinking at the bear baiting and their tempers were inflamed, but the real significance of this case is that the fight occurred in a public place where a crowd of the 'meaner sort' had gathered for bear baiting. When the case came before John Entwistle, the local justice, he regarded it as such a serious threat to public order that, despite the cost involved in transporting the prisoners to Lancaster and of maintaining them there until the next sitting, he sent them to the assize court.

A comparison can be drawn between this case and two other fights – one mentioning specifically that 'blood was drawn'[112] – brought before Ormskirk court leet, the only difference being in the setting of the fight. Although the verdict of the assize court is not recorded, the 3s 4d fine imposed by the leet was very lenient compared with the bear baiters' pre-trial ordeal, the disruption to their work, their loss of earnings and the trauma of being incarcerated in Lancaster Gaol. By refusing to deal with the 'bear baiting' offenders locally, the justice showed that in Ormskirk there was a fear of such disturbances – particularly in conjunction with cruel sports – and a determination among the local gentry to deal severely with offenders. Again, as in cockfighting, the polarisation of society is evident as the lower orders are disciplined and 'their' sport – once enjoyed by all classes – is suppressed.

The situation was slightly different in the case of bull baiting. Ungelded bulls were deemed unfit for eating unless they had been baited by dogs. The violent exercise was thought to thin the animals' blood and make their meat tender. Consequently, some civil authorities ruled that bulls had to be baited before butchering.[113] Although the same reasons applied for the ending of bull baiting as for other cruel sports, this additional consideration prolonged the sport, especially among plebeian society.

No records remain of bull baiting in Ormskirk town, possibly because it was mainly a rural pursuit. However, Nicholas Blundell recorded several baitings, and Ormskirk people were probably involved. One bull baiting was the climax of a week of celebrations following the completion of a new marl pit in July 1712. The week-long festival of barn dances and suppers, called the 'flowering' of the marl pit, concluded with the pit itself being the venue for a maypole dance and a bull bait. The whole event could be interpreted as the enactment of a half-remembered fertility rite.[114] At least it confirms that vestiges of a much earlier culture still existed in this corner of north-west England, and also that, again through traditional sports, society was reaffirming its vertical bonding. By contrast, ten years later, in 1723, Blundell forsook any idea of baiting a surplus bull for his friends and tenants and sold it to his workmen. They baited it before slaughtering it.[115] This incident graphically illustrates animal torture becoming a demoted activity. The elite abandoned the sport as the district around Ormskirk moved into the more humane Georgian era. However, although only a small section of society was involved, bull baiting continued in south Lancashire until the end of the eighteenth century.

Coursing was the reason for much litigation in our period, especially in Ormskirk. The sport was governed by the laws of the leash, formalised in Tudor times, and was a sport for the nobility and the gentry. Lower down the social scale, coursing was also enjoyed, but the attitude towards it differed, as shown by a court leet roll, where 'coursing' is crossed out and 'hunting the hare' is substituted.[116] Coursing was permissible for those holding freeholds worth over £100 a year or leaseholds worth £150 a year, or who were esquires or heirs apparent, but for lesser mortals it was not. The Game Law of 1670[117] decreed that game, such as hares, pheasants and partridges, belonged to the landed gentry and thus hunting game was their exclusive privilege. These laws caused great contention, not only because commoners had always regarded wild animals as a rightful source of food, but also because coursing was allowed over the commoners' farm land, often ruining their crops. In fact, the laws were a blatant example of privilege. Consequently, commoners were unwilling to obey them, but the justices – the administrators of those laws – were the people who benefited from them, so, unlike some other seventeenth-century laws, they were rigorously enforced.[118]

There had been a long tradition of hunting hares in the Ormskirk district,[119] nevertheless local people ignored the laws to their cost. In 1680 six men were fined by the court leet,[120] and in the 1684 quarter sessions, two Ormskirk brothers were sentenced to six months in gaol, while the following day another group were committed to gaol for three months.[121] The landed gentry were victors, but the harsh penalties had little lasting effect, for in 1696 ten men, including one of the same group, were bound over again to appear before the quarter sessions.[122] This time the charge was that they unlawfully kept greyhounds to kill and destroy hares. Evidently, the social network was so strong that no-one would testify that the offenders were coursing, and help the landed gentry claim their privilege. Significantly, although the laws continued, no more prosecutions for coursing are recorded in Ormskirk in our period.

These cases alert us to a rift in local social relations. The 'coursing' offenders were not lower class people desperate for food. Had that been so, the seventeenth-century magistrates would possibly have acquitted them or turned a blind eye, as was often their custom. On the contrary, the offenders in the assize case were a clockmaker, a joiner, an innkeeper and a corn merchant, while at the court leet the guilty included a gentleman, the local apothecary, a juryman and several well respected townsmen, whose names appear as witnesses and appraisers in probate records.[123] They had no need to kill hares for food. Their reason for coursing was to enjoy the sport and to challenge the accepted view of the social hierarchy. These members of an emerging middle class were challenging the status quo, and exerting their claims to be regarded as a group with its own identity, and with a right to one of the privileges which had previously been granted only to their immediate social superiors.

These coursing enthusiasts provide another example of the changeover from a vertically aligned society to one with a horizontal structure. These corn merchants, joiners, clock makers and apothecaries enjoyed their leisure together as members of a horizontal group and combined to challenge the privileges of another horizontal group, the landed gentry. Their longstanding acceptance of the social hierarchy and unquestioning obedience to their social superiors, characteristic of earlier times, was disappearing. Their loyalty to the lord of the manor, lawful owner of the hares, was being replaced by a middle class solidarity which was to strengthen in the ensuing century. The lack of further prosecutions was an acknowledgement by the upper echelons of society that, to avoid trouble in the Ormskirk area, the emergent class's claims to privilege should be recognised.

Gaming and gambling were very popular among all classes of society during this period (1660–1800). As we have seen, gamblers haunted racecourses and cockpits, but gaming was common even in the home. The Ormskirk grocer's inventory lists dice worth 2s 6d among his stock, but it does not mention how many dice that included. However, by comparison, 1,080 buttons – similar articles – were also worth 2s 6d, so it seems that the grocer stocked quite a number of dice for the town's gamesters.[124] As we have seen, the butcher-cum-alehouse keeper owned a

53. Entertaining in the Bedroom, 'Marriage à la Mode' scene four *by Hogarth, 1743.*[125]

shovel board, which was a very popular and familiar feature in his house, for he described two beds as being 'in the chamber where the shovel board now stands'.[126]

Undoubtedly, gaming took place in many of the town's alehouses, but its popularity and the disturbances it caused troubled many townsfolk. Consequently, the local magistrates dealt severely with those who, like Margery Hesketh, encouraged gaming. Even though Margery was disabled, John Entwistle decided that her licence should be revoked. He complained to the other magistrates that 'bad company had been harboured all that night in the jolly exercises of gaming and drinking . . . that it was a very common and usual practice . . . several other gamesters . . . frequented her house in the night time . . . and men's sons and servants haunted the place at unreasonable times'.[127] The court leet also tried to limit such practices by issuing the order that, 'if any man's servant, apprentice or children shall go about or walk in the streets or be out of the house where they dwell at or after nine of the clock in the night', they would be imprisoned and fined 12*d*.[128]

In these gaming cases a similar attitude was shown by the gentry as in the bear baiting case, again stemming from their fear of disturbances and a wish to discipline the lower classes. Again the emergence of horizontal strata in society can be identified. The lower classes' gaming was condemned by their social superiors, while the gentry and nobility gambled freely at cockfights and races.

Bowling was yet another sport enjoyed in the Ormskirk district during the seventeenth century. In 1668, 'Cavalier' Blundell referred to the visit of the Countess of Southampton – Barbara Villiers, one of the mistresses of Charles I – to Sefton, where she stayed four or five weeks, 'bowling on Sephton Green'. He recorded that 'the country came flowing in and she kept a public table at the Hall of Maile' (Maghull).[129] Ormskirk, being the nearest market town to Maghull, would benefit economically from that event. Very few references to bowling mention Ormskirk. Nevertheless, there was a green on the south side of Moor Street from 1702 until the end of our period.[130] Again the same pattern recurs: as the sport had been deserted by the gentry, few records remain. Dennis Brailsford explained that bowling was 'a great vehicle for gambling. In the late seventeenth century, the lack of decorum at bowling greens began to deter the polite. The eighteenth century was to see the game slowly slipping back to the common people'.[131] Certainly this happened in the Ormskirk district, for in 1682 the bowling green of an inn – possibly the Stanley Gate – near Ormskirk was where a gang of coiners exchanged clippings for counterfeit coins, which they 'passed' at Ormskirk Market.[132] The bowling green had completely lost its aura of gentility and its 'polite' following, so a gang of coiners met there, intermingled with the crowd of common people and, undetected, exchanged their illicit wares. Thus the sport of bowling changed and, instead of attracting trade to Ormskirk, it attracted criminals whose activities threatened to ruin the town's economy.

As the leisure scene altered in the eighteenth century, universal involvement in sports and jollification disappeared, and compartmentalised leisure gradually emerged. The upper classes gathered at specialised venues and leisure was increasingly commercialised. The lower classes found that time was no longer 'passed' but 'spent',[133] and as the nineteenth century dawned, fewer and fewer of them could afford that expense.

How was Ormskirk affected? The town failed to establish itself as a spa town, as a racing town or as a centre for other sports, yet, after all these failures, the town seemed to find its real destiny and returned to its original role as a successful market town for the rest of the eighteenth century.

Conclusion

Drawing a conclusion about the many aspects of change in seventeenth- and eighteenth-century Ormskirk is like mapping the shifting sands of an estuary. The tide of change continually ebbed and flowed, exposing successful projects, such as the spa and the races, and then swept over them, destroying them completely or reducing them to a shadow of their former selves. There was a gradual build-up in the overall prosperity of the local community, and the marketing function of the town gradually expanded into an array of shops, but at the same time component elements of that community, such as the congregations of the Quakers and Presbyterians, firmly established at the close of the seventeenth century, were slowly eroded in the course of the eighteenth.

Perhaps one of the most enduring attributes of the town was the sense of neighbourliness. Practical – sometimes passive – acts of benevolence towards neighbours of whatever creed were an automatic response to need.[1] There was a care for the less able members of the community, for instance for the the sick when a dispensary was established in the 1790s (see p. 28), and for the impoverished Quakers when the townsfolk refused to buy their distrained goods in 1676 (see p. 105). A sympathetic neighbourliness transcended differences of religious faith, as various groups suffered harassment for the sake of their religion. This sympathy often extended to a sense of neighbourly justice which prevailed over organised religious bigotries, as when the Presbyterian, Nathaniel Heywood, and members of the local Catholic community were protected and defended by neighbours of other persuasions.[2] The townsfolk's caring attitude was also evident when donations were made to the grammar school, a library was given for general use in 1690, money was left to pay for apprenticeships for poor boys[3] and, in the eighteenth century, a charity school and later a Sunday school were established for the poorer children. The well-being of all the inhabitants and visitors was safeguarded by corporatist-style orders, assuring for them the opportunity of buying good food cheaply in the market, and by indictments at the court leet to ensure their health and safety.

Yet, paradoxically, at times much of this good feeling was swept away by suspicion and competition. During times of national political crisis, suspicion led to conflict between neighbours of different religious persuasions, as when the Catholic priest's library was burnt in 1745, the year of the second major Jacobite Rebellion (see p. 113), or when Peter Andrews informed the constable about the Quaker conventicle at the height of the Exclusion crisis (see p. 105). However, these were isolated incidents, and the overall impression remains of a community determined to maintain the stability acquired so painfully by its traumatic experiences during the Civil War.

Nevertheless, the sense of unity evident in the proclamation on Charles II's return was lost to some extent, when competition for a sharply defined position among the parish hierarchy caused the parishioners to vie with one another for prestigious seatings in the church. Although this hierarchy never threatened the stability of the town, it excluded Dissenters, and another gulf appeared, dividing Anglican Conformists from the Nonconformists, both Protestant and Catholic. During the period 1662–1689, this rift separated those privileged to worship in freedom from the unprivileged deprived of that right. Yet these divisions, imposed by a distant parliament, could not destroy the innate local neighbourliness which cut across such barriers.

The interest of the earls of Derby in the town weakened during the early eighteenth century, and the inhabitants were no longer dominated by the Derbys and the local gentry. Instead, the emergent middle classes – members of the professions and wealthy tradesmen – took over those duties of patronage formerly performed by the landed classes. A clear example of this occurred when, as we have seen (see pp. 109–12), middle-class Catholics took over the leadership of the local Catholic community from the gentry and provided financial support for a Catholic priest, enabling Father Bulmer to set up a mission in the town in 1732. Other members of the middle classes co-operated to finance the schools and the dispensary (though, admittedly, Lord Derby made substantial contributions), and played a prominent part in the administration of the town through the court leet.

Social bonding through charity and patronage continued, but gradually the patronal elite came from bourgeois and professional classes rather than from the nobility and the gentry. At the same time a cultural divide opened up. The rural-based elite had shared a taste for bucolic pleasures and sports with the lower orders, but, in the eighteenth century, a new 'refined' urban culture emerged, creating a cultural chasm between the 'middle class'– with their distaste for cruel sports and their educated taste for literature and music – and the plebeians at large. The latter turned increasingly to those of their own 'class', who provided and enjoyed the same pastimes, whether it was folk music, bear baiting, cockfighting or a rough-and-tumble sports day, and the horizontal bonding of a strata in the community was thereby strengthened.

In the market-place another division was cut, not according to wealth or religion but according to residential origin. The townspeople were privileged with lower tolls and longer trading hours than those of 'strangers', and traders from outside the area were indicted more readily by the clerk of the market than were the inhabitants (see pp. 10, 12). However, as the eighteenth century progressed, the townspeople came to realise that much of their wealth depended on outsiders and, in the age of the dawning of free trade, many of the marketing restrictions were lifted.

Another feature of local change was specialisation, which was the dominating feature of English economic development in the years after the 1660s. As the period progressed, more people made a living catering for the needs of the wealthier members of society, especially for those using their affluent lifestyle as a status symbol. It was the emergent middle class which to a great extent was responsible for the growth of the consumer- and leisure-orientated society. They had sufficient wealth to demand the services of the cabinetmaker, the plasterer, the periwig maker, the breeches maker and the mantua maker to beautify themselves and their homes, and to pay for a seat on the grandstand or a box in the theatre. Innkeeping altered its image to cater for these prospering strata of society. Some specialised in up-market accommodation for visitors to the spa and for other wealthy patrons, providing for their cultural expectations by supplying pictures, books and musical instruments for their enjoyment. Others – the lower echelons of the trade, the alehouses – gradually developed as the haunts of the unruly elements, including gamblers and coiners, while yet others developed a role as the ultra-respectable venue of the adjourned court leet and the centre of much wholesale dealing.

The tide of specialisation also affected the market-place in the eighteenth century as wealthier retailers moved into independent shops where they could trade every weekday for as long as they wished, catering for their own kind of customers. The wealthy customers patronised the specialist shops, which carried large stocks and provided a wide consumer choice in a limited range of goods. The poor shopped at the general stores, where a large range of goods with a limited choice was available, and where immediate payment was seldom demanded. Credit would be expected from both types of trader, and by the trader from his supplier, which caused further polarisation, this time among the shopkeepers. Those who were considered reliably creditworthy could obtain stock from reputable dealers – often in London – while those considered less dependable had to obtain their stock from local suppliers.

Specialisation also affected the service trades. Hairdressing, rat-catching, gardening and chaise-driving emerged as full-time occupations, while dual occupations were becoming less common, though admittedly one of the town's booksellers in 1750 did not feel sufficiently confident to rely on his specialist trade to keep him solvent, and so combined it with ironmongery. Specialisation affected the leisure scene as professional jockeys, musicians, actors and artists emerged, sweeping away performances by amateurs. Within the law, too, specialisation was established in the eighteenth century. As we saw (Chapter I), barristers such as Bertie Entwistle moved from the smaller towns and their routine legal business to the larger towns, where they specialised in work for the courts.

Although the withdrawal of the Derby interest was to a great extent responsible for the demise of the spa and the races, it also caused change in other aspects of town life. As we saw (Chapter III), the gradual withdrawal of Derby leadership increased the likelihood of the townsfolk initiating improvements in urban management through the court leet. As early as 1680, a scavenger was appointed and paid: a need had been both identified and supplied for, by and for the local people. The inhabitants' sense of communal responsibility for their own environment increased in the second half of the eighteenth century as the court leet dealt with increasing numbers of cases of dereliction and dangers to public health reported by the inhabitants.

The various currents of change we have examined so far were all national trends which Ormskirk followed, possibly somewhat later than other market towns in more accessible parts of the country. Most of the changes in the town's religious life also stemmed from national alterations in attitude to various denominations. However, as we found in Chapter II, the gradual exodus of people of various professions from the town in the late eighteenth century was unusual in the experience of similar towns. Although, as Lemmings found,[4] many barristers nationwide did move to larger legal centres, it was unusual for so many other members of the various professions to move away. In the case of Ormskirk, this exodus was the result of the close proximity of Liverpool and Wigan and the lure of their professional opportunities.

Such a large percentage of non-Anglicans – Presbyterians and Catholics – was unusual in urban centres, as we saw in Chapter V. The presence of so many Catholics laid the town open to accusations of Jacobite activity, but they cannot be proved. The town's unusually high literacy rates were probably due to the presence of so many active Protestants, whose belief that bible-reading was essential in the process of salvation led to great efforts to teach reading.

Now we come to the two most pertinent questions. Was there a 'crisis' in the town during the period 1660–1800 as suggested by Peter Clark and Paul Slack (see p. viii)? Did Ormskirk start 'to shrink and stagnate'?[5] The answer to that question must be in the negative, although some aspects of the town's life did experience individual crises. However, the disappearance of the spa and the reduction in the size of both the Quaker and the Presbyterian congregations cannot be described as full-scale crises affecting the whole town. Both the Anglican and the Catholic congregations in the town steadily increased. There was continual expansion in the market, and specialist shops brought ever-increasing trade and economic opportunities into the town. In fact, progress was evident in most sections of the town's economy, while in the cultural field the inhabitants' readiness to support their own schools and theatre in the later eighteenth century indicates increasing cultural activity. Certainly, 'crisis' would not be a valid description of that situation.

Finally, how far did an 'Urban Renaissance' affect the town? The attitudes of the Enlightenment definitely influenced many spheres of the town's life. Folk wisdom of the holy well was converted into scientific explanations by the 'medical economists' of Lathom Spa. Bear baiting and cockfighting fell victims to the new attitudes to savagery against animals. Suspicion and hatred of other religions faded, and tolerance was established among the townspeople. Certainly, Ormskirk could make no claim to be a 'leisure town', as defined by McInnes in his debate with Borsay,[6] even though commercialised leisure activities increased, assemblies were held in the Town Hall and walks were constructed around the spa. As far as the townscape was concerned, there were a few beautiful Georgian buildings erected, mainly on Burscough Street, and both the 1730 church and the Town Hall had features of Palladian architecture. Durable building materials were used increasingly as the town was transformed from one of almost entirely wattle and daub cottages to a brick-built town. All considered, it can be said that the town did experience a limited 'Urban Renaissance', but then Borsay himself declared that he had 'always tried to avoid conveying the impression that the movement was one that affected all towns equally'.[7]

Thus we come to the end of our exploration of Ormskirk's changing fortunes in the period 1660–1800. Perhaps this picture of the effect of the changing currents of national trends on the small north-western market town of Ormskirk, and also of its particular experiences, will contribute towards a better understanding of the history of market towns in general during this period, as well as to a clearer and more detailed appreciation of the vigour, diversity and richness of life in urban Lancashire in those turbulent years.

Epilogue

A glance at the years following our period confirms that many of the trends already identified continued to influence the market town. Specialisation escalated among the craftsmen and traders, and more cottage property was crammed into the space at the rear of existing houses and shops with little regard for health or sanitation. The Anglican Church retained its influence over education, but its absolute control was gradually eroded in the twentieth century, and, although the social divide was very apparent in the leisure activities of the town, the Church struggled to abolish any visible signs of it within its doors.

The market continued to attract trade, despite the radical alteration in tolls and stallages imposed by Lord Derby in the 1830s.[1] Once the railway was constructed from Liverpool to Ormskirk and through to Preston in 1849, customers came from more distant places, and later in the century rail excursions were organised specifically to visit the market. Now coaches bring similar excursions to the much larger market of the twentieth century.

The weaving of cotton and fustian continued with many weavers still using handlooms and, although one cotton factory was recorded in 1839 – probably one of those established in the 1790s – by the time of the 1851 census only seven cotton workers remained in the town.[2] Later in the century two attempts were made to set up cotton factories in the town, one in 1856 and another in 1876, but both failed.[3] However, as in the later years of the eighteenth century, producers of finished textile goods, such as hatters, tailors and upholsterers, were well represented among those employed in the township.

Handloom weaving of silk was more successful, employing 224 workers in 1841, increasing to 300 in 1851, many of these supplying the Macclesfield silk industry. Two silk mills were set up in the town, but in the mid-1850s, when the English silk industry fell into recession in the face of French competition, one of the Ormskirk mills closed and the other was failing. By the time of the 1861 census the number of silk weavers had fallen to 174.[4]

The long-established leather workers ranging from saddlers to shoemakers held their place among the craftsmen of the town. Most of these workers, too, were employed in finishing products rather than in processing the raw materials, thus continuing a trend noted earlier (see p. 25). Few of the craftsmen employed many workers. In fact, the roper employing forty-two workmen was one of the largest employers in the town. Rope and leather goods were very important products of the town until the early twentieth century.

Skilled metal workers – watch and clockmakers, gold balance makers and gun makers – continued to practise their trades. The use of steam engines and coal as sources of power polluted the air with fumes and blackened property, as the steam cornmill, the steam printing works, the iron foundry and several breweries were established. Pollution increased when the gas works opened in 1833 and supplied the town with street lighting, and also when the railway expanded during the late nineteenth century.[6] Although the railway brought customers into Ormskirk, it also provided a convenient means of transport into Liverpool, and increasingly members of the professions moved their offices into the larger town. Commerce followed in their wake, leaving Ormskirk devoid of those who may have provided leadership later in the century, when the township desperately needed it.

Nevertheless, an increasing number of workers were employed providing services for those who came into the town and also for its inhabitants. As the population of the township increased – to 4,891 by 1841 – more opportunities arose for specialists. Many of these workers used the inns as a base, while those who had formerly offered services at the inns moved into their own offices. For instance, banking moved into Ormskirk Savings Bank on Lydiate Lane (Derby Street) in 1823, and later a second bank opened in Church Street.[7] Insurance companies, too, deserted the inns and moved into offices. For instance, the Phoenix, the Royal Farmers and the Atlas Fire and Life Insurance companies established offices. The first two were in Church Street and the third was in Aughton Street. The traditional sale of corn also moved from the inns to the Corn Exchange next to the Kings Arms in Moor Street. Meanwhile the inns' traditional role expanded as they provided a necessary service for the increasing number of travellers on the turnpike road north from Liverpool. Several small lodging houses were also opened, many to cater for seasonal Irish labourers who had no accommodation on the farms.

However, during the 1840s, conditions developed which threatened to sweep away all the achievements of the town's renaissance. As the court leet met only twice a year, it was incapable of effective administration in the face of the ever-increasing population, and public health in particular was neglected. The many houses at the back of older property and around courtyards had few pumps, wells or privies. In Aughton Street, middens and privies were often sited on higher land behind the houses and their effluent seeped down through the houses and onto the roadway. As we have seen (p. 57), there was no continuous system of sewers, and so the sewers' contents spilled into the brook, which emerged below the fish stones and ran down Aughton Street, onto the fields behind Church Street, or later down the railway cutting. The burial ground was so full that it could not 'be disturbed to the depth of one foot without turning up . . . mouldering remains.[8]

The crisis came when the Irish potato harvest failed and the victims of the famine fled to England, bringing with them sicknesses associated with starvation. The many seasonal labourers crowded into Ormskirk with their relatives and friends. Lodging houses, many run by Irish settlers, rapidly filled with refugees until some were so full that, for instance, forty people lived in two rooms with no windows, only a 'hole in the roof', and had the use of only two privies.[9]

Conditions deteriorated so much that a group of ratepayers asked the central board of health – established after the Public Health Act of 1848 – to send an inspector to set up a local board of health. When cholera struck the town, Robert Rawlinson, the inspector, reported that 'the rate of mortality in Ormskirk . . . [1849] . . . was higher than the worst district in London during the past year of excessive disease and cholera'. As a result of his report, a local board of health was set up, Greetby Hill reservoir was constructed to supply piped water to the town in 1853 and a sewage scheme was installed in 1854. Slowly the epidemic decreased and the dangers passed.[10]

Gradually many of the duties of the old court leet were taken over by the new board of health – despite the fact that most of its members served on both administrations – while several of its other duties were incorporated into the work of the Lancashire Constabulary. Their original police station was in Burscough Street, but in 1850 a new centre was built in Lydiate Lane (Derby Street), providing a police station and a magistrates' court, Although the quarter sessions had moved to Liverpool in 1817, the magistrates continued to meet in Ormskirk where the county court had been established in 1841. In 1874 the board of health acquired the market tolls from Lord Derby, and thus the control of the market passed from his court leet to the new authority. The court leet was then virtually redundant, so the following year it was disbanded. The residue of its funds was used together with public subscriptions to build a clock tower to replace the ruined market cross. Following the reform of local government in 1894, Ormskirk urban district council was elected to replace the board of health as the town's main administrative body, and the rural districts came under the control of the West Lancashire rural district council. These were combined later in the twentieth century to form the West Lancashire district council.

There was a second period of economic hardship in the town in the late 1880s which caused unrest among the Irish labourers, eventually leading 200 of them to terrorise Ormskirk in February 1887, marching through the streets, brandishing their sickles and threatening the inhabitants. The police, under Superintendent Jervis, had tried to alleviate the conditions by arranging for soup kitchens to cater particularly for children during the winters of 1886 and 1887, and also by distributing warm clothes to the needy, but they had been unable to placate the Irish. Earlier in the century, soup kitchens had been set up by the workhouse, but evidently it had been unable to cope with these later crises.[11]

The workhouse originated in the early 1730s when the overseers of the poor and the churchwardens of various townships in south-west Lancashire formed unions with the intention of housing their poor in workhouses instead of relieving them in their own homes. Ormskirk was chosen as the site for two workhouses. One opened in 1732 in Aughton Street to serve the area between Lydiate and Burscough, and a second opened in 1734 in Moor Street to cater for the townships immediately north of Liverpool and extending to neighbouring townships, such as Altcar and Rainford.[12] In 1839 the Aughton Street workhouse was sold and the two institutions were combined in the Moor Street premises. In 1853 a new workhouse complex to house all the paupers was opened on what is now the site of Ormskirk Hospital. In fact, some of those early buildings are still used as ancillary buildings by the modern Ormskirk Hospital. During most of the nineteenth century the workhouse was the only place in Ormskirk where the sick could be nursed.

Medicine and daily treatment were available at the dispensary, which moved in 1830 from Lydiate Lane into the neoclassical building on Burscough Street – now the farmers' club,[13] but there was a great need for a local hospital. Finally, in 1896, the cottage hospital in Hants Lane was built by public subscription, and opened by the Countess of Derby. Shortly afterwards in 1902 the infectious diseases hospital opened in Green Lane. However, post-war medical research drastically reduced the number of patients in the isolation hospital, and it became a hospital for disabled children before being demolished to make way for sheltered accommodation. Meanwhile the workhouse had evolved into the Wigan Road Hospital, which has been virtually rebuilt in the 1990s.

Friendly societies operated in the town in the early nineteenth century. Each week they collected contributions to provide for members who fell sick. Some extended their benefits to helping the unemployed and to provide for other needs. One, appropriately named the Cow Club, even compensated farmers if their animals died or fell sick. This particular club operated at the Stanley Gate inn at Bickerstaffe and no doubt similar clubs were established in the township. Other friendly societies were organised by the Sunday schools and also by the Working Men's institute. This institute originated as the Working Men's Reading and News Rooms, which opened in 1865 in Burscough Street and immediately attracted over 300 members. Three years later a purpose-built institute was erected by Thomas Riding in Moor Street on land donated by Lord Derby. It was opened by Lord Skelmersdale and housed a free library, a news room, a billiard room and a cocoa room. It was hoped that it would attract working men from the public houses and so combat the problem of drunkenness, which was rife in the town at that time. Actually there was already a public library in the town, which had opened in the vacant premises of the old charity school in 1854 and later moved into Aughton Street. Originally it had 1,200 volumes, and its popularity increased until by the 1870s it was issuing about 12,000 books each year.

THE RELIGIOUS SCENE AFTER 1800

The changing national focus of worship and also alterations in social attitudes countrywide affected the later history of the Anglican Church in Ormskirk and resulted in alterations being made both to its internal plan and to the fabric of the church. Essential maintenance escalated as the century progressed, until a major restoration was needed in the 1870s.

In the 1820s the spire was struck by lightning and was again rebuilt. Shortly afterwards the three-decker pulpit was moved to the eastern end of the nave, where it obscured the view of the altar. This alteration has significance for us as it confirms that in early nineteenth-century Ormskirk the emphasis in the services was still on preaching, as it had been in Nathaniel Heywood's day. During the winter of 1828–1829, services were held in the Town Hall while repairs were done to the church, and, in response to the bishop's campaign, several free pews were provided.[14]

The ownership of pews in the church caused great controversy during the next sixty years. An egalitarian movement within the Anglican ranks gained momentum, condemning the ostentation and segregation resulting from private pews, and yet another group complained that box pews and galleries cluttered the church and obstructed the view. The bishops appealed to the parish churches to clear the floor space and install benches, advocating a second 'uniforming' of the church, similar to that done in Ormskirk in 1634 in response to the Laudian movement.

The vicar sympathised with these opinions, but his support was less than enthusiastic for he relied on the income from pew rents to supplement his meagre stipend. Most of the pew owners agreed that the box pews impeded the view, but if they forfeited them they wanted compensation in the form of seating solely for their own use. Each party had a valid point, and this controversy continued until the 1870s, when pew rents were replaced by regular collections and the church underwent a drastic restoration programme.

The influence of the Oxford Movement also spread to Ormskirk in the mid-nineteenth century. Its members advocated a return to a medieval style of worship with a revival of ritual and an emphasis on mystery and sanctity. In fact, their aims resembled those of Archbishop Laud, who tried to restore 'the beauty of holiness' (see p. 73). Emphasis during worship was to be on the altar, the choir was to be robed and seated in the chancel, and stained glass windows were to be installed to give the churches a dim, mysterious light.

Ormskirk's first response was to install stained glass windows. Nathaniel Heywood's descendent, John Pemberton Heywood, donated glass for the east window in 1859, his widow donated a replacement after the restoration of the church and William Welsby donated the baptistry windows.[15] Then the pulpit was moved to the north-eastern side of the nave to open the view of the altar. Later Revd Sheldon, who was appointed in 1870, wore his surplice in church and turned towards the east at certain times during the service, much against the wishes of the majority of his traditionally low church congregation.[16] Other responses to the Oxford Movement were incorporated into the Gothic restoration of the church between 1877 and 1891.

However, the initial improvements were made for purely sanitary reasons. Hundreds of burials within the church had resulted in an accumulation of remains only inches below the floor and the stench permeated the building. The remains were cleared, stone flags were laid on a thick layer of concrete and a new heating system with floor-level grills was installed. Then, as the pews had been removed, they were replaced with new uniform seating. The galleries were taken down, the plaster scraped off the walls and the stonework renovated. A new pulpit, lectern and choirstalls were put in place. The old vestry was demolished and a new north-eastern part of the church was built, incorporating the old northern wall of the chancel. The eastern chancel wall and the northern walls were rebuilt, a porch was added, a new four-faced clock was put on the tower to replace the single-faced clock on the steeple and almost the whole church was reroofed – a truly major restoration.[17]

It did not meet with universal approval, for, despite acknowledging that repairs were essential, many felt that the old church incorporated the history of its own development, and the nineteenth-century Gothic restoration had destroyed that aura of antiquity. In fact, in July 1878 the great William Morris, secretary and founder of the Society for the Protection of Ancient Buildings, described the proposed alterations as 'a deliberate act of vandalism'. That was not the opinion of Lord Derby, who had contributed large sums to the project.

Since then little has been done to the structure. The gas lighting of the 1880s was replaced by electric in 1912 and updated in 1972; oil heating and, later, gas central heating was installed, and in the 1980s the lead on the aisle roofs was replaced with stainless steel. The function of certain areas within the church has been altered as first the Derby chapel, an ancient visible sign of privilege, became the War Memorial chapel after the Great War, and later the room at the base of the tower with kitchen and toilet facilities was created as a focus for social activities. In 1993 the present Church House was built to replace the one built in 1909 in Church Street, which was sold to a developer in 1988. This attractive modern building now provides accommodation for more informal services and caters for the Church's increasing social role in the modern world.

THE FREE CHURCHES

The decline of the Presbyterian congregation in Aughton Street continued. By 1851 its Unitarian minister could claim only ten members. Nevertheless, the church was not finally closed until 1886, when its minister for sixty-two years, Revd Fogg, died. During the 1920s it was used as a cookery centre by the Lancashire Education Authority, and then for several years it reverted to its former use as a place of worship, this time for the Free Evangelical Mission. Finally, in the 1960s, the church was closed and the building demolished.[18]

Although Ormskirk Methodist Church was made the head of the circuit in 1811, three years passed before they moved from their unsuitable quarters into the new church. This two-storeyed building, which cost £1,000, was in Chapel Street – possibly on the site of the old Presbyterian chapel of 1696. The group continued to hold open air meetings, and in 1824 it registered a plot of ground opposite the Wheatsheaf for public worship.[19]

During the 1840s and 1850s, the Methodist Church suffered stagnation and dissension within its ranks. However, in the following decade, worshippers filled the pews and the centre of the upper storey had to be removed to incorporate the galleries into the church and so to increase its seating capacity from 248 to 387. Despite these improvements, the caretaker and his wife were paid only £2 a quarter, a sign of the incessant financial problems experienced by the Methodists until the mid-twentieth century.

Despite this lack of finance, in 1874 the Revd Harris proposed that a new church should be built in Derby Street. Plans were made and discarded, and he moved on, but finally in 1876 he was invited back to lay the foundation stone. Two years later, amid great celebrations, the new Wesleyan Methodist church was opened. It is significant that many people from the other denominations in Ormskirk contributed towards the cost of the new church, thus continuing that co-operation and neighbourliness so evident in earlier times.

Worship and social life continued in the new church with highlights such as Sunday School treats and choir outings. However, despite many fundraising efforts, it was impossible to finance the intended upgrading of the old chapel into an acceptable Sunday School. Consequently, in 1886 the new church was partitioned behind the pulpit to provide more accommodation. The old church was sold for £285 and later became a centre for the West Lancashire Council building department, finally being demolished to make way for the new bypass in the 1990s. Meanwhile, nothing was altered in the new building until 1924, when electic lighting was installed. During the Second World War the Sunday School was taken over by a day school, and three years later the old cellar kitchen was replaced. Almost 100 years after the opening of their church, the Methodists embarked on another major building programme, resulting in the opening of Langham Hall on 6 July 1974. Today plans are afoot for further alterations, but the culmination of that scheme is far in the future.

The Ormskirk Independents or Congregationalists followed a very similar path to the Methodists. They had two attempts to establish a church: once in 1801, aborted after constant harassment, and another in 1811, which also had to be abandoned. Finally, in 1836, with the help of their fellow Congregationalists in Liverpool, they established a church to seat between 300 and 400 people in Chapel Street, nearer to Moor Street than that built by the Wesleyan Methodists. During the 1870 revival, they too renovated their buildings. In the second half of the twentieth century there was a movement towards unity in both the Presbyterian and the Congregational churches, which resulted in the two denominations combining to form the United Reformed Church. This movement had further repercussions in Ormskirk, resulting in the new group joining the Methodists to become the Methodist United Reformed Church, and their church became the community centre.

During the early years of the twentieth century, the Congregationalists let their Sunday School alongside the church to a non-denominational Evangelist. His services drew crowds of worshippers whose noisy enthusiasm disturbed those in the church next door. Chorus singing and lantern lectures were characteristic of the work of the missions in Ormskirk at this time. One had been established in the old dispensary building in Burscough Street and another, the Railway Mission, was based further down that road in the single-storey building next to the Brandreth House. Cottage Lane Mission which, from its inception in 1884, owed allegiance to the Church of England, started in a cottage before the completion of its chapel in 1888. It was finally taken over by Christ Church, Aughton, many years later. The Independent Pentecostal Gospel Mission was opened in 1957 in a converted shoe factory behind Church Street, and it still continues its work, both in the UK and abroad.

The Primitive Methodists had their first meeting in Ormskirk in 1878 in the Derby Chambers in Burscough Street, and later moved to the Exchange Rooms in Railway Road, but they did not attract many members and were forced to close. The same was not true of the Christadelphians, who also held their first meeting in 1878, in the Corn Exchange in Moor Street. They flourished and moved into their own hall in Moorgate in 1922.

THE CATHOLICS

The death of Father Crook on 10 January 1800 marked the end of an era for the Catholics. He had seen the Catholics emerge from the shadows to become a group which could proclaim its faith, practise its own religion and establish its own schools. Father Crook's position was taken by Father Talbot, who was to remain at Ormskirk for forty-five years, and was to see the township's population increase dramatically from 2,554 people in 1801 to 6,183 in 1851. Many of the newcomers were Irish Catholics who had fled from the famine in the 1840s. In fact, the Irish accounted for 10% of Ormskirk's population in 1841, and within ten years that had risen to 20%. Similarly, pupil numbers at the Catholic school increased until by 1838 there were 83 boys and 110 girls on the roll.[20]

In 1807 Father Talbot established the Ormskirk Catholic Society, a friendly society which provided for the sick, the unemployed and the elderly, and also became a focus for many social activities. By the middle of the century the Catholics desperately needed a larger church, so they embarked on many fundraising efforts and finally St Anne's church was built. It was opened on 7 August 1850 by the Right Revd Dr George Brown, who two weeks later became the first Catholic Bishop of Liverpool, when the Catholic Hierarchy was restored.

Father Hickey, who was rector at St Anne's from 1865 until his death in 1888, founded a Temperance League to combat the acute problem of drunkenness, particularly among the Irish in his parish. He also initiated fundraising for a new school, because the small school at Town End was overcrowded. Consequently, when larger premises were required to comply with the Education Act of 1870, it was possible to open the new Catholic school in 1872 in Hants Lane near the homes of many Irish families.

In the early 1890s the care of the missions, or parishes, run by the Benedictines was assigned to individual monasteries, and St Anne's became the responsibility of St Edmund's at Douai, as it is today. In 1903 the monks were expelled from France and settled in their present home at Woolhampton in Berkshire. The Ormskirk congregation struggled to clear the debts on St Anne's church, and bazaars became a regular feature of church life. One in 1907 was particularly successful, raising an amazing £1,117 17s 6d. Eventually, by 1916, the debts were cleared and St Anne's church could be consecrated. Once that had been done, gatherings of a more social nature could be organised. The highlights of the years between the wars were St Anne's annual galas instigated by Father Egerton. The processions, the Rose Queens, Morris Dancers, the sports, the side-shows and the dancing became legendary in the town.

St Anne's centenary in 1950 was celebrated with a service led by Archbishop Downey, followed by 'as much jollity as post-war rations would' allow.[21] Since then the Catholics have made great progress. St Bede's school was opened in 1965 for the older children from Hants Lane School, in the 1970s St Anne's Social Club was opened and in 1979 the new presbytery was built. The Catholic junior school followed and, as a result of an era of successful fundraising, including car-boot sales, the schools have been maintained and upgraded, a process which continues today.

EDUCATION

The successful United Charity school continued in its original building of 1724, but it became very overcrowded, and in 1828 those below the age of six were moved into an infants' school. The old building needed extensive repairs, so a new single-storey school was built alongside the savings bank in Lydiate Lane. An upper floor was added to this building in 1853, when even more space was needed.

Numbers in the school continued to increase until 1874, when a new school was opened in Aughton Street for boys between the ages of eight and fourteen. Although the cost of these premises was defrayed by public subscription, the Church of England retained a controlling interest. The girls and mixed infants remained in Derby Street until 1923, when the senior girls were transferred to the modernised industrial school in Wigan Road. The senior boys followed in 1938, while the junior boys remained in Aughton Street School until 1952, when Greetby Hill School was opened for mixed infants and juniors.

Throughout this period, private schools catered for the needs of those who could afford to pay for tuition, and most of them had preparatory classes for younger children. The more recent of these included those established by Miss Bragg, Miss Hulley and Miss Smith, but few stood the test of time.

THE GRAMMAR SCHOOL

The fortunes of the grammar school continued to ebb and flow, as periods of success were followed by recession linked to the economic condition of the township, especially during the nineteenth century. The school was not able to achieve its full potential until the curriculum was widened, adequate funding was available and its governors fully accepted their responsibilities.

As we have seen, William Naylor retired with a pension in 1821 after sixty-five years. The Anglican influence established in the 1790s continued and applicants for his post were required to belong to the Anglican Church and to be capable of teaching Greek, Latin, English 'and the lower branches of mathematics, arithmetic and writing' – a slightly wider curriculum.[22]

The next headmaster to remain for a long period was Revd Charles Forshaw (1825–1855), whose salary was £60 per annum, plus the income from fees – or, rather, a voluntary 'gratuity' of up to a guinea which he could accept – and the 7s 6d from each pupil 'for firing' (for fuel).[23] The buildings were still in a perilous state, so the number of pupils fluctuated from forty in 1828 to twenty-two in 1835. Eventually, in 1842, it was decided to demolish the old school, sell the site to the churchwardens for £100 as an extension to the graveyard, and move the children into a room above the old charity school until a new school could be built.

Meanwhile, several private schools opened to fill the need in Ormskirk. An academy was opened in Aughton Street in 1805, and in the 1820s the Classical and Commercial Academy of Kershaw and Smith was founded in Burscough Street. Possibly in that same school in 1841 George Ashburner boarded twenty-one scholars, and a very successful academy was founded in the Mansion House, St Helens Road, in 1841 by Revd Thomas Harper. He taught mathematics, book keeping, chemistry and natural philosophy – or general science. Despite losing Revd Harper in 1861, the school continued under Revd John McKechnie until 1863, when it moved to Southport.

However, in 1847 the East Lancashire Railway Company paid the the grammar school £1,034 7s 6d for property in Lydiate Lane, to be a site for their station. At last the governors had sufficient funds to build, especially when Lord Derby provided a site on Ruff Lane free of charge. The new schoolroom and master's house were completed by September 1850 at a cost of £1,234 5s 10d, and a year later pupil numbers had increased to thirty-four.

The success was not to last, for in 1855 the headmaster died and the school was closed. A new headmaster, the Revd Samuel Trueman, was appointed and more extensions were built and the school reopened, but three years later the headmaster resigned. Again the school was closed. Consequently, when it reopened, only seventeen boys remained on the roll. Immediately, Robert Scott, the new headmaster, supervised various improvements, including the installation of piped water and gas into the school. The vacant Mansion House was leased and used by the school while further extensions were made to enable over eighty scholars to be accommodated, but seldom were there more than six boarders. The curriculum was widened to include games and drill – until the parents objected.

During the 1860s, more independent schools opened, including St Leonard's Collegiate School, which was opened in 1867 by Revd Lowe in Railway Road, before moving in 1871 to the Mansion House. Three years later it too moved to Southport. The following year the Commercial School was opened in Church Street by Frederick Chittleburgh, where it prospered until 1891. With such competition, the number at the grammar school again fell, to sixty-two by 1874.

During the period 1886 to 1890 the future modernisation and funding of the grammar school were sources of great contention between the governors and the headmaster. The controversy was fuelled by an open letter in the *Ormskirk*

Advertiser expressing dissatisfaction with the school and leading to the resignation of Robert Scott. Eventually a new management scheme was approved in 1889 and the new board of governors, including William Hutton, Samuel Brighouse and Leonard Kennedy, led the school into another period of steady progress.

The buildings were further extended in 1892 to provide classroom accommodation for 125 boys, but financing the school was proving difficult because investment property had been sold. Fortunately the 1888 Local Government Act allowed councils to contribute towards technical instruction, and grants made by both Skelmersdale and Aughton enabled the teaching of applied chemistry and 'electricity' to be introduced.[24]

Finance continued to be a problem. Nevertheless, in 1889 two scholarships were offered to pupils from elementary schools. In 1891 one foundation scholarship for two years was awarded to a boy under fourteen who had attended the school for over a year. These grants acknowledged, albeit in a limited way, the intention of the grammar school's founder that education in the school should be free.

The long-serving Mr Bate became headmaster in 1901, and at his request more specialist teachers were appointed. The increased cost of salaries was met by a grant of £3,000 for scholarships made by the trustees of Peter Lathom's charity. As the only schools in the town providing higher education for girls were the private schools – at that time the Misses Valentines' Wavenley House, Tower View and the Misses Whitmores' Burscough House[25] – Mr Bate proposed to admit girls to the grammar school. More building alterations were needed to provide accommodation for them, and when Lancashire Education Committee chose the school as a centre for the instruction of pupil teachers, the extensions could not be delayed. The first girl admitted was Ellen Bate, the headmaster's sister, in May 1903. The following year, Margaret Pope was the first mistress to be appointed.

The impressive new extensions were faced with rough stone from Ruff Quarry to match the original buildings, and consisted of a chemistry laboratory, a woodwork room, a science lecture theatre, an assembly room, an art room, a music room, two practice rooms and several new classrooms, as well as more cloakrooms and toilet facilities. As a result of these improvements the school gained recognition by the Board of Education and grants from the County Education Committee. The number of scholars increased from 41 in spring 1904 to 134 (66 boys and 68 girls) when the extension opened in September 1904. Boarders were no longer admitted. Very soon even these premises were proving inadequate, and in December 1907 more extensions were opened, including a library, a cookery room and an assistant teachers' room.

At this time free places were held by 25% of the scholars, increasing to 34% by 1914, and as more pupils travelled some distance to the school, provision was made for eating packed lunches in the cookery room. Each morning one pupil would collect any pies for warming or eggs for boiling in readiness for the lunchtime break.

During the First World War, two masters, Mr P.C. Green and Mr Harry Watson, enlisted and were replaced by temporary assistant mistresses. Mr Morris, the caretaker, also enlisted, leaving the boys to stoke the boiler and do other manual work around the school. Mr Watson and twenty-two old boys were killed in action but, happily, Mr Green returned to his post. Soon the pressure of numbers – 300 by 1919 – persuaded the Board of Education to allow accommodation in the industrial school in Wigan Road to be used by the grammar school preparatory department. This annex was opened in 1920 under Mr Cliff, with Miss Thornton and Miss Booth as assistant teachers.

The school's various activities now included camping and visits to places of interest. The choir, the debating society, the scientific society and the chess club were formed, and an in-school magazine was published. Old Boys and Old Girls associations were established, and in 1926 the house system was re-formed under the names of the school's founders: Ascroft, Breres, Knowles and Stanley. Then, in 1929, more extensions were built bordering Mill Street, but the price of materials dictated that the tradition of facing the buildings with local stone had to be abandoned in favour of brick, and the architectural cohesion of the buildings was lost.

Six years later Revd Bate retired, to be replaced by Mr Dickinson. Mr Wilson and Mr Chippendale were also appointed, bringing with them a new enthusiasm for sport. The annual sports day was re-established and the traditional association football was replaced by rugby. In 1937 Mr Dickinson married Miss Cass, and together they introduced a social dimension into the children's education by regularly inviting the senior scholars to tea at their house.

During the Second World War, six of the teachers were called up and replaced by temporary teachers, while older members of staff delayed their retirement. Evacuees swelled the numbers until there were 509 on the roll, and teachers were reduced to teaching classes on the staircase for want of a room. In 1943 three large buildings were erected in Mill Street to be emergency dormitories for bombed-out refugees, but permission was granted for the school to use them as temporary classrooms. Although the 'huts' were far from ideal, they provided necessary accommodation. Wartime conditions caused many activities to be abandoned, the black-out forced many societies to close and the school day to begin later, while frequent air-raid sirens interrupted lessons. Nevertheless, the pupils gained other skills in the Air Training Corps and the Womens' Junior Air Training Corps. They laboured on the farms and also took their turn firewatching, even occasionally on the parish church roof.

In 1944 the Education Act was passed and in consequence no more fee-paying pupils were admitted to the school. Entrance depended on the results of the 11-plus examination and the preparatory department was closed, once those already attending had completed their course. The next headmaster, Mr Stevens, supervised the building of the first post-war extension, a utilitarian dining room with an asbestos roof, which was completed in 1948. Meanwhile, difficulties persisted and the first post-war prize day was held in the Regal Cinema by the light of hurricane lamps and torches, as a result of the 1947 fuel crisis.

In 1949 the concrete and glass extension, affectionately called 'the crystal palace', was opened, and later, when Mr Stevens resigned, the headmaster's house was absorbed into the school complex. In the 1960s the planned extensions, including the new hall, were finally completed. Meanwhile the curriculum was expanded still further and the scholars were featured on television making their own set, and also on radio dramatising the old barring-out custom. As part of the celebrations commemorating the school's 350th anniversary, a new sports pavilion was opened, and when interest was shown in developing computer skills, a conference was held in the school in 1966.

In 1972 it was proposed to convert the grammar school into a comprehensive school, but, after a great deal of lobbying, Mrs Thatcher rejected the idea. Nevertheless, after the formation of a Labour government in 1974, the alteration was made, but the name of the grammar school was retained to perpetuate the school's ties with the old foundation. The school's progress since then is well known, as Mr Heslegrave and then Mr Richardson have guided the school towards the millennium.

THE INDUSTRIAL SCHOOL

By 1878 the workhouse was overcrowded and it was proposed to house the children in a separate building away from the influence of the other inmates, to teach them in a special school and so 'de-pauperize' them. The new complex was built on Wigan Road and was known as the Industrial School. It had a staff of five – the schoolmaster and matron, the boys' foster father, the girls' foster mother and an industrial trainer – and accommodated seventy-nine children in the two houses. The children from the age of five learnt the three 'R's and were trained in trades such as bakery, shoemaking, gardening, farming and tailoring. The girls were trained in domestic subjects, for most of them were destined to become servants when they left at thirteen. They wore a navy blue uniform and, although discipline was very strict, treats were arranged for them, such as trips to Southport, occasional presents and special meals on Christmas Day.[26] In the late 1880s when the school became overcrowded, several Catholic pauper children were sent to Canada under the auspices of the Roman Catholic Children's Protection Society. Gradually the numbers in the school decreased and by 1914 only fifty-six children were housed there.

Consequently, when war broke out, the guardians could make fifty beds available for wounded soldiers. However, by 1917 the need was so great that the whole complex was converted into a military hospital under the control of Lord Derby's Red Cross hospital at Warrington, and the children were accommodated in other schools. The following year an annex was built, but as peace was declared immediately afterwards, the whole hospital gradually became redundant.

The complex was advertised for sale and, as the existing schools were again overcrowded, the Lancashire education authority bought it for £5,000 and embarked on a programme of modernisation. Before that could be done, the grammar school applied for permission to use the west wing and alter it according to their needs and, as we have seen, the grammar school preparatory department moved into that building. The modernisation continued, and in 1923 the older girls from the United Charities School were transferred to this new Senior Girls' Council School.

In the mid-1930s a domestic science and a woodwork centre were opened on the same site to cater for senior pupils both from Wigan Road School and from the other schools in the district. However, this arrangement was abandoned in 1938 when the senior boys from Aughton Street were transferred to join the girls and the school became Ormskirk Senior Council School. Although it was one school, it functioned as two distinct departments until 1965. In fact, an iron fence was erected down the centre of the playground to separate the two sexes.

When the Second World War broke out, two Liverpool schools, Arnot Street and Major Lester's, were evacuated to Ormskirk and shared the council school's premises. However, by December 1939, so many of the children had returned to the city that it was possible to absorb the rest into the Ormskirk School, while some of the Liverpool teachers remained to help to staff the school. This was very necessary as six of the male teachers were called up, leaving only Mr Hunter and Mr Thomas at the boys' school. Of course, women teachers were recruited to fill the vacancies. When

Liverpool endured the May blitz, the school was opened as a rest centre where weary Liverpudlians could sleep undisturbed – the women in the halls and the men in the corridors. Each morning the visitors left and the school continued as usual. In common with other schools, the children helped with the harvesting and assisted with war work, and finally celebrated the end of hostilities with a victory party.

Mr Hunter resigned in 1953 and was replaced by Mr Ellison, who was in turn followed by Mr Wagstaff in 1960. During these years the school continued to grow, extensions were added and the curriculum was continually modernised. Finally, in 1976, the school became a comprehensive school – Cross Hall High School.

NIGHT SCHOOL

Evening classes began in the mid-nineteenth century when many children left school at eleven to enter employment. Night school catered for those who wanted to continue their education in English, mathematics, technical drawing, science or shorthand. In the 1850s the classes were held in the United Charities School and later were transferred to Aughton Street. When that closed in 1938, the classes moved to Wigan Road until the outbreak of war forced their closure. Soon after peace was declared, night school reopened under the headship of Mr Thomas, who organised a variety of both vocational and non-vocational classes. That tradition continued until the present day at Cross Hall and at other centres in the town, but now most of these classes are organised by Skelmersdale College. The WEA has also presented both evening and day classes in the town since the 1940s.

THE TRAINING COLLEGE

As we have seen (p. 197), Ormskirk Grammar School became a centre for the instruction of pupil teachers in 1903. Previously they had been taught by their respective head teachers after school hours, but once that centre opened they were sent to classes in Ormskirk for a short period each week. Those who were successful in their examinations continued their training at colleges, many from Ormskirk moving on to Edge Hill College in Liverpool. Thirty years later that college moved into a splendid new building on St Helen's Road and Ormskirk became a renowned centre for the training of teachers. Since the mid-1970s the range of courses available for students has been extended until now, as Edge Hill University College it can offer over seventy undergraduate courses as well as catering for students studying for postgraduate, masters and research degrees. During the war the college moved to Bingley and the building became a military hospital.

THE LEISURE SCENE

Many of the leisure activities enjoyed by the townsfolk in the later period originated in the grammar school. In the 1860s, a dancing, deportment and fitness class was established in the school for the older boys and girls, while private classes for girls in drawing were taken by the grammar school master. Later an orchestra was formed by the town's musicians, including many ex-grammar school pupils, and in 1929 the Ormskirk Operatic Society was inaugurated at a meeting called by

Miss Harrison, the daughter of the Methodist minister. At first the group rehearsed in their homes and later they gave performances at the Institute. That centre was also the venue for early cinema shows before the Pavilion in Moorgate – now the 'Brahms and Liszt' club – and the Regal in Church Street – now Tesco's store – were built. Many balls and other celebrations were held in the upper room at the Institute until its demolition in the 1950s. Meanwhile the townspeople increasingly patronised the theatres and concert halls of Liverpool.

Parading, as in the days of the spa, gained in popularity and in 1890 Victoria Park was established, to be followed by Coronation Park. Galas and processions were organised whenever there were occasions to celebrate. In 1861 Lady Scarisbrick drove through the town in a procession to take up her inheritance; in 1872 a gala was held to celebrate the visit of the Duke and Duchess of Teck to Lathom House; and in 1885 the Prince of Wales was greeted by a procession of the townsfolk. Police Superintendant Jervis organised a pageant in 1894 portraying trades at work and including a representation of the seige of Lathom House, and each year the various friendly societies walked in procession to church, often before celebrating their particular day with a feast.

Ormskirk's tradition as a centre for military training continued when the drill hall was opened in 1900 for the local territorials. It became a public hall in the 1970s. Another centre for the youths was the YMCA, opened at the Corn Exchange in 1903. Sportsmen could join clubs for cricket, football and athletics, while plough matches, coursing, pigeon and sparrow shoots were organised in the town. Evidently cockfighting still had its followers in the early nineteenth century, for in 1821 anyone who kept a game cock was refused poor relief.[27] Nevertheless, it was definitely discouraged before finally becoming illegal in 1835. Today, clubs continue to cater for sports of various kinds and other sporting facilities are available, including the baths complex and leisure centre in Park Road and the Sporting Edge. The latter is one of the town's most recent developments, the result of a successful lottery bid, and is managed jointly by Edge Hill University College and West Lancashire District Council. This complex includes tennis courts, other courts and hockey pitches, an athletics track, soccer, rugby and cricket pitches as well as a PE laboratory, fitness suite and a sports pavilion.[28]

This cursory glance at happenings in Ormskirk since 1800 reveals that many of the achievements of the eighteenth-century urban renaissance have been swept away. The splendid Georgian buildings were split up into flats and finally demolished, while many later buildings with Victorian Gothic architecture have been replaced by twentieth-century utilitarian developments. Less to be regretted is the fact that the market-place, widened for traffic in the eighteenth century, has been closed and pedestrianised. Segregation by wealth and privilege within the church has gone, and the free grammar school where the grammars were the only subjects taught has been transformed into a comprehensive school, albeit retaining its former name.

However, the leisure activities of the townsfolk still depend on their wealth, and the cultural divide is very evident. Craftsmen and shopkeepers specialise increasingly to combat the threat posed by the supermarkets, and the attractions of Liverpool and Southport continue to lure people away from the town. Whether the town is now approaching a second urban renaissance as planners struggle to preserve, restore and recreate Ormskirk's traditional character, and the council tries to promote its ancient market and other attractions, time alone will reveal.

Notes

Preface

1. Peter Clark and Paul Slack, *English Towns in Transition* (London: Oxford University Press, 1976), p. 24; A.D. Dyer, 'Growth and Decay in English Towns', *The Urban History Yearbook* (1979), p. 66; John Patten, *English Towns 1500–1700* (Folkestone: Dawson, 1978), p. 90. Peter Borsay, 'The English Urban Renaissance: the Development of Provincial Urban Culture c. 1680–1760', *Social History*, vol. 2, no. 2, May (1977), pp. 581–603; and *The English Urban Renaissance: Culture and Society 1660–1770* (Oxford: Clarendon Press, 1989); Angus McInnes, *The English Town 1660–1760* (London: The Historical Association, 1980), p. 35.
2. Penelope Corfield, *The Impact of English Towns 1700–1800* (Oxford: Oxford University Press, 1982), pp. 20–1.
3. For Norwich see Penelope Corfield, 'A Provincial Capital in the Late Seventeenth Century: the Case of Norwich', in Peter Clark ed. *The Early Modern Town* (London: Longman/Open University Press, 1976), pp. 233–72; for Exeter see W.G. Hoskins, *Industry, Trade and People in Exeter, 1688–1800* (2nd edn, Manchester: Manchester University Press, 1968); for Warwick and Preston see Peter Borsay, *The English Urban Renaissance: Culture and Society*, passim; for Bath see David Gadd, *Georgian Summer: the Rise and Development of Bath* (Newbury: Countryside, 1987); for Shrewsbury see Angus McInnes, 'The Emergence of a Leisure Town, Shrewsbury 1660–1760', *Past and Present*, vol. 120 (1988), pp. 53–85.
4. J.D. Marshall, 'The Rise and Transformation of the Cumbrian Market Town,1660–1900', *Northern History*, vol. 19 (1983), pp. 128–9.

5. Quoted in Joan Thirsk, *The Restoration, Problems and Perspectives in History* (London: Longman, 1976), p. 200.

Introduction

1. For instance, the coins found at Ottishead Farm, Westhead in 1948: David Shotter, 'Roman Coins from North West England' (Lancaster: Centre for North West Regional Studies, Resource Paper, 1990), pp. 159–60.
2. Another interpretation is that Orm was the Scandinavian word for serpent and referred to the snake carved on the prow of a Viking ship used as a totem when the settlement was founded. I am indebted to Marion Hall for this suggestion.
3. Edward Baines, *The History of the County Palatine and Duchy of Lancaster*, two vols (Manchester: Routledge & Sons, 1870) p. 407.
4. *Victoria County History* III, p. 238.
5. A.N. Webb, ed., *An Edition of the Cartulary of Burscough Priory*, Chetham Society, vol. XVIII (1970), p. 19.
6. Ibid., p. 70.
7. The township and the manor covered the same area of land and in effect the township was the manor of Ormskirk.
8. Ibid., p. 51.
9. Ibid., p. 48
10. *VCH* III, p. 263.
11. *VCH* III, p. 262.
12. *VCH* III, p. 263.
13. Lancashire Record Office, Derby Records DDK 1455/1, Derby Property in 1653.
14. Public Record Office, DL 30/79/1073 (pepper and measure), DL 30/79/1064 (bad meat).
15. Duchy of Lancaster Petitions, Elizabeth clxxxvii A.43, as cited in *VCH* III, p. 261.

16. *VCH* III, pp. 261–3.
17. E. Broxop, *The Great Civil War in Lancashire*, (Manchester: Manchester University Press, 191█ pp. 99–148; Barry Coward, 'The Social and Political Position of th█ Earls of Derby in Later Seventee█ Century Lancashire' in J.I. Kermode and C.B. Phillips, eds, *Seventeenth Century Lancashire: Essays Presented to J.J Bagley* Transactions of the Historical Society of Lancashire and Chesh█ vol. 132, (1982), pp. 127–37.
18. LRO QSP 3/2. The 800 on the document shows signs of alteratio█ It may have been 600, later altere█ to 800.
19. LRO QSP 79/8,1653.
20. This average size of households w█ obtained by averaging the size of households in the 16 northern to█ listed by Corfield, *The Impact of Towns*, p. 129.
21. LRO, Manor Court Rolls DDK 1521/3 (1680), DDK 1521/4 (1699), DDK 1521/5 (1754), DL█ 1521/6 (1780).
22. CRO, Bishop Porteous's Visitatio█ EDV 7 1/201.
23. W.J. Hoskins, *Provincial England Essays in Social and Economic History* (London: Macmillan, 19█ p. 18.
24. *VCH* II, p. 346.
25. Liverpool increased from 2,000 i█ the 1640s to 25,000 at the end of eighteenth century; Ramsey Mu█ *History of Liverpool* (Liverpool: Liverpool University Press, 1907█ p. 180; Preston increased in the second half of the seventeenth century from approximately 6,00█ inhabitants to 11,887 in 1801; A. Hewitson, *A History of Preston in█ County of Lancaster* (Preston: Chronicle, 1883) p. 44; while Wi█ reached a population of 10,989 b█ 1801.

Chapter I

1. The phrase 'the commercial revolution' is used by D.C. Coleman in *Industry in Tudor and Stuart England* (London: Macmillan, 1975), p. 17; 'The Urban Renaissance' by P. Borsay in *The English Urban Renaissance: Culture and Society*; 'The Commercialisation of Leisure' by J.H. Plumb in *The Commercialisation of Leisure in Eighteenth Century England* (Reading: University of Reading, 1973); and 'The Birth of a Consumer Society' by McKendrick, J. Brewer and J.H. Plumb in *The Birth of a Consumer Society, the Commercialisation of Eighteenth Century England* (London: Europa, 1982).

2. J.D. Chambers *Population, Economy and Society in Pre-industrial England* (London: Oxford University Press, 1972), p. 26; G.H. Tupling, *The Origin of Markets*, vol. xlix (Transactions of the Lancashire and Cheshire Antiquarian Society 1933–4) p. 92.

3. Dyer, 'Growth and Decay', p. 66.

4. G.H. Tupling, *An Alphabetic List of Markets* vol. li *TLCAS* (1936), pp. 88–110.

5. Patten, *English Towns*, p. 206.

6. H.B. Rodgers, 'The Market Area of Preston in the Sixteenth and Seventeenth Centuries', *Geographical Studies*, vol. 3, (1956), p. 53.

7. M. Spufford, *The Great Reclothing of Rural England: Petty Chapmen and their Wares in the Seventeenth Century* (London: Hambledon, 1984), p. 76.

8. Fernand Braudel, translated by Sian Reynolds, *The Identity of France* (2 vols, London: Collins, 1988), vol. 1, p. 183.

9. Dr Richard Burn, co-author with Joseph Nicolson of *The History and Antiquities of the Counties of Westmorland and Cumberland* (London: Strahan, 1777); Cornelius Nicholson, *The Annals of Kendal* (London: Whittaker, 1861), p. 251.

10. Roy Porter, *English Society in the Eighteenth Century*, rev. edn (London: Penguin, 1982, 1990), p. 191.

11. For instance, the court leet of Manchester fined regrators in 1736: 'A Document Collection' in *Towns and Townspeople* (Milton Keynes: Open University, 1977), A322, unit 4, pp. 32, 69.

12. Anon., *An Essay to Prove that Regrators, Engrossers, Forestallers...are Destructive of Trade* (London: 1718), pp. 18–20, quoted in E.P. Thompson, 'The Moral Economy of the English Crowd in the Eighteenth Century', *Past and Present*, vol. 50 (February 1971), p. 84.

13. M.K. Noble, 'The Role of Small Towns within Regional Urban Systems', *Journal of Regional and Local Studies*, vol. 9, no. 2, (Winter, 1989), p. 33.

14. *Journal of the House of Commons*, 1733 2 March.

15. LRO DDK 1521/1.

16. Quoted in Corfield, *The Impact of Towns*, p. 20.

17. Joan Thirsk, ed., *The Agrarian History of England and Wales 1750–1850*, (8 vols, Cambridge: Cambridge University Press, 1989), vol. 6, p. 197.

18. J. Aikin, *A Description of the Country from Thirty to Forty Miles around Manchester* (1795, Reprinted Newton Abbot: David and Charles, 1968), p. 286; similar orders were made by the court leet at Ulverston 1770–1800: David Borwick, 'An English Provincial Society in north Lancashire', (PhD thesis, University of Lancaster, 1994).

19. Thompson, 'The Moral Economy', p. 88.

20. For instance, Preston fish market was moved in 1686, Liverpool fish market was built in 1670, the new market in Derby Square opened in Liverpool in 1710, and Clitheroe built a new market hall between 1700 and 1710: G.H. Tupling *Lancashire Fairs and Markets*, Part I, vol. LVIII *TLCAS* (1945–1946), pp. 14–25.

21. Quoted in Eric Pawson, *The Early Industrial Revolution: Britain in the Eighteenth Century* (London: Batsford, 1979), p. 168.

22. W. Owen, *An Account of All Fairs* (London: Owen, 1756), p. 50.

23. T.E. Gibson, ed., *Crosby Records: a Cavalier's Notebook* (London: Longmans Green, 1880), p. 138. Twinters can mean two-year-old cattle, colts or sheep, so it is unclear exactly which animals were bought by the Cavalier.

24. Frank Tyrer, ed., *The Great Diurnal of Nicholas Blundell* 3 vols (Record Society of Lancashire and Cheshire, 1968, 1970, 1972), vol. 1, p. 118; vol. 1, p. 228; vol. 2, p. 239.

25. LRO DDK 258/1, Deposition of James Davis, 1797.

26. LRO DDK 290/9/3. The Horse Fair continued in the streets of Ormskirk within living memory.

27. LRO DDK 1521/4. The spelling and punctuation has been modernised to clarify the meaning in this and all the following excerpts from contemporary documents.

28. Tyrer, ed., *The Great Diurnal*, vol. I, pp. 118, 173.

29. LRO DDK 258/1, Deposition of James Waring 1797.

30. LRO DP 385, Richard Lathom of Scarisbrick's Account Book 1722–1767.

31. S.I. Mitchell, 'Urban Markets and Retail Distribution 1730–1815', (unpublished PhD thesis, Oxford University, 1976), p. 49.

32. LRO DDK 258/1.

33. Tyrer, ed., *The Great Diurnal*, vol. II, pp. 109, 145.

34. Ibid vol. I, p. 118, (1706); vol. II, p. 145, (1715); vol. III, p. 165, (1725); vol. I, p. 173, (1708).

35. LRO DDK 153/68.

36. LRO DDK 1521/1–1521/3 (1677–1680), DDK 1521/4–1521/5 (1755–1757), DDK 1521/6–1521/17 (1779–1799).

37. LRO DDK 1746/18.

38. Richard Pococke, *Travels through England 1754–1757*, Camden Society, new series, vol. 42, (1887, reprinted by the Royal Historical Society, 1965) p. 207.

39. LRO DDK 1746/18. Orders of the clerks of the market. no. 13.

40. LRO DDK 258/1.

41. These sacks were large: a sack of barley contained 170 quarts, a sack of wheat 166 quarts, a sack of oats 204 quarts and a sack of rye 136 quarts. Out of each sackful sold, the toll gatherer claimed 1 quart – a full toll-dish. LRO DDK 258/1.

42. LRO DDK 290/9/3; R. Sharpe France, ed., 'The Will, Inventory and Accounts of Robert Walthew of Pemberton', *THSLC*, vol. 109 (1965), p. 90.

43. LRO DDK 290/9/3.

44. For instance, in the 1790s, Liverpool workhouse served thick oatmeal porridge every day for breakfast, and thin porridge three times a week in the evening; Lancaster workhouse served porridge with milk for both breakfast and evening meal every day; in Warrington it featured twice each day except Sunday and Friday: Sir Frederic Morton Eden, *The State of the Poor* (3 vols, London, 1797, reprinted London, Frank Cass, 1966), vol. 2, pp. 334, 309, 373.

45. LRO DDK 1746/18. Order no. 1.
46. LRO DDK 1521/4.
47. LRO DDK 1521/5.
48. LRO DDK 1521/12.
49. LRO DDK 1521/5
50. Thirsk, ed., *The Agrarian History*, vol. 6, p. 215.
51. It is possible that the American War of Independence was indirectly responsible for the upsurge in demand from Liverpool, for the soldiers needed food both when they assembled in the port, and during the crossing to America.
52. The relevant documents recording these restrictions are missing.
53. LRO DDK 1521/8 – 1521/16.
54. LRO DDK 1746/18. Order no. 7.
55. Ibid. Order no. 10.
56. Ibid. Order no. 8.
57. Ibid. Order no. 17.
58. LRO DDK 1521/5.
59. LRO DDK 1521/8 – 1521/16.
60. LRO DDK 1521/9.
61. LRO DDK 1521/13.
62. LRO DDK 290/9/3, the enquiry of 1830.
63. W.G. Howson, 'Plague, poverty and population 1580–1720,' *THSLC*, vol. 112 (1961), p. 53.
64. Thomas Eccleston was awarded a medal by the Royal Society in 1786 for his successful drainage of Martin Mere: W. Farrar, *The History of the Parish of North Meols* (Liverpool: Henry Young, 1903), pp. 65, 119.
65. In his 'Chronological Events', Nicholson commented: '1729–1730 Till this year potatoes were very sparingly used in Kendal'; Nicholson, *The Annals of Kendal*, p. 289.
66. A peck was a quarter of a bushel or 8 quarts; the farmers were selling the potatoes in quantities equivalent to 8 lb.
67. Arthur Young, *A Six Month Tour through the North of England 1771*, 4 vols (New York: Augustus M. Kelley, 1967), vol. 3, p. 171.
68. LRO DDK 290/9/3.
69. Tyrer, ed., *The Great Diurnal*, vol. I, p. 228, vol. II, pp. 145, 239.
70. LRO DDK 1746/18. The orders of the clerk of the market no. 9.
71. LRO DDK 290/14/5.
72. LRO DDK 290/9/3.
73. LRO WCW James Berry, 1686.
74. LRO DDK 1541/41.
75. Local soap boilers included James Moorcroft (d. 1709), Silvester Moorcroft mentioned in 1719, Edward Tatlock (1735–6) and Thomas Hareford (1786).
76. LRO QJB 7/36 Silvester Moorcroft at the suit of Catherine Ashton 5

September 1718. Discharged QJB 9/61.
77. Gibson, ed., *Crosby Records: a Cavalier's Notebook*, p. 135.
78. LRO DDK 1521/14.
79. LRO DDK 1746/18. Order no. 16.
80. LRO WCW William Livesey, (1661).
81. Joseph Wright ed. *Wright's Dialect Dictionary* (6 vols, London: Henry Frowde, for the English Dialect Society, 1904), vol. 5, R–S, p. 430.
82. LRO WCW William Watkinson (1671).
83. LRO DDK 1521/2.
84. LRO WCW James Berry, (1686).
85. The Clarke family of ropers had a shop in Burscough Street and the Rothwell family had one in Church Street in the late eighteenth century. The sites of some of the town's rope walks are identical to certain of today's long straight byways LRO DDK 1541/42. Survey for 1787.
86. LRO DDK 1455/1.
87. LRO DDK 1746/18. Order no. 3. These watering places were on the common land. An important feature of urban change during our period was the gradual disappearance of such land from within the township's boundaries. By 1797, deponents from Ormskirk were able to describe the enclosure of the last piece of 'waste' on Scarth Hill: LRO DDK 258/1.
88. LRO DDK 1746/18. Order no. 12.
89. LRO DDK 1521/4.
90. LRO DDK 1820/49.
91. LRO WCW Ann Weeming (1681), WCW Peter Swift (1686), WCW James Berry (1686), WCW Henry Tarbuck (1670).
92. LRO DDK 1746/18. Order no.4. Brass studs marking the official yard measure can still be seen on the wall of the magistrates court.
93. LRO DDK 1521/1.
94. LRO DDK 1521/5.
95. LRO DDK 1746/18. Order no. 22.
96. LRO WCW Richard Morecroft (1689).
97. LRO DDK 1521/7.
98. LRO WCW William Livesey (1661), WCW William Watkinson (1671).
99. Here gilt may mean soft leather rather than gilded leather.
100. LRO QSB 3 1661.
101. PRO E134/ 5 and 6 William and Mary/Hilary 22. (As witnesses in the Hesketh *v.* Dodd case.)
102. LRO QSP 928/2. Shoemakers' Petition.
103. Andrew Skinner, ed., *Adam Smith: the Wealth of Nations* (2 vols, Harmondsworth: Penguin, 1970), pp. 111–22.

104. L.A. Clarkson, *The Pre-Industrial Economy of England, 1500–1750* (London: Batsford, 1971), p. 101. For information on the leather industry see L.A. Clarkson, 'The Leather Crafts in Tudor and Stuart England', *The Agricultural History Review*, no. 14 (1966), pp. 25–39.
105. The resulting act again specified that the authorities in market towns 'upon pain of £40 were to appoint...yearly, two or three...persons of the most honest,and skilful men...to search...and seal' leather; Calender of State Papers Domestic Charles II vol. VIII, October 1675 (London: HMSO, 1907), p. 371.
106. Clarkson, *The Pre-Industrial Economy*, p. 99.
107. LRO WCW Henry Walton, (1691).
108. PRO E134, 13–14 William and Mary, Hilary 26.
109. LRO DDK 1820/7–1820/39.
110. Clarkson, *The Pre-Industrial Economy*, p. 15.
111. *CSPD* Chas. II, vol. VII, October, 1675, p. 369.
112. A similar site was often used for the shambles in north-western towns, for instance in Preston: John Taylor ed., *Kuerden's Preston 1682–1686* (Preston: I. Wilcockson, 1818), p.
113. Mitchell, 'Urban Markets', p. 84.
114. G.H. Tupling, *Lancashire Markets the Sixteenth and Seventeenth Centuries*, Part II, vol. 59, *TLCAS* (1947) p. 27.
115. LRO DDK 1746/18. Order Book, DDK 1521/5, DDK 1521/10. The thirty butchers of Preston Shambles were also very troublesome, slaughtering their animals and throwing 'blood, guts and garbage in ye open street': LRO CNP 3/2/4 Preston Court Leet, 23 October 17.
116. PRO PC 1/1/5, Privy Council Unbound Papers, 18 February 170
117. In Lancaster, John Lawson also opened a 'sugar house' (a refinery) the 1680s, while in Whitehaven the manufacture of snuff and tobacco was established about this time. Michael Mullett, 'Reformation and Renewal 1450–1690', in Andrew White, ed., *History of Lancaster 1193–1993* (Keele: Ryburn, 1993) p. 79.
118. See p. 89.
119. LRO WCW Henry Barton (1685).
120. In the 1680s a Peter Woosey had an alehouse near the site of the present Stanley Gate inn at Bickerstaffe. It is possible that it was also the location of this operation.

PRO PL6/34/37, PL10/103. I am indebted to Angela Barlow for drawing my attention to this case. *The Palatine Notebook*, (Liverpool: Henry Young, 1883), vol. 3, p. 273. For the storm see p. 59.
S.I. Mitchell, 'Urban Markets', p. 164.

Chapter II

For an account of the emergence of this consumer society nationwide see McKendrick, Brewer and Plumb, *The Birth of a Consumer Society*, passim. Revd. John Clayton, *Friendly Advice to the Poor in the Town of Manchester* (Manchester, 1756), quoted in Bill Williams, *The Making of Manchester Jewry 1740–1875* (Manchester: Manchester University Press, 1976), p. 6.
Sources from which the occupation data was obtained, their range of dates and the percentage of each source used when I compiled the data:
Probate Records 1600–1800, 28%; Sureties for alehouse licenses 1753–1800, 17%; Quarter Sessions Petitions 1661–1798, 9%; Marriage Bonds 1662–1752, 7%; Return of Papists 1767, 4%; Catholic Records 1674–1799, 4%; Court of the Exchequer Records 1658–1721, 3%; Grammar School Deeds and Minute Book 1662–1790, 3%; Apprenticeship Bonds and Churchwardens' Accounts 1760–1778, 2%; Catholic Register 1725–1787, 2%; Various other documents each providing 1% or less 21%.
LRO WCW Richard Woods 1667, WCW William Moorcroft 1727 and WCW Thomas Hodson 1722. James Stuart's advert appeared in the *Preston Weekly Journal*, no. 278, 8 June 1750.
Borsay, *Urban Renaissance*, pp. 54–9; McKendrick, Brewer and Plumb, *The Birth of a Consumer Society*, p. 55. Geoffrey Holmes, *Augustan England: the Professions, State and Society 1680–1730* (London: George Allen and Unwin, 1982), passim.
John Trusler, *The Way to be Rich and Respectable* (London, 1777), pp. 1–3, quoted in McKendrick, Brewer and Plumb, *The Birth of the Consumer Society*, pp. 51, 240.
Clark, ed., *The Transformation of English Provincial Towns* (London: Hutchinson, 1984), p. 30.

9. McInnes, 'The Emergence of a Leisure Town', p. 76.
10. David Lemmings, *Gentlemen and Barristers: the Inns of Court and the English Bar 1680–1730* (Oxford: Clarendon Press, 1990) pp. 126, 169; see also Holmes, *Augustan England*, p. 119.
11. *Kenyon Manuscripts*, Historical Manuscripts Commission, vol. 35 (London: HMSO, 1894), p. 153.
12. Michael Mullett, ' "A Receptacle for Papists and an Assilum": Catholicism and Disorder in Seventeenth Century Wigan', *The Catholic Historical Review*, vol. 73, no. 3 (July 1987), pp. 391–407.
13. Nicholas Blundell frequently visited lawyers in Ormskirk during the years 1702–1719: Tyrer, ed., *The Great Diurnal*, vols 1, 2, passim.
14. Henry Fishwick, *The History of the Parish of Rochdale* (Rochdale: James Clegg, 1889), p. 411.
15. W.H.R. Cook, *Joseph Brandreth, 1745–1815* (Ormskirk: Brandreth Club, 1991), pp. 1–7.
16. Ball was described by Susanna Doughty of Preston as 'a person very much made use of by several persons for the placing of their moneys at interest' at the beginning of the eighteenth century; J.R. Harris, ed., *Liverpool and Merseyside, Essays on the Economic and Social History of the Port and its Hinterland* (London: Frank Cass, 1969), pp. 70–71.
17. Photo courtesy of Liverpool Medical Institution.
18. Dr Joseph Brandreth (see p. 27) initiated the foundation of the dispensary and a secretary was appointed in 1779. In 1797 Lord Derby subscribed £2 2s as a 'gift to the newly established dispensary at Ormskirk'. This first dispensary was a small shop in Lydiate Lane, now Derby Street, and was supported by voluntary contributions, including Lord Derby's annual subscription: LRO DDK 1941, the *Derby Journal* 1795–1800.
19. Barry Coward, 'Social Change and Continuity in Early Modern England, 1500–1750', *Seminar Studies in History*, ed. R. Lockyer (London: Longman, 1988), p. 80
20. R. Davis, 'The Rise of Protection in England 1689–1786', *Economic History Review*, Second series, vol. 19, (1966), p. 315.
21. Barry Coward, 'Social Change and Continuity', p. 80.
22. Joseph Massie, *Considerations on the*

Leather Trade of Great Britain (London, 1757), p. 24, quoted in Leslie Clarkson, *Death, Disease and Famine in Pre-Industrial England* (Dublin: Gill & Macmillan, 1975), p. 28.
23. LRO QSB3.
24. PRO Exchequer Records, Hearth Tax Returns, E179 250/11 (1664), E179 250/9, E179 132/355.
25. PRO Exchequer's Records, E134, 5 and 6 William and Mary, Hilary 20.
26. LRO, WCW Margaret Billinge, Ormskirk, (1695).
27. Borsay, 'Urban Development in the Age of Defoe' in Clyve Jones, *Britain in the First Age of Party, 1650–1750*, (London: Hambledon, 1987), p. 210.
28. LRO WCW Gilbert Ambrose 1692, WCW Henry Jones 1690.
29. 'Affearing' was a reconsideration and consequent re-assessment of fines. LRO Derby Records, Bailiff's Accounts for Ormskirk, DDK 1553/68 (1687), DDK 1553/69 (1689).
30. James Dixon, ed., 'Church Expenditure two centuries ago, or Ormskirk Churchwardens' Accounts 1665–1666', *THSLC*, vol. 31 (1878) p. 177.
31. LRO Ormskirk Churchwardens' accounts, PR 2886/31.
32. LRO DDK 1553/71 (1697). *Manuscripts of the House of Lords*, The Historical Manuscripts Commission, vol. 17, 23 and 29 March (1697).
33. Tyrer, ed., *The Grand Diurnal*, vol. 2, pp. 108, 248.
34. On 13 May 1714, Blundell recorded 'Being Thomas Syer and I are the Churchwardens we dined at the Talbot in Ormskirk with Parson Letus, Parson Waring etc': Tyrer, ed., *The Great Diurnal*, vol. 2, p. 99.
35. Ibid. p. 145.
36. LRO Churchwardens accounts, PR 2886/30.
37. J. Childs, *The Army, James II and the Glorious Revolution* (Manchester: Manchester University Press, 1980), pp. 1–17.
38. A.J. Hawkes, 'Sir Roger Bradshaigh of Haigh, Knight and Baronet 1628–84', CS, New series, vol. 109 (1945) p. 51.
39. LRO WCW Thomas Barton, 1734; DDK 290/14/3, Encroachment Rental 1735.
40. Patten, *English Towns*, p. 202; Borsay, 'Urban Development in the Age of Defoe', p. 210.
41. Peter Clark, *The English Alehouse: a*

Social History 1200–1830 (London: Longman, 1983), p. 10.

42. LRO DDK 1820/50, Derby rentals for 1798.

43. PRO E 182/491, Part 1. For the figures for the northern towns see T.S. Willan, *An Eighteenth Century Shopkeeper: Abraham Dent of Kirby Stephen* (Manchester: Manchester University Press, 1970), p. 27.

44. Ian Mitchell, 'Pitt's Shop Tax in the History of Retailing', *Local Historian*, vol. 14, no. 6, May (1981), p. 349.

45. LRO WCW Peter Swift 1686.

46. Anon., *The Compleat Tradesman* (1684), quoted in N.N. Foster, 'The Peasantry and the Aristocracy: a Study of Peasant and Gentry Relations 1600–1715 with Special Reference to Lancashire', (unpublished MA thesis, University of Manchester, 1977), p. 5.

47. Williams, *The Making of Manchester Jewry, 1740–1875*, pp. 1–2.

48. PRO Kew, AO 3/371.

49. For further details of pedlars see Spufford, *The Great Reclothing of Rural England*, pp. 1–93.

50. Chester CRO EDV 7 1/101.

51. PRO RG/4/3584, register of Aughton Street Presbyterian Chapel.

52. Norman Lowe, *The Lancashire Textile Industry in the Sixteenth Century*, CS Third series, vol. 20 (1972) p. 58.

53. Ibid., p. 84.

54. N.B. Harte, 'The Rise and Protection of the Linen Trade 1690–1790', in N.B. Harte and K.G. Ponting, eds, *Textile History and Economic History: Essays in Honour of Miss Julia de Lacy Mann* (Manchester: Manchester University Press, 1973), p. 96.

55. For instance, although a considerable amount of linen was produced from the flax grown on the Fell's Swarthmoor Hall estate, none was sold commercially: Barbara Pidcock, 'Textile Manufacture in Seventeenth Century Lower Furness, its Production and Producers', (unpublished dissertation, Diploma in Local History, Lancaster, 1991).

56. James Brome, *An Account of Travels over England and Wales*, (2nd edn, London 1694, 1707).

57. LRO DDK1746/18. Order no. 12.

58. The various processes of rippling, retting, breaking, swingling or scutching and hatchelling flax are described in Tyrer, ed., *The Great*

Diurnal, vol. I, pp. 63, 269, passim. LRO DP 385, Diary of Robert Lathom, reference for 1761.

59. LRO WCW John Hill (1695).

60. J.D. Marshall, *Lancashire* (Newton Abbot: David and Charles, 1974), p. 54.

61. C. Northcote Parkinson, *The Rise of the Port of Liverpool* (Liverpool: Liverpool University Press, 1952), p. 54.

62. Tyrer, *The Great Diurnal*, vol. II, p. 39n.

63. *Journal of the House of Commons*, vol. 14, 31 January 1704/5, p. 504, and 5 February (1704/5) p. 515.

64. 12 Anne c.19, (1713); 3 Geo I c.9, (1717); 10 Geo II c.37, (1736); 15 Geo 2 c.29, (1742); Danby Pickering, *Statutes at Large*, vols 13, 17, 18.

65. Thomas Pennant, *Tour from Downing to Alston Moor in 1773* (London: E. Harding, 1801), p. 51.

66. Eden, *The State of the Poor*, vol. 2, p. 370.

67. Charles Wilson, *England's Apprenticeship 1603–1763* (London: Longman, 1965), p. 296.

68. Young, *A Six Month's Tour*, vol. III, p. 173.

69. Sheila Marriner, *The Economic and Social Development of Merseyside* (London: Croom Helm, 1982), p. 49.

70. LRO WCW William Hewitt 1723.

71. LRO WCW Anne Weeming 1681.

72. The total value of the goods in Hewitt's inventory, given as £44 11s 6d, is deceptive because much of his wealth had been dispersed for, as he declared in his will, his son George was left only 1s 'by resun he has anufe before'.

73. Janet Nelson, 'The Demand for Silk and the Waste Silk Industry in Eighteenth Century Lancaster, 1711–1780', *The Lancashire Local Historian*, no. 3, (1985), pp. 24–31.

74. Neil Cossons, *The BP Book of Industrial Archaeology* (Newton Abbot: David & Charles, 1975), p. 259.

75. Miss Martin of Ormskirk remembered as a child visiting a handloom silk weaver at work upstairs in his cottage in Chapel Street.

76. In 1825 the Independent congregation moved into part of this silk factory: B. Nightingale, ed., *Lancashire Non-Conformity or Sketches Historical and Descriptive of the Congregational and Old Presbyterian Churches in the County of Lancashire*, 6 vols (Manchester: Heywood, 1892), vol. 6, p. 200.

77. LRO WCW John Prescot 1716.

78. J. James, *The History of the Worsted Manufacture in England from the*

Earliest Times (London: Longman 1857), p. 253.

79. James, *The History of the Worsted Manufacture*, pp. 324–5. The thickness of the yarn was calculal by weight and length. For instanc sixteens meant that sixteen hanks a standard length weighed 1 lb. Tl standard length was 2,400 yd in Lower Furness, but it varied from region to region.

80. E. Pawson, 'The framework of industrial change,' in R.A. Dodgshon and R.A. Butlin, eds, *Historical Geography of England a Wales* (London: Academic Press, 1978), p. 283.

81. LRO DDK 1541/42, Survey for 1

82. He was charged £26 rental, whic suggests a large building. LRO DDK 1820/42– 1820/51, Rental for 1790–1799.

83. Eric Rideout,'Poor Law Administration in North Meols in t Eighteenth Century', *THSLC*, vol. LXXXI (1930), p. 103.

84. Ibid., p. 103.

85. This was near the site of the junction between Burscough Stre and Derby Street West.

86. British Library, Add. MS 22648.

87. Clarkson, 'Leather Crafts', pp. 3!

88. Taken from the same sources as Table 3, p. 20.

89. G.H. Tupling, *The Early Metal Trades and the Beginning of Engineering in Lancashire*, *THSL* vol. LXI (1951), p. 22.

90. McInnes, 'The Emergence of a Leisure Town', p. 64.

91. Peter Borsay, 'The English Urba Renaissance: the Development o Provincial Urban Culture', p. 58!

92. C.B. Phillips, 'Town and Countr Economic Change in Kendal *c.* 1550–1700', in Clark, ed., *The Transformation of English Provinc Towns*, p. 104.

93. Borsay, *The English Urban Renaissance*, pp. 599–602.

94. Porter, *English Society in the Eighteenth Century*, p. 82.

95. Directories often provide a biase sample, but nevertheless, with a shortage of other listings, comparisons between directory listings provide some guide to the differences between various towr John Walton, 'Trades and Professions in late Eighteenth Century England: Assessing the Evidence of Directories', *The Lo Historian*, vol. 17, no. 6, May (19 p. 343.

. Pawson, *The Early Industrial Revolution*, pp. 162–3.
. McInnes, 'The Emergence of a Leisure Town', p. 85.
. Hoh-cheung and Lorna H. Mui, *Shops and Shopkeeping in Eighteenth century England* (London: Routledge, 1989), pp. 123–4, 63–4.
. Photographs courtesy of the British Museum and J. Shaw of Chorley.
. The designer of William Haydock's token cannot have been local, for he featured Ormskirk church with the tower at the west end of the church and the spire at the east, whereas both are at the west end. The occupations of the other three token issuers (Atherton, Jackson and Haydock) were probably baker, tallow chandler and mercer.
. PRO Palatinate papers, PL 27/1.
. LRO WCW Thomas Smith 1661, WCW Henry Tarbuck 1670, WCW John Vause 1671 and WCW Isaac Woods 1677, all of Ormskirk.
. Daniel Defoe, *The Compleat Tradesman* (first published 1726, this edition 1839, reprinted Gloucester, Alan Sutton, 1987), p. 137.
. LRO Bankruptcy Papers, QJB/7/19 (Andrew Wilding), QJB/22/11 (Henry Rutter), QJB/23/23, QJB/24/2 (Peter Billinge), QJB/43/57 (James Prescott), QJB/38/11, QJB/38/21, QJB/38/22 (Robert Barton), QJB/39/10, QJB/39/40 (Henry Cook).
. LRO WCW John Windle 1673.
. Quoted by Corfield, *The Impact of Towns*, p. 97.
. A.P. Wadsworth and J. de Lacy Mann, *The Cotton Trade and Industrial Lancashire, 1600–1780,* (Manchester: Manchester University Economic History Series, 1931) p. 249.
. LRO WCW Margaret Moorcroft 1704.
. John Walton, 'Proto-Industrialisation and the First Industrial Revolution: the Case of Lancashire', in Pat Hudson, *Regions in Industries: a Perspective on the Industrial Revolution in Britain* (Cambridge: Cambridge University Press, 1989), p. 61.
. B.L. Anderson, *Capital Formation in the Industrial Revolution* (London: Dent, 1974), pp. 248–9, quoted by J.H. Plumb in McKendrick, Brewer and Plumb, *The Birth of a Consumer Society*, p. 233.
. LRO Quarter Sessions, QSB/1/284/9.

112. LRO DP.258.A. *Regarding the Douglas Navigation* no date.
113. Tyrer, ed., *The Great Diurnal*, vol. III, p. 145.
114. Ibid, p. 212.
115. LRO DDK 1649, December 1755, Stewards' Letters.
116. Young, *A Six month's Tour*, pp. 430, 434.
117. Mike Clarke, *The Leeds and Liverpool Canal: a History and Guide* (Preston: Carnegie Press, 1990), p. 254.
118. *Gore's General Advertiser* (1794) p. 656, quoted in B.L. Anderson and P.J.M. Stoney, *Commerce, Industry and Transport: Studies in Economic Change in Merseyside* (Liverpool: Liverpool University Press, 1983), p. 17.
119. M.J. Daunton, 'Towns and Economic Growth in Eighteenth Century England', in P. Abrams and E.A. Wrigley, eds, *Towns in Societies: Essays in Economic History and Historical Sociology* (Cambridge: Cambridge University Press, 1978), p. 247.

Chapter III

1. S. and B. Webb, *English Local Government: the story of the King's Highway* (London: Longman, 1913), pp. 15–22.
2. LRO, QSP 440/25, QSP 440/43.
3. LRO, QSP 1581/18.
4. PRO, DL 30/79/1072.
5. LRO DDK 1521/1, Court Roll for 1677.
6. LRO DDK 1521/1, Court Roll for 1677.
7. LRO DDK 1521/1.
8. LRO Bailiffs' Accounts, DDK 1553/67.
9. S. and B. Webb, *The King's Highway*, p. 15.
10. LRO DDK 1521/3, Court Roll for 1680.
11. The reference in the Plumbe Tempest collection is undated, but as another reference mentions James Hey, in 1703, this happened about that time. Liverpool RO 920 PLU 1; PRO P.C.1/1/5.
12. LRO DDK 1746/18. Order no. 46.
13. LRO DDK 1640, August (1746) Stewards' Letters.
14. Borsay, *English Urban Renaissance*, pp. 62–8; McInnes, 'The Emergence of a Leisure Town', pp. 70–1.
15. S. and B. Webb, *The King's Highway*, p. 14; 2, 3 Philip and Mary c.8; Pickering, *Statutes at Large*.
16. 4.3 and 4 William and Mary c.12; Pickering, *Statutes at Large*.
17. LRO DDK 1521/5 (1754)

18. LRO DDK 1521/3 (1680), QSP 480/13 (1678).
19. LRO, DDK 1746/18. Order no. 33.
20. 'Public Nuisance Considered' 1754, pp. 4–5, quoted in E.L. Jones and M.E. Falkus, 'Urban Improvement and the English Economy in the Seventeenth and Eighteenth Centuries', *Research in Economic History*, vol. 4 (1979) p. 206.
21. Pococke, *Travels through England 1754–1757*, p. 207.
22. LRO DDK 1521/8 (1783).
23. LRO DDK 1746/18. Orders of the Burleymen, no. 1.
24. LRO DDK 1521/5 (1755).
25. LRO DDK 1521/1 (1677).
26. LRO DDK 1521/5 (1755).
27. LRO DDK 1640, September (1746) Stewards' Letters, DDK 1820/3 Rental (1747).
28. DDK 1820/49 (1797).
29. LRO DDK 1746/18, Orders of the Burleymen, no. 3.
30. LRO DDK 1521/3 Court Roll, 1680.
31. LRO DDK 1746/18, Street Lookers Orders no. 2.
32. LRO DDK 1746/18, Street Lookers Orders no. 3.
33. In pre-Reformation days there was a fear that such pollution would incur the wrath of God. Possibly the Ormskirk townspeople, like those in France in the sixteenth century, sensed great danger in the defilement of objects associated with the church: Natalie Zemon Davis, *Society and Culture in Early Modern France* (Stanford, California: Stanford University Press, 1975), pp. 157–80.
34. LRO QSP 355/10.
35. LRO DDK 1746/18, Street Lookers' Orders, no. 2.
36. LRO DDK 1746/18, Street Lookers' Orders no. 5.
37. LRO DDK 1746/18, Clerk of the Market's Orders no. 7.
38. LRO DDK 1746/18, Street Lookers' Orders no. 4.
39. LRO DDK 1521/3, Court Roll 1680.
40. Jones and Falkus, 'Urban Improvement', p. 212.
41. Borsay, *The English Urban Renaissance*, p. 70.
42. McInnes, 'The Emergence of a Leisure Town', p. 71.
43. 9 Geo 11 c. 18; Pickering, *Statutes at Large*.
44. LRO DDK 1521/5, Court Roll (1755).
45. LRO DDK 1521/2 (1678), DDK 1521/5 (1754).
46. LRO DRL/3/9, Diocese of Liverpool muniments.

47. Young, *A Six Month Tour*, vol. 4, p. 430.
48. LRO, QSP 625/14.
49. LRO, QSP 551/35 (1682), QSP 956/4 (1707).
50. LRO, QSP 1260/22. As advertised in *Gore's Liverpool Directories* for 1777, 1781, 1796.
51. LRO, QSP 2197/71, QSP 2209/7, QSP 2209/6. An amusing item appeared at the end of the estimate – 'To make good mistakes £2.'
52. In several older market towns, street names perpetuate these specific market areas with such names as Sheep Street (Stow-on-the-Wold), Haymarket, Cornhill and Malthill (Northampton): Alan Everitt, 'Urban Growth 1570–1770', *Local Historian*, vol. 8, no. 4 (1968), p. 119.
53. LRO DDK 1820/1, Rentals. Presumably, here 'perch' referred to a square perch – 30.25 sq.yd.
54. For Macclesfield see Ian Mitchell, 'The Development of Urban Retailing', in Clark, ed., *The Transformation of English Provincial Towns*, p. 266; for Blandford Forum and Bath see Borsay, *The English Urban Renaissance*, pp. 67–8.
55. LRO DDK 1521/7, Court Leet Roll for 1781.
56. LRO DDK 1521/5 (1755).
57. LRO DDK 1521/13 (1793).
58. LRO DDK 1521/8 (1783) – DDK 1521/16 (1798).
59. Borwick, 'An English Provincial Society in North Lancashire'.
60. 'seller stairs are very dangerous for ye inhabitants...to pass by in ye night', October 1680: Anthony Hewitson, *Preston Court Leet Records* (Preston: George Toulmin, 1905), p. 132.
61. LRO DDK 1521/12 (1791); DDK 1521/17 (1799).
62. LRO DDK 1521/1 – DDK 1521/4 (1677–1680).
63. LRO DDK 1521/5 (1755–1757).
64. LRO DDK 1521/1 (1677) – DDK 1521/17 (1799).
65. LRO DDK 1521/8 (1784).
66. LRO DDK 1521/17 (1799).
67. LRO DDK 1521/14 (1796).
68. LRO DDK 1521/14 (1796).
69. LRO DDK 1521/12 (1791).
70. LRO DDK 1746/18. Order no. 37.
71. LRO UDOr 15/10 Robert Rawlinson, Report to the General Board of Health, 1850, p. 28.
72. In 1848, Gould Tilsley reported that he supplied 'above 100 families from his own pump': LRO UDOr 15/10 p. 25.
73. LRO DDK 1746/18, Order no. 21.

74. *VCH* vol. III, p. 261.
75. Borsay, *The English Urban Renaissance*, p. 7.
76. 14 Geo 111 c.73; Pickering, *Statutes at Large*.
77. LRO DDK 1521/10 (1787).
78. LRO DDK 1521/11 (1790).
79. LRO DDK 1521/12 (1791).
80. Described in 1819 in a collection for a proposed book, W.J. Roberts (Liverpool), *The History of Ormskirk with Antiquities, Views of Public Edificies etc.*, 1819; British Library, Add. MS, 22648, p. 157.
81. Holmes, *Augustan England*, p. 14.
82. PRO M.4.
83. LRO DDK 1455/1. The account of the Derby estates made in 1653 when they were forfeited to the Commonwealth for treason.
84. In 1652 the steward had kept the key to this inner room, and the constable complained to the justices that the room was 'necessary and useful for said town'. The steward was ordered to return the key to the constable. LRO QSP 67/39.
85. LRO DDK 1553/67 Bailiff's Accounts for 1683, DDK 1553/68 Bailiff's Accounts for 1687.
86. It was reported that it would cost more than £60 to repair the glass broken in Ormskirk. Hailstones weighing 0.75 lb fell and many of them 'rebounded two yards high'. Edmund Halley, comptroller of the mint at Chester in 1696, recorded this storm and traced its course from North Wales through Cheshire to Blackburn: Anon., *The Palatine Notebook*, vol. 3, p. 273.
87. LRO DDK 1553/71, Bailiff's Accounts 1697.
88. LRO DDK 1647–1652, Stewards' Letters: 25 August 1753, 17 April 1761, 27 August 1761.
89. LRO DDK 1553/71, Bailiff's accounts (1697), and DDK 1820/2, rentals (1747) DDK 1820/3 (1748), DDK 1820/7 (1752).
90. LRO DDK 1553/67, Bailiffs' accounts (1683).
91. LRO DDK 1650/22, Stewards' Letters (1757).
92. Borsay, 'The English Urban Renaissance', pp. 593–6.
93. LRO DDK 290/13/3, Bricklayers' Agreement (1779).
94. LRO DDK 258/1, Depositions of James Waring and Philip Heys (1797).
95. LRO DDK 258/1, Deposition of William Jones of Burscough (1797).
96. Similar arrangements applied when a new barn was built at Greetby,

Ormskirk: 'the materials were all most of them his Lordship's, wor[k] done by his Lordship's masons, carpenters etc., and four or five ca[rt] load of timber a day, ready prepar[ed] came hither from Knowsley.' Knowsley Hall, Derby Estate Pap[ers] N. 18B, n.d. eighteenth-century document. LRO DDK 290/15/1
97. LRO DDK 258/1 (1797), Deposition of James Waring.
98. LRO DDK 290/13/3. Bricklayer[s'] Agreement.
99. LRO DDK 258/1 (1797), Deposition of James Waring.
100. LRO DDK 290/15/1. This coat [of] arms can still be seen over shops [in] Church Street. LRO DDK 1941. [It] is ironic that Derby used the cana[l] which he had opposed a few years previously. *Derby Journal*, 1796, 1[?] November.
101. LRO DDK 1746/18; British Library, Add. MS 22648, p. 164.
102. LRO DDK 1521/2 (1781).
103. LRO DDK 1820/35 (1783).
104. Corfield, *The Impact of Towns*, p.
105. David Sinclair, *The History of Wigan*, 2 vols (Wigan: Wigan Observer, 1882), vol. 2, p. 213.
106. Borsay, *The English Urban Renaissance*, p. 111.
107. Hewitson, *History of Preston*, p. 357.
108. Borsay, *The English Urban Renaissance*, pp. 325–6.
109. Clarke, *The Transformation of English Provincial Towns*, p. 41.
110. McInnes, 'The Emergence of a Leisure Town', p. 84.
111. LRO DDK 1521/5 (1754).
112. LRO DDK 1521/7 (1781).
113. LRO DDK 258/1 (1797), Deposition of James Waring.
114. PRO Map 4.
115. Robert A. Philpott, *Historic Town[s of] the Merseyside Area: a Survey of Urban Settlement to c. 1800* (Liverpool: Liverpool Museum, 1988), p. 44.
116. LRO DDK 1820/1, Rental for 17[?]
117. PRO E 179/332, Hearth Tax Exemption Certificate.
118. Lydia Marshall, 'The Levying of Hearth Tax 1662–1688', *The Eng[lish] Historical Review*, vol. 51 (1936), 635; Chris Husband, 'Hearth Ta[x] Exemption Figures and the Assessment of Poverty in the Seventeenth Century Economy', Nick Alldridge, ed., *The Hearth Tax: Problems and Possibilities* (Humberside: Humberside Colle[ge] of Further Education, 1983), p. 4[?]
119. PRO E179/250/11, Exemptions

from Hearth Tax, 1664; PRO E179/383/1, Exemptions from the Hearth Tax, 1672; PRO E179 132/355, Hearth Tax Assessments for 1673.

. Nick Alldridge, 'House and Household in Restoration Chester', *Urban History Yearbook*, (1983), pp. 39–41.

. Reserved rents described properties leased for lives, rack rents property leased for a fixed term of years, while chief rents were paid on freehold properties.

. LRO DDK 1820/1 (1746).

. LRO DDK 1820/55 (1799).

. Pococke, *Travels through England*, p. 207.

. LRO DDK 1770/1 (1702).

. LRO DDK 1541/41 (1713).

. LRO DDK 1770/3 (1707).

. Liverpool Record Office Coleman Deeds no. 141.

. LRO DDK 1541/41 (1713).

. Poor durability was hardly a valid reason for replacing the 250 year old wall. CRO Visitation Records, EDV 7/1/201.

. British Library, Add. MSS 22649. Robert's Collection.

. For example, see Mona Duggan, 'Urban Change in a Lancashire Market Town 1660–1800' (PhD thesis, University of Lancaster, 1992), pp. 134–5.

. LRO DDK 1772 (1732).

. PRO E 134, 5 and 6 William and Mary, Hilary nos 20, 22, Depositions of Edward Healley and William Lathom.

. LRO WCW Thomas Gerrard 1663; Alehouse licences QSB 3 (1661).

. LRO DDK 1521/4 (1677).

. LRO DDK 1521/3 (1680).

. LRO DDK 1521/1 (1677).

. LRO QSP 832/49 (1699)

LRO WCW Thomas Houghton 1710. 'House' usually meant a kitchen in inventories.
This may have referred to the common land or it may have been part of the roadway. By 1797 the cottage had become an alehouse, the Black Horse: LRO DDK 258/1.

. LRO DDK 290/14/3, Encroachment Rentals.

LRO DDK 1820/2 (1747).

LRO DDK 290/14/3, Encroachment Rentals.

LRO DDK 1820/26 (1774), DDK 1820/36 (1786), DDK 1820/40 (1789).

LRO DDK 290/14/3, Encroachment rental.

LRO DDK 1820/12 (1758).

149. LRO DDK 258/1 (1797). Deposition of James Waring.

150. LRO DDK 290/14/1, Mr Stuart's Encroachment, 1780.

151. LRO DDK 1820/35 (1783).

152. Liverpool Record Office Plumbe Tempest Papers 920 PLU 31.

153. LRO DDK 1746/18. Order no. 11.

154. LRO WCW John Vause 1671.

155. Knowsley Hall, Estate Papers N. 18B 198 20A.

156. LRO DDK 1820/21 (1769).

157. LRO DDK 1770/15 (1777).

158. LRO DDK 1820/35 (1783).

159. LRO DDK 1820/33 (1781).

160. LRO DDK 1820/46 (1794).

161. LRO Scarisbrick Papers, DDS c.22/9.

162. LRO DDK 258/1. The deposition of John Irving.

163. LRO WCW Andrew Rutter 1781.

164. See Mona Duggan, 'Urban Change' p. 141.

165. LRO DRL 1/58.

166. This table is based on one in Priestley and Corfield's study of Norwich. Despite using a larger sample, their results show a similar pattern, and their conclusion that 'the distribution of house size changed relatively little' applies to Ormskirk: Ursula Priestley and Penelope Corfield, 'Rooms and Room Use in Norwich Housing 1580–1730', *Post-Medieval Archaeology*, no. 16 (1982), p. 100.

167. New chambers: LRO WCW William Livesey 1661, WCW Thomas Gerrard 1663, WCW Thomas Mawdesley 1682, WCW Thomas Moorcroft 1692. New parlour: WCW Roger Barton 1665. New house (kitchen): WCW Richard Wood 1668. New House (workshop): WCW Thomas Houghton 1710.

168. Jones and Falkus *Urban Improvement*, p. 201.

169. For detailed examples see Mona Duggan, 'Urban Change', p. 144.

170. Penelope Corfield, 'The Industrial Towns before the Factory, 1680–1780', in John Barrett et al., *The Rise of the New Urban Society*, (Milton Keynes: Open University Press, 1977), A322, unit 15, p. 84.

Chapter IV

1. R.C. Richardson, *Puritanism in North West England: a Regional Study of the Diocese of Chester to 1642* (Manchester University Press 1973), p. 183.

2. Nicholas Tyacke, *Anti-Calvinists: the Rise of English Arminianism*, c. *1590–1640* (Oxford Historical Monographs, Oxford: Clarendon

Press, 1987), p. 194; Patrick Collinson, *The Religion of Protestants: the Church in English Society, 1559–1625* (Oxford: Clarendon Press, 1982), pp. 31–2, and H.R Trevor Roper, *Archbishop Laud, 1573–1645* (London: Macmillan, 1940), p. 151.

3. E. Axon, 'The King's Preachers in Lancashire', *TLCAS*, vol. lvi (1944), p. 77; Richardson, *Puritanism in NW England*, p. 26.

4. CRO EDV 5 1637 Miscellaneous; Tyacke, *Anti-Calvinists*, p. 116.

5. CRO EDV 5 1637 Miscellaneous.

6. Henry Fishwick, ed., *Lancashire Church Surveys, 1650*, Part 1, *RSLC*, vol. 1 (1879) p. 89.

7. Robert S. Bosher, *The Making of the Restoration Settlement: the Influence of the Laudians, 1649–1662* (Westminster: Dacre Press, 1951, revd 1957), p. 107.

8. Nathaniel Heywood was the brother of Oliver Heywood: J. Horsfall Turner, ed., *The Reverend Oliver Heywood: his Autobiography, Diaries, Anecdotes and Event Books*, 4 vols (Brighouse: A.B. Bates, 1881), passim.

9. Frank Bate, *The Declaration of Indulgence, 1672: a Study in the Rise of Organised Dissent* (London: Constable, for Liverpool University Press, 1908), p. 4.

10. LRO PR 2886/3 Ormskirk Parish Register for 1660.

11. Thomas Wilson, Bishop of Sodor and Man, *The Practical Christian or the Devout Penitent*, 4 parts (6th edn), to which is added 'The Life of Dr Richard Sherlock, chaplain to the Earl of Derby' (London: 1713).

12. For other examples of desecration, see John Phillips, *The Reformation of Images: Destruction of Art in England 1535–1669* (University of California, 1973) pp. 190–5.

13. Bosher, *The Making of the Restoration Settlement*, p. 281.

14. Nikolaus Pevsner, ed., *The Buildings of England*, BE 37, North Lancashire (Harmondsworth: Penguin, 1969), p. 23.

15. Tyacke, *Anti-Calvinists*, p. 176.

16. Sir Henry Ashurst, *Some Remarks Upon the Life of That Painful Servant of God, Mr Nathaniel Heywood, Minister of the Gospel of Christ at Ormskirk in Lancashire, who died in the 44th Year of His Age* (London: 1695), pp. 11–12; Robert Halley, *Lancashire: its Puritanism and Nonconformity*, 2 vols (Manchester: Tubbs and Brook, 1869), vol. 2, pp. 126–7.

17. Axon, 'The King's Preachers', pp. 89–90.

18. J.R. Jones, *Country and Court, England 1658–1714* (London: Edward Arnold, 1978), p. 148.

19. James Dixon, 'Nathaniel Heywood, the Nonconformist Vicar of Ormskirk', THSLC, vol. 30 (1878), p. 160.

20. A.G. Matthews, *Calamy Revised being a revision of Edmund Calamy's 'Account of the Ministers and Others Ejected and Silenced 1660–1662'* (Oxford: Clarendon Press, 1934, reissued 1988), p. 12. Matthews claimed that thirteen more Lancashire ministers were ejected, but as the date of their ejection was uncertain he excluded them.

21. Samuel Palmer, *The Nonconformist Memorial, being an account of the ministers ejected...by Edmund Calamy D.D.*, 2 vols (London: W. Harris, 1775), vol. 2, p. 102; Halley, *Lancashire*, vol. 2, pp. 187–8.

22. Bosher, *The Making of the Restoration Settlement*, p. 273.

23. For examples, see Mona Duggan, 'Urban Change', p. 156.

24. Ashurst, *Some Remarks...on...Heywood*, pp. 14–19; Halley, *Lancashire*, vol. 2, p. 189.

25. For pluralism, salaries and the numbers ordained see Norman Sykes, *The Church and State in England in the Eighteenth Century*, (Cambridge University Press: 1932), pp. 111, 189, 215–18.

26. H.M. Luft, *A History of Merchant Taylors' School, Crosby 1620–1970* (Liverpool University Press, 1970), pp. 75–80.

27. LRO DDK 1746/18 Order of Streetlookers no. 3.

28. Dixon, ed., *The Churchwardens' Accounts for Ormskirk 1665–1666*, vol.30, pp. 170–3.

29. Ellis Gleast, whose son James later glazed the Town Hall, was paid 8s 11d 'for glazing...at several times', ibid., p. 173.

30. Borsay, *The English Urban Renaissance*, pp. 41–113.

31. 35 Eliz. cap.1. Pickering, *Statutes at Large*, vol. 7.

32. 13 Car.II stat.2 c.1 2. Ibid., vol. 8.

33. 16 Car.II c.4. Ibid., vol. 8.

34. 17 Car.II c.2. Ibid., vol. 8.

35. 14 Car.II c.33. Ibid., vol. 8.

36. Kenyon referred specifically to the Conventicle Act, but his comments apply to the whole Clarendon Code. For details see J.P. Kenyon, ed., *The Stuart Constitution, 1603–1688, Documents and Commentary*

37. (Cambridge: Cambridge University Press, 1966), p. 364.

37. R.A. Beddard, 'The Restoration Church', in J.R. Jones, ed., *The Restored Monarchy 1660–1688* (London: Macmillan, 1979), p. 166.

38. Ashurst *Some Remarks...on...Heywood*, p. 14.

39. T. Heywood, ed., *The Diary of the Rev. Henry Newcome from 30 September 1661 to 29 September 1663* CS Old Series, vol. 18 (1849), p. 23.

40. Ashurst. *Some Remarks...on...Heywood*, p. 14.

41. B. Nightingale, *The Early Stages of the Quaker Movement in Lancashire* (London: Congregational Union of England and Wales, 1921), p. 205.

42. Horsfall Turner, ed., *The Rev. Oliver Heywood*, p. 224.

43. Bate, *Declaration of Indulgence*, p. 54, quoting Western MS 28, 181, p. 58, appendix IV p. 8.

44. 22 Car.II c.1. Pickering, *Statutes at Large*, vol. 8.

45. For details of the declaration and its cancellation, see Bate, *Declaration of Indulgence*, pp. 36–75, 130–43.

46. Deposition of Robert Holland. For this and other depositions from the trial of Heywood see Anon., 'Sir Roger Bradshaigh's Letter-Book,' *THSLC* vol. LXIII (1911), pp. 168–73.

47. Ashurst, *Some Remarks...on...Heywood*, pp. 28–36; Halley, *Lancashire*, vol. 2, p. 189.

48. Ashurst, *Some Remarks...on...Heywood*, p. 35.

49. Michael Mullett, 'Popular Culture and Popular Politics', in Jones, ed., *Britain in the First Age of Party*, pp. 137–8.

50. Margaret Blundell, ed., *Cavalier: Letters of William Blundell to his Friends, 1620–1698* (London: Longmans Green, 1933), p. 210; Michael Mullett, ' "A Receptacle for Papists and an Assilum": Catholicism and Disorder in Late Seventeenth-Century Wigan', p. 391.

51. PRO Exchequer Records, E 134 13–14 William, Hilary 26. Depositions in the case Thomas Stanley v. Charles Davenport.

52. Henry Ashurst, *Some Remarks*, p. 62. Mr Starkie may have been the rector of North Meols or he may have been John Starkie, a minister ejected from Grantham and licensed in Ormskirk: B. Nightingale, ed., *Lancashire Nonconformity*, p. 8; Matthews, *Calamy Revised*, pp. 459–60.

53. British Library, Add. MS 22648, Roberts Collection.

54. Halley, *Lancashire*, vol. 2, p. 179.

55. Zachary Taylor, *The Vindication of Late Pamphlet entitled 'Obedience a Submission to the Present Governme from Bishop Overall's Convocation Book'* (London, printed for Richar Baldwin, 1691).

56. Zachary Taylor, *The Surey Impost being an answer to a late Fanatical Pamphlet – 'The Surey Demoniac'* (London 1697).

57. James Dixon, 'Notes on Certain Discoveries made during the Alteration on Ormskirk Church', *THSLC*, vol. 30 (1878) p. 145.

58. Quoted in David Cressy, *Literacy and the Social Order: Reading and Writing in Tudor and Stuart Engla* (Cambridge: Cambridge Universi Press, 1980), p. 3.

59. Alan Savidge, *The Foundation and Early Years of Queen Anne's Boun* (London: SPCK, 1955), p. 55.

60. Ashurst, *Some Remarks*, p. 11.

61. LRO PR 3385/4.

62. CRO EDV 7 1/201, Bishop Porteus's Visitation (1778).

63. Geoffrey Holmes, 'The Sachevero Riots, the Crowd and the Church' *Past and Present*, vol. 72 (1976), p 60–85.

64. British Library, Stowe Manuscrip 750 f32. Nicholas Blundell bough Steynhead's book and saw him pilloried in Liverpool, 'for writing against Dr Secheverall and the Church of England' on 21 July (1711): Tyrer, ed. *The Great Diurnal*, vol. I p. 295.

65. Collinson, *The Religion of Protesta* p. 210; Wrightson and Levine, *Poverty and Piety in an English Village*, Terling, 1525–1700 (Lond Academic Press, 1979), p. 157.

66. Armstrong, *The Church of Englan* p. 33.

67. Peter Fleetwood Hesketh, *Murray's Architectural Guide to Lancashire* (London: John Murray, 1955), p. 60 F.A. Bailey and R. Millington, *The Story of Liverpool* (Liverpool: The Corporation of Liverpool, 1957), p.

68. Jan Maria Albers, 'Seeds of Contention: Society, Politics and Church of England in Lancashire 1689–1800', (unpublished PhD thesis, Yale University, 1988), p. 5

69. In the 1720s, Liverpool (populatio approximately 12,500) and Manchester (population 8,000) had only two parish churches, while in 1730 Sheffield (population 10,000 had only one: Michael Watts, *The Dissenters, from the Reformation to French Revolution* (Oxford: Clarend

Press, 1978), p. 338; Collinson, *The Religion of Protestants*, p. 210.

89. LRO PR 3385/4.

90. James Dixon, 'Notes on Certain Discoveries', p. 147. The vestry adjoining the Bickerstaffe chapel was roofed in slate.

91. LRO PR 3385/4.

92. Sykes, *Church and State*, p. 233.

93. LRO DDK 290/2/9, Robert Scarisbrick's right to the chapel, 1721.

94. Revd F.R. Raines, *Notitia Cestriensis, or Historical Notes of the Diocese of Chester by Bishop Gastrell*, vol. 2, Part 2, Lancashire Part 2, CS, vol. 21 (1849–1850), p. 197.

95. For population totals see p. xvii.

96. LRO Quarter Sessions records, Quarter Sessions Petitions 1226/38.

97. For examples of some of the churches that contributed, see Duggan, 'Urban Change', p. 175.

98. See LRO Quarter Sessions Records, QSP 1226/31 – QSP 1226/37, for estimates given by various craftsmen.

99. Ruth Dove and Helen Segebarth, *A History of the Friends' Meeting House in Lancaster* (Preston: Snape, 1991), p. 7.

100. Today, weather-moulding on the eastern side of the tower indicates the position of the pre-1729 roof; *VCH*, vol. 111, p. 241.

101. CRO Diocesan Records, EDA 2/5.

102. For further details of this organ and of church music, see pp. 159–60.

103. Borsay, *The English Urban Renaissance*, pp. 582–96.

104. R.G.B. Bailey, *Ormskirk Parish Church* (4th edn, Gloucester: British Publishing Co., 1980), p. 3.

105. CRO EDV 1/126, Correction Book, Ormskirk (1738); PRO RG 4/3584.

106. CRO Churchwardens Presentments, EDV 5, November (1747).

107. British Library, Add. MS 36882.

108. R. Lawton, 'Population and Society, 1730–1900', in Dodgshon and Butlin, eds, *An Historical Geography of England and Wales*, p. 323.

109. J.H. Overton and F. Relton, *The English Church from the Accession of George I to the end of the Eighteenth century* (London: Macmillan, 1906), p. 139.

110. British Library Add. MS 36882; Gadd, *Georgian Summer*, p. 111.

111. The Bickerstaffe Stanleys acquired the Derby chapel when James, Tenth Earl of Derby, died in 1736, leaving no direct heir, and they inherited the title. LRO PR 3385/4; British Library, Add. MS 36882. Churchwardens' accounts, 1770.

94. LRO Ormskirk glebe terriers 1814, DRL 3/12.

95. British Library, Add. MS 22648, Roberts Collection, p. 14.

96. Albers, 'Seeds of Contention', p. 50.

97. Sykes, *Church and State*, p. 282.

98. Borsay, *The English Urban Renaissance*, pp. 596–7.

99. Anthony Armstrong, *The Church of England, Methodism and Society, 1700–1850* (University of London Press, 1973), p. 13.

100. For example, John Hurleston carved his name in 1618; CRO EDC 5 (1678), no. 9, Deposition of Gilbert Ormishaw.

101. Both Laud and Neile had objected, in the strongest terms, to worshippers sitting 'above' (eastwards) of the communion table. Sitting 'above God Almighty' was how they described it: Tyacke, *Anti-Calvinists*, p. 199; also Collinson, *The Religion of Protestants*, p. 195.

102. CRO EDC 5 (1678), no. 9, Deposition of Richard Taylor.

103. The title 'Mr' is indicative of a gentry or near-gentry family in Ormskirk's seventeenth-century records.

104. CRO EDV 5 (1678) no. 9, Deposition of Silvester Ashcroft.

105. Dixon, 'Churchwardens' Accounts 1665', pp. 170–3.

106. CRO EDC 5 (1678) Deposition of Richard Grice. Today an excellent example of an early pew, the old dog whipper's pew with a drawer for the gloves, whip and tongs stands at the back of the church. It cannot be traced in the records.

107. British Library, Add. MS 22649, Roberts Collection; LRO Derby muniments, DDK 1746/18, Order Book for Ormskirk.

108. CRO EDC 5, no. 9, 1677, Ormskirk, Deposition of Thomas Ambrose.

109. The militant Anglicanism of Charles, Eighth Earl of Derby (1651–1672), had 'exacerbated divisions in the north-west, making it...difficult...for the Stanley family to pose as the undisputed head of the local community': Barry Coward, *The Stanleys: Lord Stanley and the Earls of Derby, 1385–1672*, CS, vol. 30 (1983), pp. 181–2, p. 277.

110. CRO EDC 5 (1672), no. 29.

111. Holmes, *Augustan England*, pp. 117–18.

112. CRO EDC 5 (1677), no. 9.

113. LRO PR 3385 Acc. 7175. Churchwardens' Accounts.

114. CRO EDC 5 (1678), no. 9.

115. CRO Diocesan Records, EDC 5 no. 11, 1692, Ormskirk.

116. LRO PR 3385 Acc.7175, Churchwardens' accounts.

117. *VCH*, vol. 3, p. 243.

118. LRO Lathom Muniments, DDLm 2/1. *VCH*, vol. 3, p. 243.

119. For instance John Crosbie, a grocer, and John Heyes, a woollen draper, acquired pews in the early eighteenth century. LRO PR 3385 Acc.7175.

120. CRO, Diocesan Records, EDC 5 no. 13 (1718) Ormskirk; LRO PR 3385, Acc.7175, Churchwardens Accounts (1718).

121. CRO EDA 2/5 p. 166 (1731).

122. CRO EDA 2/6 p. 457 (1762).

123. CRO EDA 2/6 (1762), p. 456.

124. CRO EDA 2/6 (1762), p. 448.

125. CRO EDA 2/8 (1783). This tradition is recorded in the will of Thomas Greaves, 1716, who mentioned 'the burial place belonging to the house where I live'. LRO WCW Thomas Greaves (1716).

126. Collinson, *The Religion of Protestants*, p. 194.

127. LRO PR 3385, Acc.7175.

Chapter V

1. Watts, *The Dissenters*, p. 277.

2. LRO Quarter Sessions records, QSP 669/16. Although there is no mention of the Ormskirk 'Dissenters' changing their theological allegiance, their description could be misleading, for a 'Presbyterian' congregation might become a 'Unitarian' Church, and still refer to itself as 'Protestant Dissenter' or 'Presbyterian': Michael Mullett, *Sources for the History of English Non-Conformity, 1660–1830* (London: British Records Association, 1991), p. 2.

3. LRO, QSP 730/9. Registration of Dissenters' New Meeting House. Although Roger Westhead is recorded as living in Moor Street in the court roll, according to Roberts the chapel was formerly in Chapel Lane (Street) so presumably the chapel stood near the corner of the two streets, close to the site of the old Congregational church – now the community centre. LRO, Ormskirk Manor Court Roll, 1680, DDK 1521/3.

4. Alexander Gordon, ed. *Freedom after Ejection: a Review (1690–1692) of Presbyterian and Congregational Nonconformity in England and Wales* (Manchester: Manchester University Press, 1917), pp. 154–8,

184–7 (the Happy Union) and pp. 15–184 (the Common Fund); Watts, *The Dissenters*, pp. 289–97; C.G. Bolam, Jeremy Goring, H.L. Short and Roger Thomas, *The English Presbyterians from Elizabethan Puritanism to Modern Unitarianism* (London: George Allen & Unwin, 1968); pp. 101–2, 121–2.

5.   G.F. Nuttall, 'Assembly and Association in Dissent, 1689–1831', in G.J. Cuming and D. Baker, eds, *Studies in Church History*, vol. 7 (Cambridge University Press, 1971), p. 297–303.

6.   Anne Whiteman, *The Compton Census of 1676, a Critical Edition*. Records of Social and Economic History, new series, (London: for the British Academy by the Oxford University Press, 1986); for the table see pp. 179, 185, 446, 449, 538, 540, 592.

7.   Gordon, ed., *Freedom after Ejection*, p. 58.

8.   LRO WCW Edward Dicconson (1717).

9.   Horsfall Turner, ed. *Heywood's Diaries*, vol. 3, pp. 109, 152; Watts, *The Dissenters*, p. 291.

10. Joseph Hunter, *The Rise of the Old Dissent exemplified in the Life of Oliver Heywood, 1630–1702* (London: Longman, Brown and Longman, 1842), p. 301. A similar mixed denominational service was held in Devon in 1672: Nuttall, 'Assembly and Association', p. 294.

11. F. Nicholson & Ernest Axon, *The Older Nonconformity in Kendal* (Kendal: Titus Wilson, 1915), pp. 164, 546; William A. Shaw, ed., *Minutes of the Manchester Presbyterian Classis, 1646–1660*, Part 3, CS New Series, vol. 24 (1891), p. 352.

12. Shaw, ed., *Minutes*, pp. 353, 355, 357–8, 364.

13. Gordon, *Freedom after Ejection*, p. 157; Watts, *The Dissenters* p. 291.

14. LRO, QSP 795/20, QSP 988/10.

15. Halley, *Lancashire*, vol. 2, pp. 309, 316, 320.

16. For Frankland's Academy, see Nicholson and Axon, *The Older Nonconformity*, pp. 546, 617–18, and passim; Hunter, *The Rise of the Old Dissent*, pp.242–243. Frankland's Academy's successor, the Warrington Academy, was established in 1755, its first treasurer being Arthur Heywood, a direct descendent of Nathaniel Heywood: Halley, *Lancashire*, vol. 2, p. 398.

17. Mullett, *Sources*, p. 3

18. Watts, *The Dissenters*, pp. 267–89, 491–510.

19. Ibid., p. 509.

20. Raines, ed., *Notitia Cestriensis*, p. 196. This included Dissenters from the whole parish of Ormskirk.

21. See p. xvii. The fact that the population total includes only townsfolk while the Presbyterians' numbers included the parish distorts the percentage, but, as that probably applied elsewhere, the comparison is valid.

22. Watts, *The Dissenters*, p. 392; Bolam et al., *English Presbyterians*, pp. 24–7.

23. Armstrong, *The Church of England*, p. 41.

24. For the rise of Unitarianism see: R.W. Richey, 'Did the English Presbyterians become Unitarians?', *Church History*, vol. 47 (1973), pp. 58–72.

25. Russell E. Richey, 'The Effects of Toleration', *Journal of Religious History*, vol. 8, no. 4 (1974), p. 359.

26. Bolam et al., *English Presbyterians*, pp. 199, 208.

27. PRO RG/4/3584, Register of Aughton Street Presbyterian Church, Ormskirk; Watts, *The Dissenters*, p. 501. For the birth rate of 1743–1771, I have averaged the figures given by D.E.C. Eversley, while for the later period, 1771–1783, I have averaged those earlier figures: D.E.C. Eversley, 'A Survey of the Population in an Area of Worcestershire 1660–1850', *Population Studies*, vol. 10 (1957), p. 267.

28. To find the size of the congregation I divided 1,000 head of population by the number of births and multiplied them by the number of baptisms.

29. Watts, *The Dissenters*, p. 360.

30. Bolam et al., *English Presbyterians*, p. 223.

31. QSP 2009/6, Registration of Edward Pike's house, 1773.

32. British Library Add. MS 22648.

33. PRO Aughton Street Chapel Register, RG 4/3584; LRO QSP 2177/27.

34. PRO RG/4/3584, Register of Aughton Street Presbyterian Chapel, undated comment probably made *c.* 1837 when the register closed.

35. For the rise of Methodism see Rupert Davies and Gordon Rupp, eds *A History of the Methodist Church in Great Britain*, 4 vols (London: Epworth Press, 1965), vol. 1; W.J. Townsend, H.B. Workman, George Eayrs, eds *A New History of Methodism* (London: Hodder and Stoughton, 1909).

36. Armstrong *The Church of England* p. 126.

37. Ibid. p. 73.

38. Armstrong, *The Church of England* p. 127.

39. Davies and Rupp, eds, *The History the Methodist Church*, pp. 219–45.

40. For the attacks on Methodists see Jo Walsh, 'Methodism and the Mob in the Eighteenth Century', in Cuming and Baker, eds, *Studies in Church History*, vol. 8 (1972), pp. 213–27.

41. Watts, *The Dissenters*, pp. 394–464

42. Townsend et al., eds, *History of Methodism*, pp. 386–8.

43. CRO EDV 7 1/201.

44. E.A. Rose, 'Methodism in South Lancashire to 1800', *TLCAS*, vol. (1982), p. 86.

45. CRO EDV 7, 1/201.

46. Rose, *Methodism in South Lancashire*, p. 86.

47. Sylvia Jacquet, *Emmanuel: the St of Methodism in Ormskirk, 1792–19* (Ormskirk: Jacquest, 1978), p. 3.

48. Ibid., p. 3.

49. LRO DDK 1521/14 (1795). This wrecking of preaching houses also occurred at St Ives, Sheffield, Arborfield, Wolverhampton, Nantwich and Chester. Others we severely damaged: Walsh, 'Methodism and the Mob', p. 213

50. Jacquest, *Emmanuel*, pp. 4–5.

51. Barry Reay, *The Quakers and the English Revolution*, (London: Temple Smith, 1985), p. 12.

52. Ibid., pp. 44, 58.

53. Alan B. Anderson, 'A Study in th Sociology of Religious Persecutio The First Quakers', *The Journal c Religious History*, vol. 9, no. 4, December (1977), p. 255.

54. Watt, *The Dissenters*, pp. 152, 189–98, 221–3.

55. Jones, *Country and Court*, p. 146.

56. Over 200 Quakers were buried in this graveyard, in Graveyard Lan Bickerstaffe.

57. This book (LRO FRL 1/A, Lancashire Quarterly Meeting Sufferings Book, 1654–1700), unindexed and unpaged, was compiled locally by the Quaker Meeting for Sufferings to record suffering – physical and economi undergone by Friends for their beliefs.

58. Reay, *The Quakers*, pp. 43–4.

59. Rufus Jones, ed., *George Fox: an Autobiography* (London: Headley 1904), p. 165.

60. Michael Mullett, *Radical Religio Movements in Early Modern Europ*

(London: George Allen and Unwin, 1980), pp. 139–40.

LRO FRL 1/A.

Reay, *The Quakers*, pp. 91–105.

W.C. Braithwaite, *The Beginnings of Quakerism* (Cambridge: Cambridge University Press, 2nd edn, 1961), pp. 295, 474.

LRO QSP 219/7.

Revd B. Nightingale, ed., *The Early Stages of the Quaker Movement in Lancashire*, p. 40.

LRO QSP 211/36, QSP 215/14.

LRO FRL 1/A.

For examples of the sufferings see Braithwaite, *The Beginnings of Quakerism*, pp. 21–54.

G. Couthard Newstead, *Gleanings towards the Annals of Aughton* (Liverpool: C.H. Radcliffe, 1893), pp. 15–16. For other examples see Lancashire Quarterly Meetings Sufferings Book.

For other examples see Reay, *The Quakers*, pp. 39–40, 43–4, 52, 58–9.

CRO Consistory court records, EDC 5, no. 5, Ormskirk, 1674.

Michael Mullett, ed., *Early Lancaster Friends* (Lancaster: Centre for North-West Regional Studies, Occasional Paper no. 5, 1978), p. 8.

LRO FRL 1/A.

Reay, *The Quakers*, pp. 106–22; R.T. Vann, *The Social Development of English Quakerism, 1655–1755*, (Cambridge, Massachusetts: Harvard University Press, 1969), pp. 91, 102, 158.

Mullett, *Radical Religious Movements*, p. 87.

Nicholas J. Morgan, 'Lancashire Quakers and the Tithe, 1660–1730', *Bulletin of the John Rylands University Library of Manchester*, no. 70 (1988), p. 63.

Anderson, 'The Sociology of Religious Persecution', p. 254.

LRO QSP 448/12.

For further details see Arnold Lloyd, *Quaker Social History, 1669–1738* (London, Longmans Green, 1950), pp. 32–47; Vann, *The Social Development*, pp. 144–57.

LRO Lancaster Monthly Meetings, Marriage Register 1645–1800, FRL Safe 1 Shelf C, Book 756, no. 152.

J.D. Marshall, ed., *The Autobiography of William Stout of Lancaster*, CS, 3rd series, vol. 14 (1967), pp. 125–6.

LRO Derby Records, Stewards Letters, DDK 1652 August 27 (1761). WCW Hugh Crosby, Ormskirk (1761).

83. LRO QSP 726/15, Wigan (1692).

84. LRO Steward's Letters, DDK 1644 (1750).

85. CRO Bishop Porteus's Visitation (1778), EDV 7/1/201.

86. Sir John Arundell submitted this petition in 1660: M.D.R. Leys, *Catholics in England 1559–1829: A Social History* (London: Longmans Green, 1961), p. 93.

87. J.C.H. Aveling, *The Handle and the Axe: Catholic Recusants in England from the Revolution to the Emancipation* (London: Blom & Briggs, 1976), p. 206.

88. J. Miller, *Popery and Politics in England 1660–1688* (Cambridge: Cambridge University Press, 1972), p. 58.

89. Michael Mullett and Leo Warren, *Martyrs of the Diocese of Lancaster beatified on the Feast of Christ the King* (Preston: Snape, 1987), p. 10. For more details see Miller, *Popery and Politics*, pp. 121–53, 154–61, and John Kenyon, *The Popish Plot* (London: Heinemann, 1972).

90. The Lancashire Justices continued being lenient towards their Catholic neighbours until the 1680s, when, following the Popish Plot, the Privy Council summoned them *en bloc* to explain their reluctance to confiscate the Catholics' recognisances and to explain the deferment of their convictions: Kenyon, *The Popish Plot*, p. 234.

91. Sir Henry Ashurst, *Some Remarks*, pp. 37–42.

92. Mona Duggan, *A History of Scarisbrick* (Preston: Carnegie Publishing, 1996), pp. 53, 70–1. For the tightening of the penal laws in Lancashire and the Wigan riots see Mullett, *A Recepticle for Papists*, p. 391.

93. Blundell, ed. *Cavalier*, pp. 205–10.

94. LRO QSP 509/32, 1679.

95. Aveling, *The Handle and the Axe*, p. 188.

96. L.K.J. Glassey, *Politics and the Appointment of Justices of the Peace, 1675–1720* (Oxford: Oxford University Press, 1979), pp. 274–6; Miller, *Popery and Politics*, pp. 218–19, 269–72.

97. B.W. Quintrell, *Proceedings of the Lancashire Justices of the Peace at the Sheriff's Table during Assize Week, 1578–1694*, RSLC, vol. 121 (1981) p. 34.

98. D.P. Carter, 'The Lancashire Militia 1660–1688', in Kermode and Phillips, eds., *Seventeenth-Century Lancashire*, p. 180.

99. Blundell, *Cavalier*, p. 263.

100. Acts against Superstitious Uses: 1 Ed.6, c.14; 3.Jas.I c.5 and later, 11 & 12 Will.III, c.4: Pickering, *Statutes at Large*, vols 5, 7, 10.

101. E. Norman, *Roman Catholicism in England from the Elizabethan Settlement to the Second Vatican Council*, (Oxford: Oxford University Press, 1985), p. 40; John Bossy, *The English Catholic Community 1570–1850* (London: Darton, Longman & Todd, 1975), pp. 168–81.

102. T.E. Gibson, ed., *Blundell's Diary*, p. 45.

103. Dom. R.J. Stonor, *Liverpool's Hidden Story* (Billinge: Birchley Hall Press, 1957), p. 26; Leonard Hanley, *History of St. Annes', Ormskirk, 1732–1782* (Ormskirk, Causeway Press, 1982), pp. 7, 10.

104. Tyrer, ed., *The Great Diurnal*, passim.

105. John Bossy, 'Catholic Lancashire in the Eighteenth Century', in *Essays Presented to Michael Roberts sometime Professor of Modern History in the Queens University of Belfast* (Belfast: Blackstaff Press, 1976), p. 62.

106. Bossy, *English Catholic Community*, p. 261.

107. Stonor, *Liverpool's Hidden Story*, p. 27; Tyrer, ed., *The Great Diurnal*, passim.

108. J.A. Hilton, *Catholic Lancashire: a Historical Guide* (Wigan: North West Catholic History Society, 1981), pp. 14, 23.

109. Dom. F.O. Blundell, *Old Catholic Lancashire*, 3 vols (London: Burns Oates, 1925), vol. 3, pp. 93–100; *Palatine Notebook*, vol. 1, p. 87.

110. See pp. 89, 112.

111. Later, Bulmer decided that the Lancasters' request for eighty-four Masses to be said for their souls during the year was excessive and, with his superior's permission, reduced the number to twelve for Mr Lancaster and twenty-four for Mrs Lancaster: Douai Abbey, Woolhampton (Near Reading), records referring to Ormskirk.

112. LRO WCW William Lancaster (1731).

113. LRO WCW Elizabeth Lancaster (1733).

114. Rt Revd B.C. Foley, *Some People of the Penal Times* (Preston: Snape, 1991), p. 9. For further information on the financing of the English Benedictine missions see Miller, *Popery and Politics*, p. 36.

115. LRO WCW Ann Harrison (1741).

116. Records of Ormskirk Mission, Douai Abbey.
117. Tyrer, ed., *The Great Diurnal*, vol. 1, pp. 166, 169.
118. Ibid., vol. 2, pp. 144, 151–9.
119. LRO QSP 1079/22.
120. LRO WCW William Grice (1725).
121. Knowsley Hall Library, N.H. 18B, 182, no. 4, Contemporary Letters concerning 1745.
122. LRO PR 409–412, Bickerstaffe Constables' Accounts.
123. LRO QSO 2/115. April Session (1746).
124. *Palatine Notebook*, vol. I, p. 87; T.E. Gibson, *Lydiate Hall and its Associations* (Edinburgh: Ballantyne, Hanson, 1876), p. 129; Gibson ed., *Blundell's Diary*, p. 99; *State Papers Domestic*, 36/75/2.
125. Leys, *Catholics in England*, p. 120; Stonor, *Liverpool's Hidden Story*, p. 30.
126. LRO DDK 1652, August 1761, Stewards' Letters.
127. 18. George III c.46, Pickering, *Statutes at Large*, vol. 32.
128. Ibid., 31 George III c.32, vol. 37.
129. British Library Add. MS. 22648, p. 142.
130. Raines, ed., *Notitia Cestriensis*, p. 196.
131. E.S. Worrall, ed., *Returns of the Papists, 1767, for the Diocese of Chester*, 2 vols (Catholic Record Society, 1980), Occasional Publications, no. 1, vol. 1, p. 130.
132. Anon., 'Lancashire Catholicism', *THSLC*, New Series vol. 18 (1902), p. 215; Bossy, 'Catholic Lancashire', p. 62; Bossy, *English Catholic Community*, p. 424.
133. CRO EDV 7/1/201, Bishop Porteus's Visitation (1778).
134. Kenyon, *The Popish Plot*, p. 25.
135. Aveling, *The Handle and the Axe*, p. 286.
136. J. Anthony Williams, ed., *Catholicism in Bath*, 2 vols (Catholic Record Society Publications, Records Series, vol. 65, 1975), vol. 2, p. 79.
137. Miller, *Popery and Politics*, pp. 13–14.
138. J.H. Whyte, 'The Vicars Apostolic Returns of 1773', *Recusant History*, vol. 9 (1967) p. 205.
139. Dom. Gilbert Dolan OSB, 'Lancashire and the Benedictines', *THSLC*, New Series, vol. 13 (1898), p. 157.
140. Kenyon, *The Popish Plot*, p. 236.
141. Worrall, ed. *Returns of the Papists, 1767*, vol. 1, p. 130; PRO RG/4/3584 Register of Aughton Street Presbyterian Chapel, Ormskirk.
142. Beilby Porteus, *Letter to the Clergy*

in the Diocese of Chester (Chester: J. Poole, 1781).
143. For an account of the struggle for this last religious freedom, see Ursula Henriques, *Religious Toleration in England, 1787–1833* (London: Routledge and Kegan Paul, 1961).
144. Bossy, 'Catholic Lancashire', p. 54.
145. Miller, *Popery and Politics*, p. 262.
146. For instance, Albers, 'Seeds of Contention' p. 18; Jones, *Country and Court*, p. 141

Chapter VI

1. LRO Ormskirk Grammar School Agreement, DDX 191/1.
2. Holmes, *Augustan England*, p. 280.
3. Lawrence Stone, 'The Educational Revolution in England, 1560–1640', *Past and Present*, vol. 28 (1964) p. 69.
4. LRO Ormskirk Grammar School Minute Book, DDX 191/1, pp. 33, 38.
5. LRO DDX 191/2, Account Book for Ormskirk Grammar School.
6. LRO QSP 219/8 (1661).
7. J.R. Bate, 'Ormskirk Grammar School; the First Minute Book, 1613–1890', *THSLC* vol. 76 (1924), p. 94.
8. W.A.L. Vincent, *The Grammar Schools: their Continuing Tradition, 1660–1714* (London: John Murray, 1969), p. 155.
9. LRO DDX 191/1, p. 207.
10. Vincent, 'The Grammar Schools', pp. 170–1.
11. Christopher Wase, *Considerations Concerning Free-Schools* (1678) in David Cressy, *Education in Tudor and Stuart England* (London: Longmans, 1975), p. 57.
12. Marchamount Nedham, 'A Discourse Concerning Schools' (1663), pp. 3–4 in Cressy, *Education in Tudor and Stuart England*, p. 65.
13. LRO DDX 191/1, p. 206.
14. Corpus Christi College Muniments, Wase MS, 390/2 f.22.
15. W.A.L. Vincent, *The Grammar Schools*, pp. 154–5.
16. LRO DDX 191/1, pp. 212–13.
17. As we have seen, Mr Ashworth, master at Merchant Taylors' School in Crosby, experienced similar difficulties.
18. LRO, DDX 191/1.
19. LRO WCW Richard Birchall (1649).
20. C.D. Rogers, 'The Development of a Teaching Profession in England, 1547–1700' (unpublished PhD

thesis, University of Manchester, 1975), p. 333.
21. Ibid., p. 39.
22. LRO WCW Thomas Gerard (1662
23. PRO E179 132/355 25 Car.11, Hearth Tax Assessments.
24. Fishwick, *The History of the Parish of Rochdale*, p. 411.
25. 14 Car.II, c. 4: Pickering ed., *Statutes at Large*, vol. 8.
26. E. Calamy, *An Account of the Ministers, Lecturers, Masters, Fellon of Colleges and Schoolmasters who were ejected after the Restoration in 1660*, 2 vols (2nd edn 1713), vol. 2, pp. 841–5. The ejection of Thomas Hicock, usher at Merchant Taylors School of Great Crosby, was recorded: Rogers, 'Teaching Profession', p. 85; Luft, *Merchant Taylors'*, p. 76.
27. Horsfall Turner, ed., *The Reverend Oliver Heywood*, vol. 1, pp. 99–100, vol. 4, p. 79.
28. Rogers, 'Teaching Profession', appendix 11.
29. The local climate of toleration mu have changed in 1674 to allow the appointment of non-Anglicans. It reflected the limited alteration in national attitudes which encouraged Charles II to grant his short-lived Declaration of Indulgence in 1672.
30. LRO DDX 191/1, p. 214.
31. LRO DDX 191/1, p. 207.
32. Holmes, *Augustan England*, p. 79.
33. Rogers, 'Teaching Profession', p. 3
34. Although Richard Birchall died a bachelor after being wounded in 1649, he had a brother, the possible father of George, who lived in Winwick.
35. Corpus Christi College Muniment Wase MS, CCC,390/2, f.22.
36. Rogers, 'Teaching Profession', p. 3
37. LRO WCW Ellis Rycroft, schoolmaster (1675), WCW John Vause, bricklayer (1671), WCW Henry Swift (1679), WCW Richar Erby, shoemaker (1674), WCW James Barton, tailor (1677).
38. Vincent, *The Grammar Schools*, p. 1
39. Ibid., p. 56.
40. LRO DDX 191/1, p. 215.
41. Holmes, *Augustan England*, pp. 48–
42. LRO DDX 191/1, p. 218.
43. LRO WCW James Berry (1686).
44. Vincent, *The Grammar Schools*, p.
45. Henry Atherton graduated in 162 at St John's College, Cambridge: John Venn and J.A. Venn, eds, *Alumni Cantabriegiensis* (Cambridge: Cambridge Universit

Press, 1922, reprinted Nedeln, Liechtenstein: Kraus, 1974), p. 51.
Vincent, *The Grammar Schools*, p. 121.
LRO WCW Henry Atherton, schoolmaster (1685).
LRO DDX 191/1, p. 286.
Vincent, *The Grammar Schools*, p. 67.
Charles Hoole, 'A New Discovery of the old Art of Teaching School' (1660), pp. 292–3, in Cressy, *Education in Tudor and Stuart England*, p. 93.
J.A. Sharpe, *Early Modern England: a Social History* (London: Arnold, 1978), p. 267.
Tyrer, ed., *The Great Diurnal*, vol. I p. 72.
William Dobson, ed., *Extracts from the Diary of the Reverend Peter Walkden, 1725–1730* (Preston: Dobson, 1866), p. 77.
David C.J. Orritt, *The History of Ormskirk Grammar School, Lancashire* (Preston: Carnegie, 1988), p. 20.
Peter Burke, *Popular Culture in Early Modern Europe* (London: Temple Smith, 1978), pp. 192–201.
The *Gentleman's Magazine*, November (1828), pp. 403–8.
Ibid., p. 18.
LRO DDX 191/1, p. 267 (1724), p. 263 (1721).
Orritt, *Ormskirk Grammar School*, pp. 16–22.
Holmes, *Augustan England*, p. 80.
According to Rogers, by 1700, 20% of teachers in England were graduates. Although Vincent's evidence confirmed the trend, he found a higher percentage of graduate teachers than in Ormskirk – 72% in 1660–1714, falling to 66% in 1714–1770: Rogers, 'Teaching Profession', p. 168; Vincent, *The Grammar Schools*, p. 121.
LRO DDX 191/1, p. 208 (1664), p. 232 (1686), p. 261 (1723), p. 276 (1736), p. 295 (1754).
LRO DDX 191/1, p. 240 (1694), p. 253 (1719).
Orritt, *Ormskirk Grammar School*, p. 14.
LRO DDX 191/1, p. 254 (1720).
LRO DDX 191/1, p. 263 (1722).
LRO DDX 191/1, p. 313 (1798).
CRO Call Books, EDV 2/10 – EDV 2/27.
Marchamount Nedham, *A Discourse*, p. 3 quoted in Cressy, *Education in Tudor and Stuart England*, p. 39.
National figures from Vincent, *The Grammar Schools*, p. 121.
LRO DDX 191/1 p. 318.

72. Vincent, *The Grammar Schools*, pp. 95–7.
73. Nicholas Carlisle, *A Concise Description of the Endowed Grammar Schools of Lancashire and Yorkshire* (1818, reprinted Richmond: Richmond Publishing Company, 1974), pp. 639–707.
74. LRO WCW Rauffe Burnestone chapman (1612).
75. *The Charity Commissioners' Report on the County of Lancaster in 1828* (1898), p. 2016.
76. Stone, 'The Educational Revolution' *1560–1640*, p. 73.
77. Wilson, *England's Apprenticeship 1603–1763*, p. 347.
78. LRO WCW Henry Jones, innkeeper (1690). See p. 145.
79. Cressy, *Literacy and the Social Order*, p. 177. See pp. 133–4.
80. M.G. Jones, *The Charity School Movement: a Study of Eighteenth Century Puritanism in Action* (London: Cambridge University Press, 1938), pp. 5, 73.
81. Victor E. Neuburg, *Popular Education in Eighteenth Century England* (London: Woburn Press, 1971), p. 3.
82. LRO WCW Mary Winstanley (1719), WCW Archippus Kippax (1719).
83. British Library, Roberts Collection, Add. MS 22648, p. 146.
84. LRO DDHe 54/2. Hesketh Papers, Stewards Accounts.
85. LRO WCW William Grice (1725), WCW Asa Latham (1726), WCW William Unsworth (1734).
86. No exact date is given but its position among the orders suggests the early 1720s: LRO DDK 1746/18. Order no. 46.
87. CRO EDV 7/1/201, Bishop Porteus's Visitation.
88. *An Account of Charity Schools Lately Erected* (1706) p. 4, quoted by Cressy, *Education in Tudor and Stuart England*, p. 114.
89. T.W. Laqueur, *Religion and Respectability: Sunday Schools and Working Class Culture 1780–1850* (London: Yale University Press, 1976), p. 31; Jones, *The Charity School Movement*, p. 134.
90. British Library, Robert's Collection, Add. MS 22648, p. 147.
91. CRO EDV 7.
92. A.J. Hawkes, *Catalogue of Lancashire Printed Books to 1800* (Wigan Public Libraries, 1925), no. W750.
93. British Library, Add. MS. no. 22648, p. 147. *Report of the Charity Commissioners*, p. 2,017.

94. Mona Duggan, *A History of Scarisbrick*, pp. 70–1.
95. CRO EDV 5, April (1761) WA (west).
96. Hanley, *History of St Anne's*, p. 17.
97. Rogers, *Teaching Profession*, pp. 11, 333.
98. Ibid., appendix II.
99. For literacy see Cressy, *Literacy and the Social Order*; Michael Sanderson, 'Literacy and Social Mobility in the Industrial Revolution in England', *Past and Present*, vol. 56 (1972), p. 75; Thomas Laqueur, 'Debate: Literacy and Social Mobility in the Industrial Revolution in England', *Past and Present* vol. 64 (1974), p. 101; R.T. Vann, 'Literacy in Seventeenth Century England: some Hearth Tax Evidence,' *Journal of Interdisciplinary History*, vol. 5, no. 2 (1974), p. 288.
100. David Cressy, *Literacy and the Social Order*, p. 112; Wrightson and Levine, *Poverty and Piety*, p. 147.
101. R.A. Houston, 'The Development of Literacy: Northern England, 1640–1750', *Economic History Review*, vol. 35, no. 2, May (1982), p. 202.
102. David Cressy, *Literacy and the Social Order*, p. 42.
103. Various Dissenters' autobiographies from the seventeenth century confirm that 'home' teaching was common. For instance, according to Oliver Heywood's autobiography, Mrs Heywood taught her children, including Nathaniel, future vicar of Ormskirk: Margaret Spufford, 'First Steps in Literacy', *Social History*, vol. 4, no. 3, October (1979), pp. 407–35.
104. The following sources provided the literacy data. Their range of dates and the percentage of each source I used are listed. However, duplicate signatures jettisoned in the process may have influenced the final percentages to some extent.
Sources Date Range Percentage Used
Probate Records 1660–1800 89.8%
Consistory Court Records 1672–1715 3.6%
Oath of Association 1696 2.8%
Court Leet Records 1679–1796 1.8%
Quarter Sessions Petitions 1675–1724 0.9%
Diocesan Records 1663–1705 0.6%
Alehouse Licenses 1768–1784 0.5%
Bankruptcy Papers 1719–1776 0.4%
Total 100.4%.
105. Cressy, *Literacy and the Social Order*, p. 176.
106. Houston, 'Development of Literacy', p. 213.

107. Cressy, *Literacy and the Social Order*, p. 145. The parish registers used by Cressy were not as socially selective as the Ormskirk probate records, which provided much of my evidence, while Houston's totals from depositions would feature a similar group to the Ormskirk sample.

108. PRO C 213/138/1, Ormskirk Division in the Derby Hundred, Oath of Association, 1696; R.G. Dottie, 'Childwall, a Lancashire Town in the Seventeenth Century', *THSLC*, vol. 135 (1986), p. 30.

109. Houston, 'Development of Literacy', pp. 199–215; Robert Unwin, 'Literacy Patterns in Rural Communities in the Vale of York, 1660–1840', in W.B. Stephens, ed., *Studies in the History of Literacy: England and North America* (Leeds: University of Leeds, 1983), pp. 68–9; Wrightson and Levine, *Poverty and Piety*, pp. 19–25, 79, 147; R.G. Dottie, 'The People of Childwall in the Stuart Period' (unpublished MPhil thesis, University of Liverpool, 1981), pp. 425–6; Sanderson, 'Literacy and Social Mobility', pp. 56–83.

110. Houston, 'Development of Literacy', p. 206.

111. Unwin, 'Literacy Patterns in the Vale of York, 1660–1840', p. 69.

112. Wrightson and Levine, *Poverty and Piety*, p. 148.

113. Wrightson and Levine, *Poverty and Piety*, pp. 19–20, 25, 79, 147.

114. Dottie, 'The People of Childwall', pp. 425–6.

115. The population of Wigan was 4,000 compared with Ormskirk's population of approximately 1,124: Sinclair, *The History of Wigan*, vol. 2, p. 198.

116. Michael Sanderson, *Literacy and Social Mobility*, p. 83.

117. John Walton, *Lancashire: a Social History, 1558–1939* (Manchester: Manchester University Press, 1987), p. 97.

118. Jacqueline Grayson, 'Literacy, Schooling and Industrialisation 1760–1850', in Stephens, ed., *Literacy Studies: a Survey*, p. 63.

119. Lorna Weatherill, *Consumer Behaviour and Material Culture in Britain 1660–1760* (London: Routledge, 1988), p. 26; see also Cressy, *Literacy and the Social Order*, pp. 4–5.

120. Keith Wrightson, *English Society, 1580–1680* (London: Hutchinson, 1982), p. 190; Cressy, *Literacy and the Social Order*, p. 88.

121. Stephens, ed., *Literacy Studies: a Survey* p. 3.

122. Cressy, *Literacy and the Social Order*, p. 112; Borsay, *English Urban Renaissance*, p. 287; Houston, *Development of Literacy*, p. 205.

123. Ibid., p. 205

124. Sharpe, *Early Modern England*, p. 278.

125. Grayson, 'Literacy, Schooling and Industrialisation', p. 66.

126. Burke, *Popular Culture*, p. 265.

127. Houston, 'Development of Literacy', p. 215.

128. Peter Laslett, *The World We Have Lost* (London: Methuen, 1965, 2nd edn, 1971), p. 207.

Chapter VII

1. David Ogg, *England in the Reign of Charles II* (Oxford: Clarendon Press, 1936, 2nd edn), p. 515. Dorothy Davis, *A History of Shopping*, (London: Routledge & Kegan Paul, 1966) pp. 171–2. Plumb, *Commercialisation of Leisure*, p. 5.

2. LRO WCW Rauffe Burnestone, Ormskirk (1612).

3. T.S. Willan, *The Inland Trade* (Manchester: Manchester University Press, 1976), p. 80.

4. Wrightson and Levine, *Poverty and Piety*, p. 17.

5. LRO WCW Ambrose Jackson, Ormskirk (1683).

6. Henry Wheatley ed., *The Diary of Samuel Pepys*, 8 vols (London: George Bell, first published 1893, reprinted 1923), vol. 3, p. 216.

7. LRO WCW Margery Clarkson, Ormskirk (1693).

8. Burke, *Popular Culture*, pp. 253–4; Margaret Spufford, *Small Books and Pleasant Histories: Popular Fiction and its Readership in Seventeenth Century England* (Cambridge: Cambridge University Press, 1981), pp. 111–28.

9. LRO William Grice, Ormskirk, 1725; *Preston Journal*, no. 278, 8 June (1750).

10. LRO WCW Thomas Pemberton (1783), WCW Mary Prescott (1788), WCW Robert Oakes (1674), WCW Thomas Keaquicke (1680), all of Ormskirk.

11. Weatherill, *Consumer Behaviour*, p. 207.

12. LRO WCW Henry Lathom (1667), WCW Thomas Pemberton (1783), WCW John Glover (1791), all of Ormskirk.

13. LRO PR 3385 Acc.7175. Dissenters often took notes during the sermon and transcribed them on their return home, as Roger Lowe was commissioned to do for his neighbours in the 1660s. 'Extract from a Lancashire Diary, 1663–1678' (reprinted from 'Local Gleanings' in *The Manchester Courier*, 1876), p. 14.

14. British Library, Add. MS 22648 Robert's Collection. A copy of this sermon is at Dr Williams' Library, London.

15. *The Palatine Notebook*, vol. 4, p. 54

16. LRO WCW Richard Sutch (1691), WCW Elizabeth Wilson (1735), both of Ormskirk.

17. LRO PR 3385 Acc. 7175; *Dictionary of National Biography*.

18. Hawkes, *Lancashire Printed Books*, no. W750.

19. *DNB*.

20. *DNB*.

21. *DNB*. When Foxe served under Bishop Jewel, he objected to wearing a surplice, as Broxopp of Ormskirk did in 1633 (see p. 73).

22. *DNB*.

23. *DNB*.

24. LRO PR 3385 Acc. 7175.

25. *British Museum General Catalogue Printed Books* (1965), vol. 84, p. 49

26. LRO WCW William Farrington, Ormskirk (1693).

27. LRO WCW John Entwistle (1710), WCW Henry Lathom (1667), WCW Thomas Knowles (1777), WCW Richard Sutch (1691), all of Ormskirk.

28. Alan Everitt, ed., *Perspectives in Urban History*, (London: Macmillan, 1973), pp. 104–13.

29. First published by A. Millar in London in 1755, *British Museum General Catalogue*, vol. 30, p. 351. LRO WCW Thomas Knowles, Ormskirk (1777).

30. LRO WCW William Grice (1725)

31. *British Museum Catalogue*, vol. 82, p. 749.

32. Weatherill, *Consumer Behaviour*, p. 26.

33. LRO WCW Henry Jones, Ormskirk (1690).

34. Borsay, *The English Urban Renaissance*, pp. 214, 144–5; Peter Clarke, *The English Alehouse*, pp. 154–5; Weatherill, *Consumer Behaviour*, p. 26, p. 168.

35. J.H. Plumb, 'The Public, Literature and the Arts', in Paul Fritz and David Williams, eds., *The Triumph of Culture: Eighteenth Century Perspectives* (Toronto: A. M. Hakkert, 1972), pp. 38–9.

The Preston Journal, no. 104, 24 September (1742).

Plumb,'The Public', pp. 38–9.

LRO WCW Henry Tyrer (1738), WCW Anne Bold (1705), WCW Ellen Rogers (1733), WCW Jane Walsh (1710), all of Ormskirk.

LRO WCW Thomas Tatlock, Ormskirk (1731).

LRO WCW Hannah Taylor, Ormskirk (1789).

LRO WCW Thomas Bradshaw (1717).

Preston Journal, no. 104, 24 September (1742).

W.A. Abram, ed., *Memorials of the Preston Guilds*, (Preston, George Toulmin, 1882) pp. 72–3.

Everitt, ed., *Perspectives in Urban History*, p. 117.

LRO WCW Thomas Tatlock (1683), WCW Thomas Grice (1686), WCW Gilbert Ambrose (1692), WCW Thomas Moorcroft (1693), WCW James Bastwell (1694), all of Ormskirk.

LRO Mary Stanley, Ormskirk (1743).

Plumb, in Fritz & Williams, eds, *The Triumph of Culture*, pp. 38–9 (1727).

LRO WCW William Bryan, WCW Thomas Crane (1737), both of Ormskirk.

J.J. Bagley and A.G. Hodgkiss, *Lancashire: a History of the County Palatine in Early Maps* (Manchester: Neil Richardson, 1985), pp. 12–20, 30.

LRO WCW Thomas Crosby (1690), WCW John Crosby (1703), WCW William Grice (1725), all of Ormskirk.

LRO WCW Henry Oliverson, barber, Ormskirk (1698).

LRO WCW John Cuquitt, husbandman, Ormskirk (1704).

LRO WCW Thomas Crosby (1690), WCW John Crosby (1703), WCW William Grice (1725), WCW James Berry (1686), shopkeepers, WCW Christopher Gibson, vicar (1727), WCW William Fryer, plasterer (1734), all of Ormskirk.

Marjorie Plant, *The English Book Trade: an Economic History of the Making and Sale of Books* (London: George Allen and Unwin, 1939, 2nd edn 1965), p. 184.

British Library, Add. MS 22648, Roberts Collection, p. 19. The 'paste' eggs were derived from Paschal or Easter eggs, but whether the dance had antique origins or whether it was merely a strange antic is unclear.

Burke, *Popular Culture* , p. 216.

Sybil Rosenfeld, *Strolling Players*

and Drama in the Provinces, 1660–1765 (New York: Octagon Books, 1970), p. 21.

58. LRO QSB 1/106 no. 72.

59. Local tradition states that, in his youth, Shakespeare belonged to a troupe of players whose patron was Sir Thomas Hesketh of Rufford Hall (near Ormskirk). Perhaps this influenced the players' decision to present this play locally; Ernest Honigman, *Shakespeare: the Lost Years* (Manchester: Manchester University Press, 1985) pp. 31–9.

60. A.L. Beier, *Masterless Men: the Vagrancy Problem in England, 1560–1640* (London: Methuen, 1985), p. 96.

61. 11 Geo 11 c.28: Pickering, *Statutes at Large*, vol. 17; Glynne Wickham, *A History of the Theatre* (Oxford: Phaidon Press, 1985), pp. 165–7.

62. Joan Parkes, *Travel in England in the Seventeenth Century* (London: Oxford University Press, 1925), pp. 268, 331; Rosenfeld, *Strolling Players* pp. 7–8.

63. Ibid., p. 6.

64. Lowe, *Extracts from a Lancashire Diary 1663–1678*, p. 30.

65. Tyrer ed., *The Great Diurnal*, vol. 2, p. 132 (Formby), p. 207 (London).

66. Brand, *Observations on Popular Antiquities of Great Britain*, 2 vols (London: F.C. and J Rivington, 1813), vol. 1, pp. 315–24.

67. Liverpool Record Office: Plumbe Tempest Papers, 920 PLU 24.

68. In 1795, Tate Wilkinson, a strolling player referring to his performances at York, declared that his 'winter tradesmens' bills [were] dependent for payments arising from the profits of the Assize and Races yearly at that city': Tate Wilkinson, *The Wandering Patentee*, 4 vols (Yorks: Wilson, Spence and Mawson, 1795, reprinted London: Scholar Press, 1973), vol. 4, p. 68.

69. *Kendal Weekly Courant*, 17 June (1732), quoted in Margaret Eddershaw, *Grand Fashionable Nights, Kendal Theatre, 1575–1985* (Lancaster: Centre for North West Regional Studies, University of Lancaster, 1988), p. 3.

70. British Library, Add. MS 22648, Roberts Collection, p. 164.

71. C.W. Chalklin, 'Capital Expenditure on Building for Cultural Purposes in Provincial England, 1730–1830', *Business History*, vol. 22, no. 1 (1980), p. 53.

72. Adrienne Rosen, 'Winchester in

Transition, 1580–1700', in Peter Clark, ed., *Country Towns in Pre-Industrial England* (Leicester: Leicester University Press, 1981), p. 180; McInnes, 'The Emergence of a Leisure Town', p. 69.

73. *Kendal Weekly Courant*, 17 June (1732) in Eddershaw *Grand Fashionable Nights*, p. 3; Cecil Price, *Theatre in the Age of Garrick* (Oxford: Basil Blackwell, 1973), pp. 187–8.

74. LRO DDK 1820/2 (1747) – DDK 1820/11 (1756).

75. Tyrer, ed., *Great Diurnal*, vol. 1, p. 180, 26 July 1708; vol. 3, p. 77, 15 May 1722, and passim.

76. Price, *Theatre in the Age of Garrick*, p. 187.

77. Liverpool Record Office, R.J. Broadbent manuscript, 'On the Early Theatres in Liverpool'. Moore Street became Tithebarn Street. Possibly the tithebarn later became the theatre.

78. The original Ship Inn can be seen in the photograph of the market (illustration no. 10, p. 18). The gabled building with the sign 'Ablett's' on it was the Ship Inn.

79. Eddershaw, *Grand Fashionable Nights*, p. 4.

80. Liverpool Record Office, Hq 792 (72) BRO, R.J. Broadbent, Collection of Cuttings Regarding Local Theatres; the *Ormskirk Advertiser*, 1 April 1926, 12 August 1926.

81. Price, *Theatre in the Age of Garrick*, p. 192. A few theatres had decorative exteriors, such as Birmingham's Theatre Royal of 1774 with its facade bearing the sculpted heads of Garrick and Shakespeare – a display of the town's new prosperity and civic pride. Douglas Reid, 'Popular Theatre in Victorian Britain,' in Louis James and David Bradley, eds, *Performance and Politics in Popular Drama* (Cambridge: Cambridge University Press, 1980), p. 66.

82. Liverpool Record Office, Hq 792 (72) BRO, R.J. Broadbent.

83. By courtesy of Harvard Theatre Collection, Harvard University, USA.

84. There is the possibility, not proven, of a link with the Wigan Entwistle family originally from Foxholes near Rochdale, the family of Bertie Entwistle, lawyer and later vice-chancellor of the Duchy of Lancaster.

85. Broadbent, 'The Old Ormskirk Theatre', the *Ormskirk Advertiser*, 1 April (1926).

86. Plumb, *The Commercialisation of Leisure*, p. 13.

87. A Kendal playbill for 4 April 1783 advertised such a concert, during which three plays were to be presented *gratis* between the items: Eddershaw, *Grand Fashionable Nights*, p. 10.

88. Price, *Theatre in the Age of Garrick*, pp. 175–6.

89. 28 Geo.IIIc.30: Pickering, *Statutes at Large*, vol. 36.

90. Price, *Theatre in the Age of Garrick*, p. 85.

91. Frank Tyrer defined a 'gigg' as 'a humorous entertainment often acted after the main play'. According to Peter Burke, the 'jig' (the same word spelt differently) originated in Elizabethan times and was a satirical song-and-dance act which waned in popularity after the Restoration. Tyrer, ed., *The Great Diurnal*, vol. 1, p. 173 (Great Crosby 1708), vol. 2, p. 8 (Ann Rothwells, 1712); Burke, *Popular Culture*, p. 277.

92. R.M. Wiles, 'Provincial Culture in Early Georgian England', in Fritz and Williams, eds, *The Triumph of Culture*, p. 67; Donald Greene, *The Age of Exuberance* (New York: Random House, 1970); LRO WCW John King, Ormskirk (1591). As servant of the Stanleys, he was buried in the high chancel.

93. Wheatley, ed., *The Diary of Samuel Pepys*, vol. 5, p. 395. For example, on 6 July 1660, Pepys visited his Lord's and 'did sing extemporys' (vol. 1, p. 180). Virginals were described as 'a pair' and the name was often used for other keyboard instruments.

94. Plumb, *The Commercialisation of Leisure*, p. 14; Sharpe, *Early Modern England*, p. 296.

95. Innkeepers' inventories were excluded for examination later (pp. 158–9).

96. LRO WCW Jane Tipping (1667), WCW Hannah Thompson (1676), WCW Samuel Andrews (1689), all of Ormskirk.

97. LRO WCW William Hewitt, Ormskirk (1723).

98. W.B. Boulton, *Amusements of Old London* (London: Benjamin Blom, 1901 reprinted 1969), p. 205.

99. Margaret Pelling, 'Appearance and Reality in London 1500–1700: Barber Surgeons the Body and Disease', in A.L. Beier and Roger Finlay, eds, *London 1500–1700: the Making of Metropolitan London* (London: Longmans, 1986), p. 95. An old woodcut portrays a barber's

shop where one customer is entertaining the others by playing his 'ghittern' 'according to the old custom'. Wheatley, ed., *Diary of Samuel Pepys*, vol. 1, p. 159. n. 4. A ghittern or cittern was a medieval stringed instrument. The modern 'guitar' is derived from the word.

100. British Library, Add. MS 22648, Robert's Collection, 1819.

101. Tyrer, ed., *The Great Diurnal*, vol. 1, p. 40.

102. Holmes, *Augustan England*, p. 29.

103. Borsay, *The English Urban Renaissance*, pp. 191–4.

104. LRO DDK 1650, 1757 22 May. Stewards' Letters.

105. Plumb, *Commercialisation of Leisure*, p. 15.

106. LRO WCW Henry Jones, Ormskirk (1690).

107. LRO WCW Thomas Barton, Ormskirk (1734).

108. Wheatley, ed., *The Diary of Samuel Pepys*, vol. 1, p. 19.

109. Clark, *The English Alehouse*, p. 155.

110. Clark, *The English Alehouse*, p. 154.

111. LRO WCW Hugh Standish (1700), WCW Mary Stanley (1734), both of Ormskirk.

112. Watts, *The Dissenters*, p. 309.

113. Wheatley, ed., *The Diary of Samuel Pepys*, vol. 1, p. 181, n.1.

114. Lowe, *Extracts from a Lancashire Diary 1663–1678*, pp. 5, 29, 63–4.

115. Wheatley, ed., *The Diary of Samuel Pepys*, vol. 1, p. 255.

116. J.E. Bailey, 'Church Goods 1552', CS, vol. 113 (1888), p. 113.

117. LRO PR 3385 Acc.7175

118. LRO DDK 290/2/14.

119. LRO DDK 290/2/18–19.

120. LRO DDK 290/2/21.

121. LRO WCW Jane Brooke Ormskirk (1742).

122. LRO DDK 290/2/20.

123. British Library, Add. MS 22648, Robert's Collection 1819. This organ was probably a reconstruction of the earlier one.

124. Owen Ashmore, 'Inventories as a source of Local History', *The Amateur Historian*, vol. 4, no. 5 (1959) p. 160.

125. LRC DDK 290/2/20.

126. Burke, *Popular Culture*, pp. 270–81.

Chapter VIII

1. For information on spas see Phyllis Hembry, *The English Spa 1560–1815: a Social History* (London: Athlone Press, 1990).

2. Edmund Borlase, *Lathom Spaw in Lancashire with some Reasonable Case and Cures effected by it* (London: Robert Clavel, 1670), dedicatory section, unpaged. Edmund Borlase, son of Sir John Borlase, a lord justice in Ireland, was educated in Dublin, obtained his degree of Doctor of Physic at Leyden in 1650, his degree of Doctor of Medicine at Oxford in 1660, and practised medicine in Chester till his death in 1682(?): *DNB*

3. Thomas Short, *The Natural, Experimental and Medicinal History of the Mineral Waters of Derbyshire, Lincolnshire and Yorkshire* (Sheffield: Short, 1740), Supplementary volume included the north-western counties (1743–1750), p. 34; Short (1690?–1772), physician, practised in Sheffield: *DNB*

4. Letter from William Blundell to Edmund Borlase 1672, reproduced *The Lancet*, 6 March (1897), p. 688.

5. Pococke, *Travels through England, 1754–1757*, p. 207.

6. Borlase, *Lathom Spaw*, p. 4.

7. Short, *History of the Mineral Water* p. 34.

8. Borlase, *Lathom Spaw*, p. 7.

9. Ibid., p. 3.

10. Ibid., p. 3.

11. L.W.B. Brockliss, 'The Development of the Spa in Seventeenth-Century France', *Medical History*, Supplement no. 10 (1990), p. 32.

12. Short, *The Natural History of Mineral Waters*, p. 34.

13. In the 1660s, Bath had two seasons spring and autumn – later merged into one summer season. In the 1720s the two seasons returned, but by the 1780s these had merged into a winter season: Borsay, *The English Renaissance*, pp. 141–2.

14. Short, *The Natural History of Mineral Waters*, p. 34.

15. Borlase, *Lathom Spaw*, p. 6.

16. Borsay, *The English Renaissance*, pp. 350–4. The passion for parading in Bath was described in 1762 by Oliver Goldsmith: 'When...Church...is done some of the company appear upon the parade or the other public walks, where they continue to chat and muse each other...After dinner...the company meet...at the pump house. From this they retire to the walks.' Oliver Goldsmith, *Life of Beau Nash* (London: Sisleys, 1762, reprinted Panel Books, 1907), p. 38.

7. Tyrer, ed., *The Great Diurnal*, vol. 1, p. 40.

8. Here Borlase meant either the dowager countess, the heroine of the siege of Lathom Hall, who had travelled widely in Europe, or the wife of the Eighth Earl of Derby – formerly Helena de Rupa, once maid of honour to Elizabeth of Bohemia.

9. Borlase, *Lathom Spaw*, The Epistle, unpaged.

10. Charles I often visited Bath; his son, the Prince of Wales, stayed there in 1645, and Henrietta Maria patronised Tunbridge Wells. In 1663, Charles II visited both Tunbridge Wells and Bath, and extended his patronage to Epsom – popular because of its proximity to London. Royalty patronised Bath spa throughout our period. Cheltenham was a favourite resort of George III: Hembry, *The English Spa*, pp. 46, 66, 113, 133, 192.

11. Tobias Smollet, *The Expedition of Humphrey Clinker* (London: Johnston, 1771, reprinted London: Oxford University Press, 1966), p. 181.

12. *DNB*. The earl's copy of the book in the library at Knowsley is inscribed, 'ex dono authoris' and signed 'Derby'.

13. Short, *The Natural History of Mineral Waters*, p. 34.

14. N.G. Coley,' Physicians and the Chemical Analysis of Mineral Waters in Eighteenth Century England', *Medical History*, vol. 26 (1982) p. 124.

15. Borlase, *Lathom Spaw*, p. 20.

16. Jon Eklund, ' "Of a Spirit in the Water" : Some Early Ideas on the Aerial Dimension', *Isis*, vol. 67 (1976) p. 530.

17. As Jon Eklund wrote ('Of a Spirit', p. 530), 'we will not find the sharpness of definition...of later generations'. Alum often indicated only a salty taste, while vitriol was a universal acid. Later, vitriol was the name used for sulphates.

18. Borlase, *Lathom Spaw*, p. 14.

19. E.S. Turner, *Taking the Cure* (London: Michael Joseph, 1967), p. 44.

20. Charles Leigh, *The Natural History of Lancashire, Cheshire and the Peak in Derbyshire* (Oxford: 1700), pp. 28–35. Charles Leigh, 1662–1701?, MD at Cambridge, 1689, practised in London, Manchester and throughout Lancashire: *DNB*.

21. Dr Leigh denounced Lister's 'germinating pyrites'. Chalybeate meant impregnated with iron. According to Eklund ('Of a Spirit',

p. 542), in 1734, a chemist analysing Scarborough water used the word 'vitrified' to mean 'volatile'. Probably this was meant here.

32. Leigh, *The Natural History*, p. 28.

33. Dr John Woodward (1665–1728), trained in 1684 under Dr Peter Barwick, Charles II's physician, became professor of physic at Gresham College in 1692, and published a volume containing theories about the origin of springs. *DNB*.

34. When Blauegate Colliery was extended to mine this coal seam in the 1850s, the well was covered and a drain laid to carry the water into the colliery. Marcella Holland, 'Lathom Spa', in Peter Smith, ed., *A Short History of Lathom* (St Helens: Chalon Press, 1981), p. 52.

35. Borlase, *Lathom Spaw*, Dedication, unpaged.

36. Christopher Morris, ed., *The Journeys of Celia Fiennes* (London: Cresset Press, 1947), p. 184.

37. For example, see LRO QSP 844/6, 856/10, 1024/19.

38. John Floyer, *The History of Cold Bathing, both Ancient and Modern* (London: W. Innys & R. Manby, first published 1702, 6th edn 1732), p. 320; Hembry, *The English Spa*, pp. 159–78. The site of the plunge bath is possibly Bath Lodge, a ruined, highly ornamented building north of Ormskirk. Its site plan shows a well rising in the centre of the building and traces of walks laid out around it; John Addy and Peter McNiven, eds, *The Diary of Henry Prescott LLB, Deputy Registrar of Chester Diocese*, 3 vols, RSLC (1994), p. 318.

39. John Barrett, 'Spas and Seaside Resorts, 1660–1780', *The Rise of the New Urban Society* (Milton Keynes: Open University, 1977) A322, Unit 14, p. 42; Corfield, *The Impact of Towns*, p. 61.

40. Morris, ed., *The Journeys of Celia Fiennes* p. 103.

41. Hembry, *The English Spa*, p.47.

42. Borlase, *Lathom Spaw*, p. 6.

43. Letter from William Blundell to Borlase, 1672; *The Lancet*, 6 March (1897) p. 688.

44. Gibson, ed., *A Cavalier's Notebook*, p. 298.

45. Borlase, *Lathom Spaw* (2nd edn) with *A Further Account of Lathom Spaw* (unpaged, 1872).

46. Short, *The Natural History of Mineral Waters*, p. 34.

47. Gibson, ed., *Cavalier's Notebook*, p. 298. Corfield found at least 225

spas were listed in 1740; Corfield, *The Impact of Towns*, p. 62.

48. The *London Gazette*, 8 June (1685) in J. Fairfax-Blakeborough, *Northern Turf History*, 2 vols (London: J.A. Allen, 1948), vol. 2, p. 189. The usual venue for the Ormskirk Race was along what is now Long Lane, Aughton.

49. I am indebted to Lord Derby for permission to read this document in his archives at Knowsley Hall. no. 18B 209.

50. Fairfax-Blakeborough, *Northern Turf*, vol. 2, p. 189.

51. According to local oral tradition, Grandstand Farm on Formby Lane and Standhouses on Aughton Brow were the sites of grandstands on the racecourse.

52. Entrance fees to the course could not be charged because it was common land.

53. Gibson, ed., *A Cavalier's Notebook*, p. 268; LRO Molyneux muniments, DDM/11/68.

54. Tyrer, ed., *The Great Diurnal*, vol. 3, pp. 135, 164.

55. The Library, Knowsley Hall, nos H85 A and B.

56. LRO Letters of Lord Strange, DDX 334/8.

57. LRO Subscribers to a Plate, DDX 244/1.

58. Millard Cox, *Derby, the Life and Times of the Twelfth Earl of Derby, Edward Smith Stanley, 1752–1834* (London: J.A. Allen, 1974), p. 18.

59. Knowsley Hall Library, H.85.B: The Weather Journal of James, Tenth Earl of Derby.

60. Stanley interest revived between 1807 and 1815, when enclosure schemes threatened the racecourse and finally forced its closure: Audrey Coney, 'Aughton Enclosure in the Eighteenth and Early Nineteenth Centuries: the Struggle for Superiority', *THSLC*, vol. 136 (1986), pp. 59–80.

61. Fairfax-Blakeborough, *Northern Turf*, vol. 2, p. 189.

62. Tyrer, ed., *The Great Diurnal*, vol. 1, p. 257; vol. 3, pp. 161, 164, 187.

63. Fairfax-Blakeborough, *Northern Turf*, vol. 2, p. 190.

64. 'Lawyer' Starkey arranged Blundell's secret financial transactions with the Abbess of the Gravelines Convent of the Poor Clares in Flanders from his chambers in Preston: Tyrer, ed., *The Great Diurnal* vol. 2, pp. 19, 165. In 1734, he was one of the few

barristers willing to act for his
clients in any branch of the law – or
outside it (see p. 26); Holmes,
Augustan England, p. 119;
Lemmings, *Gentlemen and
Barristers*, pp. 126, 168.

65. Lord Cholmondley was then Lord
Lieutenant of Cheshire and later
became Lord Lieutenant of North
Wales: Tyrer, ed., *The Great Diurnal*
vol. 1, p. 257, vol. 2, p. 19.

66. Ibid., vol. 3, p. 161.

67. Ibid., vol. 1, pp. 3–4.

68. G. Scott Thomson, ed., *Letters of a
Grandmother, 1732–1735* (London:
Cape, 1943), p. 58.

69. LRO *London Gazette* 1696, UDOr
15/1.

70. LRO Subscribers to a Plate, DDX
244/1.

71. E.P. Thompson, 'Patrician Society,
Plebeian Culture', *Journal of Social
History*, vol. 7 (1974), p. 394.

72. LRO *London Gazette* 1696, UDOr
15/1.

73. Gibson, ed., *A Cavalier's Notebook*,
p. 214.

74. LRO WCW Mary Smith (1704),
WCW Richard Johnson (1716), both
of Ormskirk.

75. Borsay 'The English Urban
Renaissance', pp. 343–8; also *The
English Urban Renaissance* pp. 184, 304.

76. H. Fielding, *An Enquiry into the
Causes of the Late Increase of Robbers*
(London: 1751), quoted by R.W.
Malcolmson in *Popular Recreations
in English Society, 1700–1850*
(London: Cambridge University
Press, 1973), p. 157.

77. Malcolmson, *Popular Recreations*, p. 152.

78. LRO DDX 244/1.

79. LRO DDX 334/8, 334/10.

80. LRO PR 58, PR 59.

81. This leisure culture appeared in the
diaries of both Blundell and
Tyldesley: Tyrer, ed., *The Great
Diurnal*; Joseph Gillow and Anthony
Hewitson, eds, *The Tyldesley Diary,
1712–1714* (Preston: Hewitson, 1873).

82. Many doubted Monmouth's motives
in visiting Wallasey – only about 10
miles from Ormskirk. Dr Matthew
Fowler wrote to the Secretary of State
that Monmouth 'came not hither
barely on account of a horse race':
CSPD, 1682, p. 389. Later he repeated
his suspicions: 'You may be assured
there was more in this meeting than a
horse race.': *CSPD* (1682), p. 409.

83. One witness, John Lighburn, swore
'that being then a carrier, he brought
several packs of arms from London
to Standish in December 1691 and

there saw Sir William Gerard, Sir
Thomas Clifton, Mr Dicconson, Mr
Blundell and others and that they
discoursed of King James' landing
and then divided the arms and that
Mr Dicconson and Mr Blundell
took their share of the arms': LRO,
Kenyon Muniments, DDKe.8/13.

84. Revd T.C. Porteus, 'New Light on
the Lancashire Jacobite Plot,
1692–1694', *TLCAS*, vol. L (1935)
pp. 1–64; William Beaumont,
'Jacobite Trials at Manchester 1694',
CS, Old Series, vol. 28 (1853).

85. Samuel Hibbert Ware, *Lancashire
Memorials of the Rebellion, 1715*, CS,
1st Series, vol. V (1845) p. 162.

86. LRO Scarisbrick Muniments,
DDSc 44/15. A letter dated 25
November 1745, from Mrs Standish
to her sister Mrs Dicconson and
containing the news that 'my Lord
Darby was to be burnt in effigie
today at Liverpool...for deserting
them on this occasion', establishes
her Stuart loyalties and her
contempt for Lord Derby for failing
to support the Stuart cause.

87. LRO, Hesketh Muniments, DDHe
28/47.

88. LRO DDK 1541/41, DDK
1770/14. Cockpit Lane has only
recently been lost in a road-
widening scheme.

89. Tyrer, ed., *The Great Diurnal*, vol. 1,
pp. 51, 87.

90. LRO Letters from Lord Strange,
DDX 334/10, DDX 334/14.

91. LRO Letters from Lord Strange,
DDX 334/14.

92. LRO Subscribers to a Plate, DDX
244/1.

93. Tyrer, ed., *The Great Diurnal*, vol. 1,
p. 51.

94. LRO DDX 334/10–12. A 'main'
was a series of fights: a 'short main'
lasted two days, a 'long main' a week
and a 'Welch main' – usually
involving fourteen pairs of cocks –
was a knock-out competition, the
surviving cock from one fight
fighting the survivor of another,
until one remained. A 'battle royal'
involved putting all the cocks into
the pit together until only one bird
survived. A 'battle' was one fight. A
'bye', or 'bye battle', was a
secondary fight, between younger
and less experienced birds.

95. Cox, *Derby, the Life and Times*, p. 83.

96. LRO Derby Muniments, DDK
835/20.

97. Richard, Lord Braybrooke, ed.
*Diary and Correspondence of Samuel

Pepys, vol. II (6th edn, London:
Henry G. Bohn, 1858), p. 77.

98. By courtesy of the Victoria and
Albert Museum.

99. Boulton, *Amusements of Old London*,
p. 206.

100. Keith Thomas, *Man and the Natural
World: Changing Attitudes in England*
(London: Penguin, Allen Lane,
1983), p. 15.

101. Thomas, *Man and the Natural
World*, p. 150.

102. Thompson, 'Patrician Society,
Plebeian Culture', p. 393.

103. On Monday 16 July 1666. W. Sachs,
ed., *The Diary of Roger Lowe of
Ashton in Makerfield 1663–1674*
(London: Longmans, Green, 1938),
p. 105.

104. Boulton, *Amusements of Old London*,
p. 196.

105. Ibid., p. 205.

106. Ibid., pp. 201.

107. LRO WCW Ralph Whitestones
(1622).

108. LRO QSB/1/194.

109. PRO PL 27/1.

110. Charles Madeley, 'The Roll of the
Mock Corporation of Farnworth in
Widnes', *THSLC*, New Series, vol.
XXXI (1916), p. 29. This ceremony
is recorded in the minutes dated
1714–1761.

111. Thomas, *Man and the Natural
World*, p. 186.

112. LRO, Court Roll, DDK 1521/3.

113. Thomas, *Man and the Natural
World*, pp. 93, 153.

114. Tyrer, ed., *The Great Diurnal*, vol. 2
p. 26.

115. Ibid., vol. 3, p. 121.

116. The sport was called 'coursing'
when the participants were upper
classes following rigid rules, but was
dismissed as 'hunting the hare'
when done in plebeian circles. LRO
DDK 1521/3.

117. 1670: Car. 11, c. 25: Pickering,
Statutes at Large, vol. 8.

118. P.B. Munsche, 'The Game Laws in
Wiltshire 1750–1800', in J.S.
Cockburn ed., *Crime in England,
1500–1800* (London: Methuen,
1977), pp. 210–212; E.P. Thompson
*Whigs and Hunters: the Origin of the
Black Act* (London: Penguin, Allen
Lane, 1975), pp. 59–63.

119. Hare coursing for the Waterloo Cup
continues today at Altcar, 5 miles
from Ormskirk.

120. LRO DDK 1521/3.

121. LRO QSP 594/7.

122. LRO QSP 778/25.

123. The 'gentleman' in question was n

landed gentry or he would have had the right to course. For the appraisers and witnesses see LRO WCW Henry Oliverson (1698), WCW James Berry (1686), WCW Peter Swift (1686), WCW Edward Darbyshire (1697).

24. LRO WCW James Berry (1686).
25. By courtesy of the trustees of the National Gallery.
26. LRO WCW Hugh Standish (1700). It was usual in the eighteenth century for the bedroom to serve also as an entertaining room.
7. LRO QSP 590/23 (1684).
8. LRO DDK 1746/18. Order no. 12.
9. Gibson, ed., *A Cavalier's Notebook*, p. 41.
0. LRO Rentals and Surveys, DDK 1770/8, DDK 1770/9, DDK 1770/15, DDK 1820/1, DDK 1770/2.
1. Dennis Brailsford, *Sport and Society: Elizabeth – Anne* (London: Routledge & Kegan Paul, 1969), p. 212.
2. PRO PL 27/1.
3. E.P. Thompson, 'Time, Work-Discipline and Industrial Capitalism', *Past and Present*, vol. 38, August (1967) p. 61.

Conclusion

K. Wrightson, *English Society, 1580–1680*, pp. 51–63, and *passim*. During his captivity and trial in 1663, Heywoood was defended by people of other persuasions; see p. 79. For an instance of Protestant helping Catholic, see p. 107.
For instance by John Crosby; LRO WCW John Crosby (1703).

4. Lemmings, *Gentlemen and Barristers*, pp. 126, 169.
5. Clark and Slack, *English Towns in Transition*, p. 24.
6. Angus McInnes in Peter Borsay and Angus McInnes, 'Debate: the Emergence of a Leisure Town: or an Urban Renaissance?', *Past and Present*, no. 126 (1990), p. 201.
7. Borsay and McInnes, 'Debate', p. 190.

Epilogue

1. LRO DDK 290/9/3.
2. P.E. Bradshaw, 'A Study of the township of Ormskirk in the mid-nineteenth century', unpublished BA dissertation, Edge Hill (1977) p. 45.
3. F.W. Stacey, 'Ormskirk, the development of a nineteenth century town' (unpublished, Edge Hill College, 1977), p. 7.
4. *Ormskirk Advertiser*, 6 December 1855, quoted in Stacey, 'Ormskirk,' p. 6.
5. See p. 000.
6. British Library Add. MS 22648, Robert's Collection; George Lea, *Handbook to Ormskirk* (Ormskirk: Hutton, 1893), p. 16.
7. Ordnance Survey map for 1850, 5 ft to 1 statute mile.
8. LRO UDOr 15/10, Robert Rawlinson, 'Report to the General Board of Health' 1850).
9. Lancs CRO UDOr 15/10, p. 19.
10. Audrey Coney, 'Mid-Nineteenth-Century Ormskirk: Disease, Overcrowding and the Irish in a Lancashire Market Town.' *TLCHS*, vol. 139 (1989), p. 102.
11. Stacey, 'Ormskirk', p. 48.

12. LRO PR 445; The graves of those who lived in these workhouses are in the graveyard near the south porch of the parish church.
13. The Brandreth family made a large contribution towards these new premises and Lord Lathom gave stone from a quarry in Lathom Park for the building; Lea *Handbook*, pp. 23–24.
14. For further details see Michael Ockenden, 'The Development of Ormskirk Church' (unpublished PhD thesis University of Liverpool, 1996), pp. 94–108.
15. Ockenden, 'The Development of Ormskirk Church,' p. 113.
16. Ibid., p. 150.
17. Ibid., pp. 145–240.
18. Jacquest, *Emmanuel*, pp. 38–9.
19. For a more detailed account see Jacquest, *Emmanuel*, passim.
20. For further details of St Anne's Church, see Leonard Hanley, *History of St Anne's*.
21. Hanley, *History of St Anne's*, p. 25.
22. Orritt, *Ormskirk Grammar School*, p. 22.
23. The Report of the Charity Commissioners, 1898, p. 2, 17.
24. Orritt, *Ormskirk Grammar School*, p. 61.
25. Ibid., p. 91.
26. For further information see L. Malcolm Hall, *A Century of Progress* (Ormskirk: Cross Hall School, 1977).
27. LRO QJD 1/209.
28. For further information on Edge Hill College see Fiona Montgomery, *Edge Hill University College: A History, 1885–1997* (Chichester: Phillimore, 1997).

Bibliography

Books

Abrams, Philip & Wrigley, E.A. (eds), *Towns in Societies: Essays in Economic History and Historical Sociology* (Cambridge: Cambridge University Press, 1978).

Addison, William. *English Fairs and Markets* (London: B.T. Batsford, 1953).

Alldridge, Nick. (ed.) *The Hearth Tax; Problems and Possibilities*. Papers submitted to the CORAL Conference, 1983 (Humberside: Humberside College of Further Education, 1983).

Anderson, B.L. & Stoney, P.J.M. *Commerce, Industry and Transport, Studies in Economic Change on Merseyside* (Liverpool: Liverpool University Press, 1983).

Anon. *The Palatine Notebook*, vols 1–4 (Liverpool: Henry Young, 1881–4).

Armstrong, Anthony. *The Church of England, Methodists and Society* (London: University of London Press, 1973).

Aveling, J.C.H. *The Handle and the Axe. Catholic Recusants in England from the Revolution to the Emancipation* (London: Blond & Briggs, 1976).

Bagley, J.J. & Hodgkiss, A.G. *Lancashire: A History of the County Palatine in Early Maps* (Manchester: Neil Richardson, 1985).

Bailey F.A. & Millington R. *The Story of Liverpool* (Liverpool: The Corporation of Liverpool, 1957).

Bailey, R.G.B. *Ormskirk Parish Church* (Gloucester: The British Publishing Co., 1965).

Baines, E. *The History of the County Palatine and Duchy of Lancaster* (Manchester: Routledge, 1870).

Barley, M.W. *The English Farmhouse and Cottage* (London: Routledge and Kegan Paul, 1961).

Bate, Frank. *The Declaration of Indulgence, 1672. A Study of the Rise of Organised Dissent* (London: Constable for Liverpool University Press, 1908).

Beales, A.C.F. *Education under Penalty; English Catholic Education from the Reformation to the Fall of James II* (University of London, The Athlone Press, 1963).

Beier, A.L. & Finlay, R. (eds), *London 1500–1700. The Making of the Metropolis* (London: Longman, 1986).

Beier, A.L. *Masterless Men: The Vagrancy Problem in England, 1560–1640* (London & New York: Methuen, 1985).

Betjeman, John. *Collins Pocket Guide to English Parish Churches* (London: Collins, 1968).

Bewes, W.A. *Church Briefs* (London: Adam & Black, 1896).

Blundell, Dom, F.O. *Old Catholic Lancashire* (vol. 3, London: Burns Oats, 1925).

Bolam, C.G., Goring, J., Short, H.L., & Thomas, R. *The English Presbyterians from Elizabethan Puritanism to Modern Unitarianism* (London: George Allen & Unwin, 1968).

Borsay, Peter. *The English Urban Renaissance; Culture, and Society in the Provincial Town, 1660–1770* (Oxford: Clarendon Press, 1989).

Borsay, Peter, (ed.) *The Eighteenth-Century Town. A Reader in English Urban History, 1688–1820* (London: Longman, 1990).

Bosher, Robert. *The Making of the Restoration Settlement; The Influence of the Laudians, 1649–62* (Westminster: Dacre Press, 1951, reprinted 1957).

Bossy, John & Jupp, Peter, (eds) *Essays presented to Michael Roberts sometime Professor of Modern History in the Queen's University of Belfast* (Belfast: Blackstaff Press, 1976).

Bossy, John. *The English Catholic Community, 1570–1850* (London: Darton, Longman & Todd, 1975).

Boulton, W.B. *The Amusements of Old London* (London: Benjamin Blom, 1901, reprinted 1969).

Brailsford, Dennis. *Sport and Society, Elizabeth to Anne* (London: Routledge & Kegan Paul, 1969).

Braithwaite, W.C. *The Beginnings of Quakerism* (Cambridge: Cambridge University Press, second edition 1961).

——. *The Second Period of Quakerism* (2 vols, London: Cambridge University Press, 2nd edition 1961).

Braudel, Fernand, (translated by Sian Reynolds). *The Identity of France* (2 vols, vol. 1, London: Collins, 1988).

Brewer, John, & Styles, John, (eds) *An Ungovernable People: the English and their Law in the Seventeenth Century* (London: Hutchinson, 1980).

Broxop, E. *The Great Civil War in Lancashire* (Manchester: Manchester University Press, 1910).

Burke, Peter. *Popular Culture in Early Modern Europe* (London: Temple Smith, 1978).

Burne, R.V.H. *Chester Cathedral from its founding by Henry VIII to the Accession of Queen Victoria* (London: SPCK, 1958).

Carlisle, Nicholas. *A Concise Dictionary of the Endowed Grammar Schools of Lancashire and Yorkshire* (London: Baldwin, Cradock & Joy, 1818, republished Richmond: Richmond Publishing Co., 1972).

Chambers, J.D. *Population, Economy, and Society in Pre-Industrial England* (London: Oxford University Press, 1972).

Childs, J. *The Army, James II and the Glorious Revolution* (Manchester: Manchester University Press, 1980).

Clark, Peter. *The Transformation of English Provincial Towns, 1600–1800* (London: Hutchinson, 1984).

——. *The English Alehouse; A Social History, 1200–1830* (London: Longmans, 1983).

——, (ed.). *Country Towns in Pre-Industrial England* (Leicester: Leicester University Press, 1981).

——, (ed.). *The Early Modern Town* (London: Longman, Open University Press, 1976).

Clark, Peter, & Morgan, Phillip, et al. *English Urban History, 1500–1780* Course material for A322 (Milton Keynes: Open University Press, 1977).

Clark, Peter, & Slack, Paul. *English Towns in Transition* (London: Oxford University Press, 1976).

Clark, Peter, & Slack, Paul, (eds). *Crisis and Order in English Towns* (London: Routledge & Kegan Paul, 1972).

Clarke, Basil & Betjeman, John. *English Churches* (London: Vista Books, 1964).

Clarke, Mike. *The Leeds and Liverpool Canal: A History and Guide* (Preston: Carnegie, 1990).

Clarkson, Leslie. *Death, Disease and Famine in Pre-Industrial England* (Dublin: Gill & Macmillan, 1975)

Clarkson, L.A. *The Pre-Industrial Economy of England, 1500–1750* (London: Batsford, 1971).

Cockburn, J.S., (ed.). *Crime in England, 1550–1800* (London: Methuen, 1977).

Coleman, D.C. *Industry in Tudor and Stuart England* (London: Macmillan Press, 1975).

Collinson, Patrick. *The Religion of Protestants. The Church in English Society, 1559–1625*, The Ford Lectures, 1979 (Oxford: Clarendon Press, 1982).

Cook, W.H.R. *Joseph Brandreth, 1745–1815* (Ormskirk: Brandreth Club, 1991).

Corfield, P.J. *The Impact of English Towns, 1700–1800* (Oxford: Oxford University Press, 1982).

Coward, Barry. *Social Change and Continuity in Early Modern England, 1500–1750*, Seminar Studies in History, R. Lockyer (ed.) (London: Longman, 1988)

——. *The Lords Stanley and Earls of Derby, 1385–1672* (C.S. Third Series, vol. 30, 1983).

Cox, Millard. *Derby, The Life and Times of the Twelfth Earl of Derby, Edward Smith Stanley, 1752–1834* (London: J.A. Allen, 1974).

Cressy, David. *Education in Tudor and Stuart England* (London: Longmans, 1975).

——. *Literacy and the Social Order: Reading and Writing in Tudor and Stuart England* (Cambridge: Cambridge University Press, 1980).

Davies, R. & Rupp, G. (eds) *A History of the Methodist Church in Great Britain* (4 vols, vol. 1, London: Epworth Press, 1965).

Davis, Dorothy. *A History of Shopping* (London: Routledge & Kegan Paul, 1966).

Davis, Natalie Zemon. *Society and Culture in Early Modern France* (Stanford, California: Stanford University Press, 1975),

Dodgshon, R.A. & Butlin, R.A. *A Historical Geography of England and Wales* (London: Academic Press, 1978).

Dove, Ruth & Segebarth, Ruth. *A History of the Friends Meeting House in Lancaster* (Preston: Snape, 1991).

Duggan, Mona. *A History of Scarisbrick* (Preston: Carnegie, 1996).

Eddershaw, Margaret. *Grand Fashionable Nights, Kendal Theatre 1575–1985* (Lancaster: Centre for North West Regional Studies Lancaster University, 1988).

Everitt, Alan. *Perspectives in English Urban History* (London: Macmillan, 1973).

Fairfax-Blakeborough, J. *Northern Turf History* (2 vols, vol. 2, London: J.A. Allen, 1948).

Farrer, W. & Brownbill, J. (eds). *The Victoria History of the County of Lancaster* (vol. 2 & 3, London: University of London, 1907).

Fishwick, Henry. *The History of the Parish of Rochdale* (Rochdale: James Clegg, 1889).

Fleetwood Hesketh, Peter. *Murray's Lancashire Architectural Guide* (London: John Murray, 1955).

Foley, Rt Revd B.C. *Some People of the Penal Times* (Preston: Snape, 1991).

Foster, Joseph. *Alumini Oxoniensis* (1891, reprinted Neneln, Liechtenstein: Kraus, 1968).

Fritz, P. & Williams, D. (eds). *The Triumph of Culture; Eighteenth-Century Perspectives* (Toronto: A.M. Hakkert, 1972).

Gadd, David. *Georgian Summer, The Rise and Development of Bath* (Newbury: Countryside Books, 1987).

Gibson, Revd T.E. *Lydiate Hall and its Associations* (Edinburgh: Ballantyne, Hanson, 1876).

Glassey, Lionel K.J. *Politics and the appointment of Justices of the Peace, 1675–1720* (Oxford: Oxford University Press, 1979).

Gordon, Alexander. *Freedom after Ejection: A Review (1690–1692) of Presbyterian and Congregational Nonconformity in England and Wales* (Manchester: Manchester University Press, 1917).

Green, I.M. *The Re-Establishment of the Church of England, 1660–1663* (Oxford: Oxford University Press, 1978).

Halley, Robert. *Lancashire, its Puritanism and Nonconformity* (2 vols, vols 1 & 2, Manchester: Tubbs and Brook, 1869).

Hanley, Leonard. *A History of St Anne's, Ormskirk (1732–1982)* (Ormskirk: Causeway Press, 1982).

Harris, J.R. (ed.). Liverpool and Merseyside, Essays on the Economic and Social History of the Port (London: Frank Cass, 1969).

Harte, N.B. & Ponting, K.G. (eds). *Textile History and Economic History* (Manchester: Manchester University Press, 1973).

Hawkes, A.J. *Lancashire Printed Books to 1800* (Wigan: Public Library, 1925).

Hembry, Phyllis. *The English Spa 1560–1815: A Social History* (London: Athlone Press, 1990).

Henriques, Ursula. *Religious Toleration in England, 1787–1833* (London, Routledge & Kegan Paul, 1961).

Hewitson, A. *Preston Court Leet Records* (Preston: George Toulman & Sons, 1905).

Hewitson, Anthony. *The History of Preston* (Preston: Preston Chronicle, 1883).

Hill, Christopher. *The World Turned Upside Down. Radical Ideas during the English Revolution* (London: Temple Smith, 1973).

Hilton, J.A. *Catholic Lancashire, a Historical Guide* (Wigan: North-West Catholic History Society, 1981).

Holmes, Geoffrey. *Augustan England: The Professions, State and Society* (London: George Allen & Unwin, 1982).

Honigman, Ernest. *Shakespeare, the Lost Years* (Manchester: Manchester University Press, 1985).

Hoskins, W.G. *Provincial England. Essays in Social and Economic History* (London: Macmillan, 1964).

——. *Industry, Trade and People in Exeter, 1688–1800* (Exeter: University of Exeter, 1935, second edition, Manchester: Manchester University Press, 1968).

Hudson, Pat. *Regions and Industries. A Perspective on the Industrial Revolution in Britain* (Cambridge: Cambridge University Press, 1989).

Hunter, Joseph. *The Rise of the Old Dissent exemplified in the Life of Oliver Heywood, 1630–1702* (London: Longman, Brown & Longman, 1842).

Hutton, T. *Ormskirk Dispensary, Cottage Hospital and Home for Nurses Report* (Ormskirk: *The Advertiser*, 1915).

Jacquest, Sylvia. *Emmanuel, The Story of Methodism in Ormskirk, 1792–1978* (Ormskirk: Jacquest, 1978).

James, J. *The History of Worsted Manufacture in England from the Earliest Times* (London: Longmans, 1857).

James, Louis and Bradley, David. (eds). *Performance and Politics in Popular Drama* (Cambridge: Cambridge University Press, 1980).

Jessop, Augustus. (ed.). *The Lives of the Norths* (3 vols, vol. 3, London: George Bell & Sons, 1890).

Jones, Clyve. (ed.). *Britain in the First Age of Party, 1650–1750* (London: The Hambledon Press, 1987).

Jones, J.R. *Country and Court: England 1658–1714* (London: Edward Arnold, 1978).

Jones, J.R., (ed.). *The Restored Monarchy, 1660–88* (London: Macmillan Press, 1979).

Jones, M.G. *The Charity School Movement: A Study of Eighteenth-Century Puritanism in action* (London: Cambridge University Press, 1938).

Jones, E.L. & Mingay, G.E. (eds). *Land, Labour and Population in the Industrial Revolution: Essays presented to J.D. Chambers* (London: Edward Arnold, 1967).

Kenyon, J.P. (ed.). *The Stuart Constitution 1603–1688. Documents and Commentary* (Cambridge: Cambridge University Press, 1966).

Kenyon, John. *The Popish Plot* (London: Heinemann, 1972).

Kermode, J.I. & Phillips, C.B., (eds). *Seventeenth-Century Lancashire, Essays presented to J.J. Bagley* (Liverpool: TLCHS, 1983).

Laqueur, Thomas Walter. *Religion and Respectability: Sunday Schools and Working-Class Culture, 1750–1850* (London & New York: Yale University Press, 1976).

Laslett, Peter. *The World We Have Lost* (London: Methuen, 1965, second edition 1971).

Le Roy Laduire, Emmanuel, (translated by John Day). *The Peasants of Languedoc* (Urbana, Illinois: University of Illinois Press, 1966, translated 1976).

Lea, George. *Handbook to Ormskirk* (Ormskirk: Hutton *Ormskirk Advertiser*, 1893).

Lemmings, David. *Gentlemen and Barristers, The Inns of Court and the English Bar, 1680–1730* (Oxford: Clarendon Press, 1990).

Leys, M.D.R. *Catholics in England 1559–1829: A Social History* (London: Longmans, Green, 1961).

Lloyd, Arnold. *Quaker Social History, 1669–1738* (London: Longmans Green, 1950).

Loomes, Brian. *Lancashire Clocks and Clockmakers* (Newton Abbot: David and Charles, 1975).

Lowe, Norman. *The Lancashire Textile Industry in the Sixteenth Century* (C.S. third series, vol. 20, 1972).

Luft, H.M. *A History of Merchant Taylors' School, 1620–1970* (Liverpool: Liverpool University Press, 1970).

Malcolmson, R.W. *Popular Recreations in English Society, 1700–1850* (London: Cambridge University Press, 1973).

Marriner, Sheila. *The Economic and Social Development of Merseyside* (London: Croom Helm, 1982).

Marshall, J.D. *Kendal 1661–1801. The Growth of the Modern Town* (Kendal: CWAAS, 1975).

——. *Lancashire*, City and County Histories (Newton Abbot: David and Charles, 1974).

Matthews, A.G. *Calamy Revised; being a Revision of Edmund Calamy's Account of the Ministers and Others Ejected and Silenced, 1660–2* (Oxford: Clarendon Press, 1934).

Mathias, Peter. *The Brewing Industry in England, 1700–1830* (Cambridge: Cambridge University Press, 1959).

McKendrick, N., Brewer, J. & Plumb, J.H. *The Birth of a Consumer Society; The Commercialization of Eighteenth-Century England* (London: Europa Publications, 1982).

McInnes, Angus. *The English Town, 1660–1760* (London: The Historical Asssociation, 1980).

Miller, John. *Popery and Politics in England, 1660–1688* (Cambridge: Cambridge University Press, 1973).

Minchinton, W.E. (ed.). *The Growth of English Overseas Trade in the Seventeenth and Eighteenth Century* (London: Methuen, 1969).

Montgomery, Fiona. *Edge Hill University College: A History, 1885–1997* (Chichester: Phillimore, 1997).

Morrill, J.S. *Cheshire 1630–60, County, Government and Society during the English Revolution* (London: Oxford University Press, 1974).

Morris, Christopher. (ed.). *The Journeys of Celia Fiennes* (London, Cresset Press, 1947).

Mui, Hoh-cheung & Lorna H. *Shops and Shopping in Eighteenth-Century England* (London: Routledge, 1989).

Muir, Ramsey. *A History of Liverpool* (Liverpool: Liverpool University Press, 1907).

Mullett, Michael. *Sources for the History of English Nonconformity, 1660–1830* (London: British Records Association, 1991).

——. *Martyrs of the Diocese of Lancaster Beatified November 22 1987* (Preston: T. Snape, 1987).

—— (ed.). *Early Lancaster Friends* (Lancaster: Centre for North West Regional Studies, University of Lancaster, 1978).

——. *Radical Religious Movements in Early Modern Europe* (London: George Allen & Unwin, 1980).

Neuburg, Victor E. *Popular Education in Eighteenth-Century England* (London: Woburn Press, 1971).

Newstead, G. Couthard. *Gleanings towards the Annals of Aughton General, Ecclesiastical and Architectural* (Liverpool: C.H. Radcliffe, 1893).

Nicholson, Cornelius. *The Annals of Kendal* (London: Whittaker, 1861).

Nicholson, F. & Axon, E. (eds). *The Old Nonconformity in Kendal* (Kendal: Titus Wilson, 1915).

Nightingale, Revd B. *Lancashire Nonconformity* (Manchester: Heywood, 1892).

Nightingale, Revd B. (ed.). *Early stages of the Quaker Movement in Lancashire* (London: Congregational Union of England and Wales, 1921).

Norman, E. *Roman Catholicism in England from the Elizabethan Settlement to the Second Vatican Council* (Oxford, Oxford University Press, 1985).

Notestein, W. *A History of Witchcraft in England 1558–1718* (New York: Russell, 1965).

Ogg, David. *England in the Reign of Charles II* (Oxford: Clarendon Press, 1936, 2nd edition).

Open University Course Team. *English Urban History, 1500–1780*, Course A322 (Milton Keynes: Open University Press, 1977).

——. *The Enlightenment*, Course A204 (Milton Keynes: Open University Press, 1980).

Orritt, David C.J. *The History of Ormskirk Grammar School Lancashire* (Preston: Carnegie Press, 1988).

Overton J.H. & Relton F. *The English Church from the Accession of George I to the end of the Eighteenth Century* (London: Macmillan, 1906).

Parkes, Joan. *Travel in England in the Seventeenth Century* (London: Oxford University Press, 1925).

Parkinson, C. Northcote. *The Rise of the Port of Liverpool* (Liverpool: Liverpool University Press, 1952).

Patten, John. *English Towns, 1500–1700* (Folkestone: Dawson, 1978)

Pawson, Eric. *The Early Industrial Revolution: Britain in the Eighteenth Century* (London: Batsford, 1979).

Pevsner, N. *The Buildings of England, Lancashire* vol. 2, *The Rural North*, BE37 (Harmondsworth: Penguin Books, 1969).

Phillips, John. *The Reformation of Images: Destruction of Art in England, 1553–1660* (Berkeley: University of California Press, 1973).

Philpott, Robert A. *Historic Towns of the Merseyside Area. A Survey of Urban Settlement to c. 1800* (Liverpool: Liverpool Museum, 1988).

Picton, J.A. (ed.). *City of Liverpool, Municipal Archives and Records* (2 vols, Liverpool: Gilbert Walmsley, 1886).

Plant, Marjorie. *The English Book Trade: an Economic History of the Making and Sale of Books* (London: George Unwin and Allen, 1939, second edition 1965).

Plumb, J.H. *The Commercialisation of Leisure in Eighteenth-Century England* (Reading: University of Reading, 1973).

Porter, Roy. *English Society in the Eighteenth Century* (Harmondsworth: Penguin Books, Allen Lane, 1982, revised edition 1990)

Porter, Roy. (ed.). *The Medical History of Waters and Spas*, Medical History Supplement, no. 10 (London, Wellcome Institute, 1990).

Price, Cecil. *Theatre in the Age of Garrick* (Oxford: Basil Blackwell, 1973).

Priestley, Ursula and Fenner, Alayne. *Shops and Shopkeepers in Norwich, 1660–1730* (Norwich: Centre for East Anglian Studies University of East Anglia, 1985).

Reay, Barry. *The Quakers and the English Revolution* (London: Temple Smith, 1985).

Richardson, R. *Puritanism in North-West England* (Manchester: Manchester University Press, 1973).

Roberts, Robert. *The Classic Slum: Salford Life in the First Half of the Century* (Manchester: Manchester University Press, 1971).

Rosenfeld, Sybil. *Strolling Players and Drama in the Provinces, 1660–1765* (New York: Octagon Books, 1970).

Russell, Elbert. *The History of Quakerism* (Richmond, Indiana: Friends United Press, 1979).

Sagar, John H. *The Bickerstaffe Quakers, 1650–1800* (Ormskirk Family History Society, 1984).

Savidge, Alan. *The Foundation and Early Years of Queen Anne's Bounty* (London: SPCK, 1955).

Sharpe, J.A. *Early Modern England: a Social History* (London: Edward Arnold, 1978).

Shotter, David. *Roman Coins from North-West England* (Lancaster: Centre for North West Regional Studies, resource paper, 1990).

Sinclair, David. *The History of Wigan* (vol. 2, Wigan: Wall, *Observer* Office, 1882).

Smith, Peter. (ed.). *A Short History of Lathom* (St. Helens: Chalon Press, 1981.

Spufford, Margaret. *The Great Reclothing of Rural England. Petty Chapmen and their Wares in the Seventeenth Century* (London: Hambledon Press, 1984).

——. *Small Books and Pleasant Histories: Popular Fiction and its Readership in Seventeenth Century England* (Cambridge: Cambridge University Press, 1981).

Stell, Christophe. *An Inventory of Nonconformist Chapels and Meeting Houses in Central England* (London: HMSO, 1986)

Stephens, Sir Leslie & Lee, Sir Sidney. (eds). *The Dictionary of National Biography* (22 vols, London: Oxford University Press, 1917–1960).

Stephens, W.B. (ed.). *Studies in the History of Literacy: England and North America* (Leeds: University of Leeds, 1983).

Stonor, R.J. *Liverpool's Hidden Story* (Billinge: Birchley Hall Press, 1957).

Sykes, Norman. *Church and State in England in the Eighteenth Century* (Cambridge: Cambridge University Press, 1934).

Thirsk, Joan. *The Restoration: Problems and Perspectives in History* (H.F. Kearney (ed.)) (London: Longman, 1976).

——, (ed.). *The Agrarian History of England and Wales* (vol. 6 Cambridge: Cambridge University Press, 1989).

Thomas, Keith. *Man and the Natural World: Changing Attitudes in England* (London: Penguin Books, Allen Lane, 1983).

Thompson, E.P. *Whigs and Hunters. The Origin of the Black Act* (London: Penguin Books, Allen Lane, 1975).

Townsend, W., Workman, H.B. & Eayrs, G. (eds.) *A New History of Methodism* (London: Hodder and Stoughton, 1909).

Trevor Roper, H.R. *Archbishop Laud, 1573–1645* (London: Macmillan, 1940).

Turner, Ernest Sackville. *Taking the Cure.* (London: Michael Joseph, 1967).

Tyacke, Nicholas. *Anti-Calvinists, The Rise of English Arminianism, c. 1590–1640* (Oxford: Clarendon Press, 1987).

Vann, Richard T. *The Social Development of English Quakerism, 1655–1755* (Cambridge, Massachusetts: Harvard University Press, 1969).

Venn, John & Venn, J.A. (eds). *Alumini Cantabriegiensis* (Cambridge: Cambridge University Press, 1922 reprinted Nedeln, Liechtenstein: Kraus, 1974).

Vincent, W.A.L. *The Grammar Schools: Their Continuing Tradition, 1660–1714* (London: John Murray, 1969).

Wadsworth, A.P. and Mann, J. de Lacy. *The Cotton Trade and Industrial Lancashire, 1600–1780* (Manchester: Manchester University Econ. Hist. Series, 1931).

Walsh, John. *Methodism and the Mob in the Eighteenth Century*, Studies in Church History, vol. 8 (Cambridge: Cambridge University Press, 1972).

Walton, John K. *Lancashire, a Social History* (Manchester: Manchester University Press, 1987).

Ware, Samuel Hibbert. *Lancashire Memorials of the Rebellion, 1715* (C.S. first series, vol. 5, 1845).

Watts, Michael. *The Dissenters* (Oxford: Clarendon Press, 1978).

Weatherill, Lorna. *Consumer Behaviour and Material Culture in Britain, 1660–1760* (London: Routledge, 1988).

Webb, Sidney and Beatrice. *English Local Government. The Manor and the Borough* (London: Longmans, Green, 1908).

——. *English Local Government. The Story of the King's Highway* (London: Longmans, 1913).

White, Andrew. *A History of Lancaster, 1193–1993* (Keele: Ryburn Publishing Keele University Press, 1993).

Whiteman, Anne. (ed.). *The Compton Census of 1676: A Critical Edition* (London: for the British Academy by the Oxford University Press, 1986).

Whiteman, Anne, et al. *Statesmen, Scholars and Merchants: Essays in Eighteenth-Century History presented to Dame Lucy Sutherland* (Oxford: Clarendon Press, 1973).

Wickham, Glynne. *A History of the Theatre* (Oxford: Phaidon, 1985).

Willan, T.S. *The Inland Trade* (Manchester: Manchester University Press, 1976).

——. *An Eighteenth-Century Shopkeeper, Abraham Dent of Kirkby Stephen* (Manchester: Manchester University Press, 1970).

Williams, Bill. *The Making of Manchester Jewry, 1740–1875* (Manchester: Manchester University Press, 1976).

Williams, J. Anthony. (ed.). *Catholicism in Bath* (Catholic Record Society Publications, Records Series, vol. 65, 1975).

Wilson, John. *The Chorleys of Chorley Hall* (Manchester: Sherratt and Hughes, 1907).

Wilson, John. *The Story of the Old Parish Church of Chorley* (Edinburgh: Ballantyne Press, 1914).

Wright, Joseph. (ed.). *Wright's Dialect Dictionary* (6 vols, London: Henry Frowde, 1904).

Wrightson, Keith and Levine, David. *Poverty and Piety in an English Village* (New York: Academic Press, 1979).

Wrightson, Keith. *English Society, 1580–1680* (London: Hutchinson, 1982).

Articles

Addy, John. 'Bishop Porteus Visitation of the Diocese of Chester, 1778', *Northern History*, no. 13, 1977.

Alldridge, Nick. 'House and Household in Restoration Chester', *Urban History Yearbook*, 1983.

Anderson, Alan, B. 'A Study in the Sociology of Religious Persecution: the First Quakers', *The Journal of Religious History*, vol. 9, nos 1–4, 1977.

Arkell, Tom. 'Multiplying Factors for Estimating Population Totals from the Hearth Tax', *Local Population Studies*, no. 28, spring 1982.

Ashmore, Owen. 'Inventories as a Source of Local History, 1. Houses', *Amateur Historian*, vol. 4, no. 5, 1959.

Aveling, J.C.H. 'Some Aspects of Yorkshire Catholic : Recusant History, 1558–1791', in Cuming, G.J. (ed.) *Studies in Church History*, vol. 4, 1967.

Axon, E. 'The King's Preachers in Lancashire', *TLCAS*, vol. 56, 1944.

Bate, Revd J.R. 'Ormskirk Grammar School; the First Minute Book, 1613–1890', *TLCHS*, vol. 76, 1924.

Beaumont, William. 'Jacobite Trials at Manchester 1694', *CS*, vol. 28, 1853.

Bennett, G.V. 'The Convocation of 1710: an Anglican Attempt at a Counter-Revolution', in Cuming, G.J. & Baker, Derek. (eds). *Studies in Church History*, vol. 7, 1971.

Blackwood, B.G. 'Plebeian Catholics in Later Stuart Lancashire', *Northern History*, no. 25, 1989.

Borsay, Peter. 'Culture, Status and the English Urban Landscape', *History*, vol. 67, no. 219, Feb. 1982.

Borsay, Peter. The English Urban Renaissance: The Development of Provincial Urban Culture, *c. 1680–1760*', *Social History*, vol. 5, May, 1977.

Borsay, Peter, & McInnes, Angus. 'Debate The Emergence of a Leisure Town: or an Urban Renaissance?' *Past and Present*, vol. 126, 1990.

Bossy, John, 'More Northumbrian Congregations', *Recusant History*, vol. 10, 1969–70.

——. 'Four Catholic Communities in Rural Northumbria 1750–1850', *Recusant History*, vol. 9, 1967.

Chalklin, C.W. 'Capital Expenditure on Building for Cultural Purposes in Provincial England, 1730–1830', *Business History*, vol. 22, no. 1. 1980.

Chartres, J.A. 'Road Carrying in England in the Seventeenth Century: Myth and Reality', *Economic History Review*, 2nd series, vol. 30, no. 1, 1977.

Cheetham, F.H. 'Lancashire Briefs in a Rutland Parish', *TLCHS*, vol. 84, 1932.

——. 'Notes on Some Ormskirk Watch and Clock Makers', *TLCAS*, vol. 51, 1936.

Clarkson, L.A. 'The Leather Crafts in Tudor and Stuart England', *Agricultural History Review*, no. 14, 1966.

——. 'The Organisation of the Leather Industry in the late Sixteenth and Seventeenth century', *Economic History Review*, 2nd series, vol. 13, no. 2, 1960.

Coley, Noel G. 'Physicians and the Chemical Analysis of Mineral Waters in Eighteenth Century England', *Medical History*, vol. 26, April 1982.

Coney, Audrey, P. 'Mid-Nineteenth-Century Ormskirk: Disease, Overcrowding, and the Irish in a Lancashire Market Town', *TLCHS*, vol. 139, 1990.

——. 'Aughton Enclosure in the Eighteenth and Early Nineteenth Century: The Struggle for Superiority', *TLCHS*, vol. 136, 1987.

Coward, Barry. 'The Social and Political Position of Earls of Derby in Later Seventeenth-Century Lancashire', *Essays Presented to J.J. Bagley*, *TLCHS*, vol. 132, 1982.

Cressy, David. 'Literacy in the Seventeenth-Century', *Journal of Interdisciplinary History*, vol. 8, no. 1, 1977.

Davis, R. 'The Rise of Protection in England, 1689–1786', *Economic History Review*, 2nd series, vol. 19, no. 2, 1966.

Dixon, James. 'Nathaniel Heywood, the Nonconformist Vicar of Ormskirk', *TLCHS*, vol. 30, 1878.

——. 'Notes on Certain Discoveries during the Alteration of Ormskirk Church', *TLCHS*, vol. 30, 1878.

Dolan, Dom Gilbert, OSB. 'Lancashire and the Benedictines', *TLCHS*, New Series, vol. 13, 1898.

Dottie, R.G. 'Childwall; a Lancashire Town in the Seventeenth Century', *TLCHS*, vol. 135, 1986.

Dyer, A.D. 'The Growth and Decay of English Towns', *Urban History Yearbook*, 1979.

Eklund, Jon. ' "Of a Spirit in the Water": Some Early Ideas on the Aerial Dimension', *Isis*, vol. 67, 1976.

Everitt, Alan. 'Urban Growth, 1570–1770', *Local Historian*, vol. 8, no. 4, 1968.

Eversley D. 'A Survey of the Population in an Area in Worcestershire 1660–1850', *Population Studies*, vol. 10, 1957.

Hawkes, A.J. 'A Find of Roman Coins near Ormskirk', *TLCAS*, vol. 61, 1949.

——. 'Sir Roger Bradshaigh of Haigh', *CS*, New Series, vol. 109, 1945.

Heywood, Nathan. 'Tokens of the Seventeenth Century', *TLCAS*, vol 5, 1887.

——. 'Further Notes on Lancashire and Cheshire Tokens', *TLCAS*, vol. 30, 1912.

Hill, J.E. Christopher. 'Puritans and the Dark Corners of the Land', *TRHS*, Series 5, vol. 13, 1963.

Holmes, Geoffrey. 'The Sacheverell Riots. The Crowd and the Church', *Past and Present*, vol. 72, 1976.

Houston, R.A. 'The Development of Literacy: Northern England 1640–1750', *Economic History Review*, 2nd series, vol. 35, no. 2, 1982.

Howson, W.G. 'Plague, Poverty and Population', *TLCHS*, vol. 112, 1961.

Jarvis, R.C. 'The Rebellion of 1745', *TLCAS*, vol. 56, 1944.

——. 'The Forty-Five and Local Records', *TLCAS*, vol. 65, 1955.

Jeans, Susi. 'Three Lancashire Organs', *The Organ*, vol. 59, no. 234, October 1980.

Jones, E.L. & Falkus, M.E. 'Urban Improvement and the English Economy in the Seventeenth and Eighteenth Centuries', *Research in Economic History*, vol. 4, 1979.

King, Walter, F. 'The Regulation of Ale Houses in Stuart Lancashire', *TLCHS*, vol. 129, 1980.

Langton, J. & Laxton, P. 'Parish Registers and Urban Structure; the Example of Eighteenth-Century Liverpool', *Urban History Yearbook*, 1978.

Laqueur, Thomas. 'Debate: Literacy and Social Mobility in the Industrial Revolution in England', *Past and Present*, vol. 64, 1974.

Latham, R.C. 'Roger Lowe, Shopkeeper and Nonconformist, 1663–1669', *History*, 2nd series, vol. 26, 1941–2.

Lemire, Beverley. 'Consumerism in Pre-industrial and Early Industrial England: The Trade in Secondhand Clothes', *Journal of British Studies*, vol. 27, January 1988.

Madeley, Charles. 'The Roll of the Mock Corporation of Farnworth in Widnes', *TLCHS*, new series, vol. 31, 1916.

Marshall, Lydia M. 'The Levying of the Hearth Tax, 1662–1688', *English Historical Review*, vol. 51, 1936; *Northern History*, no. 19, 1983.

Marshall, J.D. 'The Rise and Transformation of the Cumbrian Market Town, 1660–1900', *Northern History*, no. 19, 1983.

McInnes, Angus. 'The Emergence of a Leisure Town: Shrewsbury 1660–1760', *Past and Present*, vol. 120, 1988.

Mitchell, Ian. 'Pitt's Shop Tax in the History of Retailing', *Local Historian*, vol. 14, no. 6, May 1981.

Mitchell, Ian, S. 'Retailing in Eighteenth and Early Nineteenth-Century Cheshire', *TLCHS*, vol. 130, 1981.

Morgan, Nicholas J. 'Lancashire Quakers and the Tithe, 1660–1730', *Bulletin of the John Rylands University Library of Manchester*, vol. 70, 1988.

Mullett, Michael. 'A Receptacle for Papists and an Assilum', *The Catholic Historical Review*, vol. 73, no. 3, 1987.

——. 'The Internal Politics of Bedford, 1660–1688', *Bedfordshire Historical Records Society*, vol. 59, 1980.

——. 'To Dwell Together in Unity: the Search for Agreement in Preston Politics, 1660–1690', *TLCHS*, vol. 125, 1974.

Nelson, Janet. 'The Demand for Silk and the Waste Silk Industry in Eighteenth-Century Lancaster, 1711–1780', *Lancashire Local Historian*, no. 3, 1985.

Noble, M.K. 'The Role of Small Towns within Regional Urban Systems: Some Thoughts and Considerations', *Journal of Regional and Local Studies*, no. 9, no. 2, winter 1989.

Nuttall, G.F. 'Assembly and Association in Dissent, 1689–1831', in Cuming, C.J. and Baker, Derek. (eds). *Studies in Church History*, vol. 7, 1971.

Peyton, S.A. 'The Religious Census of 1767', *English Historical Review*, vol. 68, 1933.

Porteous, Revd T.C. 'New Light on the Lancashire Jacobite Plot, 1692–4', *TLCAS*, vol. 50, 1934–5.

Priestley, Ursula and Corfield, Penelope. 'Rooms and Room Use in Norwich Housing, 1580–1730', *Post Mediaeval Archaeology*, no. 16, 1982.

Reay, Barry. 'Popular Hostility towards Quakers in Mid-Seventeenth Century England', *Social History*, vol. 5, no. 3, Oct. 1980.

Richey, Russell, E. 'Did the Presbyterians become Unitarians?' *Church History*, vol. 47, 1973.

——. 'The Effects of Toleration', *Journal of Religious History*, vol. 8, no. 4, 1974.

Rideout, Eric. H. 'Poor Law Administration in North Meols', *TLCHS*, vol. 81, 1930.

Rodgers, H.B. 'The Market Area of Preston in the Sixteenth and Seventeenth Centuries', *Geographical Studies*, vol. 3, 1956.

Rose, E.A. 'Methodism in South Lancashire to 1800', *TLCAS*, vol. 81, 1982.

Sanderson, Michael. 'Literacy and Social Mobility in the Industrial Revolution in England', *Past and Present*, vol. 56, 1972.

Sogner, Solvi. 'Aspects of the Demographic Situation in Seventeen Parishes in Shropshire, 1711–1760; and Exercise based on Parish Registers', *Population Studies*, vol. 17, 1963–4.

Spalding, J.C. 'The Demise of the English Presbyterianism 1660–1760', *Church History*, vol. 28, 1959.

Spufford, Margaret. 'First Steps in Literacy', *Social History*, vol. 4, no. 3, Oct. 1979.

Stone, Lawrence. 'The Educational Revolution in England 1560–1640', *Past and Present*, vol. 28, 1964.

Thompson, E.P. 'Patrician Society, Plebeian Culture', *Journal of Social History*, vol. 7, 1974.

——. 'Time, Work and Industrial Capitalism', *Past and Present*, vol. 38, August 1967.

——. 'The Moral Economy of the English Crowd in the Eighteenth Century', *Past and Present*, vol. 50, 1971.

Tupling, G.H. 'Early English Markets and their Tolls', *TLCAS*, vol. 50, 1934.

——. 'Lancashire Markets in the Sixteenth and Seventeenth Centuries', *TLCAS*, part I, vol. 58,1945–6; part II, vol. 59, 1947.

——. 'The Early Metal Trades and the Beginning of Engineering in Lancashire', *TLCAS*, vol. 61, 1951.

——. 'Alphabetic List of Markets and Fairs in Lancashire recorded before 1700', *TLCAS*, vol. 51, 1936.

——. 'The Origin of Markets and Fairs in Medieval Lancashire', *TLCAS*, vol. 49, 1933.

Vann, R.T. 'Literacy in Seventeenth-Century England', *Journal of Interdisciplinary History*, vol. 5, no. 2, 1974.

Walsh, John. 'Methodism and the Mob', in Cuming, G.J. & Baker, Derek. (eds). *Studies in Church History*, vol. 8, 1972.

Walton, John. 'Trades and Professions in late Eighteenth Century England: Assessing the Evidence of Directories', *Local Historian*, vol. 17, no. 6, May 1987.

Ware, Samuel Hibbert. 'Lancashire Memorials of 1715', *CS*, first series, vol. 5, 1845.

Whiteman, Anne. 'The Church of England, 1660–1663', *TRHS*, 5th series, vol. 5, 1955.

Whyte J.H. 'The Vicar's Apostolic Returns, 1773', *Recusant History*, vol. 9, 1967.

Index